Teaching Environmental and Natural Resource Economics

T0327390

ELGAR GUIDES TO TEACHING

The Elgar Guides to Teaching series provides a variety of resources for instructors looking for new ways to engage students. Each volume provides a unique set of materials and insights that will help both new and seasoned teachers expand their toolbox in order to teach more effectively. Titles include selections of methods, exercises, games and teaching philosophies suitable for the particular subject featured. Each volume is authored or edited by a seasoned professor. Edited volumes comprise contributions from both established instructors and newer faculty who offer fresh takes on their fields of study.

Titles in the series include:

Teaching Environmental and Natural Resource Economics

Paradigms and Pedagogy

Edited by

John C. Bergstrom

Department of Agricultural and Applied Economics, University of Georgia, USA

John C. Whitehead

Department of Economics, Appalachian State University, USA

ELGAR GUIDES TO TEACHING

Edward Elgar
PUBLISHING

Cheltenham, UK • Northampton, MA, USA

Published by
Edward Elgar Publishing Limited
The Lypiatts
15 Lansdown Road
Cheltenham
Glos GL50 2JA
UK

Edward Elgar Publishing, Inc.
William Pratt House
9 Dewey Court
Northampton
Massachusetts 01060
USA

Paperback edition 2023

A catalogue record for this book
is available from the British Library

Library of Congress Control Number: 2021949004

This book is available electronically in the **Elgar**online
Economics subject collection
http://dx.doi.org/10.4337/9781788114288

ISBN 978 1 78811 427 1 (Hardback)
ISBN 978 1 78811 428 8 (eBook)
ISBN 978 1 03532 203 9 (Paperback)

Printed and bound by CPI Group (UK) Ltd, Croydon, CR0 4YY

Contents

PART II   PEDAGOGY

Figures

Tables

Boxes

Contributors

David A. Anderson is Professor of Economics at Centre College, Danville, Kentucky.

John C. Bergstrom is Professor at the Department of Agricultural and Applied Economics, University of Georgia, Athens, Georgia.

Jim Casey is Professor of Economics at Washington and Lee University, Lexington, Virginia.

Tim Haab is Professor at the Department of Agricultural, Environmental, and Development Economics, Ohio State University, Columbus, Ohio.

Amy Henderson is Associate Professor of Economics at St. Mary's College of Maryland, St. Mary's City, Maryland.

Robert J. Johnston is Professor at the Department of Economics, Clark University, Worcester, Massachusetts.

Stephan Kroll is Professor at the Department of Agricultural and Resource Economics, Colorado State University, Fort Collins, Colorado.

Kathleen Lawlor is Assistant Professor at the Department of Economics, University of North Carolina Asheville, Asheville, North Carolina.

Leah Greden Mathews is Professor at the Department of Economics, University of North Carolina Asheville, Asheville, North Carolina.

Shana M. McDermott is Associate Professor at the Department of Economics, Trinity University, San Antonio, Texas.

David McEvoy is Professor at the Department of Economics, Appalachian State University, Boone, North Carolina.

Peter W. Schuhmann is Professor at the Department of Economics and Finance, University of North Carolina, Wilmington, North Carolina.

John C. Whitehead is Professor at the Department of Economics, Appalachian State University, Boone, North Carolina.

Preface

John C. Bergstrom and John C. Whitehead

The first teaching-focused article on the topic of this book appeared in the *Journal of Economic Education* five years after John Krutilla's (1967) influential 'Conservation reconsidered' article appeared in the *American Economic Review* and two years after the first Earth Day and the founding of the U.S. Environmental Protection Agency. Carter (1972) suggests that the production possibilities curve (with environmental quality on one axis and market goods on the other) as the foundational theory for teaching courses related to environmental and natural resource economics. The article provides a reading list for instructors, sans formal textbooks, including books that could supplement a micro principles text and other readings. Over a decade and a half later, Christiansen (1988) reviewed progress in the field with a review of the most influential environmental and natural resource economics textbooks.

Since that time, almost 50 economic education journal articles have been published addressing the field of environmental and natural resource economics (González-Ramírez et al., 2021). In one of the first articles in this literature since Carter (1972), Walbert and Bierma (1988) described a classroom game that illustrated two important points in environmental economics: (1) the optimal pollution level is not zero and (2) tradeable permits can be a more cost-effective approach to regulation. Following Walbert and Bierma (1988) the number of articles has been increasing linearly with five, 15, and 25 articles published in the 1990s, 2000s, and 2010s. Most of these articles have considered classroom games with others describing innovations in computer-assisted instruction and the use of the contingent valuation method as a student project.

It is within this scholarly context that this book has emerged. The chapters within this book make several significant contributions to the economic education literature. In the first chapter of the book, a brief survey of the history of thought in environmental and natural resource economics is presented which helps provide context for the rest of the book. In addition, when teaching our own courses, we have found that sprinkling a typical course with some background historical theory and personalities often helps set the stage for the modern innovations that we teach with the additional benefit of enhancing students' interest in and understanding of course content.

The rest of the book is divided into two parts: paradigms and pedagogy. In Part I on paradigms are five chapters that provide models for teaching the variety of courses that have emerged in university curricula. We find that while there are a number of environmental and natural resource economics textbooks, there is little guidance for how to approach the course topics and outline. This part helps to fill that void.

Part II on pedagogy consists of eight chapters that contribute to the practice of teaching environmental and natural resource economics. These chapters can be further classified into those that approach the teaching of a particular topic and those that use a particular teaching method. The topical chapters include approaches to teaching environmental justice, nonmarket valuation, and climate change. The methods chapters describe the use of classroom experiments, data analysis, policy briefs, technology, and a variety of supplemental materials.

The first two chapters in Part I on paradigms cover the more traditional, neoclassical approaches to the topics in the course. In Chapter 2, David McEvoy describes a positive economics course that focuses on environmental and resource policy to achieve economic efficiency. This chapter discusses approaches to teaching the economic concepts of optimal environmental and natural resource management with theory and classroom experiments. In Chapter 3, John Bergstrom describes an applied welfare economics teaching paradigm (approach) that focuses on theory and tools for evaluating natural resource and environmental policy and management decisions. Examples of assignments that demonstrate the usefulness of this approach including benefit–cost analysis exercises are described.

The next two chapters in Part I consider less traditional approaches to teaching environmental and natural resource economics. Robert Johnston, in Chapter 4, presents the key components of an interdisciplinary ecosystem services and sustainability approach. The chapter includes teaching tips and examples. On the other end of the science spectrum, Kathleen Lawlor describes an institutional approach to the course in Chapter 5, with a focus on climate change. The chapter includes teaching resources and strategies that could be used in the classroom.

In Chapter 6, Tim Haab describes an approach to teaching an environmental and natural resources course as a micro principles course. For example, he asks why are market failures taught secondarily when they are pervasive and the competitive market is the unusual situation? In short, he thinks we've been teaching principles of micro with a misplaced emphasis.

Considering first the topical chapters in Part II on pedagogy, in Chapter 7 Amy Henderson addresses environmental justice by describing how data can be used to develop active learning exercises to determine if minority or low-income populations bear a disproportionate share of the costs of pollution. Peter Schuhmann, in Chapter 12, describes an approach to teaching non-market valuation to undergraduates including where to place the topic in the outline of the course, tips for motivating the need for valuation, and ways to deal with the more technical nature of the topic. Jim Casey describes a teaching module focused on climate change in Chapter 14. He describes a model that considers the full costs of producing and consuming energy resources.

Considering next the chapters that contribute to teaching practice in Part II, Stephan Kroll describes five classroom experiments in Chapter 8 including those on externalities, public goods, willingness-to-pay versus willingness-to-accept, tradable emissions permits, and the problems with eco-labelling. In Chapter 9, John Whitehead describes research activities that range from a single class day in an introductory course to a semester length project in an advanced course. The research topics include the valuation of public goods, environmental policy, and natural resources. Leah Greden Mathews describes her policy briefs assignment as one that engages students, bringing the real world to the course, and improves writing skills (Chapter 10). In Chapter 11, Shana McDermott describes assignments using smartphone technologies related to sustainability and encourages students to interact with the outdoors which might lead to the co-benefit of pro-environmental behavior. David Anderson describes the need for triangulated teaching (Chapter 13). Supplements to the textbook and lectures can include educational videos, active-learning exercises, field trips, guest lectures, and blogs.

While we are more than satisfied with the contents of the book, it is not encyclopedic. Inevitably, there are chapters that we would have liked to include that did not make it for various reasons. For example, another useful chapter would have provided a review of the textbooks in the field as an update to Christiansen (1988). The enormity of this task precluded its inclusion. We also would have like to have included a paradigms chapter focused on teaching the intertemporal allocation of natural resources (e.g., energy, fisheries, forestry). Finally, as we were trying to wrap up this project, the COVID-19 pandemic hit and many courses moved online. Whitehead's own second-year course transitioned from face-to-face to hybrid during the 2020–21 academic year to consistently online beginning in the 2021–22 academic year. A chapter on teaching environmental and natural resource economics online would have made a useful contribution to the literature – or maybe that is the topic for another book given all that we as an educational profession have experienced and learned over the past unforgettable two years teaching online asynchronous, online synchronous and hybrid formats.

Finally, we thank the authors of the chapters for excellent contributions and their patience as the COVID-19 pandemic delayed the editors in putting the final touches on the book (e.g., writing this preface). We hope that instructors of environmental and natural resource economics find the book useful when doing this important work.

REFERENCES

Carter, W. (1972), 'Teaching environmental economics', *Journal of Economic Education* **4** (1), 36–42.

Christiansen, G.B. (1988), 'The natural environment and economic education', *Journal of Economic Education* **19** (2): 185–197.

González-Ramírez, J., J. Caviglia-Harris, and J.C. Whitehead (2021), 'Teaching environmental and natural resource economics: A review of the economic education literature', *International Review of Environmental and Resource Economics* **15** (3): 235–369.

Krutilla, J.V. (1967), 'Conservation reconsidered', *American Economic Review* **57** (4): 777–786.

Walbert, M.S., and T.J. Bierma (1988), 'The permits game: Conveying the logic of marketable pollution permits', *Journal of Economic Education* **19** (4): 383–389.

1. Reflections on the historical development of natural resource and environmental economics

John C. Bergstrom

INTRODUCTION

There are many perspectives on the historical development of natural resource and environmental economics, and what constitutes the main ingredients of the body of knowledge and associated teaching in the field. This introductory chapter, and outline of this book as a whole, represents the author's personal perspectives on these topics.[1] Also, since this is a book about teaching natural resource and environmental economics, in this chapter I also attempt to highlight the academic heritage of natural resource and environmental economics including key contributors and programs. Teachers of environmental and resource economics can enhance their lectures with some history of thought story telling. This chapter, which is heavily influenced by the author's own teaching and research experience provides a brief introduction. Thus, I do not claim that this chapter covers everything and everybody that may be important components of an overview and history of natural resource and environmental economics. The interested reader should also see Spash (1999), Pearce (2002), Heal (2007), Kling et al. (2010), Lichtenberg et al. (2010), Sandmo (2015), Brown et al. (2016), and Groom and Talevi (2020) for fuller treatments from different perspectives.

Historically, natural resource economics and environmental economics developed, for the most part, as separate sub-disciplines of the general discipline of economics. However, as discussed later in this chapter, more holistic, ecological thinking about natural resource and environmental issues and problems led to somewhat of a merging of these two sub-disciplines. But I first consider the historical development of these sub-disciplines as separate fields of study and teaching.

THE "CONSERVATION MOVEMENT" AND NATURAL RESOURCE ECONOMICS

I took my first natural resource economics class in 1979 at the University of Maryland, College Park. The instructor for the course was Dr. Ivar Strand and the textbook for the class was Ciriacy-Wantrup's classic book, *Resource Conservation: Economics and Policies*, first published in 1952. This classic book by Ciriacy-Wantrup contributed to the emergence of "natural resource economics" as a sub-discipline in the 1950s. This book also contains themes and concepts reflected in modern-day environmental economics which by many accounts emerged as a sub-discipline in the 1970s. Professor Ciriacy-Wantrup is also credited for starting a long history of teaching and research in natural resource and environmental economics in the Department of Agricultural Economics at the University of California, Berkeley (Brown et al., 2016).

The fact that the title of Ciriacy-Wantrup's 1952 book prominently displayed the word "conservation" reflects a longer history and concerns regarding natural resource scarcity and conservation. For many students of natural resource and environmental economics, the idea that natural resources are scarce and therefore pose limits to economic growth and human welfare is introduced and illustrated by the "Malthusian Doctrine." The main tenants of this doctrine, named after its 18th-century originator, a classic political economist by the name of Thomas Malthus (1766–1834), are that human population growth will exceed the ability of the natural resource base (what may now be called "natural capital") to support essential life-support services such as food production (Malthus, 1798). That is, according to the Malthusian Doctrine, natural resource scarcity will ultimately lead to catastrophe.

Thomas Malthus was writing from the perspective of living in 18th-century England when it was experiencing rapid population growth that was straining this island nation's limited land base for agricultural production. One way out of the Malthusian Doctrine trap which many people from crowded European countries in the 18th and 19th centuries pursued was to emigrate to the sparsely populated, natural-resource-rich "New World" in the Americas. When newly arrived European immigrants settled in the Americas, many believed that the vast natural resources of the "New World" were inexhaustible, literally. However, eventually it became clear that rapid and extensive economic growth and development was depleting natural supplies of minerals, timber, and fish and wildlife at a rate where complete exhaustion was feasible. For example, at least until about the mid-19th century in the United States, huge flocks of millions of passenger pigeons darkened the sky and made a "thunderous noise that made it difficult for people to hear each other talking in normal conversation." In those days, it was inconceivable by most people that birds of such abundance could ever disappear, or even be depleted by a significant amount. However, by the end of the 19th century, the vast flocks were gone due to extensive hunting. The last known passenger pigeon died in the Cincinnati Zoo in 1914 (Yeoman, 2014).

The demise of the passenger pigeon and other similar examples of natural resource depletion showed people that natural resources were not inexhaustible, at least not in one place. However, in the U.S. in the 19th century, a "frontier mentality" going back to colonial days still persisted. This mentality envisioned the continued existence of new frontiers endowed with abundant resources ready for the taking including U.S. states and territories in the 19th century West and later into the 20th century the "last frontier," Alaska. The timber harvesting industry in the 19th-century U.S. illustrated the "frontier mentality" model of resource use whereby once timber resources were depleted in one region of the U.S., timber companies abandoned the cut-over land and moved on to new stands of timber in different regions of the U.S., generally moving from the Eastern U.S. to the Western U.S.

Growth of Nature Appreciation

However, not all Americans in the 19th century bought into the frontier mentality which de-emphasized the conservation of natural resources in one place. One such person was Henry David Thoreau (1817–1862). Thoreau was many things including abolitionist, author, business inventor, land surveyor, social activist, and both an early "conservationist" and "environmentalist." He attended Harvard College (later Harvard University) from 1833 to 1837 taking classes in rhetoric, classics, philosophy, and math & science. His later writings reflected the general academic field of moral philosophy including a focus on nature (environmental ethics) influenced by one of his mentors, Ralph Waldo Emerson (1803–1882) whose moral/nature philosophy is reflected in his book entitled *Nature*.

Thoreau is probably best known, especially among students of the conservation and environmental movements in the U.S., for his book, *Walden: Life in the Woods* (Thoreau, 1854).[2] In his writings and actions including extensive hikes in the countryside around Concord, Massachusetts, Thoreau advocated appreciation of nature for its aesthetic qualities during a time in America where nature was much more commonly viewed as a source of raw materials to fuel economic production and growth. Thus, Thoreau's writings and actions foreshadowed the concepts of non-consumptive and nonrival use values of natural resources (e.g., recreational hiking, wildlife observation) which are now core concepts in natural resource and environmental economics teaching programs. Thoreau may also have anticipated the also now-familiar concepts in natural resource and environmental economics, and environmental ethics, of intrinsic values and passive or non-use values including existence values when he wrote in his essay entitled "Walking": "in wildness is preservation of the world" (Thoreau, 1862).

The moral/nature philosophy of Emerson and Thoreau laid the groundwork for more scientific and practical treatises directly related to natural resource conservation starting with the very influential book by George Perkins Marsh entitled, *Man and Nature: Physical Geography as Modified by Human Action*, first published in 1864 (Marsh, 1864). In this book, Marsh described the relationships between environmental degradation, natural resource depletion, and the fall of ancient human civilizations in the Mediterranean. He used these examples to illustrate the reality of natural resource exhaustion (e.g., natural resources are not inexhaustible) and the negative consequences to human societies who poorly manage their natural resource base (natural capital) including over-exploitation.[3]

In 1869, after the publication of Marsh's book, *Man and Nature*, a personality well-known to almost all students in the natural resource and environmental fields of study, John Muir, traveled to the high Sierra Mountains of California helping to shepherd a flock of sheep into their summer grazing grounds. Muir described his experiences during this summer in one of his first essays, "My First Summer in the Sierra" (Muir, 1911). Much of this essay is devoted to describing the plants, animals, and landscape of the Sierra Mountains in California which he found beautiful and fascinating. He provided even more detailed descriptions of the high Sierra Mountains' natural resources and environment in the article, "The Mountains of California" published in 1894 (Muir, 1894). In this article, Muir theorized that the high Sierra valleys such as Yosemite Valley were developed through glacial actions. Leading scientists of the day scoffed at this glacier valley sculpting theory, which of course turned out to be supported by later geological studies and mainstream scientists.

John Muir's writings took on the moral-nature philosophical tones of Thoreau, and also the practical, scientific tones of George P. Marsh. The scientific nature of his writing reflects his academic training at the University of Wisconsin-Madison where he studied chemistry, geology, and botany for two years. The moral-nature philosophical nature of his writings is reminiscent of spiritual themes in the Bible (which Muir knew well) as in the following bit of prose in "My First Summer in the Sierra" describing the Sierra Mountains:

> Through a meadow opening in the pine woods I see snowy peaks about the headwaters of the Merced above Yosemite. How near they seem and clear their outlines on the blue air, or rather *in* the blue air; for they seem to be saturated with it. How consuming strong the invitation they extend! Shall I be allowed to go to them? Night and day I pray that I may, but it seems too good to be true. Someone worthy will go, able for the Godful work, yet as far as I can I must drift about these love-monument

mountains, glad to be a servant of the servants is so holy a wilderness. (Muir, 1911, p. 22)

The writings and actions of George P. Marsh and John Muir in the late 19th century helped to change the public's thinking with respect to natural resources and the environment in fundamental ways. This helped spark the "conservation movement" in the U.S. which began developing in earnest in the early 20th century (Albright, 1988). Both Marsh and Muir helped lead the public away from thinking that the natural resources of the New World (North America in particular) were inexhaustible, and towards thinking about the need to actively conserve natural resources for the betterment of present and future generations of people. They also helped the public, Muir especially, to think about natural resources and the environmental settings not just as sources of raw materials for economic production and growth, but also as sources of aesthetic enjoyment, recreation, and restoration of personal physical, emotional, and spiritual health.[4] Such broad viewpoints on the values of nature that are commonplace to students studying natural resource and environmental economics in this day and age, were quite unconventional and ground-breaking at the turn of the 20th century.

Conservation as Wise Use

Other ground-breaking views related to natural resource conservation around the turn of the 20th century were practiced, voiced, and written about by Gifford Pinchot. Pinchot attended Yale University as an undergraduate student, graduating in 1889. He then did postgraduate studies at the French National School of Forestry. In 1892, upon the recommendation of Frederick Law Olmstead (designer of Central Park in New York City and one of the founders of American landscape architecture), Pinchot was hired by George Vanderbilt to manage the forests which were part of his 125,000-acre estate in western North Carolina near Asheville. Much of the Vanderbilt estate forest lands that Pinchot managed are now part of the Pisgah National Forest. Another part, the Biltmore House and Gardens, still owned by descendants of the George Vanderbilt family, are open to the public for viewing and guided tours.

As George Vanderbilt's private forester, Pinchot implemented professional forest management practices on a large scale for the first time in the U.S., earning the title held today by Pisgah National Forest as the "cradle of forestry" in America. Pinchot went on to become the first Chief of the U.S. Forest Service from 1905 to 1910. Pinchot's guiding principles for natural resource management and conservation are documented in his book entitled *The Fight for Conservation* and include the need for national development, reduction of waste, and working towards the common good (Pinchot, 1910).

With respect to conservation of natural resources, Pinchot described the "common good" as working to achieve the "greatest good for the greatest number of people for the longest time" (Pinchot, 1910). This philosophical–moral basis for this principle goes back to the 18th-century English philosopher, Jeremy Bentham, who wrote, "Nature has placed mankind under the governance of two sovereign masters, *pain* and *pleasure*" (Bentham, 1789). Thus, Bentham considered "happiness" to be associated with the presence of pleasure and the absence of pain, and as early as 1776 stated as a matter of moral philosophy that "it is the greatest happiness of the greatest number that is the measure of right and wrong" (Bentham, 1776). John Stuart Mill popularized Bentham's moral philosophy of seeking and maximizing happiness individually and collectively, or utilitarianism, that is one of the foundations of modern economic theory. Of special note to students of natural resource and environmental economics, utilitarianism provides the philosophical–moral basis for using benefit–cost analysis, and by association the potential Pareto improvement criterion (see Chapter 3 in this book) to evaluate natural resource and environmental policy and management decisions and policies.

Pinchot's principles for natural resource conservation also encompass the ideas (or ideals) that natural resource conservation entails the wise use of natural resources over time for multiple purposes. Pinchot's focus on the wise *use* of natural resources provided some of the foundation for later theories and practices of economic conservation in the form of economic theory for optimal depletion of exhaustible, nonrenewable resources (e.g., minerals) over time, and optimal sustainable management of exhaustible, renewable resources (e.g., forests, fish and wildlife) over time. His focus on *multiple* values of natural resources helped provide the foundation for the "multiple use doctrine" followed to this day by the U.S. Forest Service and other federal and state natural resource management agencies (e.g., U.S. Bureau of Land Management, U.S. Army Corps of Engineers).

National Parks and Natural Resource Conservation and Preservation

Another major, ground-breaking development in the American conservation movement occurred on March 1, 1872 when President Ulysses S. Grant signed into law the Congressional bill establishing the world's first national park, Yellowstone National Park, which stretches across parts of Montana, Wyoming, and Idaho. The national park concept, however, has earlier roots back to June 30, 1864 when President Abraham Lincoln signed legislation providing federal protection to the Yosemite Valley and the Mariposa Grove of Giant Sequoias in California for "public use, resort, and recreation."

Yellowstone National Park was established primarily to protect the unique landscape and geologic features of the area including natural geysers (e.g., what is now known as "Old Faithful" geyser). The second national park was established on September 25, 1890 when President Benjamin Harrison signed the Congressional bill establishing Sequoia National Park in California. Sequoia National Park was the first national park established primarily to protect living, biological resources – the gigantic Sequoia trees (Sequoiadendron giganteum).

President Harrison also signed legislation establishing Yosemite National Park as the nation's third national park on October 1, 1890. When Sequoia and Yosemite National Parks were established in 1890, a national park service with park rangers who manage the parks did not yet exist. Thus, management of these two national parks, along with Yellowstone National Park, was assigned to the U.S. Army. An African American company of soldiers under the command of Captain Charles Young, who was a commissioned African American U.S. Army Officer (in fact, the only one of such at the time), was given the task of protecting and managing the natural resources in Sequoia and Yosemite National Parks.·

It took until the early 1900s before significantly more national parks were established through many "grassroots" efforts and the political will and action at the national level and in Washington, D.C. led by President Theodore Roosevelt. Roosevelt's interests in and commitment to protecting public lands in the western U.S. as national parks and monuments were inspired by a buffalo hunting trip to North Dakota in 1883, a family vacation to Yellowstone National Park in 1890, a later visit and tour of Yellowstone National Park with well-known at the time naturalist John Burroughs, and a particularly impactful three-day camping trip with John Muir in Yosemite Valley in 1903. Muir took full advantage of this unprecedented time alone with the President in nature to share his philosophy and passion for protecting the natural wonders and "cathedrals" of America. President Roosevelt's contributions to the conservation movement included signing legislation creating five national parks and establishing 51 bird reserves, four game reserves, and 150 national forests (working with Gifford Pinchot). In 1906, he also signed into law the U.S. Antiquities Act which he used extensively, and not without controversy, to proclaim 18 new national monuments.

The establishment of national parks, national monuments, and other units of the national park system has had much influence on natural resource and environmental economics. For example, origins of the travel cost method can be traced back to a letter written by Harold Hotelling to the National Park Service suggesting such a method for estimating the demand for national park visits. The letter was in response to an appeal initiated by the Director of the National Park Service for ideas on how to value national park services (Hotelling, 1947). The Director was interested in, as are many government administrators to this day, obtaining data about the economic benefits of national parks in order to help justify federal budget expenditures (costs) on national parks (Hanemann, 1992).

With respect to natural resource use, national parks and the national park system also moved away from the "multiple-use doctrine" advocated by Gifford Pinchot and followed by the U.S. Forest Service to focusing more on non-consumptive recreational uses of natural resources. One of the earliest advocates of preserving natural resources in the U.S. for their aesthetic and scenic values was John Muir. The "preservationist" approach/environmental ethic in the tradition of John Muir and the "conservationist" approach/environmental ethic in the tradition of Gifford Pinchot came to philosophical blows and practical management conflicts in the Hetch Hetchy Valley (California) preservation debate in the early 1900s. In the end, the practical needs of the City of San Francisco for municipal water supplies won the day and resulted in the building of a dam and reservoir in the Hetch Hetchy Valley resulting in the flooding and loss of what John Muir called the second Yosemite Valley – actually the valley is still there, it is just under a lot of water and technically could be restored someday if the dam were to be removed (something Hetch Hetchy Valley advocates have pushed for in recent years).

Development of Formal Economic Models of Optimum Resource Use

The conservationist approach to natural resource management is consistent with the concept of economic conservation pioneered by Ciriacy-Wantrup (1968) in his classic book *Resource Conservation: Economics and Policies*. More specifically, he defined the optimal state of conservation as the rate of resource use that would maximize the present value of net revenues over time (Ciriacy-Wantrup, 1968; Brown et al., 2016). This general rule is the basis for the dynamic optimization approach for analyzing economically optimal natural resource use and management – which is a core component of natural resource economics teaching programs.

In the case of exhaustible, non-renewable resources, the concept of an optimal time path of consumption can be traced back further to Harold Hotelling. Hotelling was a mathematician turned economist who was a professor at Stanford University, Columbia University, and the University of North Carolina-Chapel Hill until he retired in 1966. He was one of the early pioneers in the fields of mathematical economics and econometrics (Arrow and Lehman, 2012). Heal (2007) also credits Hotelling as "in many ways, the founder of analytical resource and environmental economics." In his seminal 1931 paper on the economics of exhaustible resources, Hotelling formulated what is now known as Hotelling's Rule which states that the optimal price path and extraction rate for exhaustible resources occurs where the resource output price is increasing at the market interest rate. Such a price path maximizes net returns from extraction over time (Hotelling, 1931; Heal, 2007).

In the case of renewable resources, theory and methods for optimal resources use and management is rooted in forestry and fisheries management. Optimal management of forests and fisheries introduced the concept of "sustainable use" into natural resource and environmental economics. Because trees and fish can reproduce themselves through biological growth, it is possible to harvest a given level of these resources on a sustainable basis, year after year. As with non-renewable resources, the optimal harvest of renewable resources from an economic perspective is the rate of harvest that maximizes net returns over time. Early pioneering contributors to the economic theory of fisheries economics, an example of common pool resources, include H. Scott Gordon, Anthony Scott, and James Crutchfield (Gordon, 1954; Scott, 1955; Crutchfield, 1961; Brown et al., 2016). Faustmann (1849) and Hartman (1976) are credited with the development of forestry economics (Brazee, 2001).

The development of natural resource and environmental economics over time has also been heavily influenced by the need to assess and provide practical solutions to the use and allocation of water. Griffin (2012) provides a comprehensive review of the "origins and ideals" of water resource economics, including major contributors to theory and techniques especially during what he terms the "classic era" of water resource economics (1945–1969). In the U.S., he traces the development of water resource economics back to the early 1900s when federal legislation was passed to deal with national problems and needs related to flood control, navigation, and irrigation (especially in the arid Western U.S.).[5] This early legislation resulted in the system of federal water management projects we see today throughout the U.S., particularly dams and reservoir systems.

Eventually, outdoor recreation became a formally recognized benefit of federal water projects which resulted in the development of economic theory and techniques for estimating use values of water-based outdoor recreation – in particular, revealed preference techniques such as the travel cost method. Today, in addition to use values, passive use or non-use values are recognized as important benefits of water resources contributing, for example, to preservation of critical wildlife habitat (e.g., wetlands) and existence values of wildlife species that depend on this habitat. The need to value passive use or non-use values for inclusion in policy and project assessment (e.g., benefit–cost analysis) spurred on development of stated preference theory and techniques for measuring these values such as contingent valuation and choice experiments (Banzhaf, 2010; Griffin, 2012).

The "conservationist" philosophy and concept of economic conservation historically (and in many ways up to today) tends to focus on consumptive use values of natural resources and the environment (e.g., think optimal extraction rate of crude oil from a privately-owned well, optimal harvest of trees from a privately-owned forest, optimal commercial harvest rate of fish from a common-property fishery). As mentioned above, the conservationist philosophy and arguments of Gifford Pinchot and allies prevailed over the preservationist philosophy and arguments of John Muir in the fight to save the Hetch Hetchy Valley in the Sierra Nevada Mountains of California from flooding for a water reservoir. In his arguments for preserving the valley in its natural, unflooded state, John Muir emphasized non-consumptive use and non-use of the valley. For example, he foresaw that Yosemite Valley would eventually become crowded with recreational users and argued that the nearby Hetch Hetchy Valley would provide a needed, and near equal, substitute site for hiking, camping, and other forms of non-consumption outdoor recreational activities (even though John Muir and Teddy Roosevelt were generally allies in the National Park movement, Muir did not share Roosevelt's passion for consumptive outdoor recreational activities such as hunting).

Muir also emphasized the need to preserve the rare aesthetic beauty of the Hetch Hetchy Valley in its natural form. John Muir's writings in which he reflects upon the natural beauty and majesty of the Sierra Nevada Mountains suggest that he also recognized intrinsic and non-use (or passive use) values of natural resources and the environment. He, himself, certainly spent time off-site (e.g., at home) thinking about and reflecting on the beauty and majesty of natural environments, contributing perhaps to his own enjoyment from what natural resource and environmental economists now call existence value. His essays describing the natural wonders of the Sierra Nevada Mountains to readers in the populated (and crowded) cities of the East Coast may have also contributed to these readers holding existence values for places such as the Yosemite and Hetch Hetchy Valleys. Formal theoretical recognition by economists of the existence of existence value would come much later as described below.

THE "ENVIRONMENTAL MOVEMENT" AND ENVIRONMENTAL ECONOMICS

The conservation movement in the U.S. of the late 19th century and early 20th century eventually developed and expanded into a broader environmental movement in the 1960s and 1970s.[6] The need for a broad environmental movement was, in part, catalyzed by the Cuyahoga River catching fire in 1969 due to uncontrolled dumping of industrial waste.[7] In addition, I recall during my undergraduate college days in the 1970s, there was also much concern expressed inside and outside of the classroom about the human "population explosion" leading to growing resource scarcity and limits to economic growth and social well-being. A very influential Club of Rome report entitled, *The*

Limits to Growth (Meadows et al., 1972) contributed to these Malthusian type concerns. As every student of natural resource and environmental economics knows (or should know), concerns over human population and resource scarcity leading to a "day of reckoning" where human population growth outstrips natural resource availability with dire consequences for humanity and society dates back at least to Thomas Malthus and what we now call the "Malthusian Doctrine" discussed earlier in this chapter.

The *Limits to Growth* report and other ensuing related papers and discussion spurred economists in the 1970s to think more deeply and broadly about the values of scarce natural resources. At that time and before, economists were familiar with the relationships between natural resource scarcity and economic rent introduced by David Ricardo, who was another classical economist living and writing about the same time and place as Thomas Malthus (e.g., England in the 18th century and early 19th century). Ricardo theorized that scarce agricultural land in England should command a surplus economic value or rent we now refer to as "land rent" – and the scarcer, the higher should be the land rent associated with agricultural production (Ricardo, 1817).[8]

In modern neoclassical economic theory, land rent is akin to the concept of producer surplus which is used to measure the net benefits to firms of producing goods and services. The concept of consumer surplus is used to measure the net benefits to consumers of consuming goods and services. Consumer surplus, like producer surplus (e.g., land rent) is affected by resource scarcity. For example, *ceteris paribus*, we would expect the net benefits (consumer surplus) a person receives from hiking at a highly unique and beautiful natural area (e.g., Yosemite Valley or Grand Canyon) to be higher as compared to hiking at a common, non-unique site such as a local park (with perhaps the exception of Central Park in New York City and the like).

In addition to consumer surplus values arising from active uses of natural resources, natural resource and environmental economists nowadays recognize that people can derive consumer surplus values even when not actively using a natural resource – what we now call non-use values. The clearest example of a non-use value is *existence value* defined as the value (consumer surplus) a person places merely thinking about and reflecting on the existence of a natural resource independent of any type of actual use. The more formal recognition and definition of existence value is usually attributed to the classic article written by John Krutilla entitled "Conservation reconsidered" (Krutilla, 1967), although the genesis of the idea can also be traced back to Ciriacy-Wantrup's *Resource Conservation* book (Brown et al., 2016). Later theoretical developments led to more formal definitions of use and non-use values and associated theoretically appropriate welfare measures (e.g., Hicksian compensating and equivalent surplus) based on applied welfare economics (e.g., see Randall and Stoll, 1980; Hanemann, 1984; and Chapter 3 in this book). These theoretical developments provided the theoretical grounding for the parallel development of nonmarket valuation techniques for measuring use and non-use values.

Recognition of Market Failures

In addition to a recognition of the broad values of natural resources and the environment to include both use and non-use values, the environmental movement of the 1960s and 1970s ushered in a new era of applying economic theory to the solution of negative externality problems such as air and water pollution. Rachel Carson's famous book, *Silent Spring*, was a major contributor to popular recognition of externality problems, both within and outside of academia. In this book, in a very readable and relatable way (often tough for scientists to do), Carson showed how DDT spraying for mosquitos led to the negative externality and unintended consequence of harming bird eggs and reproduction which would eventually lead to spring without the singing of birds, or a silent spring (Carson, 1962).

The DDT negative externality problem described by Carson in *Silent Spring* is a type of "market failure" or "market inefficiency" defined as the failure or inability of private markets to satisfy the conditions necessary and sufficient for a competitive market equilibrium to be Pareto efficient. Toxic chemical contamination of the environment, such as from DDT, is a "public bad." In such cases, the private market results in "too much" of the public bad from a Pareto efficiency (economic efficiency) standpoint. Market failure also can occur in the case of positive externalities such as "public goods." Examples of public goods include clean water and clean air. In general, private markets will provide "too little" of the public good from a Pareto efficiency (economic efficiency) standpoint. As pointed out by Samuelson in his seminal article on public goods, in the case of public goods that are nonrival in consumption (e.g., everyone can consume the same amount, of say, clean air in a day), Pareto efficiency involves vertical summation of demand curves – which is not easily done in practice due to the "free rider" problem and associated difficulty in measuring consumers' true willingness-to-pay for public goods (Samuelson, 1954).

In the 1970s and beyond, the application of economics to environmental policy-making such as developing and implementing market-like solutions to air and water pollution problems (e.g., tradable pollution permits) proliferated. The first Earth Day, which occurred on April 22, 1970, has been credited with raising national environmental awareness and helping to launch federal environmental regulation. Earth Day was one of several major environmental events in 1970 including passage of the Clean Air Act and the National Environmental Policy Act (NEPA). In addition to the Clean Air Act, the 1972

Federal Water Pollution Control Act (which was renamed the Clean Water Act with its 1977 amendments), the Endangered Species Act, the Safe Drinking Water Act, and several other major pieces of legislation were passed in the 1970s. These policies helped to stimulate an explosion of research in the area of environmental and resource economics (Freeman, 2002; Pearce, 2002; Fouquet, 2019).

Correcting for Market Failures

When teaching about environmental economics and policy, a usual starting point is introducing students to the neoclassical economist Arthur Pigou and the concepts of Pigouvian taxes and subsidies as a means for correcting negative externalities (Pigou, 1920; Pearce, 2002). Pigouvian taxes, for example, are the theoretical basis for current proposals to use carbon taxes to reduce carbon emissions, say by industrial factories and power plants. Allen Kneese, an environmental economist at Resources for the Future, was instrumental in the application of Pigouvian pricing in environmental economics (Banzhaf, 2020). Kneese first laid out the notion that later became known as "green taxes" could be used to achieve the efficient amount of pollution cost effectively relative to command-and-control policy.

Ronald Coase offered an alternative approach (now known as the "Coase Theorem") to solving externality problems based on voluntary transactions whereby the party generating the externality and the party affected by the externality negotiate the externality away (Coase, 1960). For example, given all the right conditions, the Coase Theorem suggests that a downstream farmer whose use of river water is impaired by nutrient run-off from an upstream farmer, could pay the upstream farmer to modify agricultural operations on the upstream farm to reduce nutrient run-off. The end theoretical result of applying the Coase Theorem is a Pareto-efficient level of negative externality (e.g., pollution) abatement, as with Pigouvian taxes and subsidies. The Coase Theorem is primarily applicable to externalities with only a few parties that are affected such that they can negotiate over internalizing the externality. However, most policy relevant externalities such as urban air pollution or pollution of interstate waterways involve thousands, if not millions of people, and hence the Coase Theorem does not provide a practical solution in these cases.[9]

Since the decade of the 1970s federal environmental regulation has moved away from rigid standards and become more incentive-based and flexible. Tom Crocker (1966) and Dales (1968) introduced the concept of tradeable pollution permits for air (Crocker) and water (Dales) pollution. Hahn (1989) reviews a number of these early efforts. The first large-scale implementation of tradeable pollution permits was with the Acid Rain Program in the 1990 Clean Air Act Amendments. This "grand experiment" in tradeable pollution permits has been credited with achieving more reductions in acid rain at lower cost than expected (Stavins, 1998).[10]

With respect to making efficient natural resource and environmental management and policy decisions, economists have long recognized that individual and group (societal) decisions do not occur in an institutional vacuum. In reality, institutions, especially property rights, heavily influence the economic outcomes of individual and group decisions affecting natural resources and the environment. This "institutional economics" school of thought has origins in natural resource and environmental economics in the field of "land economics" which focuses on "the economic relationships people have with others respecting land" (Barlowe, 1986, p. 3). Barlowe traces the origins of land economics back to a seminar on landed property taught by Richard Ely at the University of Wisconsin in 1892. Formal recognition of land economics as a separate field of economics, according to Barlowe, occurred in 1919 with the establishment of the Division of Land Economics in the U.S. Department of Agriculture (ibid.). Although some universities still offer stand-alone courses in land economics, in many applied economics departments, concepts from land and institutional economics are taught as components of broader natural resource and environmental economics.

For example, in my "Principles of Resource Economics" undergraduate course, I teach a section on institutions affecting natural resource use, allocation, and management focusing on property rights. Considering property rights and physical characteristics affecting production and consumption, natural and environmental resources can be grouped into four broad categories: (1) rival, exclusive; (2) rival, nonexclusive; (3) nonrival, exclusive; and (4) nonrival, nonexclusive. Rival, exclusive resources include pure private goods such as crude oil, natural gas, and other minerals. Nonrival, nonexclusive resources include pure public goods such as clean ambient air. Rival, nonexclusive resources include "open access" resources with *res nullius* property rights such as fish in international waters and minerals on Earth's moon.

Nonrival, exclusive resources include "common property" resources with *res communis* property rights such as public timber land in the U.S. managed by the U.S Forest Service (National Forests), public livestock grazing land in the U.S. managed by the U.S. Bureau of Land Management, and ocean fisheries controlled and managed by different countries within their 200-mile territorial limits (Bergstrom and Randall, 2016, Chapters 9 and 10). Probably every student who has taken a natural resource or environmental course at a college or university around the world has read or at least heard about the "tragedy of the commons." The tragedy of the commons, popularized by Garrett Hardin his classic 1968 *Science* article, refers to depletion and exhaustion of "open access" type resources with little or no property rights governing use. In the absence of property rights or other institutions (e.g., customs, commonly accepted "rules of the game"), there is an incentive for people to want to "capture" and consume a resource before somebody else does which can lead to a "free for all" and overexploitation of a resource from economic, environmental, and social (ethical) perspectives (e.g., the "triple bottom line").

One solution to open-access resource problems is to establish private property rights over the resource (e.g., privatize the resource) with the main idea being that private owners will have an economic incentive to use and manage the resource in a wise and efficient manner – for example, a farmer/landowner should have an economic incentive to follow "best practice" soil and water conservation farming techniques on the land. This "privatize the resource" approach is consistent with the Austrian economics school of thought which promotes the benefits of private property institutions and free markets, and Nobel laureate James Buchanan's "public choice theory" which questions whether imperfect, self-interested government officials operating in imperfect government institutions can do a better job of achieving Pareto-efficient outcomes as compared to imperfect, self-interested producers and consumers operating in imperfect private markets (Anderson, 1982; Randall, 1985).

In contrast, other economists in the tradition of land/institutional economics have argued that natural and environmental resources can (and perhaps should) be efficiently managed as "common property" resources if the common owners and users of the resource effectively cooperate together to achieve mutually beneficial ends such as conservation of soil and water resources (Bromley, 1982; Randall, 1985). For example, Nobel laureate Elinor Ostrom studied small communities around the world and found that social norms and other "grass root" institutional arrangements could prevent overexploitation and exhaustion of common property or common pool resources. Based on theoretical insight including from game theory and empirical observation, Ostrom developed eight fundamental design principles for stable use and management of common property or common pool natural resources including shared grazing land and fisheries (Ostrom, 1990, 2010).

Concern over natural resource depletion and environmental degradation has led to another school of thought in economics focusing on ecosystems and ecosystem goods and services – ecological economics. Pearce (2002) traces ecological economics back to Kenneth Boulding's classic "spaceship Earth" essay (Boulding, 1966). In this essay, Boulding described the Planet Earth as a "closed system" akin to a closed ecosystem subject to positive and negative feedback loops and cycles (e.g., chemical cycles). In a closed ecosystem or economy, for example, human-induced air and water pollution could cause a negative feedback loop affecting the health and integrity of ecosystems and their ability to provide ecosystem goods and service of value to people. Viewing coupled ecosystems and economies in the nature of closed economies suggests the need for a proper balance of natural capital inputs and environmental outputs (including pollution) in order to sustain both healthy ecosystems and economies.[11]

Pearce (2002) discusses the extent to which ecological economics is a "new paradigm" as compared to environmental economics based on neoclassical economic theory and models. As far as I know, very few economics and applied economics departments teach separate ecological economics courses. However, concepts emerging from or highlighted by ecological economics such as natural capital, materials balance, ecosystem services, and sustainable development are often incorporated into natural resource and environmental economics teaching and research programs.

CONCLUDING REMARKS

This chapter highlights the academic history and heritage of natural resource and environmental economics including key contributors and programs. The chapter integrates this history and heritage with the rise and development of the "conservation movement" and "environmental movement" in the United States. The story is told from the personal perspective and reflections of the author who began his own journey into the field and natural resource and environmental economics as an undergraduate student in the 1970s. The chapter serves two purposes for this book. First, I and my co-editor John Whitehead hope that this historical overview is useful as a teaching resource. In the classes we teach in natural resource and environmental economics, we have found that brief discussions of the history of economic thought stimulates students' interest in the textbook material, and helps them to better understand the material by reference to the original sources and reasons why particular theories, concepts, and methods came about. Second, this chapter provides context for the remainder of this book with respect to appreciating and passing on the rich heritage and modern content of natural resource and environmental economics to current and future students of the field.

NOTES

1.   I gratefully acknowledge John Whitehead (the other co-editor of this book) and John Loomis for many very helpful comments and edits on this chapter. I am also indebted to many colleagues who graciously responded to my request on the Land & Resource Economics Network listserve (RESECON) for input and references related to the historical development of natural resource and environmental economics.
2.   I recall that during the 1970s, Thoreau's *Walden* was one of the philosophical and practical "guidebooks" for "back-to-the-land"-type young people seeking a more simple, natural, and environmentally friendly lifestyle whose heritage has been passed on to modern-day rural and urban "homesteaders."

3. One of the chapter authors of this book, Robert Johnston, is Research Professor and Director of The George Perkins Marsh Institute at Clark University in Worcester, MA. The Marsh Institute and the natural resource and environmental research it supports reflects the ongoing legacy of George P. Marsh.

4. The popular film by Ken Burnes, *The National Parks: America's Best Idea*, provides an excellent and interesting documentation of John Muir's nature philosophy as well as an overview of the conservation movement in the United States. I have used this film in a freshman seminar course at the University of Georgia designed to introduce students to conservation and resource management historical thought and practice.

5. The Reclamation Act of 1902 was passed in response to the demand for irrigation water by farmers in the Intermountain West region of the U.S. which led to the establishment of the Bureau of Reclamation, which built and manages large water development in this region including one of its first and most well-known projects, the Hoover Dam and Reservoir (Lake Mead Project). In addition to irrigation water, the project was built to provide flood control and hydroelectricity benefits. Today, outdoor recreation is also a major benefit of Lake Mead including the first and largest national recreation area in the U.S., Lake Mead National Recreation Area (https://www.nps.gov/lake/index.htm).

6. For exposition purposes, I have divided this chapter into sections on the "conservation movement" and natural resource economics and the later "environmental movement" and environmental economics. However, over time, both the conservation and environmental movements influenced developments in both the fields of natural resource economics and environmental economics. Also, even in my own thinking, it is often difficult to draw a clear line between the conservation and environmental movements and the fields of natural resource economics and environmental economics. That is, as I "pan out" to a broader "birds-eye view," the conservation movement, environmental movement, natural resource economics, and environmental economics tend to merge together into a more holistic and interconnected paradigm (which also includes ecological economics).

7. I am grateful to John Loomis for this additional insight on the origins of the environmental movement.

8. Johann Heinrich von Thünen, the name of another classical economist which should be familiar to students of natural resource and environmental economics, conceptualized scarcity rent as deriving from geographical location whereby land closest to the "city center" would command the highest economic surplus value (von Thünen, 1826).

9. My thanks to John Loomis for the reminder and addition of this practical limitation of Coase-type solutions to broad externality problems.

10. I appreciate John Whitehead's addition of this paragraph and other insights on the history of environmental policy and its relationships with environmental economics.

11. Pearce (2002) points out that such a "material balance" model of an economy was first formalized by Ayres and Kneese (1969).

REFERENCES

Albright, H.M. (1988), 'Great American Conservationists', in *Conservators of Hope: The Horace M. Albright Conservation Lectures*, Moscow, ID: University of

Idaho Press in Cooperation with the Board of Regents of University of California, Berkeley.

Anderson, T.L. (1982), 'The new resource economics: Old ideas and new applications', *American Journal of Agricultural Economics*, **64** (5): 928–934.

Arrow, K.J. and E.L. Lehmann (2012), 'Harold Hotelling', in *Selected Works of EL Lehmann*, Boston, MA: Springer, pp. 903–915.

Ayres, R., and A. Kneese (1969), 'Production, consumption, and externalities', *American Economic Review*, **59** (3): 282–297.

Banzhaf, H.S. (2010), 'Consumer surplus with apology: A historical perspective on nonmarket valuation and recreation demand', *Annual Review of Resource Economics*, **2**: 18.1–18.25.

Banzhaf, H.S. (2020), 'A history of pricing pollution (or, why everything you thought you knew about it is wrong and Pigouvian taxes are not necessarily Pigouvian)', unpublished manuscript, June.

Barlowe, R. (1986), *Land Resource Economics*, Fourth Edition, Englewood Cliffs, NJ: Prentice-Hall.

Bentham, J. (1776), *A Fragment on Government: Being an Examination of What is Delivered, on the Subject of Government in General in the Introduction to Sir William Blackstone's Commentaries: With a Preface, in Which is Given a Critique of the Work at Large*, London: Printed for T. Payne, P. Elmsly and E. Brooke.

Bentham, J. (1789), *An Introduction to the Principles of Morals and Legislation. Printed in the Year 1780, and Now First Published. By Jeremy Bentham.* London: Printed for T. Payne and Son.

Bergstrom, J.C. and A. Randall (2016), *Resource Economics: An Economic Approach to Natural Resource and Environmental Policy*, Cheltenham, UK and Northampton, MA, USA: Edward Elgar Publishing.

Boulding, K. (1966), 'The economics of the coming spaceship Earth', in H. Jarett (ed.), *Environmental Quality in a Growing Economy*, Baltimore: Johns Hopkins University Press, pp. 3–14.

Brazee, R. (2001), 'The Faustmann formula: Fundamental to forest economics 150 years after publication', *Forest Science*, **47** (4): 441–442.

Bromley, D.W. (1982), 'Land and water problems: An institutional perspective', *American Journal of Agricultural Economics*, **64** (5): 834–844.

Brown, G.M., V.K. Smith, G.R. Munro and R. Bishop (2016), 'Early pioneers in natural resource economics', *Annual Review of Resource Economics*, **8**: 25–42.

Carson, R. (1962), *Silent Spring*, Boston, MA: Houghton Mifflin.

Ciriacy-Wantrup S.V. (1952), *Resource Conservation: Economics and Policies*, Oakland, CA: University of California Press.

Coase, R. (1960), 'The problem of social cost', *Journal of Law and Economics*, **3** (1): 1–44.

Crocker, Thomas D. (1966), 'The structuring of atmospheric pollution control systems', in H. Wolozin (ed.), *The Economics of Air Pollution*, New York: Norton, pp. 61–86.

Crutchfield, J.A. (1961), 'An economic evaluation of alternative methods of fishery regulations', *Journal of Law and Economics*, **4**: 131–43.

Dales, J. (1968), *Pollution, Property and Prices*, Toronto: University Press.

Emerson, R.W. (1836), *Nature*, Boston, MA: James Munroe.

Faustmann, M. (1849), 'On the determination of the value which forestland and immature stands pose for forestry', Reprinted in the *Journal of Forest Economics*, **1**: 7–44 (1995).

Fouquet, R. (2019), 'Introduction', in R. Fouquet (ed.), *Handbook on Green Growth*, Cheltenham, UK and Northampton, MA, USA: Edward Elgar Publishing.

Freeman, A.M. (2002), 'Environmental policy since Earth Day I: What have we gained?', *Journal of Economic Perspectives*, **16** (1): 125–146.

Gordon H.S. (1954), 'The economic theory of a common property resource: The fishery', *Journal of Political Economy*, **62**: 124–142.

Griffin, R.C. (2012), 'The origins and ideals of water resource economics in the United States', *Annual Review of Resource Economics*, **4** (1): 353–377.

Groom, B. and M. Talevi (2020), 'How does economics address the environment?', Chapter 14, in K. Deane and E.V. Waeyenberge (eds), *Recharting the History of Economic Thought*, London, UK: Red Globe Press, pp. 247–268.

Hahn, R.W. (1989), 'Economic prescriptions for environmental problems: How the patient followed the doctor's orders', *Journal of Economic Perspectives*, **3** (2): 95–114.

Hanemann, W.M. (1984), 'Welfare evaluations in contingent valuation experiments with discrete responses', *American Journal of Agricultural Economics*, **66** (3): 332–341.

Hanemann, W. Michael (1992), 'Preface', in S. Navrud (ed.), *Pricing the European Environment*, New York: Oxford University Press, pp. 9–14.

Hardin, G. (1968), 'The tragedy of the commons', *Science*, **162** (3859): 1243–1248.

Hartman, R. (1976), 'The harvesting decision when a standing forest has value', *Economic Inquiry*, **14** (1): 52–58.

Heal, G. (2007), 'A celebration of environmental and resource economics', *Review of Environmental Economics and Policy*, **1** (1): 7–25.

Hotelling, H. (1931), 'The economics of exhaustible resources', *Journal of Political Economy*, **39** (2): 137–175.

Hotelling, H. (1947), *Letter to the National Park Service*, Published in Prewitt (1949), *The Economics of Public Recreation: The Prewitt Report*, Washington, D.C.: U.S. Department of the Interior.

Kling, C.L., K. Segerson and J.F. Shogren (2010), 'Environmental economics: How agricultural economists helped advance the field', *American Journal of Agricultural Economics*, **92** (2): 487–505.

Krutilla, J.V. (1967), 'Conservation reconsidered', *American Economic Review*, **57** (4): 777–786.

Lichtenberg, E., J. Shortle, J. Wilen and D. Zilberman (2010), 'Natural resource economics and conservation: Contributions of agricultural economics and agricultural economists', *American Journal of Agricultural Economics*, **92** (2): 469–486.

Malthus, T.R. (1798), 'An essay on the principle of population', in *Oxfords World Classics* reprints.

Marsh, G.P. (1864), *Man and Nature: Physical Geography as Modified by Human Action*, New York, NY: Charles Scribner.

Meadows, D.H., D.L. Meadows, J. Randers and W.W. Behrens III (1972), *The Limits to Growth: A Report for the Club of Rome's Project on the Predicament of Mankind*, New York: Universe Books.

Muir, J. (1894), *The Mountains of California*, New York: The Century Company.

Muir, J. (1911), *My First Summer in the Sierra*, Boston: Houghton Mifflin Company.

Ostrom, E. (1990), *Governing the Commons: The Evolution of Institutions for Collective Action*, Cambridge, UK: Cambridge University Press.

Ostrom, E. (2010), 'Beyond markets and states: Polycentric governance of complex economic systems', *American Economic Review*, **100** (3): 1–33.

Pearce, D. (2002), 'An intellectual history of environmental economics', *Annual Review of Energy and the Environment*, **27** (1): 57–81.

Pigou, A.C. (1920), *The Economics of Welfare*, London: Palgrave Macmillan.

Pinchot, G. (1910), *The Fight for Conservation*, New York, NY: Doubleday, Page & Company.

Randall, A. (1985), 'Methodology, ideology, and the economics of policy: Why resource economists disagree', *American Journal of Agricultural Economics*, **67** (5): 1022–1029.

Randall, A. and J.R. Stoll (1980), 'Consumer's surplus in commodity space', *American Economic Review*, **71** (3): 449–457.

Ricardo, David (1817), *On the Principles of Political Economy and Taxation*, London: John Murray, Albemarle Street.

Samuelson, P.A. (1954), 'The pure theory of public expenditure', *Review of Economics and Statistics*, **36** (4): 387–389.

Sandmo, A. (2015), 'The early history of environmental economics', *Review of Environmental Economics and Policy*, **9** (1): 43–63.

Scott, A.D. (1955), 'The fishery: The objectives of sole ownership', *Journal of Political Economy*, **63** (2): 116–124.

Spash, C. (1999), 'The development of environmental thinking in economics', *Environmental Values*, **8** (4): 413–435.

Stavins, R.N. (1998), 'What can we learn from the grand policy experiment? Lessons from SO2 allowance trading', *Journal of Economic Perspectives*, **12** (3): 69–88.

Thoreau, H.D. (1854), *Walden: Life in the Woods*, Boston, MA: Ticknor & Fields.

Thoreau, H.D. (1862), 'Walking', *The Atlantic Magazine*, May.

Viitala, E.J. (2013), 'The discovery of the Faustmann formula in natural resource economics', *History of Political Economy*, **45** (3): 523–548.

von Thünen, Johann Heinrich (1826), *Der isolierte Staat* (*The Isolated State*), Hamburg: Wirtschaft & Finan.

Yeoman, B. (2014), 'Why the passenger pigeon went extinct', *Audubon Magazine*, May–June.

PART I

Paradigms

2. Positive economics, economic efficiency, environmental economics and policy

David McEvoy

2.1 INTRODUCTION – THE RENAISSANCE 'ECONOMIC' MAN

Managing environmental and natural resources is a balancing act. On the one hand everyone benefits from a cleaner environment and better protection of natural resources. On the other hand, reducing pollution and protecting the environment is potentially costly and the trade-off is that society may have to reduce investment in other activities. When economists think about the optimal amount of environmental protection they often rely on the concept of efficiency; that is, maximizing the difference between the benefits and the costs of managing resources. This chapter discusses approaches to teaching the economic concepts of optimal environmental and natural resource management and the policies designed to achieve these goals. In my teaching and research, I like to complement theory with experiments, and I take the same approach in this chapter.

One of the most interesting aspects about being an economist is that we do all kinds of different things. Economists are social scientists who study human behavior, and have close ties to psychologists and anthropologists. Economists are also focused on social policies with a keen interest in how resources are allocated in society, having overlapping agendas with our political science colleagues. Economists are theorists, mathematicians, data scientists and experimentalists, and communicate with the 'hard' sciences and statisticians. The domain of environmental and resource economists spreads even farther, and these economists often rub shoulders with environmental scientists, environmental engineers, and environmentalists.

This broad set of skills and interests sometimes makes it hard to succinctly describe what an economist does. Any economist with experience answering questions during a college open house will understand this point. Students interested in studying economics (more often the parents standing behind them) will ask the million-dollar question: what kind of jobs do economists get? It's hard not to sound facetious when the economist answers truthfully with 'just about any job they want'.

One of the most helpful approaches I have found in the classroom is to start off my course in environmental economics by describing some of the many roles economists play in helping solve big social problems. I use climate change as the overarching example, but any topic can be explored. I borrowed this general approach in my teaching from the late David Pearce, who among many accomplishments coauthored the *Blueprint for a Green Economy* (Pearce et al. 1989) which was an early influential text on environmental and resource economics. The goal with this approach is to get students thinking about the myriad of issues surrounding a social problem like climate change and along the way point to where economists can help out. It is also a good opportunity to introduce some foundational concepts and definitions that will be used throughout the course.

2.1.1   What *Is* and What *Ought* To Be

Even the most successful politicians can confuse positive and normative statements about climate change. On the positive side (what *is*), the writing is on the wall. Anthropogenic climate change is occurring, it is well documented and understood. Over 200 distinct scientific organizations have published public positions that climate change has been caused, in part, by human activity.[1] For the most part economists stay out of the earth science and climate research debate and rely on those experts to make and articulate the connections between greenhouse gasses and climate.

That climate change is happening, however, does not necessarily mean society should do anything about it. The 'should' part of the discussion is of course normative (what *ought to be*). The question of what to do about climate change is a value judgement. One person's optimal management of the climate may be fundamentally different from his or her neighbors. Economists play a role here through the concepts of social choice, a topic that triggers lofty questions regarding how society should determine the allocation of resources. Of course, much attention will be paid to *efficiency*, the workhorse of modern economics.

This part of the course is conducive to a broad discussion of established social choice theories, including Rawls, Bentham and Pareto. The topic of social choice can lead to very interesting and lively discussions, and in particular having students consider Rawl's (1971) 'veil of ignorance' as a thought experiment is always provocative. The idea is for students to imagine they have to make policy decisions without having any information about their own particular race, social class, gender, skills or tastes in larger society. Rawls argues that the policies that would result under this level of ignorance would be moral and just since decision makers would not be making policies biased toward their individual interests.

A takeaway message for students is that determining goals for environmental and resource management is a *normative* question. There is no objectively correct answer on how best to manage the environment. However, once environmental goals are established, the economist plays an important role in helping shape policy design.

2.1.2   The Costs and Benefits of Managing a Changing Climate

Economists are often misunderstood. To most people outside of the profession the view is that economists just care about money. On one hand this is completely unwarranted considering that economists are primarily focused on how resources are managed. On the other hand, it often does ring true. Not that economists care that much about money, but money turns out to be a convenient measuring rod, and if society needs to manage resources it needs to understand the costs and benefits of doing so. Since many of the damages associated with climate change are environmental, it is here where the professor introduces the taxonomy of values people get from environmental and natural resources. Those include direct use values and non-use values, which include option, bequest and existence values.

Instructors can highlight the unique role economists play in valuing non-market resources (and pointing out the values from these techniques as examples of *positive economics*). Entire courses can be dedicated to techniques for environmental valuation, but the goal is to introduce the concepts in order to get students thinking about how to quantify the value of things that are not typically bought and sold in markets. Of course, the damages associated with climate change become the benefits of reducing climate change. These potential benefits need to be compared with the costs associated with mitigating climate change, and here the concepts of greenhouse gas mitigation are introduced. Economists play a big role in this area, and the students should be familiar with the implications of the integrated assessment models (e.g., RICE, DICE developed by William Nordhaus[2]) that attempt to aggregate the benefits and costs of mitigating climate change.

2.1.3   Discounting the Future

Any consideration of the costs of meeting climate objectives requires confronting one of the thorniest issues in all climate-change economics: how should we compare present and future costs and benefits? [...] A full appreciation of the economics of climate change cannot proceed without dealing with discounting. (Nordhaus, 2013)

It is remarkable how important the discount rate is for determining policy paths toward management of climate change. Given a high enough discount rate the implication from a cost–benefit analysis could easily be for society to do nothing to change its current emissions path. On the flip side, a zero (or very low) discount rate can lead to nonsensical policy prescriptions. There is a large and growing literature in economics on the choice of discount rates for climate change. Later in this chapter we explore the concept of the 'social cost of carbon', which is determined in part by how much we choose to discount future costs and benefits.

2.1.4   Environmental and Natural Resource Policies

The majority of the material in a course in environmental economics and policy is focused on a detailed examination of the various policy options to achieve environmental goals. The climate change example lends itself to a smooth transition to the more general problems of pollution control. Here the instructor introduces the concepts of command and control, market-based policies and voluntary approaches. The market-based policies are further segmented into price-based policies (taxes, subsidies) and quantity-based policies (tradeable permits). Once again, economists play a fundamental role in both the development of the theories of emissions control policies and empirical tests of those theories (*positive economics*). Throughout, concepts in behavioral economics can be highlighted.

In the remainder of this chapter I discuss approaches to teaching a few of the areas highlighted above – in particular: market efficiency, externalities and market-based environmental policy.

2.2   EFFICIENT ENVIRONMENTAL MANAGEMENT

A course in environmental and natural resource economics is really a course focused on externalities. For this reason, it is useful to start by considering competitive markets – those without externalities – in order to later showcase how the introduction of externalities can lead to inefficiencies. Competitive markets and social welfare are typically topics that take center stage in undergraduate courses in microeconomics, and therefore many students are familiar with the basic ideas. However, I have taught many courses in environmental and natural resource economics in which students have no prior education in economics. One of the most effective ways to introduce competitive markets and social welfare is through a simple classroom experiment based on a paper by Charles Holt (1996). Holt's experiment is a 'paper and pencil' exercise and can be done anywhere without relying on sophisticated technology, but is geared toward smaller classes (30 or less). There are other software-based variants of Holt's experiment that can easily accommodate classes with hundreds of students.[3]

2.2.1   Trading in a Classroom Market

This classroom experiment is best implemented after introducing individual and market supply and demand schedules, but before introducing competitive market equilibria and social welfare. The goal is to have students participate in a market in which very little is known beyond their own personal values and then observe aggregate market outcomes. Using the results of the experiment as a point of departure, the theory of competitive market equilibrium and the efficient market hypothesis can be introduced. Even with very few students, the empirical results from the classroom experiment will almost always closely match the theoretical predictions.

Although the full experiment and instructions can be found in Holt (1996), for convenience I include a summary of the approach here. I also include data from a previous course to help illustrate the topics.

The students in the class are divided (as evenly as possible) into buyers and sellers. There is one good in the market that is perfectly homogenous. The buyers are given their individual value for each unit of the good they purchase. Likewise, the sellers are given the marginal cost of selling each unit. Their objective is to make as much money as possible.

Following Holt, one way to quickly and randomly introduce the values and costs to the participants is through a deck of cards. Red cards can convey the buyer's value for each unit they purchase and black cards are the costs sellers face when they produce each unit. Buyers and sellers are free to make any deal they want with whomever they want. To facilitate this, the instructor announces that the market is 'open' for trading and students congregate in the front (or clear area) in the classroom and try to negotiate a sale. When a deal is struck, both parties report the price at which each unit was sold and the instructor makes note of the buyer's value and the seller's cost. At that point the instructor announces the price to the trading room so that information becomes common knowledge.

As an example, suppose a buyer named Bob strikes a deal with a seller named Sally. Bob's value for one unit of the good is $8 (e.g., he was given an eight of hearts) and Sally's cost for producing the unit is $4 (e.g., she was given a four of spades). Note that both Bob and Sally can keep their personal information private when negotiating. Suppose the two agree on a transaction for a price of $5.50. In this case Sally earns $1.50 on the deal ($5.50 − 4) and Bob earns $2.50 ($8 – 5.50). At that point Bob and Sally report the price and their respective values/costs to the instructor and the price of $5.50 is announced to the trading room floor.

When all possible transactions are made (or when the allotted time runs out) the trading stops. At this point all of the prices have been posted for all of the units sold on the market. Multiple rounds of trading can be implemented as a way to give participants some experience buying and selling goods and to help smooth out the results.

It is best practice for the instructor to set up the market supply and demand schedule for the experiment prior to the start of class. Suppose there are 20 students in the class, ten are assigned as buyers and ten as sellers. Each can buy or sell only one unit.

As an example, the demand schedule for buyers is: 4,5,6,6,7,8,9,9,10,10. The supply schedule for sellers is: 2,2,3,3,4,5,6,6,7,8, and both are graphed in Figure 2.1.

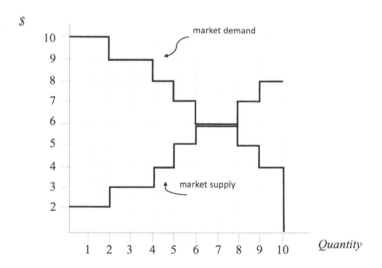

Figure 2.1   Market demand and supply

I include results from the first three periods of a previous classroom experiment with 20 students in Figure 2.2. The prices tend to start off with higher variability and then quickly trend toward the equilibrium price of $6. The instructor should not expect perfect 'price taking' at $6, but the variance will be low after a few trading periods.

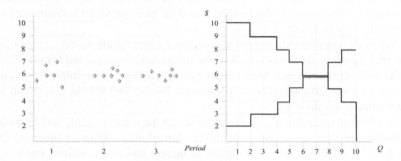

Figure 2.2   Results from first three periods of a classroom trading experiment in relation to the market supply and demand curves

Figures 2.1 and 2.2 can be used to introduce the theory of competitive market equilibria and social welfare. Students can clearly see the intersection of both curves and the predicted price and quantities sold (a price of $6 and quantities between 6 and 8 units). Following this, the concepts of consumer and producer surplus can be illustrated and a measure of social welfare can be introduced and calculated.

For the uninitiated in economics, the results of the classroom experiment and the efficiency of competitive markets can be linked to Adam Smith's (1776) famous metaphor of an 'invisible hand' guiding self-interested individuals to optimal social outcomes. The concepts of consumer, producer and total surplus can be introduced and easily calculated by hand given the step functions. The instructor can calculate total surplus in each period of the experiment and compare it with maximum surplus levels. It is easy to show that if a government wanted to set a fixed price lower or higher than the $6, total surplus in the market would be strictly lower than under an unregulated competitive market.

At this point in the class I like to discuss how we move from the stepwise supply and demand curves that we generate by hand to the smooth curves we observe in our textbooks. This typically involves a discussion of hundreds or thousands of buyers and sellers, each making a tiny step on the curve which can be safely approximated with a smooth line. The continuous functional forms and graphs allow for simplicity and clarity in our calculations moving forward. (See Appendix, Student Exercise 1: Competitive Market Equilibrium.)

2.2.2   Externalities and Market Failures

The niceties of an unregulated market, of course, break down quickly when externalities are present. When the production or consumption of a good imposes an unintended external cost or benefit on others, market outcomes will likely not result in the maximum surplus for society. The supply and demand paradigm that was introduced through the classroom experiment can easily be generalized to demonstrate the losses society faces from ignoring externalities, or on the other hand the gains society can capture by appropriately regulating the economy.

As an example, consider the stylized market for gasoline in Figure 2.3. The market demand curve depicts the marginal willingness to pay (marginal benefit) of all gasoline consumers and the market supply curve is the private marginal cost of producing the good and bringing it to market. The consumption of gasoline, however, produces external costs (carbon emissions and other air pollutants) on society. The line above the market supply curve is called the social marginal cost curve. It includes the private marginal cost that firms face supplying gasoline *plus* the external cost from the consumption of gasoline. In an unregulated market – one in which the external costs imposed on society are ignored by the market participants – the predicted outcome is denoted by q^m (and a corresponding price not depicted in the graph). However, at a quantity of q^m, the social marginal cost of gasoline exceeds the marginal benefit when taking into account the external costs. The efficient quantity and price of gasoline – the one that maximizes the net benefits to society – occurs at point q^*. That point q^* is what economists consider the social optimum.

We can use welfare estimates (total surplus) to demonstrate the inefficiencies from an unregulated market in the presence of externalities. At quantity q^m, the *total benefit* of consuming gasoline is depicted as the entire area under the demand curve (total willingness to pay), which is $A + B + C + D + E$. Meanwhile, producers incur a private cost of production denoted by areas $D + E$ (the area under the supply curve). However, because of the negative externality in consumption society faces an additional cost of $B + C + F$ at quantity q^m. Therefore, total costs from unregulated production and consumption equal $D + E + B + C + F$. Putting this altogether yields the following equations:

Total Surplus in Unregulated Market = Total Benefits – Total Costs, Total Surplus in Unregulated Market = (A + B + C + D + E) – (D + E + B + C + F) = A – F.

Now consider total surplus at point q^*, where the private marginal benefits equal the *social* marginal costs. At q^* the total benefit of consumption is $A + B$

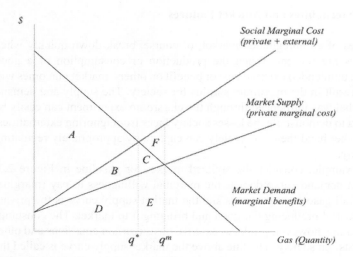

Figure 2.3   Social cost of negative externalities

+ *D*. The total cost, including both private and external costs is *B* + *D*, which yields:

Total Surplus in Social Optimum = (A + B + D) – (B + D) = A.

The area *F* is the loss in welfare under the unregulated market outcome relative to the socially optimal outcome. Understanding area *F* is extremely important in environmental economics and policy. The loss depicted by area *F* exists because there is a disconnect between what is individually optimal for gasoline producers and consumers and what is socially optimal. The primary goal of policies to better manage environmental resources is to reduce area *F* by guiding firms and consumers to make decisions that better align individual and collective goals.

See Box 2.1 for an estimate of the external damages caused by carbon emissions. This exercise demonstrates that because of the external costs of pollution caused by burning fossil fuels, the optimal amount of gasoline bought and sold on the market is lower than the unregulated market, and the optimal price is higher than the unregulated price.

Classroom discussion question*: Why isn't it optimal to reduce the quantity of gasoline (and its associated pollution) to zero?*

BOX 2.1 THE SOCIAL COST OF CARBON

The social cost of carbon (SCC) is the monetary estimate of the external damages that result from emitting an additional ton of carbon dioxide into the atmosphere. Rennert and Kingdon (2019) provide a nice review of the SCC and its use in policy design. They conveniently summarize the steps required to calculate the SCC, which include: (1) predicting future paths of carbon emissions, (2) predicting how emissions will impact climate, (3) estimating the economic impact climatic changes will have on all aspects of the economy, and (4) calculating the present value of the stream of future damages. Every step is tremendously challenging. Economists in particular have contributed significantly to our understanding and implementation of steps (3) and (4).

The SCC is not just an interesting calculation found in academic journal articles. It is very practical. Benefit–cost analysis is a required part of all regulatory policies in the United States, and the SCC is utilized to capture the monetary value of the external damages associated with carbon and greenhouse gas emissions. The SCC is also used by many states in regional policy analyses and energy use decisions. Most carbon offset programs, including those administered by commercial airlines, rely on the SCC to determine appropriate pricing.

While there is great uncertainty about what the 'right' number is, regulatory analysis in the United States uses $42 per metric ton of CO_2 (in 2007 dollars), based on a 3 percent average discount rate (Interagency Working Group on Social Cost of Greenhouse Gases, 2016). This is equivalent to roughly $50 in 2020 terms.

2.3 POLICIES TO REGULATE THE ENVIRONMENT

Although economists tend to focus on efficient environmental and resource management, efficiency is just one possible goal. In practice, environmental policy objectives tend not to focus on economic efficiency, but on improving the environment relative to a chosen baseline. For international climate change policies, the goal is often to reduce emissions in order to bring temperatures to pre-industrial levels. In some cases, the goal is to reduce emissions relative to the year in which policy discussions were initiated (e.g., a 25 percent reduction of greenhouse gas emissions relative to 1990). While the specific goals may differ, the objective is to improve the environment relative to a target level or 'business as usual'.

Regardless of the environmental goals, economists have a lot to offer in how to approach the design of policies to reach those goals. While economists disagree on much, we typically agree that given an environmental target, policies should be designed to reach their objectives in the least cost manner. This is the concept of *cost effectiveness* in environmental policy.

When teaching environmental economics and policy, cost effectiveness is the key to understanding why economists prefer market-based solutions – like emissions taxes and permits – to solve environmental problems rather than rely on more traditional command-and-control regulation. To explore this in detail, we turn our attention to the kinds of decisions firms make when facing different regulatory regimes. We move away from the market equilibrium analysis in the previous section and analyze the decisions of individual firms in a market that generates pollution.

There are many ways polluting firms can reduce their emissions. The simplest way, though potentially very costly, is to restrict the quantity of the good produced and sold. However, in most situations there are often more profitable options. Firms can change the inputs to production (e.g., an electric utility moving from coal to natural gas) or install end of line technologies (e.g., a 'scrubber' to remove sulfur dioxide). Firms can often decrease emissions by reducing inefficiencies in their operations (e.g., more effective supply chain management) or through better training of their employees. The point is that for every industry there is a portfolio of options available to reduce emissions, and not all firms are the same. Some firms will be able to reduce emissions cheaper than others. This is important because for a policy to be cost effective, the environmental goals must be reached in the least cost manner. If some firms can reduce emissions cheaper than others, a policy that requires equal emissions reductions cannot be cost effective.

The analysis starts with a stylized graph of a firm's marginal cost of abating emissions – see Figure 2.4. The graph shows the marginal abatement cost (MAC) of a single firm producing carbon emissions from burning fossil fuels to generate electricity. The point where the curve intersects the horizontal axis is the status quo, or baseline. At this point – labeled e^u – the firm is not abating emissions. This point can also be thought of as the profit maximizing level of emissions for a firm in the absence of regulation. The curve increases at an increasing rate as emissions move from the unregulated level toward zero (or as abatement moves from zero to 100 percent).

A few points are worth noting. The first units of emissions abatement are the least expensive. These are the low-hanging fruit. Profit-maximizing firms can be expected to exhaust the cheapest abatement options first before moving to the more expensive scenarios. Abating the last units of emissions are always the most expensive.

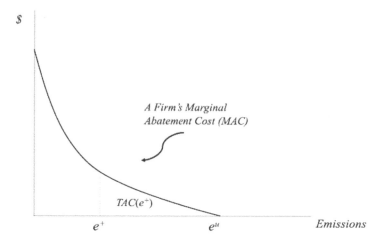

Figure 2.4   *A representative firm's marginal abatement cost (MAC) curve and the total abatement cost of emissions control*

As firms move from the unregulated level of emissions (e^u) to a lower level, the total abatement cost (TAC) for the firm is the area under its MAC curve from e^u to the new level. For an emissions level of e^+, for example, the total abatement cost is $TAC(e^+)$ in Figure 2.4.

The graph can be expanded by including the marginal abatement costs for multiple different firms in the industry and the aggregate marginal abatement cost (AMAC) curve (which is the horizontal sum of each MAC curve).

2.3.1   Emissions Taxes

One way to reduce a negative externality is to tax the activity that generates the negative externality. An emissions tax, often called a Pigouvian tax (after Arthur Pigou, the economist credited with the idea), imposes a price per unit of emissions released by a regulated firm. When an emissions tax is zero, firms would maximize their profit by emitting at point e^u in Figure 2.4. When a per-unit tax is positive, there is an incentive for firms to reduce emissions. The question is by how much?

Suppose, for example, a per-unit tax is set as t in Figure 2.5. Under the tax regime, each firm would be required to pay \$$t$ for each unit of emissions released into the environment. If a firm continued to emit e^u, then the total tax bill paid to the regulator (government) would be $t \times e^u$. Given the tax, the firm has a new profit maximizing level of emissions. It determines this by comparing the amount it has to pay in taxes for each additional unit of emissions (t) with the cost it would incur for abating an additional unit of emissions. The profit-maximizing level of emissions, e', occurs where $t = MAC$.

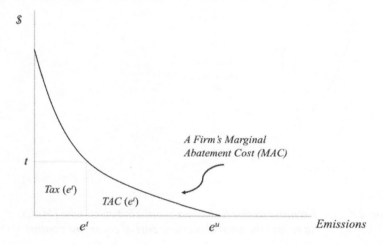

Figure 2.5   A firm's emissions decision when facing a per-unit tax of t

Students may wonder why $t = MAC$ is the optimal point. One way to shed light on this is to consider points where $MAC < t$. When it is cheaper to reduce emissions rather than pay the tax on those emissions, a firm will abate emissions. When $MAC > t$, it is more profitable for firms to emit pollution and pay the tax rather than incur the higher cost of abatement. At the point where $MAC = t$ the per-unit tax exactly equals the per-unit cost of abatement, and therefore a firm's profits are maximized.

Classroom discussion question: Environmental policies are often considered 'sticky'; that is, there is a tendency for them to remain unchanged for long periods of time. If the tax stays at t, do firms have an incentive to try and discover ways to lower their marginal abatement costs?

2.3.2   Classroom Example on Command and Control vs Emissions Taxes

Let us consider two firms in a market that produces emissions (e.g., electric utility). The two firms' MAC curves are shown in Figure 2.6 along with the aggregate marginal abatement cost (AMAC) curve for the two firms. From the points where the two individual MAC curves intersect the horizontal axis, it is clear that the aggregate level of emissions in the absence of regulation is 10 + 20 = 30 units. That is, Firm 1 emits 10 units and Firm 2 emits 20 units.[4]

Suppose a regulator has an environmental goal to cap aggregate emissions at 15 units (i.e., cut total emissions in half). One option is for the regulator to set a standard for each firm that their emissions cannot exceed 7.5 units. This kind of simple regulation falls under the category of command and control, and in practice there is almost always an overwhelming tendency for regulators to apply the same emissions standards to all sources of pollution.

Under a regulation that caps emissions at 7.5 units for each firm, the total abatement cost is $6.25 for Firm 1 (darker shaded triangle) and $78.13 for Firm 2 for a total of $84.38 in aggregate abatement costs.

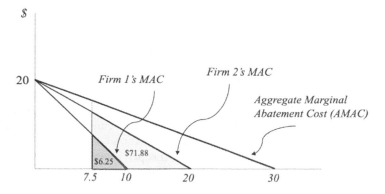

Figure 2.6   Abatement costs given a uniform emissions standard of 7.5 units

Now let us consider an emissions tax that would lead to an aggregate emissions level of 15 units. Since we know each firm will choose emissions so that $t = MAC$, we can simply plug 15 for the total emissions level into the AMAC curve and solve. This yields an emissions tax of $t = 10$ (Figure 2.7). Under an emissions tax of 10, Firm 1 emits 5 units of emissions and Firm 2 emits 10 units. The total abatement costs are $25 and $50 for Firms 1 and 2 respectively, leading to an aggregate of $75.

A simple comparison of $84.38 and $75 illustrates that while both policies led to 15 units of emissions (or, alternatively, 15 units of abatement), the tax did so with a lower total abatement cost.

Why are aggregate abatement costs lower under the tax regime? The short answer is because of what is called the *equi-marginal principle*. The equi-marginal principle states that to reach emissions targets in the lowest cost

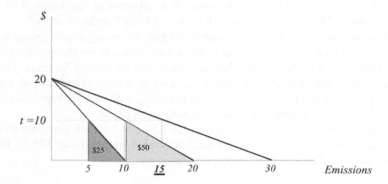

Figure 2.7   *Emissions levels and abatement costs given a per-unit tax of $10*

way (i.e., cost effectively), the marginal abatement costs (MACs) for all firms must be equal at their choice of emissions.

At this point in my course I usually say something like 'if you can only retain one thing from this class, it should be understanding the equi-marginal principle'. It is actually quite intuitive. The idea is that if the marginal abatement costs of all firms are *not* equal at their choice of emissions, then it must be the case that at least one firm can abate the next unit of emissions cheaper than another firm. And if someone *can* do it cheaper, it means that there exists a less expensive way to reach the target. Until the MACs are equivalent there is always a way to increase the net benefits to society (assuming continuous choices).

It is easy to demonstrate that the equi-marginal principle is achieved under any emissions tax. All firms in the regulated industry face the same per-unit emissions tax, and we know each firm will choose an emissions level where the tax equals their marginal abatement cost curve (recall, Figure 2.6). Therefore, in equilibrium $t = MAC1 = MAC2 = \ldots = MACn$. The equi-marginal principle is satisfied for any tax level and the abatement target is reached in the least cost method.

It is important to stress to students what this does not mean. It does not mean firms will take on equal levels of emissions abatement. It also does not mean firms will incur the same total abatement costs. It simply means that at the margin, the cost to abate the next unit of emissions is equivalent for all firms facing the tax.

It should also be clear that there are reasons why firms would prefer command-and-control regulation (emissions standards) over emissions taxes. One big reason is that firms have to pay the tax bill to the regulator. Since this tax is simply a transfer from one actor in society to others, we don't consider this a loss (or gain) to society, but it is undoubtedly an additional expense for the firms. Another reason there may be opposition to the tax is that for some firms, equal emissions standards (or caps) would mean less abatement compared to the tax regime (as is the case for Firm 1 in our example). See Box 2.2. for a description of the British Columbia carbon tax system.

BOX 2.2   BRITISH COLUMBIA CARBON TAX

In 2008 British Columba enacted the first carbon tax in North America. The overarching goal was to reduce greenhouse gas emissions by 33 percent (relative to 2007 levels) by 2020. The tax applies to the purchase and use of all fossil fuels and covers roughly 70 percent of all greenhouse gas emissions. The tax started at $10 (Canadian dollars) per ton of carbon dioxide equivalent emissions and has risen to a current tax of $30 per ton.

Tax revenues are used to offset (reduce) other distortionary taxes, including corporate income tax and personal income tax.

The authors of a 2015 study on the effectiveness of the carbon tax write 'the British Columbia carbon tax may provide the purest example of the economist's carbon tax prescription in practice' (Murray and Rivers, 2015).

A number of studies have examined the impact the tax has had on emissions levels and the economy. It is estimated that the tax has reduced greenhouse gas emissions by 5–15 percent relative to a world without a tax (Beck et al., 2015; Murray and Rivers, 2015; Elgie and McClay, 2013). In terms of the impact on the economy, Murray and Rivers (2015) conclude that the tax has had little impact in either direction.

2.3.3   Tradeable Emissions Permits

The emissions tax regulates pollution by imposing a price on emissions. By setting the tax higher (lower), the quantity of emissions decreases (increases). An alternative market-based approach to environmental policy involves directly manipulating the quantity of emissions through individual tradeable permits. Suppose a regulator has an aggregate emissions target that is less than the status quo and issues a permit for each unit of allowable emissions. Those permits are then allocated to the firms in the industry, and holding a permit allows the firm to emit a unit of emissions. In its simplest form (and assuming adequate enforcement), as long as the total number of permits equals the emissions target, then firms will have to abate emissions beyond the permitted amount and the environmental target will be reached.

Handing out permits, however, does not necessarily mean the environmental target will be reached cost effectively. Since some firms will be able to abate emissions cheaper than others, the distribution of permits and abatement responsibilities will differ across the industry. This is why it is important the permits are tradeable. Trading ensures that the permit system is cost effective because those firms that need them the most (i.e., those firms with the highest cost of abatement) will purchase them from firms that need them the least (i.e., those firms with the lowest cost of abatement).

Before formally introducing the theory of how trading permits will result in an equilibrium market permit price that will result in cost-effective emissions control, I like to have students participate in a classroom experiment on permit trading. The experiment is a variation of the one published by Anderson and Stafford (2000). The point of the experiment is to have students participate in a very simple tradeable permit system so they can actively observe how trading leads to cost effective emissions control. I outline the basic steps and instructions here and include additional resources in an appendix.

2.3.4   Classroom Experiment on Permit Trading

I start the experiment by informing students in the class that they are each assuming the role of a firm that produces a good that can be sold on the open market for $12 per unit. The good costs nothing to produce (to keep it simple) but results in one unit of emissions per unit produced. Each student has the capacity to produce up to two units of the good. I inform the students there will be multiple periods to the experiment.

Baseline
The first period of the experiment establishes a baseline by having students make decisions without any regulations. Note that in this case the profit-maximizing decision is simple, each firm should produce two units and earn $24. In this baseline case there would be $2n$ units of pollution emitted in total, where n is the number of students in the class.

Non-tradeable permits
In the second period I let the students know that I (the instructor) am assuming the role of an environmental regulator and I want to reduce total emissions from ____ units to ____ units. The exact numbers depend on how many students are in the class and what makes sense to the instructor. To reach the target, the regulator issues that many permits (Figure 2.8) and one permit allows its owner to emit one unit of emissions. For each unit produced, a firm must

either submit a permit or pay the cost of cleanup (abatement) if they are short on permits.

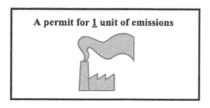

Figure 2.8   *Permit to release one unit of emissions*

Each firm will have a different cost of reducing each unit of emissions (i.e., different marginal abatement costs) depending on the technology that the firm employs and the age of its plant. Each producer will be dealt a playing card that represents their marginal abatement cost.

I typically start by allocating the permits by dividing them evenly (or as close as possible) between the students. In this period students are not allowed to trade the permits, so the result is the same as in any emissions standards regime or command and control; that is, the abatement responsibilities are the same for all firms.

At the end of the decision period the students must commit to a level of production, submit any permits that they have to the instructor, and pay abatement costs for any units that are produced without accompanying permits (their marginal abatement cost is on their card).

After this period concludes, the instructor tallies up the total cost of reaching the emissions target and shares it with the class.

Tradeable permits
In the next set of periods, permits are again allocated uniformly to students and the students are given time (usually three minutes) to buy and sell permits from one another. If a student pair wishes to make a trade, they come to the trading area in the front of the classroom to complete the transaction. The transaction price immediately gets recorded by the instructor and posted for all participants to observe.

After all trades have been made (or the time runs out), students fill out the appropriate cells in their ledger and tally up their earnings. The instructor again tallies up total abatement costs for the industry (classroom) and reports the summary statistics to the class.

It is best to repeat this round a number of times as it will take a bit of time for the price to stabilize and approach the theoretical permit price. It's also fun and informative to change the way permits are allocated at the start of the period. The instructor can switch from uniform allocations to randomly giving some firms two permits and others zero.

The experiment is simple, but it does take some preparation before it is implemented during class. I typically map out the AMAC curve ahead of time by choosing the individual MACs for each student. As an example, for a class of $n = 16$ students I use: 10,9,9,8,8,7,7,6,6,5,5,4,4,3,3,2. Given 16 students each producing two units, in the baseline there are 32 units of pollution. If the regulator wants to cut emissions in half, that means issuing 16 permits. Given 16 permits, the equilibrium permit price is \$6 and firms with MACs 2 through 6 should be selling permits (and abating), and firms with MACs 6 through 10 should be buying permits and polluting.

The experiment provides a nice introduction and segue into the theory of tradeable emissions permits. Because the students actively participated in a permit market that converged on the theoretical permit price (\$6 in our example), they can appreciate why firms can be considered price takers in a permit market. And once students understand that concept, it's easy to see that the permit price and the tax can both achieve the same environmental goals cost effectively.

If the instructor has time, the experiment can be expanded to include subsidies and taxes, and comparisons can be made between all three regulatory regimes. (See Appendix, Student Exercise 2: Market-based Environmental Policies.)

2.3.5   Extensions

The approach and exercises introduced in this chapter are just starting points. The economics of environmental policy becomes increasingly more interesting when exploring components in more detail. These include the double dividend of environmental taxation (Pearce, 1991), dual systems under uncertainty (Roberts and Spence, 1976), prices vs. quantities (Weitzman, 1974), enforcement (Stranlund and Dhanda, 1999), permit auctions, non-uniform emissions (Muller and Mendelsohn, 2009) and much more.

2.4   CONCLUSION

Economists spend a great deal of time thinking deeply about efficient environmental and resource management, maximizing the net benefits to society. While efficiency is a lofty goal, the harsh reality of practical environmental regulation is that not everyone thinks like an economist. I have not witnessed a constituency of voters that are particularly concerned about maximizing net benefits. When I first started teaching courses in environmental economics,

I could tell many students appreciated the idea of efficiency but were suspect about its importance in policy making. What I've learned over the years is that is alright. Economists have so much more to offer in the policy debate on environmental policy. Even if the overarching environmental targets are determined completely ad hoc, or by committee, or by environmental engineers, or environmental scientists, the economist can help shape policy design. The concepts of cost effectiveness and the equi-marginal principle are instrumental in making sure environmental goals are met without wasting resources. Economists have developed the unique tools to value environmental resources that are not typically bought and sold in traditional markets. As strange as it sounds, economists must help explain that sometimes market failures can be solved with market solutions. My approach to teaching the topics has always been to get students actively involved by participating in classroom experiments. I hope this chapter proves useful for instructors starting out teaching environmental economics and policy.

NOTES

1. See http://www.opr.ca.gov/facts/list-of-scientific-organizations.html.
2. See https://williamnordhaus.com/dicerice-models.
3. See Kiviq for a free, web-based program for a classroom trading experiment: https://www.kiviq.us/info.
4. While going over this example, it is useful to describe the underlying functions in the graph shown in Figure 2.6. Firm 1 has a $MAC = 20 - 2e_1$, Firm 2 has a $MAC = 20 - e_2$ and $AMAC = 20 - 2/3E$, where $E = e_1 + e_2$.

REFERENCES

Anderson, L.R. and S.L. Stafford (2000), 'Choosing winners and losers in a classroom permit trading game', *Southern Economic Journal*, **67** (1): 212–219.
Beck, M., N. Rivers and H. Yonezawa (2015), 'A rural myth? The perceived unfairness of carbon taxes in rural communities', Manuscript.
Elgie, S. and J. McClay (2013), 'BC's carbon tax shift is working well after four years (attention Ottawa)', *Canadian Public Policy*, **39** (2): 1–10.
Holt, C.A. (1996), 'Classroom games: Trading in a pit market', *Journal of Economic Perspectives*, **10** (1): 193–203.
Interagency Working Group on Social Cost of Greenhouse Gases (2016), 'Technical support document: Technical update of the social cost of carbon for regulatory impact analysis – under Executive Order 12866', United States Government.
Muller, N. and R. Mendelson (2009), 'Efficient pollution regulation: Getting the prices right', *American Economic Review*, **99** (5): 1714–1739.
Murray, B. and N. Rivers (2015), 'British Columbia's revenue-neutral carbon tax: A review of the latest "grand experiment" in environmental policy', *Energy Policy*, **86**: 674–683.
Nordhaus, W. (2013), *The Climate Casino: Risk, Uncertainty, and Economics for a Warming World*, Yale University Press.

Pearce, D.W. (1991), 'The role of carbon taxes in adjusting to global warming', *Economic Journal*, **101** (407): 938–948.

Pearce, D.W., A. Markandya and E. Barbier (1989), *Blueprint for a Green Economy*, Earthscan, London.

Rawls, J. (1971), *A Theory of Justice*, Oxford University Press, Oxford, England.

Rennert, K. and C. Kingdon (2019), 'Social cost of carbon 101: A review of the social cost of carbon, from a basic definition to the history of its use in policy analysis', *Resources for the Future*, https://media.rff.org/documents/SCC_Explainer.pdf.

Roberts, M.J. and M. Spence (1976), 'Effluent charges and licenses under uncertainty', *Journal of Public Economics*, **5**: 193–208.

Smith, A. (1776), *An Inquiry into the Nature and Causes of the Wealth of Nations*, W. Strahan and T. Cadell, London.

Stranlund, J.K. and K.K. Dhanda (1999), 'Endogenous monitoring and enforcement of a transferable emissions permit system', *Journal of Environmental Economics and Management*, **38** (3): 267–282.

Weitzman, M.L. (1974), 'Prices vs. quantities', *Review of Economic Studies*, **41** (4): 477–491.

APPENDIX: STUDENT EXERCISES

1.   Competitive Market Equilibrium

Consider a competitive market for Snozberries (a luxury candy). The market demand for Snozberries is $Q^D = 50 - P$, where Q^D is quantity demanded (the unit is cartons) and P is the price (in $s). The market supply for Snozberries is $Q^S = 4P$, where Q^S is quantity supplied and P is the price.
Answer the following questions:

[a]   Draw a graph of the market demand and supply.
[b]   What is the competitive market equilibrium price and quantity of Snozberries?
[c]   What is the value of Consumer Surplus (CS), Producer Surplus (PS) and Total Surplus (TS)?
[d]   Is there any price that a government could impose in the market to increase Total Surplus beyond the value calculated in [c]? Why or why not?

2.   Market-based Environmental Policies

Consider two firms in an industry that each emit a uniformly mixed air pollutant (e.g., carbon dioxide). The marginal abatement costs for Firms 1 and 2 are $MAC_1 = 100 - e_1$ and $MAC_2 = 100 - 4e_2$, respectively.

[a]   What is the unregulated level of emissions for each firm?

Suppose a regulator wants to reduce aggregate emissions from the two firms to a total of 25 units. To do so, it issues 25 tradeable permits (free allocation) to the firms.

[b]   What price will the permits sell for assuming a competitive trading market?
[c]   How many permits does each firm buy and/or sell?
[d]   Alternatively, what could the regulator choose for a per-unit emissions tax to achieve the goal of 25 units of emissions?

3. An applied welfare economics approach to teaching natural resource and environmental economics[1]

John C. Bergstrom

INTRODUCTION

An early inspiration in my university teaching and research career was an essay written by John Krutilla entitled "Reflections of an applied welfare economist." The essay published in the *Journal of Environmental Economics and Management* (Krutilla, 1981) was Krutilla's Presidential Address presented at the Annual Meetings of the Association of Environmental and Resource Economists in 1980. At the time of this presidential address I was just starting graduate school studying natural resource and environmental economics.

Throughout graduate school I developed interests in policy and project analysis and economic valuation of natural resource and environmental goods and services. Krutilla's essay helped me to see the connections between applied welfare economics, economic valuation, and natural resource and environmental policy and management. Other professional mentors, notably Alan Randall, John Stoll, and many colleagues in the USDA Regional Research Project ("Costs and Benefits of Natural Resources on Public and Private Lands," originally numbered W-133) over the past 30-plus years have also influenced my thinking and applied welfare economics approach to teaching (and research) in natural resource and environmental economics. In the rest of this chapter, I will discuss this approach to teaching from conceptual and practical perspectives.

FOUNDATIONAL CONCEPTS

I primarily teach two courses, one undergraduate and one graduate, at the University of Georgia in the natural resource and environmental economics area. The undergraduate course is entitled, "Principles of Resource Economics" (ENVM 3060) and utilizes Bergstrom and Randall (2016) *Resource Economics: An Economic Approach to Natural Resource and*

Environmental Policy as a textbook (published in its fourth edition as of the writing of this book). Even though the short titles of this textbook and my undergraduate course are *Resource Economics*, both the course and the textbook provide foundational concepts relevant in general to natural resource and environmental economics, policy, and management.

My graduate class is entitled, "Nonmarket Economic Valuation Techniques and Applications" (AAEC 8100) and utilizes Champ et al. (2017) *A Primer on Nonmarket Valuation* as a textbook (published in its second edition as of the writing of this book). This textbook and my graduate class both start out presenting the conceptual basis for economic valuation of price and imposed quantity changes in microeconomics theory in general, and applied welfare economics in particular.

At the beginning of the semester, I tell the students in my graduate class that before they learn how to apply nonmarket valuation techniques (e.g., travel cost method, contingent valuation method, choice experiments), they need to have a firm understanding of what they are measuring theoretically and the intended use of their valuation estimates in natural resource and environmental decision-making (e.g., benefit–cost analysis). I make a similar pitch to my undergraduate students without the more technical jargon. I emphasize to both my undergraduate and graduate students that natural resource and environmental economics broadly deals with how people and society allocate scarce resources between alternative uses ("states of the world") to enhance individual and group welfare or well-being.

Whether speaking in general to undergraduate students, or more technically to graduate students, I find that the maximization of social well-being (or welfare) problem in applied welfare economics is a good place to start. Undergraduate students especially (but also some graduate students) have misconceptions about the overall purpose of the field of natural resource and environmental economics. Thus, I have found it useful and often enlightening to students to emphasize that the study of natural resource and environmental economics is ultimately about improving the well-being of people at the individual, local, state, national, and global levels. However, I explain further that individuals (including themselves) or societies (including the communities in which they live or will live) are constrained by scarce natural resource and environmental goods and services (in short, ecosystem goods and services).

Thus, I go on to explain further that to obtain the highest levels of well-being (utility, welfare in economics jargon) possible, society (e.g., communities at the local, state, and national levels) must allocate, use, and manage ecosystem goods and services wisely (e.g., in an economically efficient and sustainable manner using economics jargon). Here, economic efficiency refers to Pareto efficiency, or a situation where it is not possible to reallocate scarce inputs to production and scarce outputs (goods and services) to consumers in a way that increases the well-being of one individual or group without simultaneously reducing the well-being of some other individual or group (Bergstrom and Randall, 2016, Chapter 5).

Pareto efficiency is a necessary condition for maximization of social well-being. In an economy such as the U.S. economy, there is theoretically no one unique, Pareto-efficient (PE) combination of inputs going into production and outputs (goods and services) going to consumers – in fact, there are theoretically an infinite number of PE input and output mix combinations in any economy. Thus, I explain to my students, Pareto efficiency can answer positive economics questions, such as: "What is an economically efficient allocation of land and water to the production of food and housing in a given economy?" However, Pareto efficiency cannot answer normative economic questions such as: "How should food and housing be allocated to different consumer groups in a given economy?" (Bergstrom and Randall, 2016, Chapters 5 and 8).

In the standard maximization of social well-being problem posed by Bator (1957), we need a social welfare function to answer normative economic questions dealing with the distribution of goods and services and, ultimately, well-being across different individuals or groups. A social welfare function shows a society's subjective preferences for the distribution of goods and services and well-being (utility, welfare) across individuals or groups (Bator, 1957; Buchanan, 1959). Given a social welfare function, we can theoretically identify the unique Pareto Efficient combination of inputs going into production and outputs (goods and services) going to different individuals or groups that maximizes social well-being (Bator's "Bliss Point") (Bergstrom and Randall, 2016, Chapter 8).

The maximization of social well-being problem illustrates many important concepts in natural resource and environmental economics. First, because Pareto efficiency is necessary for maximizing social well-being, the problem illustrates how a society grapples with the question of: "How do we get the most output (goods and services) from limited inputs including natural resources?" That is, the problem shows that a society faced with limited resources should seek to produce along its production possibilities frontier. Furthermore, the problem shows that in order to produce more goods and services for the benefit of society, the society must find new resources and/or improve production technology (e.g., "smart" irrigation technology that allows farmers to produce more crops with the same amount of or even less water). Thus, the problem illustrates that economically efficient use of productive inputs can be good for the environment since scarce natural resource inputs such as water are not employed in production in a wasteful manner (e.g., using more water than is needed to produce a given amount of food crops).

The maximization of social well-being problem also illustrates that what is good for the health of the environment (e.g., getting the most food crop output from the least amount of water input) is also good for the bottom-line profitability of businesses and the economic health of the economy as a whole. For example, by producing the same level of food crops with less water or other inputs such as fertilizers and pesticides, farm businesses (producers) save money. When farmers use less chemicals (e.g., fertilizers, pesticides, herbicides), there is also less risk of excess chemicals contaminating ground water and surface water supplies through leaching and run-off into rivers, lakes, and oceans.

When talking with students about the relationships between the environment and the economy, I find it helpful to refer to the "triple bottom line" of, colloquially speaking, "planet, profit, and people." Since "planet" and "people" are quite broad terms, and as this book illustrates, economics involves much more than just "profit," I prefer to state the triple bottom-line as the three E's of natural resource and environmental policy and management: Environment, Economics, and Ethics. I have already discussed above how the maximization of social well-being problem illustrates environmental and economic issues and concerns. The problem also illustrates the ethical/social component of the triple bottom line as discussed below.

As noted above, Pareto efficiency can only answer positive economics questions related to natural resource and environmental economics, policy, and management such as: "What are allocations of natural resource inputs to the production of goods and services that are efficient in production?" And, "What are allocations of goods and services to consumers that are efficient in consumption?" When consumption and production efficiency are achieved simultaneously, an economy or society will be operating at some point along its grand utility frontier (GUF).

A GUF between two parties (Party 1 and Party 2) is illustrated in Figure 3.1. The utility (well-being) of Party 1 (U_1) is measured on the horizontal axis and the utility (well-being) of Party 2 (U_2) is measured on the vertical axis. The GUF in Figure 3.1 shows all of the PE distributions of well-being (utility) between Party 1 and Party 2 (which can be individuals or groups) subject to the constraints faced by an economy or society at a given point in time and space, such as the economy's or society's given endowment of natural resource inputs, other inputs (e.g., labor, capital), technology, and human populations and preferences. Theoretically, there are an infinite number of PE points an economy or society could be located at along its GUF (Bergstrom and Randall, 2016, Chapter 5).

The question of, "Where *should* an economy or society be located at on its GUF (or which point is best)?" is a normative question requiring the imposition of ethical value judgements embodied in the society's social welfare (well-being) function. Given a particular society's (e.g., community, state, nation) social welfare function, we can define which point on the society's or

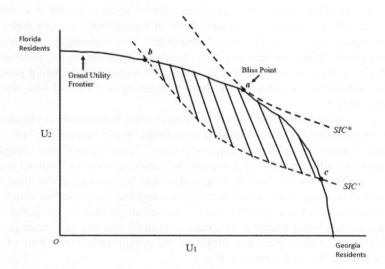

Figure 3.1   Illustration of maximum social well-being (social welfare)

economy's GUF is best defined as Bator's bliss point or point of maximum social well-being. As illustrated in Figure 3.1, the bliss point is determined graphically by the tangency between the GUF and maximum social indifference curve attainable (SIC*) at point *a*. Once at the bliss point or any other point on the GUF, any move to another Pareto-efficient point on the society's or economy's GUF involves additional ethical value judgements related to economic injury.

Real economic injury refers to a situation where an individual or group is made absolutely worse-off by a change in natural resource or environmental policy or management. For example, for the past three decades, the states of Alabama, Florida, and Georgia have been embroiled in what has become commonly known in the southeastern U.S. as the "Tri-State Water Wars." The three states have been in conflict over the allocation of water managed by a system of U.S. Army Corps of Engineers water projects (e.g., dams, reservoirs) mainly along the Chattahoochee River, which forms part of the western border between Alabama and Georgia before flowing into the Apalachicola Bay on the Gulf Coast of Florida.

A major dispute is the claim by the State of Florida that too much Chattahoochee River water is being held in the State of Georgia, which harms the Apalachicola Bay shellfish industry by disturbing the delicate ecology of the bay (in particular, the right mix of saltwater and freshwater needed for shellfish to survive and thrive). Ecological (environmental) harm to the Apalachicola Bay shellfish industry, the Florida dispute claims, results in real economic injury in the form of reduced income, and in turn well-being, to Florida shellfish-related business owners and employees, especially those tied to the oyster industry.[2]

Abstracting away from the State of Alabama's interests and focusing just on Florida and Georgia, Pareto efficiency can answer the question of, "What is an efficient allocation of Chattahoochee River water to Florida and Georgia?" Pareto efficiency, however, does not help us to compare between the infinite number of possible PE allocations of Chattahoochee River water to Florida and Georgia – that is, alternative PE water allocations cannot be compared using the Pareto criterion. The Pareto criterion, also termed a Pareto improvement or the Pareto safety criterion, states that a change in policy or management is an improvement if at least one party (individual or group) is made better-off without making some other party worse-off (Herbener, 1997; Bergstrom and Randall, 2016, Chapter 8).

Moving from one PE point to another PE point along a society's or economy's GUF will always involve making at least one party worse-off. For example, assume that in Figure 3.1, State of Georgia residents represent Party 1 whose utility (well-being) is measured on the horizontal axis, and State of Florida residents represent Party 2 whose utility (well-being) is measured on the vertical axis. A move from the PE allocation of Chattahoochee River water between Georgia and Florida represented by point *b* to the PE river water allocation represented by the bliss point (point *a*) will benefit Georgia residents but harm Florida residents. Therefore, such a move is not considered a Pareto improvement. Similarly, a move from the PE allocation of Chattahoochee River water between Georgia and Florida of Chattahoochee River water represented by point *c* to the river water allocation represented by the bliss point (point *a*) will benefit Florida residents but harm Georgia residents. In general, a move from one PE point to another along the GUF will always make at least one party worse-off.

When a change in natural resource or environmental policy and management involves both gainers (those who are made better-off) and losers (those who are made worse-off), we are faced with the ethical problems related to the distribution of well-being or income and equity concerns. Such distribution and equity concerns ultimately involve underlying theoretical and empirical problems related to interpersonal comparisons of utility (Chipman and Moore, 1978; Cooter and Rappoport, 1984). The fundamental root question is, "How do we weigh gains to gainers against losses to losers?" This question does not have an easy answer, since for one, every individual is unique with unique preferences defined by their individual utility function. Thus, we cannot directly compare, for example, the utility a Florida resident obtains from eating a dozen Apalachicola Bay oysters to the utility another Florida resident (or Georgia resident for that matter) receives from eating an identical dozen oysters. Similarly, we cannot for example, directly compare the utility a Georgia resident gains from utilizing some unit measure of Chattahoochee River water quantity or quality to the losses a Florida resident suffers from not being able to utilize an equivalent unit measure of Chattahoochee River water quantity or quality.

Another fundamental problem posed by interpersonal comparisons of utility is that, in theory, utility is generally thought to be unobservable. That is, for example, we do not have an accurate and reliable "utility meter" that can be hooked to a person's brain to measure how many "utils" of satisfaction the person obtains from eating a dozen oysters or using some unit measure of Chattahoochee River water quantity or quality.[3] However, in an effort to measure satisfaction psychologists and economists have made significant strides over the years in developing and applying subjective well-being or happiness survey measurement tools (Kahneman and Krueger, 2006; Ferreira and Moro, 2010).

Assuming we were able to measure individual utility (well-being), would we then be able to aggregate individual utility into a theoretically consistent and coherent social welfare function? Based on Arrow's impossibility theorem, the standard answer to this question is "No" when two or more individuals are faced with three or more alternatives/options (Arrow, 1951; Herbener, 1997; Bergstrom and Randall, 2016, Chapter 8). Such a situation could occur, for example, when a group of U.S. national forest stakeholders (e.g., people who utilize the forest for logging, hunting, fishing, birdwatching, hiking, etc.) are asked to rank three or more national forest plans in order of preference. Arrow's impossibility theorem shows that the aggregate or group ranking of management plans compared to individual rankings may violate basic preference axioms such as transitivity, independence of irrelevant alternatives, and the Pareto criterion (Arrow, 1951). Such preference axiom violations cast doubt on the ability of economists, for example, to be able to aggregate individual values (e.g., individual willingness to pay) into an aggregate value (e.g., aggregate willingness to pay) function capable of providing theoretically consistent and coherent rankings of three or more policy or management alternatives (such as three or more national forest management plans).

PRACTICAL APPLICATIONS OF APPLIED WELFARE ECONOMICS AND ECONOMIC VALUATION

Despite the theoretical challenges including measuring and aggregating individual preference and values, applied welfare economic theory and economic valuation techniques have been widely applied to evaluate natural resource and environmental policy and management decisions, especially since the 1960s and 1970s when the U.S. began passing and implementing new and far-reaching natural resource and environmental legislation including the Clean Air Act (1963, 1970), the Wilderness Act (1964), the National Environmental Policy Act or NEPA (1970), the Clean Water Act (1972), the Endangered Species Act (1973), and the Forest and Rangeland Renewable Resources Planning Act (1974). Implementation of these new policies spurred the need for theory and techniques for evaluating and making social choices between alternative "states of the world" brought about by the implementation of these and other natural resource and environmental policies (Krutilla, 1981; Gowdy, 2004). Examples include evaluating and comparing: (1) air quality levels before and after implementation of regulations controlling sulfur dioxide (SO_2) emissions from fossil-fuel powered electricity generation plants; (2) designating part of a national forest currently managed for non-consumptive uses (e.g., birdwatching, hiking) and consumptive uses (e.g., logging, mining, hunting, fishing) to a new official wilderness area that restricts consumptive uses; (3) placing restrictions on logging in private forests in order to protect old-growth trees used for habitat by an endangered species; and (4) the quantity and quality of water and wetlands in a national wildlife refuge before and after new or proposed nearby mining activity.

Actually, as pointed out by a number of economists including Krutilla (1981), the need for practical theory and techniques for evaluating changes in environmental policy and natural resource management dates as far back as the Flood Control Act of 1936, which authorized federal engineering water projects such as dams, reservoirs, dikes, and levees designed to control river water flows and mitigate flood risks. This legislation includes one of the earliest references to required benefit–cost analysis (BCA) of federal natural resource and environmental-related projects by stating that the benefits of such projects to whomsoever they accrue should be at least as great as the costs to whomsoever they accrue.

The theoretical basis for BCA in applied welfare economics is the Kaldor/Hicks compensation test which states that a policy or project change is an improvement if the gainers from the change could compensate the losers and still be better off, and the losers could not pay (bribe) the gainers to give up the change (Chipman and Moore, 1978; Gowdy, 2004, 2005; Bergstrom and Randall, 2016, Chapters 8 and 12). As applied by federal natural resource management agencies such as the U.S. Forest Service (national), U.S. Army Corps of Engineers (eastern U.S.), and Bureau of Land Management (western U.S.), BCA is based on the narrower Kaldor compensation test, which states that a policy or management change is an improvement if the gainers of the change could compensate the losers and still be better off (Bergstrom and Randall, 2016, Chapters 8 and 12).

The operative word in the Kaldor compensation test is *could*. For example, the Kaldor compensation test does not require losers to be compensated – it only requires that it be shown that gainers *could* compensate the losers and still be better off. If losers were actually compensated for their losses and made whole, the policy or management change would represent a Pareto improvement. Thus, a policy or management change that passes the Kaldor compensation test represents a *potential* Pareto improvement (PPI).

Obviously, dropping the requirement to compensate losers for their losses makes application of the Kaldor compensation test and identification of PPIs more practical when evaluating "real-world" environmental policy and natural resource management changes. However, because compensation is not paid resulting in real economic injury to losers, BCA with its Kaldor compensation test and PPI theoretical underpinnings is subject to criticism based on distributional and equity concerns.

Despite distributional and equity concerns over real economic injury, applications of BCA have proliferated in the U.S. and in other countries. Application of BCA generally involves evaluating and comparing only two "states of the world" – the "with" policy or management change scenario vs. the "without" policy or management change scenario. Such pairwise comparisons and choices help to overcome the Arrow impossibility theorem which is mainly problematic when more than two "states of the world" or choices are being evaluated and compared. Another advantage of BCA is that application of the Kaldor compensation test is consistent with theoretically appropriate individual welfare change measures defined in applied welfare economics including Hicksian compensating and equivalent surplus (Bergstrom and Randall, 2016, Chapters 12 and 13).

When evaluating imposed changes in natural resource or environmental quantity or quality under the Kaldor compensation test, say changes that would improve water quantity or quality where stakeholders have presumed rights to the status quo or "without" change "states of the world," the theoretically appropriate measure of gains (benefits) would be Hicksian compensating surplus (Randall and Stoll, 1980; Bergstrom and Randall, 2016, Chapter 12). For those who gain from the change, Hicksian compensating surplus would be interpreted as their willingness to pay (WTP) for the improvement. For those who lose from the change, Hicksian compensating surplus would be interpreted as their willingness to accept compensation (WTA) for the change.

If aggregate WTP for the change is greater than aggregate WTA for the change, then the gainers could compensate the losers and still be better off – e.g., the benefits (gains=WTP) of the policy or management change would be greater than the costs (losses=WTA). Thus, the change would pass the Kaldor compensation test and also represent a PPI. Hicksian compensating surplus (WTP and WTA) can be measured empirically using economic valuation techniques including nonmarket valuation techniques (see Chapter 12 in this book for a discussion of economic valuation techniques).

Using aggregate WTP and WTA to implement the Kaldor compensation test and BCA avoids (skirts) theoretical problems related to interpersonal comparisons of utility by employing a famous (or maybe infamous!) tool in the economist's toolbox – making *assumptions*! First, in order to aggregate WTA or WTP across individuals, economists assume that all individuals have identical preferences (e.g., utility functions) so that we can evaluate policy and management changes employing a "representative agent" (Gowdy, 2004). Second, we assume there exists an underlying, latent social welfare function which shows that a community or society is indifferent as to the distribution of well-being (utility, welfare) across individuals or groups. Following the second assumption, there is no call for differential weighting of benefits (gains) and costs (losses) based on socio-economic characteristics of gainers and losers such as their levels of income.

When teaching students about evaluating natural resource and environmental policy and management changes using BCA, in addition to making the above underlying assumptions clear, following the triple bottom line rubric, we should also make our implicit value judgement explicit and clear (Gul and Pesendorfer, 2007). In the case of the BCA in general, a strong value judgement is that policy and management decisions based on the philosopher Jeremy Bentham's utilitarian goal of "providing the greatest good to the greatest number of people" are socially acceptable from an distributional equity perspective.

Another strong value judgement in the case of the BCA in general is that all members of a community affected by a policy or management decision are equally deserving of enjoying benefits or suffering costs, regardless of their socioeconomic status. For example, when applying traditional BCA, we make the value judgement that it would be socially acceptable from an equity perspective for a policy or management change to, say, reduce the incomes of economically poor people in the community, so long as income gains to economically rich people in the community (benefits) are greater than the income losses to the relatively poor people in the community (costs).

When gains and losses are measured in terms of the value of goods and services produced in an economy or income, the assumption of society's indifference to the distribution of well-being implies we are dealing with a special case of the maximization of social well-being (welfare) criterion – the maximization of social product criterion. Under this special case, social well-being is measured by the sum of the value of goods and services produced in an economy (e.g., GDP) or the sum of incomes across individuals or groups (e.g., aggregate income). Implementation of the maximization of social product criterion to evaluate environmental policy and natural resource management changes can result in both gainers and losers (e.g., economic injury). Following this criterion, however, so long as the net change in social product is positive (e.g., social product goes up), the policy or management change would be considered an improvement (Bergstrom and Randall, 2016, Chapter 8).

For example, suppose in the case of national forest management, social product is narrowly defined as the sum of incomes to commercial loggers that harvest trees in a national forest plus the sum of incomes to commercial recreational outfitters who lead guided hunting or fishing trips in the same national forest. Suppose a change in management plans would place more restrictions on logging in the national forest in favor of opening up more areas dedicated to fish and wildlife management resulting in more recreational hunting and fishing opportunities. Such a change would benefit recreation outfitters by increasing their incomes but impose real economic injury on commercial loggers by decreasing their incomes. However, the management change would be considered an improvement under the maximum value of social product criterion as long as the net change in aggregate income to the recreation outfitters and commercial loggers is positive – e.g., recreation outfitters gain more than commercial loggers lose. I use this simple example in both of my undergraduate and graduate classes of trade-offs between managing a national forest for alternative purposes under the "multiple-use doctrine," illustrating again the usefulness of an applied welfare economics approach to teaching natural resource and environmental economics which highlights the triple bottom line implications of policy and management decisions.

LEARNING MODULES AND CASE STUDIES

In my undergraduate class, I expand upon the simple trade-off example described in the paragraph above in the form of a learning module[4] featuring a hypothetical case study where students evaluate pairwise forest management scenarios (e.g., current management situation vs. management alternative A; current management situation vs. management alternative B; and current management situation vs. management alternative C) using several different decision criteria including the Pareto efficiency, Pareto improvement (Pareto safety), potential Pareto improvement (Kaldor compensation test), and maximum value of social product criteria. Given valuation information, students determine if a move from the current management situation to one of the management alternatives is an improvement according to these decision criteria.

They also evaluate the economic efficiency and equity implications/characteristics of each decision criterion as applied to the case study. With respect to economic efficiency, students answer the questions: (1) is economic efficiency (Pareto efficiency) necessary for an improvement in the short run?; and (2) is economic efficiency (Pareto efficiency) necessary for maximizing total benefits of forest management in the long run? With respect to equity, students answer the questions: (1) do the decision criteria allow real economic injury?; and (2) do the decision criteria allow relative economic injury?

In the case of the Pareto efficiency, potential Pareto improvement, and maximization of social product criteria, economic efficiency (Pareto efficiency) is not necessary in the short run for a policy or management change to be considered an improvement. In the long run, however, with all three of these criteria, economic efficiency is necessary for obtaining a point of maximal total benefits. This result has desirable environmental and economic implications, say for national forest and other public lands management. With respect to economics, obtaining Pareto efficiency would mean that the public land management agency is allocating scarce inputs (e.g., national forest land and water resources, labor, and budget) to the provision of national forest outputs, including consumptive uses (e.g., logging, mining, hunting and fishing) and non-consumptive uses (e.g., hiking, birdwatching, photography) in an economically efficient manner. It also means that the public land management agency is providing national forest outputs to consumers and other stakeholders in an economically efficient manner.

Pareto-efficient management of national forests and other public lands is also good for the environment as it helps to prevent wasteful and perhaps damaging use and management of natural resources. For example, achieving economic efficiency would result in allocating the minimum amount of national forest land resources needed to achieve a given level of logging or mining (termed a "desired future condition" in national forest management jargon). Achieving economic efficiency would also result in allocating the minimum amount of water stemming from a national forest watershed needed for downstream agricultural irrigation and/or municipal drinking water.

The Pareto efficiency, potential Pareto improvement, and maximization of social product criteria all allow for real economic injury; that is, one or more individuals or group can be made absolutely worse off (e.g., decrease in benefits however they are measured) by a policy or management change. The Pareto improvement (Pareto safety) criterion does not allow real economic injury – that is, no individual or group can be made absolutely worse off by a policy or management change (e.g., at least one party must be made better off, and none worse off). The Pareto improvement criterion, however, does allow for relative economic injury which occurs when one party is made relatively worse off compared to another party.

Relative economic injury can occur even in the absence of real economic injury. For example, return to the simple example of national forest benefits distributed to commercial loggers vs. recreation outfitters in the form of income, and assume the total benefits (social product) of these outputs to stakeholders is measured by the sum of income to commercial loggers and recreation outfitters. Further assume in the current management situation commercial loggers have 60 percent of the total benefit "pie" and recreation outfitters have 40 percent of the total benefit "pie." Now, suppose a change in national forest management will increase benefits to both parties by increasing the size of the total benefit "pie" (e.g., through allocation of more land and water resources to both), but the distribution of the total benefit "pie" changes such that commercial loggers now have 70 percent of the total pie and recreational outfitters have 30 percent of the total pie. Although they have been made absolutely better off by the management change, recreation outfitters may feel that they have been made unfairly worse off by the change, *relative* to commercial loggers (since their "slice" of the total benefit pie has been reduced from 40 percent to 30 percent and the loggers "slice" has been increased from 60 percent to 70 percent).

In my undergraduate class, I also assign a case study type homework exercise to provide students with practical training and experience in conducting a BCA using Microsoft Excel. The study area for this case study type homework exercise is a state park/conservation area in the State of Georgia – Smithgall Woods State Park in the northeast Georgia mountains. For the assignment, the students are asked to assume that the managers of Smithgall Woods State Park have determined that their objective in managing the park/conservation area is to provide two primary services valued by people: (1) on-site recreation, and (2) off-site preservation services such as clean drinking water and fish and wildlife existence values. The managers have also determined that there are two primary "stakeholder" groups they are concerned about: (1) people who live near Smithgall Woods State Park who have a relatively higher demand for on-site recreation as compared to off-site preservation services (locals), and (2) people who live far away from Smithgall Woods (such as in the downstream City of Atlanta) who have a relatively higher demand for off-site preservation services as compared to on-site recreation (nonlocals). Students are provided with economic values (e.g., willingness to pay) these stakeholders place on on-site recreation visitor days (RVDs) and off-site preservation services, and the quantities of these RVDs and preservation services they demand. This "price" and "quantity" data allows the students to calculate the total value (total benefits) of on-site recreation RVDs and off-site preservation services to both stakeholder groups over a 25-year time horizon.

In the exercise, students are also provided with information on the up-front, lump-sum costs (e.g., construction costs), recurring annual costs (e.g., operation, maintenance) over the 25-year time horizon, and one-time, lump-sum costs incurred at the end of the 25-year time horizon (e.g., environmental restoration costs). With the benefit and cost data and a given, assumed discount rate, the students are then asked to calculate the benefit–cost ratio and net present value using Microsoft Excel for a change in management from the "current management" scenario to a "new management" scenario. Students are then asked to state/explain whether moving to the new management scenario from the current management scenario represents a potential Pareto improvement.

In my graduate class, I provide practical experience to students on application of applied welfare economics and economic valuation theory and techniques through a semester long case study of a "wicked problem" in natural resource and environmental policy and management.[5] Historically, the term "wicked problems" is not been well recognized in the field of applied economics (Batie, 2008). Normally used to describe situations or scenarios that are difficult to solve using standard modeling methods, these problems are often highly complex and span multiple disciplines (Rittel and Webber, 1973; Dentoni et al., 2012). By their nature, wicked problems cannot be divided into smaller more manageable parts based on any prior maintained assumptions (Weber and Khademian, 2008). Thus, the standard reductionist analytical tools favored by most applied economists may not suffice when attempting to manage and find solutions to wicked problems. In addition, currently, the broader and perhaps more holistic problem-solving skills necessary to undertake and properly examine these types of problems are not typically taught in applied economics graduate programs which focus on quantitative analysis techniques.

In response, the following case study exercise is used in my graduate class as a method to teach, train, and educate graduate-level applied economics students how to deal with, account for, and "solve" wicked-type policy problems in agricultural, natural resource, and environmental economics. In contrast to the previous literature, this case study approach uses an interactive classroom exercise where students are divided into groups, representing consulting teams who have been "hired" to evaluate a wicked-type policy problem. The focus on the case study is a single, but highly timely and relevant wicked-type policy problem, namely: "What is the socially preferred size of the Bear's Ears National Monument in Utah?"

The Bears Ears National Monument was originally established by President Barak Obama in December 2016 as one of his last acts in office. Under the authority granted to him via the Antiquities Act of 1906, President Obama sought to add an additional layer of protection to lands already in the public domain (public lands), and in particular the cultural legacy of these lands, by establishing these lands as a new national monument. This new Bears Ears National Monument originally encompassed about 1.35 million acres to be managed jointly by the U.S. Forest Service and U.S. Bureau of Land Management (BLM). However, almost exactly one year later in December 2017, after reviewing recommendations from the Secretary of the Interior at the time, Ryan Zinke, President Donald Trump took executive action to reduce the size of the Bears Ears National Monument to encompass just over 201,000 acres which includes the Bears Ears buttes (so named by Native Americans since these natural buttes resemble bears' ears) and other significant Native American cultural sites. Subsequent to another review of the Bears Ears National Monument, on October 8, 2021, the Biden Administration restored the monument back to about the size set originally by the Obama Administration.

The resizing of the Bears Ears National Monument represents a wicked-type policy problem for three main reasons. First, there are many sides to the issue and thus, many diverse key stakeholders involved, all of whom have their own opinions and ideas on how the monument should be managed. Secondly, there is considerable risk and uncertainty involved in many of the economic values associated with the area, especially the potential economic value and environmental risks associated with proposed uranium mining. Third, the context of the problem, which involves changing the designation and size of a national monument by different U.S. presidents under the Antiquities Act, involves complicated legal issues which influence proposed and final solutions to and outcomes of the resizing problem.

In order to address the Bears Ears National Monument resizing problem, students in my graduate class were asked to role-play as members of a private consulting firm hired to evaluate the Bears Ears National Monument and provide policy recommendations with respect to what is the socially preferred size of the monument. Prior to the start of the case study, students completed a pre-survey, the results of which were used to access their level of understanding of wicked-type policy problems, prior to participating in the case study. Students were then presented with four in-class case study exercises and some background information on the Bears Ears National Monument wicked policy problem. The objective of the in-class exercises was to guide students through a traditional, quantitative economic problem-solving process, including how to identify goods and services supported by an area of interest, how to determine theoretically appropriate welfare measures to be used, how to assign economic values, and how to compare benefits and costs via traditional benefit–cost analysis.

Following the completion of the in-class case study exercises, we assigned an individual take-home assignment to students, the results of which were used to gauge each student's ability to determine the economic values associated with changes in goods and services brought about by a proposed policy change. The values identified for the individual take-home assignment were then used to conduct BCA using net present value calculations for the final group presentations. In the final group presentations, students also identified additional quantitative and qualitative techniques for assessing the policy problem.

The final group presentations can be thought of as formal "policy briefs," which are commonly delivered by economists who are hired to evaluate policy changes. For the presentations, students were asked to first present information on the economic value of eight specific changes in nonmarket and market goods and services they identified. Each team of "private consultants" then presented their recommendations as to what constitutes the socially preferred size of the Bears Ears National Monument, based on their quantitative and qualitative assessments.

During the final presentations, students were also asked to explain in detail any limitations of their results, and how they adjusted for these limitations given the wicked nature of the Bears Ears National Monument resizing debate. To discourage the free-rider problem, students were asked to complete individual evaluations for each member of their team, the scores of which were factored into each student's final grade. The final group presentations were accompanied by a post-survey, the results of which were used to reassess each student's perceived understanding of wicked-type policy problems after participating in the semester-long project.

FINAL THOUGHTS

As indicated by the different chapters in this book, different instructors take different approaches to teaching natural resource and environmental economics, which is okay by me, and I think healthy for maintaining diversity of academic thought. These different approaches also reflect the fact that natural resource and environmental economics is a very nuanced field of study. Also, at the college level, the way we professors teach courses tends to reflect our diverse academic backgrounds and training and current areas of research and outreach. For example, throughout my career my research program has focused on application of applied welfare economics theory and nonmarket valuation techniques for evaluation of public policy and management decisions affecting natural resources and the environment.

At the college level, I believe it benefits both instructors and their students for professors to integrate their research (and outreach) programs into their teaching programs. I have found that both my undergraduate and graduate students appreciate it when I talk about how my research projects relate to the material we are discussing in class. Thus, using an applied welfare economics approach to teaching natural resource and environmental economics has come quite naturally to me over the years. And because the academic field of natural resource and environmental economics is so heavily related to policy and management decisions, I have found an applied welfare economics approach to be a professionally satisfying, and I hope effective, way of passing on knowledge to students and preparing them to help evaluate and solve natural resource and environmental issues and problems in the future.

NOTES

1.   Comments and suggestions on this chapter from John Whitehead and Amanda Harker Steele are gratefully acknowledged.
2.   This dispute between Florida and Georgia eventually made its way to the docket of the U.S. Supreme Court. On April 1, 2021, the U.S. Supreme Court ruled unanimously in favor of Georgia stating that "Florida failed to prove by clear and convincing evidence that the collapse of its oyster fisheries was caused by Georgia's overconsumption" (of water). The Court also found no "clear and convincing evidence that Georgia overconsumption has harmed river wildlife and plant life by disconnecting tributaries, swamps, and sloughs from the Apalachicola River, thereby drying out important habitats for river species." Even though this dispute has now been settled by the U.S. Supreme Court, it still provides a good case study for illustrating important applied welfare economics concepts, "triple bottom line" considerations, and the intersection between law and economics.
3.   I tell my students to contemplate that maybe in their lifetimes such a utility-detecting device could be developed, considering recent technological advances in human brain scans that allow scientists to observe different "pleasure centers" in the human brain lighting up in response to different positive and negative stimuli such as aesthetically-pleasing (positive) landscape photos or disturbing or scary (negative) photos such as snakes and spiders (at least generally disturbing or scary to most humans!).
4.   Full text of the learning module available at the companion website for this book: https://osf.io/dujas/.
5.   This case was developed and implemented in conjunction with Amanda Harker Steele, former PhD student in the Department of Agricultural and Applied Economics, University of Georgia, and current Senior Economist, KeyLogic, Morgantown, WV. For more details on the case study, see Steele, A.H. and J.C. Bergstrom (2021), 'Teaching by the case method to enhance graduate students' understanding and assessment of wicked-type problems: An application involving the Bears Ears National Monument', *Applied Economics Teaching Resources*, 3 (3): 1–78.

REFERENCES

Arrow, K.J. (1951), *Social Choice and Individual Values*. New York: Wiley.
Batie, S.S. (2008), 'Wicked problems and applied economics', *American Journal of Agricultural Economics*, **90** (5): 1176–1191.
Bator, F.M. (1957), 'The simple analytics of welfare maximization', *American Economic Review*, **47** (1): 22–59.
Bergstrom, J.C. and A. Randall (2016), *Resource Economics: An Economic Approach to Natural Resource and Environmental Policy*, Cheltenham, UK and Northampton, MA, USA: Edward Elgar Publishing.
Buchanan, J.M. (1959), 'Positive economics, welfare economics, and political economy', *Journal of Law and Economics*, **2** (October): 124–138.

Champ, P.A., K.J. Boyle, and T.C. Brown (eds) (2017), *A Primer in Nonmarket Valuation*, Springer.

Chipman, J.S. and J.C. Moore (1978), 'The new welfare economics 1939–1974', *International Economic Review*, **19** (3): 547–584.

Cooter, R. and P. Rappoport (1984), 'Were the ordinalists wrong about welfare economics?' *Journal of Economic Literature*, **22** (2): 507–530.

Dentoni, D., O. Hospes and R.B. Ross (2012), 'Managing wicked problems in agribusiness: The role of multi-stakeholder engagements in value creation', *International Food and Agribusiness Management Review*, **15**, Special Issue B: 1–12.

Ferreira, S. and M. Moro (2010), 'On the use of subjective well-being data for environmental valuation', *Environmental and Resource Economics*, **46** (3): 249–273.

Gowdy, J.M. (2004), 'The revolution in welfare economics and its implications for environmental valuation', *Land Economics*, **80** (2): 239–257.

Gowdy, J.M. (2005), 'Toward a new welfare economics for sustainability', *Ecological Economics*, **53** (2): 211–222.

Gul, F. and W. Pesendorfer (2007), 'Welfare without happiness', *American Economic Review*, **97** (2): 471–476.

Herbener, J.M. (1997), 'The Pareto rule and welfare economics', *Review of Austrian Economics*, **10** (1): 79–106.

Kahneman, D. and A.B. Krueger (2006), 'Developments in the measurement of subjective well-being', *Journal of Economic Perspectives*, **20** (1): 3–24.

Krutilla, J.V. (1981), 'Reflections of an applied welfare economist', *Journal of Environmental Economics and Management*, **8** (1): 1–10.

Randall, A. and J.R. Stoll (1980), 'Consumer's surplus in commodity space', *American Economic Review*, **70** (3): 449–455.

Rittel, H.W. and M.M. Webber (1973), 'Dilemmas in a general theory of planning', *Policy Sciences*, **4** (2): 155–169.

Weber, E.P. and A.M. Khademian (2008), 'Wicked problems, knowledge challenges, and collaborative capacity builders in network settings', *Public Administration Review*, **68** (2): 334–349.

4. An ecosystem services approach to natural resource and environmental economics

Robert J. Johnston

INTRODUCTION

Ecosystem services are defined as the outputs of natural systems that contribute to social welfare (Daily 1997; Millennium Ecosystem Assessment 2005; Brown et al. 2007; Fisher et al. 2008, 2009; Polasky and Segerson 2009; Bateman et al. 2011). In the same way that traditional economic production combines capital, labor and technology to produce goods and services valued by people, ecosystems combine natural capital and processes to produce ecosystem goods and services valued by people. Ecosystem "goods" are generally defined as tangible or material products created by ecosystems, such as fish and trees. Ecosystem "services," in contrast, are usually considered to be intangible (or less tangible) flows, such as natural flood control or pollination (Brown et al. 2007).[1] However, distinguishing ecosystem goods from ecosystem services is not always straightforward, and for ease of communication these goods and services are typically grouped under the general term "ecosystem services." Perspectives and evaluations grounded in the concept of ecosystem services are becoming influential worldwide, and government agencies in the U.S. and elsewhere are seeking to formalize the role of ecosystem services information in decision-making (National Research Council 2005; Turner and Daily 2008; Polasky and Segerson 2009; Lipton et al. 2014; Olander and Maltby 2014; Guerry et al. 2015; Hanley et al. 2015; Ruckelshaus et al., 2015; Olander et al. 2017, 2018). Hence, the relatively low visibility of ecosystem services perspectives in traditional economic textbooks and curricula belies the increasing importance of this type of work to decision-making.

Ecosystem services can benefit people in different ways, either directly or in combination with other inputs such as human labor. The complexity of these interactions can pose challenges for the interdisciplinary work necessary to predict, quantify and value changes in these services (Polasky and Segerson

2009). Although ecosystem services (or goods produced directly from these services) are sometimes bought and sold in markets, they also support *nonmarket values*—values for outcomes that cannot be purchased directly on markets[2] (Freeman et al. 2014; Champ et al. 2017). Some types of ecosystem services are valued directly by individuals and firms—these are often called "final" ecosystem services or endpoints. Other services provide value only indirectly, through the production of other valued ecosystem goods and services. These are often denoted "intermediate" services.[3] As noted above, ecosystem services are sometimes tangible and easily measured, such as the quantity of timber produced by a forest. Other ecosystem services are more difficult to quantify, such as the aesthetic benefits provided by a natural landscape or the direct and indirect effects of genetic diversity on human health.[4]

The concept that systems of natural production provide valued goods and services is not new. Economists began to develop formal methods for non-market valuation of natural resources in the 1940s (Hotelling 1947). There is also a long history of bioeconomics research grounded in concepts of ecological production, extending back to pioneering work in forestry (e.g., Faustmann 1849; Hartman 1976) and fisheries (e.g., Gordon 1954; Scott 1955; Schaefer 1957). The economic theory and methods that enable ecosystem service valuation (or welfare analysis) are the same as those applicable to other types of market and non-market goods (Brown et al. 2007; Freeman et al. 2014; Champ et al. 2017). This similarity is explained by Hanley and Barbier (2009, p. 206): "ecosystems are assets that produce a flow of beneficial goods and services over time. In this regard, they are no different from any other asset in an economy, and in principle, ecosystem services should be valued in a similar manner."

So, what makes ecosystem services analysis different? Despite similarities to other areas of economic study, ecosystem services analysis is not the same as traditional economic analysis or valuation. One of the most fundamental differences relates to how models and questions are framed. The ecosystem services paradigm implies a focus on values provided through ecosystem structures and functions—it is an interdisciplinary perspective focusing on natural systems of production that influence human welfare. The traditional emphasis of economic analysis has been on the use and value of individual resources or goods provided (at least in part) using natural inputs, or on the valuation of non-market goods and services related to the environment (Polasky and Segerson 2009). For example, traditional economic valuation typically emphasizes the estimation of values provided by market or non-market goods—where production of these goods may require a combination of ecosystem services with human capital and labor (Freeman et al. 2014). The specific natural or human processes that produce those valued non-market goods are generally of secondary interest, assuming that one is able to quantify or predict the changes for which values are to be estimated.

In contrast, ecosystem services analyses give greater focus to the ecological processes through which ecosystem services are produced. For example, ecosystem services modeling may seek to disentangle the benefits provided by natural systems alone and/or to estimate the value of changes in these systems. Hence, where traditional economic valuation focuses primarily on changes in the final goods and services that influence welfare, ecosystem services analysis often seeks to trace those values back through systems of human and ecological production to (a) isolate the values provided by natural systems, and (b) understand how changes in these natural systems affect the provision of valued services. Although the applicable methods for economic analysis may be similar if not identical (e.g., methods for non-market valuation), ecosystem services analysis requires additional steps to identify, quantify and isolate services provided by ecosystem functions. It also involves greater attention to the biophysical production functions that translate ecosystem structures, processes and functions to valued goods and services.[5]

Ecosystem services analyses integrate theory and methods from multiple disciplines. Understanding this type of analysis requires a foundation in economic theory and methods (e.g., welfare economics and valuation), together with at least a basic familiarity with the natural sciences. For some applications, a more in-depth understanding of specific valuation methods and natural science disciplines (and modeling) is also required. Unlike some forms of economic valuation—that require expertise primarily in economics—ecosystem service valuation requires integrating knowledge and methods from one or more natural sciences. Because of this, instructional methods for ecosystem service valuation differ in both style and substance from those typically encountered in economics courses.

This chapter provides an overview of the ecosystem services approach to natural resource and environmental economics, emphasizing basic concepts, theory, and methods. Although the chapter highlights the fundamentally interdisciplinary nature of ecosystem services analysis, it retains a focus on ecosystem services as related to the study of *economics*.[6] The chapter begins with an overview of the general paradigm. This is followed by a discussion of key components in ecosystem services analysis, including causal chains, ecosystem service definitions, and production functions (biophysical and economic) necessary to quantify ecosystem services provision and value. These sections emphasize aspects of ecosystem services analysis that differ from those in other areas of economics. The chapter concludes with a review of ecosystem services valuation, again focusing on the dimensions that distinguish ecosystem services value estimation from other types of market and non-market valuation.

THE ECOSYSTEM SERVICES PARADIGM

As described by Polasky and Segerson (2009, p. 417), "a fundamental element of the ecosystem services paradigm is the recognition that changes in ecosystem structure or function, in turn, influence the provision of ecosystem services enjoyed by humans." Accordingly, ecosystem services research is grounded on at least an implicit conceptual framework that links systems of natural production embodied in ecosystems (biophysical or ecological production functions) to the various ways that these systems provide direct and indirect social benefit.

Conceptual Frameworks

Conceptual frameworks for ecosystem services may be summarized using stylized diagrams such as that in Figure 4.1. Similar frameworks, illustrations and accompanying discussions may be found in works such as Brown et al. (2007), Dale and Polasky (2007), Turner and Daily (2008), Fisher et al. (2009), Polasky and Segerson (2009), Bateman et al. (2011) and Johnston et al. (2014). Although the details, terminology and emphasis of these conceptual models differ somewhat, they all reflect the various ways that ecosystem structures, processes, functions, and services contribute (directly and indirectly) to human benefits.

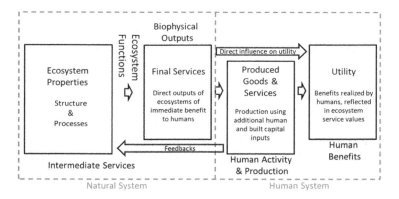

Figure 4.1   Conceptual diagram of ecosystem service linkages

Grounded in previous works such as De Groot et al. (2002) and Brown et al. (2007) we distinguish between ecosystem structures, processes and functions. Borrowing the definition of Brown et al. (2007), "[e]cosystem structure refers to the abiotic and biotic components of an ecosystem and the ecological connections among these components. Ecosystem process refers to the cycles and interactions among those abiotic and biotic components." De Groot et al. (2002, p. 394) further define ecosystem functions as "a subset of ecological processes and ecosystem structures" that "provide goods and services that satisfy human needs, directly or indirectly." Hence, "each [ecosystem] function is the result of the natural processes of the total ecological sub-system of which it is a part." Commonly cited examples of ecosystem functions include regulation and habitat functions, among others.

Ecosystem functions, in turn, generate biophysical outputs that directly enhance human welfare or well-being. Outputs that directly affect welfare in this way are defined as final ecosystem services or ecological endpoints (Boyd and Banzhaf 2007; Brown et al. 2007; Fisher et al. 2009; Johnston and Russell 2011; Boyd and Krupnick 2013; Boyd et al. 2016). Intermediate services are ecological outcomes (e.g., processes or functions) that only benefit humans through effects on other, final ecosystem services (i.e., they are not valued by people directly). These may be viewed as inputs into the biophysical production of final services. The status of an ecological outcome as a final versus intermediate service may vary across individuals or firms (Johnston and Russell 2011).[7]

Even at this superficial level, a framework such as this demonstrates that an ecosystem services analysis may require consideration of a potentially complex set of interactions though which ecosystems influence human welfare. These interactions determine the data and models that are required to conduct economic analysis. Based on this framework, one can also see that *valuation of market goods and services produced using ecosystem services* as inputs is not necessarily the same as *valuation of ecosystem services*. In many cases, the final product sold in a market, and hence most easily valued, does not represent an ecosystem service. Rather, ecosystem services often serve as inputs to market or household production of other goods and services. Distinctions of this type are generally less important for traditional economic valuation—wherein it is not typically crucial whether an outcome to be valued is of natural or human origin. However, these distinctions are important if one wishes to distinguish the benefits derived from ecosystems from the benefits derived from human production (Bateman et al. 2011; Johnston and Russell 2011).

BOX 4.1   TEACHING TIP: MOVING BEYOND THE TERMINOLOGY

There is inconsistency across publications regarding ecosystem service classifications and terminology. This inconsistency can lead to confusion for those new to the study of ecosystem services. For example, some publications eschew the final versus intermediate terminology, using terminology such as "ecological endpoints" or "linking indicators" (Boyd and Krupnick 2013; Boyd et al. 2016). Some works distinguish between ecosystem processes and functions, whereas others do not make this distinction. There is also at least some inconsistency regarding the point at which ecosystem production is distinguished from human production. For example, some researchers would consider a harvested fish (a fish in the boat) to be a final ecosystem service or endpoint, whereas others would consider this to be the product of human production (Boyd and Krupnick 2013; Boyd et al. 2016). For the latter group, the final ecosystem service would be the fish in the water, *prior* to harvest by humans. Differences such as these, however, primarily concern *terminology and categorization*—the underlying methods for analysis typically remain the same. If one understands the system itself, the terminology and categories used to describe that system are of lesser importance (although shared terminology can be critical for communication and comprehension across or within disciplines). Communicating this message to students can help prevent confusion when publications use inconsistent classifications and nomenclature to describe the same (or similar) concepts.

To help inform practical applications of ecosystem services analysis, there have been multiple attempts to create standardized and comprehensive ecosystem service classification systems. For example, the United States Environmental Protection Agency (U.S. EPA) has created the National Ecosystem Services Classification System (NESCS) (U.S. EPA 2015) and the competing Final Ecosystem Goods and Services Classification System (Landers and Nahlik 2013). Although generic typologies and classification systems such as these can be a useful starting point to understanding the services provided by particular ecosystems in specific locations, they are not a substitute for in-depth, case-specific understanding of the human and natural systems under study. This is in large part due to the inability of any single, fixed classification system to fully capture the complexity of ways that people interact with (and value) ecosystems across different contexts. Box 4.1 provides simple teaching tips related to the different classification systems and nomenclatures used to describe ecosystem services.

TYPES OF ECOSYSTEM SERVICES ANALYSIS

Economists conduct many different types of ecosystem services analysis. For example, models can be developed to estimate human behavioral responses to ecosystem service (or disservice) changes, such as the effect of fish species abundance and water quality on recreational fishing (e.g., Parsons and Hauber 1998; Jakus and Shaw 2003; Melstrom et al. 2015). Some research attempts to quantify changes in ecosystem service provision, for example that may occur under future policy scenarios or as part of backward-looking sustainability analysis. Models can be designed to inform policy design or conservation that optimizes ecosystem service provision or value (e.g., Polasky et al. 2008; Leroux et al. 2009; Wainger et al. 2010; Duke et al. 2014, 2015; Duran Vinent et al. 2019), or to characterize ecosystem service trade-offs, substitutability or roles in different types of production (e.g., Polasky et al. 2008; Bauer 2014; Simpson 2014; Drupp 2018). This large body of work includes analyses that predict the effect of, or otherwise evaluate, payment for ecosystem services (PES) programs (Claassen et al. 2008; Jack et al. 2008; Gómez-Baggethun et al. 2010; Pattanayak et al. 2010). An ecosystem services framework can also be used as the foundation for natural capital or ecosystem accounting (Boyd and Banzhaf 2007; Warnell et al. 2020).

These and other types of economic analysis, however, are predicated on the foundational idea that ecosystem services provide value to people. As a consequence, a particularly large body of research applies various types of *economic valuation methods* (Freeman et al. 2014; Champ et al. 2017) to ecosystem services analysis—seeking to estimate the social benefits provided by ecosystem services and natural capital. General discussions and summaries of this work are provided in multiple books and articles, including National Research Council (2005), Brown et al. (2007), Hanley and Barbier (2009), Polasky and Segerson (2009), Holland et al. (2010), Bateman et al. (2011), and National Ecosystem Services Partnership (NESP 2016), among many others. A later section of this chapter (Valuation of Ecosystem Services) introduces the theory and methods for this type of analysis.

FOUNDATIONS FOR ECONOMIC ANALYSIS

Although goals and methods of the different types of ecosystem services analysis vary, most have similar conceptual and theoretical foundations. This section outlines the foundations that underpin the different types of ecosystem services analysis conducted by economists.

Ecosystem Service Causal Chains

Although generic diagrams such as Figure 4.1 above can help communicate the general ecosystem services paradigm, they are of insufficient detail to guide empirical analyses. For this reason, ecosystem services analysis is often grounded in a more detailed causal chain (or path model) that illustrates conceptually how a management action or policy is expected to propagate through natural and social systems to effect ecosystem service provision, human behavior, and associated benefits or costs to affected human beneficiary groups (Olander et al. 2018). These diagrams can be constructed at different levels of resolution (or conversely, abstraction) and are typically developed at the beginning of an ecosystem services analysis to guide subsequent exploration of the natural and human systems under study. They may then be adapted over time, as more is learned about these systems and their interactions.

Development of causal chains is an important component of ecosystem services modeling, as it encourages analysts to document their initial understanding of the system under study, including the complete set of linkages from ecosystem changes through to human values. This documentation identifies the principal aspects of biophysical production, human behavior and human value(s) that must be elucidated. It can also help to identify gaps in data and understanding that must be addressed to provide the desired ecosystem services information. Through the development of ecosystem services causal chains, analysts can answer questions such as: How does a policy, management decision, or program action affect ecological conditions? How do changes in ecological conditions lead to changes in the delivery of ecosystem services (defined as ecological changes that directly influence people)? How do changes in the delivery of ecosystem services affect human behavior? How do these combined changes affect benefits or costs to individuals or groups? Answers to these questions are used to identify the types of ecosystem services and social outcomes relevant to a decision, thereby informing subsequent development of empirical methods (Wainger and Mazzotta 2011; Olander et al. 2018).

An illustrative causal chain is shown in Figure 4.2, for an example of mechanical thinning of forests used to address forest fire risk. This figure adapts an earlier example provided by Olander et al. (2018). The diagram provides a conceptual depiction of how the policy or behavior under consideration (here, mechanical thinning) is expected to propagate through ecological and human systems to influence various types of human benefits realized through ecosystem service changes. It shows the key channels through which anticipated human benefits (and costs) are realized and can thereby help analysts identify the type of information necessary to understand the system and calculate outcomes of interest (such as ecosystem service values). It also shows the different ways that individual ecological changes can influence human behavior and values. For example, changes in species populations can influence human values through multiple channels, including recreation (hunting and wildlife viewing) as well as direct existence or nonuse values.[8]

Agreement on the causal chain by those involved in an ecosystem services project (often including both ecologists and economists) can ensure consensus on the key relationships that define the system under study. Such agreements can be critical at the outset, as disciplinary differences can often lead to subtle but important divergences in how individual researchers perceive these integrated systems, and the key elements that must be characterized. An ecosystem services analysis does not need to evaluate every relationship within a causal chain and can commence at any point along the illustrated means–ends pathways.

Another important role of the causal chain is to help ensure that each desired ecosystem service or associated economic value is counted once and only once—avoiding omissions or *double counting* (Fisher et al. 2008, 2009; Johnston and Russell 2011). In concept, ecosystem services values can be quantified at any node along a causal chain. If estimated appropriately, the total value of the change at any node incorporates the values of all causally connected "downstream" changes (i.e., to the right on the chain).[9] Common double-counting errors include efforts to add values of intermediate and final services along the same pathway of a causal chain.

It is possible to illustrate the distinction between intermediate and final services more formally using a simple conceptual model, drawing from the framework described in Johnston et al. (2013). Models of this type can be used to illustrate the double-counting problem (and how to avoid it). Here, we show relationships in "utility space," in which a set of ecosystem services directly influences the utility (or welfare) of households. For illustration, assume that household h has a utility function of the form $U_h(X, Y(X, Z))$, where $\partial U / \partial X > 0$, $\partial U / \partial Y > 0$, $\partial Y / \partial Z > 0$, and $\partial Y / \partial X > 0$. Within this simple model, X and Y are measurable ecological conditions or outputs. $Y = Y(X, Z)$ reflects a biophysical production function through which changes in X and Z cause biophysical changes in Y, via ecological processes. In this way, the biophysical (or ecological) production function is embedded structurally within the utility function.

Here, both X and Y are direct arguments in $U_h(\cdot)$; they do not require further ecological transformation to influence utility and are hence classified as "final" ecosystem services or ecological endpoints. In contrast, Z is an intermediate service. Its influence on $U_h(\cdot)$ occurs only through its effect on Y, realized through the biophysical function $Y(\cdot)$. This illustrative model also illustrates that an ecological outcome, X, can affect utility both directly (and hence be a final service) and indirectly through its contribution to the production of another final service, Y (and hence simultaneously be an intermediate service). Thus, equation (4.1) clarifies the status of X as both a final and an intermediate service, i.e., with both direct and indirect influences on utility. The marginal utility (or household value) of a change in X is calculated

$$dU \,/\, dX = \partial U \,/\, \partial X + (\partial U \,/\, \partial Y) \cdot (\partial Y \,/\, \partial X) > 0. \qquad (4.1)$$

The total derivative in equation (4.1) reflects the direct and indirect effects of the change in X.

A simple model of this type can be used to illustrate the double-counting problem that can occur if causal relationships such as these are overlooked. Imagine that an attempt to value the "total" ecosystem service value caused by a change in X (dX) first calculates the value for a change in X (i.e., based on a money metric of the utility change dU/dX) and then adds the value of Y caused by the change in X (i.e., a money metric of the utility change $(\partial U \,/\, \partial Y) \cdot (\partial Y \,/\, \partial X)$). From equation (4.1), it is easy to see that this counts the argument $(\partial U \,/\, \partial Y) \cdot (\partial Y \,/\, \partial X)$ twice—once as part of dU/dX and once by itself. The result of this double counting will be an overestimate of ecosystem service value. Although this simple illustration is shown in terms of household utility, parallel examples can be shown for monetary values.

Drawing a more concrete example from Figure 4.2, a comprehensive value for changes in "populations of species of interest to people" (the total value for the change) should reflect and aggregate all values associated with resulting changes to (a) opportunities for wildlife watching, (b) access to game species, and (c) species existence. Hence, it would *not* be conceptually appropriate to quantify (independently) and add ecosystem service values associated with (a) changes in populations of species of interest to people, and (b) changes in opportunities for wildlife watching. Doing so would double count the same values (here, values related to wildlife watching), because changes in opportunities for wildlife watching only occur because of the underlying change in species populations. As a result, a correctly estimated total value for species population changes would include causally downstream values for wildlife watching.

Double counting of this type is a common error in ecosystem services analysis (for discussion see Fisher et al. 2008, 2009 and Johnston and Russell 2011), and is sometimes encouraged unintentionally by publications in the ecosystem services literature. Consider, for example, ecosystem services typologies or classifications such as that in the Millennium Ecosystem Assessment (MEA 2005). This typology (e.g., MEA 2005, p. 50) presents an illustrative list of different "regulating," "provisioning" and "cultural" ecosystem services

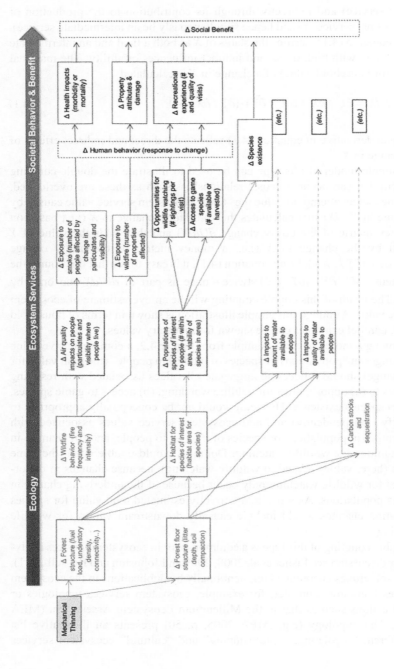

Figure 4.2   Illustrative causal chain for a case study of mechanical forest thinning

within the same level of the typology. Building on this implied structure, many past analyses have sought to quantify and aggregate values linked to these different types of services. Such efforts are often misguided from the perspective of consistent measurement of economic values. The problem is described by Fisher et al. (2008, p. 2051):

> While [the typology in the MEA] is useful as a heuristic tool, it can lead to confusion when trying to assign economic values to ecosystem services. For example, in the Millennium Ecosystem Assessment, nutrient cycling is a supporting service, water flow regulation is a regulating service, and recreation is a cultural service. However, we see the first two as providing the same service, usable water, and the third (e.g., recreation on a clean, navigable river) turning the usable water into a human benefit (i.e., the endpoint that has a direct impact on human welfare). If all three Millennium Ecosystem Assessment services were to be individually valued and added to a cost–benefit analysis, we would commit the error of double counting, as the intermediate services are by default included in the value of the final service.

Double counting of this type can be avoided through the careful use of causal chains to underpin empirical work (Olander et al. 2018). Avoiding the double-counting trap should also be a key message to students when teaching ecosystem service valuation.

Defining Ecosystem Services: Benefit Relevant or Linking Indicators

Economists often give minimal attention to the formal definitions of biophysical variables used within their models. This is often justifiable in "textbook" economics because it is easy to observe and define most types of goods and services produced and consumed in traditional markets (e.g., cars, pizzas, televisions). However, ecosystem service analysis (and teaching) requires clear biophysical definitions of the services under consideration, and (unlike traditional market goods) the ways that we should identify and quantify ecosystem services are not always obvious. Even seemingly simple ideas such as how one defines and measures an ecosystem service can be a source of considerable confusion to students.

Specific criteria for ecosystem service definitions and measurements are required to ensure validity, reliability and consistency in subsequent models.[10] For example, the capacity of a causal chain to inform subsequent research and modeling depends on the extent to which it incorporates well-defined measures of ecosystem services. Although seemingly obvious in concept, many ecosystem services analyses have been predicated on ambiguous or poorly defined ecosystem service indicators—such that the results have no clear economic and/or ecological interpretation (Johnston et al. 2012; Boyd et al. 2016). For example, as explained by Johnston et al. (2012), some economic valuation exercises have quantified values for services defined in broad categorical terms such as "high," "medium" and "low," with insufficient information to link these categories to explicit biophysical measurements. In other cases, ecological analyses have presented biophysical measures of (ostensible) "eco-system services" that have no clear link to human behavior or welfare (Boyd et al. 2016; Olander et al. 2018).

Well-defined biophysical measures (or indicators) of ecosystem services are a precursor for valid and reliable ecosystem service models. Olander et al. (2018) refer to these types of well-defined ecosystem service measures as *benefit relevant indicators* (or BRIs).[11] Among other characteristics of BRIs, two are particularly important. First, BRIs must have a clear and precise inter-pretation from the perspective of biophysical science—they must be defined using a scale that is unambiguous, measurable, and replicable (Schultz et al. 2012; Olander et al. 2018). Second, BRIs must have demonstrable and rela-tively direct relevance to human welfare—the connection to human behavior and/or welfare must be clear and proximate (Boyd et al. 2016; Olander et al. 2018). The latter characteristic implies that human access is often relevant. For example, a measurable change in recreational fish abundance may not reflect an ecosystem service if these fish are located in an area where they cannot be accessed by anglers, and hence provide no recreational benefits. As described above, indicators of final ecosystem services are directly proximate to human behavior and value, and are hence often the best type of indicators for economic analysis.

As described by Olander et al. (2018), well-defined BRIs can be continuous (e.g., board feet of merchantable timber available from a specified land parcel), discrete (e.g., the number of species providing pollination services), or categor-ical (e.g., the presence/absence of a particular species). Categorical measures can also reflect key thresholds or officially defined categories—for example, whether a population is considered endangered or threatened according to gov-ernmental listings. In contrast, categorical scales such as "low," "medium" and "high" (or good, fair, poor, etc.) fail to meet standards of ecosystem service clarity (they are not unambiguous, measurable, and replicable), unless such terms are clearly linked to well-defined and communicated thresholds and underlying measures. For example, "high biodiversity" is not a well-defined measure of an ecosystem service, without clearly defined underlying measures and definitions of both "high" and "biodiversity" (e.g., what index is used to measure biodiversity, what level of this index is associated with the "high" category, and how is this index linked to human welfare?). Before continuing with subsequent phases of an ecosystem services analysis, it is important to ensure that the measures of ecosystem services under consideration are well defined. Although one need not apply the specific nomenclature of BRIs, some approach must be used to ensure that measures of ecosystem services are valid for the intended types of analysis.

Identifying Final Ecosystem Services in Practice

Identification of final ecosystem services is straightforward in theory—they are any direct (ecosystem services) argument in a utility or economic production function. This definition implies that final ecosystem services are also the most relevant to the behavior of (and benefits or costs realized by) individuals and firms. Hence, identification of final ecosystem services is a precursor to many (if not most) types of ecosystem service analysis. However, because utility and production functions cannot be directly observed (one cannot "see" a utility function—it is a theoretical construct), identification of final ecosystem services is not always simple in practice. To address this challenge, Johnston and Russell (2011) identify a simple set of theoretically grounded, intuitive rules that can be used to identify and teach about final ecosystem services.

This approach relies on four simple rules that are combined to identify final ecosystem services and distinguish them from intermediate ecosystem services or processes.

- *Rule one:* For any biophysical outcome h to serve as final ecosystem service for individual (or firm) j, changes in h must influence the welfare of individual j, so that a fully informed, rational person j would be willing to pay for increases in h rather than go without. This guideline reflects the necessary but not sufficient condition that h must somehow—directly or indirectly—influence the welfare of at least one individual or firm. Cast in terms of utility as given in equation (4.1) above, this simply implies that $dU / dX > 0$ (assuming a positively valued service rather than a negatively valued disservice).
- *Rule two:* For biophysical outcome h to serve as an ecosystem service for individual (or firm) j, h must represent the output of an ecological system prior to any combination with human labor, capital or technology. This condition recognizes the crucial distinction between ecological (biophysical) production and economic production, and that an ecosystem service (as usually defined) must reflect an outcome of natural rather than human production.
- *Rule three:* For biophysical outcome h to serve as a final ecosystem service for individual (or firm) j, the rational individual must be willing to pay for increases in h, assuming that all other ecosystem outputs and conditions $i \neq h$ are held constant. Individual j must benefit from, and be willing to pay for, the change in endpoint h, even if everything else in the ecosystem remains unchanged. Assuming that rules one and two apply, rule three is

a sufficient guideline distinguishing intermediate from final services. Returning to the simple utility example in (4.1), this implies that $\partial U / \partial Y > 0$, such that X has a direct and immediate effect on utility, holding all else constant.

• *Rule four:* An ecosystem outcome h can simultaneously represent a final service and an intermediate service, if it affects utility or production in multiple ways. Returning to the stylized utility example in (4.1), this final rule reflects the fact that X can influence utility directly ($\partial U / \partial X$) and indirectly ($(\partial U / \partial Y) \cdot \partial(Y / \partial X)$), with the sum of all direct and indirect effects comprising the total value (dU / dX).

Consistent use of guidelines such as these can provide insight on whether any given ecosystem service (or biophysical measure) represents a final service to a particular individual or firm. Such distinctions are important in practice, because they identify the arguments that should, in most cases, be included in subsequent economic modeling and empirical analysis.

Ecological Production Functions

Grounded in ecosystem service causal chains and clear definitions of ecosystem services, it is often necessary to identify or estimate the *biophysical* (or *ecological*) *production functions* that link different nodes in the causal chain. Knowledge of these relationships is necessary to quantify the change in ecosystem services that is expected to result from a change in the ecosystems that provide those services—that is, to estimate relationships on the left-hand side of an ecosystem services causal chain (those associated with ecological or biophysical causality). Note that specific knowledge of these production functions is not a necessary precursor to all types of ecosystem services analysis. As an illustration, one can estimate the value of an ecosystem service change conditional on that change being provided (e.g., scenario analysis), without explicit analysis of underlying biophysical processes. Many economic analyses estimate values for hypothetical but feasible changes in ecosystem services, but do not provide biophysical models necessary to predict the specific conditions under which these changes might actually occur. However, for ecosystem services analyses that seek to link changes in ecosystems (or human actions affecting ecosystems) to changes in ecosystem services, knowledge of biophysical production functions is required.

Various types of biophysical production functions may be relevant to an ecosystem services analysis, depending on the type of information required. Wainger and Mazzotta (2011) describe three different types of biophysical functions that may be relevant to an ecosystem services analysis, each operating on a different aspect of a causal chain. These are (1) impact functions that connect human actions to changes in stressors, (2) response functions that relate changes in these stressors to changes in ecosystems, and (3) ecoservice production functions that translate ecosystem changes to changes into final ecosystem services. Biophysical functions such as these may be estimated using multiple approaches and types of data, and reported at different degrees of detail. For example, many ecosystem service analyses rely on biophysical production functions embedded within models such as the Integrated Valuation of Ecosystem Services and Tradeoffs (InVEST) tool (e.g., Nelson et al. 2009; Tallis and Polasky 2009), or extant models of land use/cover and ecosystem change (e.g., Bateman et al. 2011; Ferrini et al. 2015). In such cases, publications often describe the underlying biophysical functions in general or conceptual terms (because the structural details of these models are reported elsewhere).

In other cases, the structure, derivation, and data underlying biophysical production functions are developed for individual economic analyses and are described in detail. For example, Johnston et al. (2002) describe an expert elicitation approach used to derive a biophysical production function translating changes in salt marsh land cover to habitat suitability for particular types of marsh species. In another salt marsh example, Duran Vinent et al. (2019) describe a structural, biophysical model of marsh migration used to predict changes in marsh area that would result from a combination of sea-level rise and human actions to preserve marsh migration zones. This biophysical production function underpins an economic portfolio model that optimizes marsh ecosystem service benefits by diversifying marsh preservation actions. Reduced form econometric estimates of biophysical relationships may also be used.[12] For example, Johnston et al. (2017c) develop a simple econometric model to estimate relationships between freshwater mussel abundance, chlorophyll-a concentrations and water clarity, using data from a watershed in Rhode Island (see Box 4.2 below).

BOX 4.2   EXAMPLE: ESTIMATING A BIOPHYSICAL PRODUCTION FUNCTION FOR ECONOMIC VALUATION

As part of an ecosystem services valuation exercise, Johnston et al. (2017c) illustrate how existing data and previously published results were used to estimate a reduced-form biophysical production function linking freshwater mussel abundance (an intermediate ecosystem service) to water clarity (a final service) for a watershed in Rhode Island (USA). Freshwater clarity improvements are commonly attributed to biofiltration provided by bivalve mollusks such as mussels. The approach is based on a regression model that relates inverse Secchi depth (a biophysical indicator of water clarity) to chlorophyll-a concentration, using water sample data from the Pawtuxet Watershed. A random-effects regression model is used to estimate the function Ln *(Inverse Secchi depth)* $= -0.910 + 0.164$ *(Ln Chlorophyll a)*. This equation is combined with an assumed 1:1 inverse monotonic relationship between mussel abundance and chlorophyll-a concentrations (grounded in prior findings from the ecological literature) to derive approximate relationships between changes in mussel abundance and changes in water clarity used as a foundation for stated preference survey design and subsequent economic analysis. This illustrates reduced-form estimation of a very simple biophysical production function.

Economic Production Functions

Biophysical production functions are not the only type of production functions that may be relevant. Many ecosystem services are not consumed or enjoyed directly by people—rather they provide value as inputs to other types of goods and services produced in markets. For example, the growth of certain types of trees in forests may be valued in part due to timber production, where raw timber is used as an input to the production of other valued goods and services. In cases such as these, estimating the value of the ecosystem service requires an understanding of the *economic production functions* that link ecosystem service inputs to valued market outputs. Deriving the relationship between the value of a final market product and the value of an ecosystem service used in production requires an understanding of production functions that govern (1) how the ecosystem service combines with market-purchased inputs to produce the final good, and (2) the degree to which the ecosystem service and market inputs can serve as substitutes for each other within production. These functions are similar in structure to those encountered in other areas of microeconomics (Silberberg 1990), in that they determine how different sets of inputs combine to produce valued outputs (market goods and services).

To illustrate the relevance of economic production functions for ecosystem services analysis, we adapt a simple illustration provided by Bateman et al. (2011). This illustration begins with a stylized production function of the general form $q = f(m, n)$, where q is a valued market good (the output), m is a market input (such as labor) and n is an ecosystem service input. The function $f(m, n)$ can take many different forms and can incorporate multiple different market and ecosystem service inputs. For example, a production function with two market inputs (m_1 and m_2) would be specified $f(m_1, m_2, n)$. For illustration, Bateman et al. (2011) use a Cobb–Douglas specification for this production function, such that $q = f(m, n) = m^\alpha n^\beta$.

Production functions of this type provide multiple types of information within an ecosystem services analysis. For example, they can be used to determine the *marginal rate of technical substitution* between market and ecosystem service inputs—the increase (decrease) in a market input that would be required to offset a one-unit decrease (increase) in the ecosystem service within production. For the illustrative production function shown here, this is calculated as $\dfrac{\partial q / \partial n}{\partial q / \partial m} = \left(\frac{\beta}{\alpha}\right)\left(\frac{m}{n}\right)$. Notice that for the illustrated Cobb–Douglas specification, the rate of technical substitution depends on the ratio of inputs used in production ($\frac{m}{n}$). This relationship implies that as an ecosystem service input becomes more scarce (n is smaller), an increasingly large quantity of the market input is required to offset further ecosystem service losses. The degree to which input substitutability changes as a function of input levels is denoted the *elasticity of technical substitution*[13]—and is critical to understanding the value of ecosystem services within the production of market goods (Bateman et al. 2011). Different types of economic production functions allow different substitution possibilities between market inputs and ecosystem services. For example, some types of production functions (called Leontief production functions) allow no input substitution, as all inputs are used in fixed proportions. Economic production functions can also be used to determine the quantity of output change that would result from a change in ecosystem service availability, holding all other inputs constant.

When ecosystem service values are derived (at least in part) through the production of market goods, knowledge of economic production relationships is required to estimate values. It is also required to predict how firms might react to changes in ecosystem service provision, e.g., by substituting other inputs, altering outputs, or both. Production functions of this type can be estimated empirically using firm- or industry-level data. For example, Babin et al. (1982) illustrate a model that estimates the extent to which other production inputs can be substituted for water in U.S. industrial production. Discussions of the implications of production relationships within different types of ecosystem services analysis are provided by the National Research Council (2005), Bateman et al. (2011), Bauer (2014) and Simpson (2014), among many others. Analyses that fail to account for how ecosystem services are used within production (for example by attributing 100 percent of the value of particular market goods to an ecosystem service used in their production, or allowing no possibility for input substitution by firms) will typically produce invalid results (Bateman et al. 2011).

As an exercise, it can be useful to have students explore the implications of different types of common production functions encountered within microeconomics for the value and substitutability of ecosystem services within different types of market production (e.g., calculating measures such as the marginal rate of technical substitution or marginal revenue product[14] and explaining their interpretations). These include both structural and reduced-form models (see Box 4.3). As illustrated by Bateman et al. (2011) for a simple Cobb–Douglas specification, these exercises can follow a parallel mathematical and theoretical structure to those used commonly in economic textbook exercises applied to other types of stylized production inputs (e.g., capital and labor).

BOX 4.3   UNDERSTANDING THE DIFFERENCE BETWEEN STRUCTURAL AND REDUCED-FORM MODELS

When using or estimating biophysical and economic production functions, one will often encounter discussions of *structural* and *reduced-form models*. It is important for students to understand the difference between these two approaches, as applied across the literature. The distinction between these two approaches in neoclassical economics has its roots in simultaneous equation modeling, but contemporary economists (and non-economists) often interpret these terms more broadly. Differences in the formal definitions and colloquial usages of these terms across distinct areas of the literature can sometimes cause confusion.

In general terms, structural models characterize a system using underlying behavioral equations that are assumed to govern how that system operates. These functions may be used to mathematically derive empirical equations and parameters of interest, which may be subsequently estimated, simulated, calibrated, or validated using observable data. In economics, structural models have been described as approaches that specify "complete models of economic behavior and [estimate or calibrate] the primitives of such models" (Chetty 2009, p. 1), or as "any empirical model where one recovers the parameters of behavioral functions—e.g., demand and supply equations, indirect utility functions of individuals, or the cost structures of firms" (Timmins and Schlenker 2009, p. 353). For example, one might mathematically derive ecosystem service demand (or WTP) functions based on an assumed, underlying utility function that describes individuals' choices over different goods and services, presuming budget-constrained utility maximization. These resulting demand equations might then be estimated using econometric methods and observable data. In ecology, one might specify a set of biophysical equations that represent how a natural system is assumed to function, which might then be calibrated or validated using observed ecological data. For example, the ecosystem service models of Duran Vinent et al. (2019) are based on structural models of salt marsh evolution (biophysical) and dynamic utility maximization (economic).

Reduced-form models, in contrast, specify an equation or set of related equations that describe hypothesized empirical relationships between a dependent variable and a set of exogenous explanatory variables.[15] These equations are typically designed to capture and test causal relationships between variables or to predict empirical outcomes—not to reflect the structural function of the underlying systems. Reduced-form equations are typically estimated based on observable data using statistical methods such as maximum likelihood or least-squares regression. Functional forms for the equations are often specified based on hypothesized *general* relationships suggested by theory, intuition, past empirical findings, and other considerations, but are usually recognized as empirical approximations from a formal structural perspective (see, e.g., Bergstrom and Taylor 2006). Unlike structural models, reduced-form models typically seek to avoid structural assumptions to obtain transparent, robust and identified empirical results (Timmins and Schlenker 2009). For example, in economics, one might estimate a reduced-form hedonic function in which housing price in a market is explained as a function of ecosystem service indicators, among other factors.

A TEACHING ILLUSTRATION—BIOECONOMIC MODEL OF A FISHERY

Classroom teaching in economics is often oriented around illustrative graphs and models. Following this tradition, this section illustrates some of the basic concepts discussed above using a standard, static bioeconomic model of the fishery (Anderson and Seijo 2010). Similar illustrations can be used in the classroom to help convey ecosystem services concepts.

We begin with a simple model of a fishery whose growth rate per period (the net quantity of fish added naturally to the stock each time period) is given by a standard logistic growth function

$$g(x) = \gamma x \left(\frac{K - x}{K} \right) = \gamma x \left(1 - \frac{x}{K} \right). \tag{4.2}$$

Here, $g(x)$ is the per period growth of stock x, K is the natural carrying capacity of the ecosystem (the maximum stock it can support with zero harvest), and γ is a parameter reflecting the intrinsic ecological growth rate of the stock. Introducing potential human harvest (q) into the model, the net change in the stock, $\frac{dx}{dt}$, is then equal to net natural growth in equation (4.2) (what is added to the stock each period) minus harvest (what is removed from the stock each period by fishing firms), so that

$$\frac{dx}{dt} = g(x) - q = \gamma x \left(1 - \frac{x}{K} \right) - q. \tag{4.3}$$

Sustainable, or steady-state harvest is defined as the harvest rate at which the stock remains constant over time, or at which $\frac{dx}{dt} = 0$. This occurs where $g(x) = q$ so that

$$q = \gamma x \left(1 - \frac{x}{K} \right). \tag{4.4}$$

How is this simple model viewed from an ecosystem services perspective? Here, ecosystem *structure* is reflected in the underlying characteristics of the ecosystem that give rise to the growth function in (4.2). The ecosystem *function* of interest is the growth function itself—a biophysical process through which the ecosystem provides harvestable fish. The resulting ecosystem *service* is defined as the resulting fish in the water, or the stock of fish that may be harvested at any given time x, as shown by (4.3). If one harvests this stock in a sustainable manner $(g(x) = q)$, the sustainably harvestable flow of this ecosystem service (or how much fish is provided at each time period) is given by growth function $g(x)$. This situation is implied by equation (4.4).

From this foundation, one can add elements of economic behavior and production. For example, in fisheries, firms cannot simply "produce" fish at will—rather they apply fishing "effort" (such as boats and labor) to harvest fish from the ecosystem. For illustration, assume that we can model harvest during any time period as a simple linear function of industry effort, $q = aEx$, where a is a catchability coefficient (how easy the fish are to catch), and E is the aggregate effort of all fishing firms (boats). If we combine this equation with (4.4), simple mathematical manipulations can then be used to obtain the following equation,

$$q = KaE\left(1 - \frac{aE}{\gamma}\right). \tag{4.5}$$

This "yield–effort function" reflects equilibrium (or sustainable steady-state) harvest as a function of effort and the biophysical parameters a, γ, and K. Note that (4.5) can also be interpreted as *economic production function* which maps the industry's effort input (E) to the realized harvest of the ecosystem service (q), conditional on steady-state harvest. One can also disaggregate E into a sub-function of inputs such as capital and labor, if desired.

The total revenue from this harvest can be quantified by multiplying this ecosystem service harvest by the dockside price at which it can be sold on the market (which can be calculated using a market demand function for dockside fish). If we make a simplifying assumption that dockside prices are fixed in the relevant range (p), then total revenues may be represented by $TR = pq$, with q specified as in equation (4.5). A further textbook assumption that fishing cost is a linear function of effort allows the total cost of fishing to be represented as $TC = cE$, where c is the per unit cost of effort. Further derivations grounded in this basic bioeconomic framework can be used to analyze many different aspects of fishery behavior and supply, ecosystem service value, management effects or other dimensions of interest. For example, one can calculate the level of fishery effort that optimizes the sustainable harvest value of the fishery.

Illustrations such as this can help students understand the ecosystem service paradigm using the same type of stylized models included in economic textbooks, and thereby amenable to illustrative classroom exercises. They can also help to clarify the differences between key concepts such as biophysical and economic production, and ecosystem services versus market products. Although illustrated here for a classic fisheries model, similar examples can be developed for many other types of ecosystem services.

VALUATION OF ECOSYSTEM SERVICES

As noted above, a large proportion of economic research on ecosystem services is oriented around *ecosystem services valuation*—the estimation of social (typically economic) value associated with different types of ecosystem service changes in different contexts (National Research Council 2005). Basic concepts of ecosystem service valuation are summarized by multiple publications (e.g., National Research Council 2005; Brown et al. 2007; Hanley and Barbier 2009; Holland et al. 2010; Bateman et al. 2011; NESP 2016). There is a mature literature on underlying economic valuation methods (e.g., Haab and McConnell 2002; Bockstael and McConnell 2010; Freeman et al. 2014; Champ et al. 2017). Grounded in this work, this section introduces some of the basic conceptual and theoretical foundations for economic valuation as applied to ecosystem services.

Economic benefits (values) and costs may be realized by individuals or firms (e.g., businesses). They are quantified in comparative terms, relative to a well-defined baseline, and reflect the welfare (or well-being) of individuals or groups. For individuals, ecosystem service values are generally measured as the maximum amount of other goods that the individual is willing to forego to obtain additional units of the ecosystem service under study. This reflects the individual's willingness to pay (WTP). Value may also be quantified in terms of willingness to accept (WTA), defined as the minimum amount that a person or group would be willing to accept in order to give up a specified quantity of an ecosystem service (or a related natural asset) that is already possessed. Economic values or benefits, therefore, reflect trade-offs: what people are willing to give up in order to obtain something else, either in or out of organized markets. The resulting values are denoted *market* and *nonmarket values*. Economists' ability to monetize market or nonmarket benefits in this way relies on the concept of *substitutability*—that the welfare gained through increases in one commodity (here an ecosystem service) can be offset by decreases in other commodities or money (this is similar to substitution in production by firms, discussed above). Ecosystem services that are not substitutable in this way, at least on the margin, are not candidates for economic valuation.

Economic values are meaningful only for a particular quantity of a (well-defined) market or nonmarket ecosystem service or natural asset, relative to a specific baseline. If these changes are large (i.e., non-marginal), value estimation must account for the fact that per unit values for any good or service generally diminish as one obtains more of that good or service (i.e., diminishing marginal utility). For example, a recreational angler is usually willing to pay more per fish to increase his or her catch from 0 to 1 fish than from 99 to 100 fish; the value of a marginal fish depends on how many fish have already been caught.

Different economic measures can be used to quantify ecosystem service values. One common (but approximate) measure of value is Marshallian *consumer surplus*, which may be interpreted as the difference between what an individual or group would be willing to pay for an ecosystem service (measured off the demand curve) and what is actually paid, summed over all units. This is measured as the area below the demand curve but above the market price for all units consumed (or the entire area underneath the demand curve if an ecosystem service is provided by nature without the need for market purchases). A parallel benefit measure for firms is *producer surplus*, which is similar, but not identical to, economic profits.[16]

Exact theoretical welfare measures of surplus for individuals are called *Hicksian welfare measures*; these include compensating and equivalent surplus or variation (Silberberg 1990; Just et al. 2004). Hicksian welfare measures, however, are difficult to measure using data on observed behavior. For this reason, economists will frequently use alternative estimates that can provide close approximations to exact Hicksian welfare measures. Common among these is Marshallian (consumer) surplus, as discussed above. These concepts are identical to those applied in standard neoclassical welfare economics, merely applied to ecosystem services. Hence, they are not discussed in greater detail here.

Grounded in concepts such as these, economists have developed different methods for quantifying market and nonmarket values, including values for ecosystem services (National Research Council 2005; Hanley and Barbier 2009; Holland et al. 2010; Freeman et al. 2014; Johnston et al. 2015a; Champ et al. 2017). These valuation techniques are all based on a foundation of microeconomic theory. This internally consistent model of human behavior and welfare allows benefit and cost measures to be quantified, aggregated and compared in common monetary terms. The theoretical basis of economic valuation (at least when conducted in a valid manner) allows one to link these estimated monetary values (e.g., benefits, costs, and WTP) with consistent measures of welfare for individuals, households, or groups.

The choice of ecosystem service valuation method(s) is determined by the type of values that are likely to be present (and relevant to the questions being addressed), the type of data that are available to support the analysis, and whether the situation for which values are desired is currently observable. Table 4.1 provides a concise summary of valuation methods commonly applied to ecosystem services. *Market valuation methods* are applicable when ecosystem services are bought and sold directly in markets or are used directly as inputs into the production activities of firms. In such cases, traditional approaches based on consumer demand analysis and firm production (see discussion of economic production functions above) can be used to quantify ecosystem service values—for example using measures such as Marshallian consumer surplus or Hicksian compensating variation to quantify welfare changes associated with market goods (Silberberg 1990; Just et al. 2004).

Non-market revealed preference methods are based on analyses of human behavior under observable conditions. Examples include recreation demand models, hedonic property value models and averting behavior methods (Bockstael and McConnell 2010; Freeman et al. 2014; Champ et al. 2017). Because these methods are grounded in observable behavior (or ecosystem service uses), they can only measure *use values*—or values related to the

Table 4.1   *Common valuation methods applied to ecosystem services*

	Valuation method	Description
Market valuation	Market analysis and transactions	Derives value from household or firm demand functions, estimated using data on market transactions and prices.
	Production function	Derives value based on the contribution of ecosystem services to the production of market goods by firms (see discussion of economic production functions above).
Revealed preference	Hedonic price method	Derives an implicit value for ecosystem services using data on observed prices of related market goods. An example is the hedonic property value method, which estimates ecosystem service values using patterns in observed housing property values.
	Recreation demand methods	Derives value based on observed recreational behavior.
	Averting behavior/ defensive expenditures	Derives value based on models of averting and defensive behavior and expenditures incurred in response to ecosystem service changes.
Stated preference	Contingent valuation (open-ended and discrete choice)	Estimates values using responses to survey questions in which respondents are asked to state their WTP or WTA for an ecosystem service outcome (open-ended), or whether they would vote for or choose an action or policy with specific outcomes and costs (discrete choice).
	Choice modeling/ experiments	Estimates values using responses to survey questions in which respondents are asked to choose among multi-attribute policy alternatives, with associated costs and ecosystem service outcomes.
Other/hybrid	Benefit transfer	Estimates values for ecosystem service changes at one or more sites (or situations) where valuation has not been conducted, using valuation results from other sites (or situations) where values have been estimated.
	Revealed/stated preference	Valuation that combines data and/or methods from revealed and stated preference valuation techniques.
Avoided and replacement costs[a]	Damage costs avoided	Value is inferred from the direct and indirect expenses incurred as a result of damage to the built environment or to people.
	Replacement/ restoration cost	Value is inferred from potential expenditures incurred to replace or restore ecosystem services.

Note: Avoided and replacement cost methods provide theoretically well-defined (valid) measures of economic value only under restrictive conditions and assumptions. In most cases, these approaches do not provide well-defined measures of economic value.

consumptive or non-consumptive use of the ecosystem service. Moreover, they can only be applied to situations in which the requisite types of behavior and ecosystem service conditions can be observed. Revealed preference methods are sometimes called "indirect" valuation methods, because they use data on observed behavior to infer (indirectly) values for goods that are not bought and sold directly in markets.

In contrast, *stated preference methods* are based on the analysis of responses to carefully designed survey questions that are designed to elicit values directly—hence these are sometimes called "direct" valuation methods (Bateman et al. 2002; Kanninen 2010; Champ et al. 2017; Johnston et al. 2017b; Hanley and Czajkowski 2019). Examples of stated preference methods include *contingent valuation* and *discrete choice experiment* (or *choice modeling*) methods. Stated preference methods, while sometimes more controversial because of their reliance on survey responses rather than observed behavior, can measure both use and *nonuse values*. Nonuse values may be defined as values that do not require use of a commodity or related behavior, or that cannot be calculated using observations of ecosystem service uses. An example would be the value that individuals often hold for the continued existence of rare wildlife species, apart from any direct or indirect use of that species. When these values are expected to be significant, stated preference methods are required to obtain comprehensive measures of total ecosystem service value. Stated preference methods are also the only approaches capable of estimating values for situations that do not yet exist, and hence cannot be evaluated using data on observed behavior. Therefore, for some types of ecosystem service applications, stated preference methods are the only available means (other than benefit transfer of prior stated preference results) to estimate values.

There are also *hybrid* or *other valuation* methods that do not fit neatly into other categories. Among these is *benefit transfer*, defined as the use of pre-existing empirical estimates from primary studies at one or more sites or contexts where research has been conducted (called study sites) to predict welfare estimates such as willingness to pay (WTP) at other, typically unstudied sites or contexts (called policy sites) (Johnston and Rosenberger 2010; Johnston et al. 2015a, 2018b; Rosenberger and Loomis 2017). Typically, benefit transfer uses measures of WTP (or other economic values) derived from a primary study in one location to approximate values at other locations where valuation has not been conducted. Benefit transfers are used when time, funding, data or other constraints prevent the use of primary research to estimate values. The increasing focus among government agencies and others on the estimation of ecosystem service values, combined with a lack of time and resources required for primary valuation research, has led to increasing use of benefit transfer to quantify these values (Plummer 2009; Johnston and

Wainger 2015; Richardson et al. 2015). Multiple types of benefit transfer are possible, from simple unadjusted unit value transfers, through unit or benefit function transfers adjusted for core measures such as purchasing power or income elasticity, to complex preference calibrations and meta-analyses that allow multiple adjustments to improve transfer accuracy and ensure consistency with theory (Johnston et al. 2015b, 2018b).

Revealed/stated preference methods supplement data on observed behavior with stated preference data—usually on how those behaviors would change under hypothetical future conditions. These approaches enable predicted (stated) behavior to be calibrated to observed (revealed) behavior within a unified theoretical framework, enabling forecasts of behaviors outside of observed conditions while mitigating concerns associated with survey data on anticipated or hypothetical behaviors (Whitehead et al. 2008, 2011).

Finally, *cost-avoided methods* seek to estimate values using data on the cost of restoring or replacing services that are damaged or lost. Examples include *replacement cost methods*, which provide a proxy of value for a nonmarket good or service based on the cost of "replacing" that good or service using technological or other means; *damage cost methods*, which seek to quantify the protective value of ecosystem services (such as wetlands that protect homes from flooding) based on the monetary damages they prevent. Although these methods can be easier to apply than other valuation methods, they provide theoretically valid measures of economic value only under narrow circumstances (and with restrictive assumptions) (National Research Council 2005). Among the shortcomings of these methods is that they do not distinguish between costs and values (i.e., that the cost of replacing an ecosystem service is not the same as the value of that service). Hence, economists generally recommend that such methods should be used with caution, and with attention towards the validity and interpretation of resulting value estimates (Holland et al. 2010; Bateman et al. 2011).

Scope and Scale in Ecosystem Service Valuation

One of the most misunderstood and misused aspects of ecosystem service valuation involves the scaling of ecosystem service value estimates over populations, affected areas, or quantities of change (Brander et al. 2012). General discussions of the role of scope and scale in valuation are provided by Heberlein et al. (2005), Rolfe and Wang (2011) and Glenk et al. (2020), among others. Regardless of the method applied, the validity of ecosystem service valuation depends on the extent to which value estimates reflect the effect of the scope (magnitude) and geographical scale of ecosystem service changes. With rare exceptions, economic theory suggests that welfare estimates should be affected by the scope of the change in the good or service, spatial dimensions such as the location of people with respect to the ecosystem service in question, and the availability of substitutes and complements. Other factors such as household income are also typically relevant.

Economic theory further suggests that *diminishing marginal utility* should apply to ecosystem services in many circumstances. That is, each successive unit of an ecosystem service consumed (or enjoyed) is expected to provide less value, on the margin, than the previous unit. This expectation is the foundation for downward sloping demand curves observed for both market and non-market goods. For example, a birder will typically value the first sighting of a rare bird species more than the 100th sighting of the same species (and would be willing to pay more to obtain the first sighting, *ceteris paribus*).

Concerns related to the treatment of scope and scale are particularly relevant to ecosystem services analysis due to the common (but frequently abused) practice of "scaling up" ecosystem service values (Bockstael et al. 2000; Brander et al. 2012; Johnston and Wainger 2015). That is, per unit value estimates from studies over small areas are sometimes scaled up (or multiplied) over much larger scopes, scales or market areas. This scaling often (explicitly or implicitly) relies on some form of benefit transfer. Although benefit transfer in general can be used in valid and reliable ways, scaling or multiplication of values by a different quantity or area than was evaluated by the original study requires strong and often unrealistic assumptions (Johnston et al. 2015b). Unless the estimated benefit functions allow adjustments to account for scope and scale effects, the result will often be large errors and invalid value estimates.

Figure 4.3 illustrates the importance of scope and scale for ecosystem service valuation. For illustration assume that a study at site A estimates WTP (or another measure of economic value), per unit change, for a marginal change in an ecosystem service x, beginning at a current (baseline) level x_0. This is shown by wtp_A. For illustration, Figure 4.3 depicts three possible shapes for the underlying marginal benefit (WTP) function, given by MB_1, MB_2, and MB_3. This figure illustrates possible demand (or marginal value) functions for an ecosystem service, as a function of the quantity of the ecosystem service available. For any given quantity of the ecosystem service, these curves show a representative individual's marginal benefit (or MB) for the last, or marginal unit consumed or enjoyed. Because all of these curves intersect at point A, all result in the same marginal WTP measure evaluated at x_0.

Curve MB_1 reflects a standard, downward-sloping marginal benefit curve; this is a common pattern that one might expect for ecosystem service values, reflecting diminishing but still positive marginal WTP as the quantity of the service increases. Curve MB_2 reflects the type of marginal benefits that might

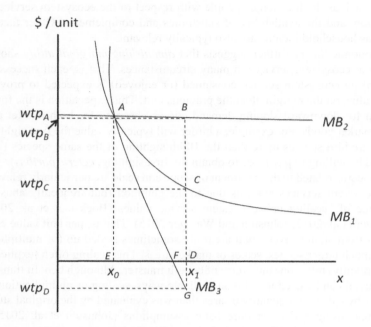

*Figure 4.3   Illustrative marginal benefit functions for an ecosystem
              service*

be expected for local, small-scale changes in an ecosystem service valued at
a global level (such as carbon sequestration) or whose outputs are sold on
large-scale global markets (such as agricultural commodities[17]). In such cases,
marginal WTP for additional units of the service will decline slowly, leading
to a nearly flat marginal benefit curve. Finally, benefit curve MB_3 reflects
quickly diminishing WTP for an ecosystem service, such that marginal WTP
becomes negative after a certain threshold quantity. An example of an ecosystem service with a marginal benefit curve of this type would be water quantity
in a river. Up to a certain threshold, the marginal benefit of additional river
water is often positive. Once the river reaches flood stage, however, additional
water can impose costs due to flooding, so that marginal benefits become
negative.

Now assume that an analyst scales up a marginal benefit estimate from the
original study conducted for a small change at x_0 (yielding an estimate of
wtp_A per unit) to a much larger quantity or scope of change. For illustration,
consider a *non-marginal change* from x_0 to x_1 (so that the total ecosystem
service change is $x_1 - x_0$). First, assume that the marginal benefit curve is

given by MB_1. Along MB_1, the true marginal WTP (value for the last unit obtained) for the ecosystem service at x_1 is wtp_C —this is different from the assumed, scaled-up per unit value wtp_A. The true total benefit of this non-marginal change is the entire area under MB_1 between x_0 and x_1, or area ACDE. However, were one to scale up the marginal value per unit value estimated above (wtp_A) and apply it to the total non-marginal change, the result would be $wtp_A \times (x_1 - x_0)$, or area ABDE. This estimate would overstate the true, scaled-up value.

Now assume a benefit function with a shape such as MB_2 (a flat demand function). In this case, if the ecosystem service is provided at a level of x_1, the true WTP (or value) for the marginal unit is wtp_B. This is a good proxy for wtp_A. In this case, scaling wtp_A over all units from x_0 to x_1 would yield a reasonable approximation of the true total value of the change.

Finally, consider an example such as the steep demand function MB_3. For a curve of this shape (where value for the marginal unit declines rapidly with increases in quantity), the marginal value of the ecosystem service at x_1 is *negative* (wtp_D for the marginal unit along MB_3). In this case, scaling up marginal WTP (wtp_A) would lead to the misguided conclusion that marginal WTP is positive (and equal to wtp_A) for the entire change from x_0 to x_1 — when the true marginal value becomes negative for all $x > F$. As described above, the incorrectly scaled estimate of total value would be equal to $wtp_A \times (x_1 - x_0)$, or area ABDE. This estimate would grossly overstate the true total value along demand function MB_3 (moving from x_0 to x_1), which would be equal to the area of triangle AFE *minus* the area of triangle FDG. Examples such as this demonstrate that failure to consider the shape of the marginal benefit curve and the current level of a service can lead to gross misunderstanding of value.

Errors such as these occur frequently when one seeks to scale-up values calculated per unit area (e.g., ecosystem service values per acre) to much larger areas than the original primary study. Extreme examples involve scaling of benefit measures in attempts to quantify the total benefits of ecosystem services or natural capital at a planetary, nation, statewide, or ecosystem scale (see critiques of such practices in Toman 1998; Bockstael et al. 2000 and National Research Council 2005). These attempts ignore diminishing marginal utility (i.e., the cause of downward-sloping demand curves) and the fact that economic values are meaningful only for clearly specified changes in a good, service, or asset relative to a known baseline. Some justify these applications under the guise that some number is better than no number, or that raising awareness of the value of ecosystems is more important than the validity or reliability of empirical results (National Research Council 2005). However, errors that dramatically inflate values can erode confidence in the validity of ecosystem services analysis in general—causing decision makers to ignore all types of economic value estimates. Errors that deflate values by failing to consider location-specific or unique conditions can lead to decisions that fail to reflect the full value provided by ecosystems. In either case, inaccurate results can promote policies or actions that reduce human welfare.

Similar concerns apply to geospatial scale and distance. For example, it is well established that individuals are often willing to pay less for ecosystem service improvements that are located at a greater distance from their homes (Hanley et al. 2003; Bateman et al. 2006; Ferrini et al. 2015; Glenk et al. 2020). Hence, any aggregation, transfer, or scaling of ecosystem service values that fails to consider potentially relevant geospatial aspects of value—such as where ecosystem services are located, where people live, and the geographical area over which ecosystem service changes occur—can lead to errors in value estimates (Johnston et al. 2018a).

Issues such as these are discussed in the literature devoted to ecosystem service benefit transfer (e.g., Bateman et al. 2006; Plummer 2009; Ferrini et al. 2015; Johnston and Wainger 2015; Richardson et al. 2015; Johnston and Bauer 2019). This literature demonstrates ways that variations in scope and scale can be accommodated when transferring or approximating values based on primary valuation studies conducted in particular locations. For example, individual primary valuation studies or meta-analyses[18] can be specified to incorporate effects of distance and other spatial factors when predicting estimates of per household value. Examples of such functions are illustrated by Hanley et al. (2003), Bateman et al. (2006), Ferrini et al. (2015) and Johnston et al. (2017a, 2018a), among many others. Glenk et al. (2020) provide a literature review discussing spatial dimensions in valuation more generally, with a focus on stated preference valuation. Schaafsma (2015) reviews spatial and geographical aspects of benefit transfer applicable to all types of environmental and natural resource values.

As a general rule, scope and scale concerns such as these imply that ecosystem service valuation should *not*, at least in most applications, seek to calculate fixed measures of value per unit area (e.g., ecosystem service value per hectare), and then scale or multiply these per-unit-area estimates by large ecosystem areas. As discussed earlier, scaling up of this type (especially when conducted over large areas) often overlooks fundamental patterns expected in well-defined measures of ecosystem service value. More valid approaches typically provide benefit functions that predict *per household value* as a function of the scope (or quantity) of ecosystem service change and mediating factors such as geospatial dimensions. These per household values can then be adjusted for ecosystem service and household characteristics in particular areas (e.g., income differences) to generate aggregate population-scale estimates of value for particular types of ecosystem service changes. An illustrative example of this process is provided by Johnston and Bauer (2019) for scenarios of water quality change due to riparian restoration in the Great Bay Watershed of New Hampshire, USA.

CONCLUSION

Ecosystem services perspectives towards natural resource and environmental economics are influential worldwide. Well-conceptualized ecosystem services analysis—whether through valuation or other perspectives—can help clarify trade-offs necessary to enhance and sustain the benefits that humans realize from ecosystems and can provide information unavailable through other economic methods. Although economic components of ecosystem service modeling and valuation rely on the same microeconomic foundations as many other types of economic analysis, the interdisciplinary, systems-based focus of this work requires approaches not frequently encountered in mainstream economics. At the same time, enthusiasm for the ecosystem services concept in policy and practice has led to some empirical applications that sacrifice scientific rigor in ways that provide inaccurate information.

The ecosystem services paradigm can provide significant insight to inform human decisions. This type of work is grounded in decades of work by economists, ecologists, and others seeking to model interactions between natural and human systems. Exemplary ecosystem services research efforts are an evolution of these methods. From this perspective, the prospective validity of the underlying methods has already been established, and the primary challenge is recasting and/or adapting methods and results to an ecosystem services framework. Among the most important hurdles for economists learning about ecosystem service approaches is to understand how these approaches differ from (and/or are similar or identical to) those in other areas of environmental and natural resource economics. When highlighting the novelty of these ecosystem services approaches, publications in the literature sometimes underappreciate foundations in (and similarities to) other areas of work.

At the same time, the integration of economics and ecology required by the ecosystem services framework can impose challenges that are distinct from those encountered in other areas of economics, and there have been many poorly conceived and implemented efforts at ecosystem services analysis. Challenges to valid analysis expand as one moves beyond well-defined, marginal analyses to more ambitious attempts to characterize all services, linkages, and values in large-scale systems. Even though the underlying economics and ecology may be well-developed, the integration and scale of these large-scale models can require methodological innovations, as well as (sometimes) sacrifices that threaten validity. Valid theory and methods are precursors to all valid economic analysis of ecosystem services. The ongoing challenges of ecosystem services analysis, together with the likelihood that the resulting information will be an important part of future decision-making, underscore the need for future contributions by economists in this important area of work.

NOTES

1. There are also ecosystem "disservices," or natural outputs that reduce human welfare.
2. For example, market value is provided through the market production and consumption of wild-capture fish. Nonmarket values are provided by recreational fishing. Hence, the same ecosystem service (natural fish production in aquatic ecosystems) can support both market and nonmarket benefits.
3. For a discussion of these concepts, see Boyd and Banzhaf (2007), Fisher et al. (2008), Fisher and Turner (2008), Johnston and Russell (2011), and Johnston et al. (2013).
4. Boyd et al. (2016) provide a detailed discussion of ecosystem services indicators and measurement.
5. Distinctions between processes, functions and services are discussed in greater detail below.
6. Discussions of non-economic (or non-anthropocentric) perspectives and/or critiques of standard economic approaches to ecosystem services are provided in various works, including Polasky and Segerson (2009) and Gómez-Baggethun et al. (2010).
7. Like all diagrams of this type, Figure 4.1 is best interpreted as a stylized conceptual framework rather than a universally applicable structural model. For example, although not captured directly in Figure 4.1, some ecological outputs also influence human welfare both directly and indirectly—Boyd and Krupnick (2013) refer to these as "dual" ecosystem services. There can also be overlaps and/or fuzzy boundaries between some categories. For example, some ecosystem structures can be valued by people directly (e.g., as a source of nonuse values), and hence also serve as final ecosystem services.
8. Nonuse or passive use values are often defined as values that cannot be quantified using data on observed behaviors, or (more broadly) as values that do not require observable use of a good or service.
9. Conceptually, this relationship is similar to that between input and output values within traditional microeconomic theory of the firm. For example, elementary theory dictates that the marginal value of any production input (such as an additional unit of labor) to a firm reflects the causally related marginal revenue product (MRP) of that input—or the additional value of production output made possible via the additional input usage. Explanation of such relationships may be found in almost any introductory microeconomics textbook.
10. For a discussion of validity and reliability in environmental economics, see Bishop and Boyle (2019).
11. Boyd et al. (2016) refer to similar types of measures as *Linking Indicators*.
12. See structural versus reduced-form models in Box 4.3 below.

13. For a technical discussion of this concept, see Silberberg (1990).
14. Within this context, the marginal revenue product (MRP) of an ecosystem service would reflect the additional revenue, on the margin, generated by the use of one more unit of an ecosystem service as an input within a firm's production activity, *ceteris paribus*.
15. A confusion over terminology sometimes arises because the term "reduced-form model" can also refer to the "reduced form" of a structural economic model (Chetty 2009). In this usage, structural models are used to derive a subsequent "reduced form" model that is subsequently estimated, where each parameter in the reduced form model reflects a mathematical function of one or more primitive parameters from the structural equations.
16. The difference between producer surplus and economic profits lies in the treatment of fixed costs of production.
17. Note that agricultural commodities *themselves* are not generally classified as final ecosystem services, because these commodities are produced through the combination of a purely ecological output with human labor, capital and technology. Rather, agricultural commodities are produced using ecosystem services.
18. Meta-analysis is a "study of studies." In valuation, meta-analyses are often used to synthesize information from many prior studies of specific types of ecosystem service value. This synthesis often relies on meta-regression models and generates umbrella valuation functions able to predict similar values across different types of sites and ecosystem service changes (Nelson and Kennedy 2009; Boyle and Wooldridge 2018; Johnston and Bauer 2019).

REFERENCES

Anderson, L.G. and J.C. Seijo (2010), *Bioeconomics of Fisheries Management*, Wiley-Blackwell.

Babin, F.G., C.E. Willis, and P.G. Allen (1982), 'Estimation of substitution possibilities between water and other production inputs', *American Journal of Agricultural Economics*, **64**, 148–151.

Bateman, I.J., R.T. Carson, B.H. Day, W.M. Hanemann, N. Hanley, T. Hett, M. Jones-Lee, G. Loomes, S. Mourato, E. Özdemiroglu, and D.W. Pearce (2002), *Economic Valuation with Stated Preference Techniques: A Manual*, Cheltenham, UK and Northampton, MA, USA: Edward Elgar Publishing.

Bateman, I.J., B.H. Day, S. Georgiou, and I. Lake (2006), 'The aggregation of environmental benefit values: Welfare measures, distance decay and total WTP', *Ecological Economics*, **60**, 450–460.

Bateman, I.J., G.M. Mace, C. Fezzi, G. Atkinson, and K. Turner (2011), 'Economic analysis for ecosystem service assessments', *Environmental and Resource Economics*, **48**, 177–218.

Bauer, D.M. (2014), 'Valuation of pollination services: A comparison of approaches', Chapter 7 in K.N. Ninan (ed.), *Valuing Ecosystem Services: Methodological Issues and Case Studies*, Cheltenham, UK and Northampton, MA, USA: Edward Elgar Publishing.

Bergstrom, J.C. and L.O. Taylor (2006), 'Using meta-analysis for benefits transfer: Theory and practice', *Ecological Economics*, **60**, 351–360.

Bishop, R.C. and K.J. Boyle (2019), 'Reliability and validity in nonmarket valuation', *Environmental and Resource Economics*, **72** (2), 559–582.

Bockstael, N.E. and K.E. McConnell (2010), *Environmental and Resource Valuation with Revealed Preferences: A Theoretical Guide to Empirical Models*, Dordrecht, The Netherlands: Springer.

Bockstael, N.E., A.M. Freeman, R.J. Kopp, P.R. Portney, and V.K. Smith (2000), 'On measuring economic values for nature', *Environmental Science and Technology*, **34**, 1384–1389.

Boyd, J. and S. Banzhaf (2007), 'What are ecosystem services? The need for standardized environmental accounting units', *Ecological Economics*, **63** (2–3), 616–626.

Boyd, J. and A. Krupnick (2013), 'Using ecological production theory to define and select environmental commodities for nonmarket valuation', *Agricultural and Resource Economics Review*, **42**, 1–32.

Boyd, J., P. Ringold, A. Krupnick, R.J. Johnston, M.A. Weber, and K. Hall (2016), 'Ecosystem services indicators: Improving the linkage between biophysical and economic analyses', *International Review of Environmental and Resource Economics*, **8**, 359–443.

Boyle, K.J. and J.M. Wooldridge (2018), 'Understanding error structures and exploiting panel data in meta-analytic benefit transfers', *Environmental and Resource Economics*, **69**, 609–635.

Brander, L.M., I. Bräuer, H. Gerdes, A. Ghermandi, O. Kuik, A. Markandya, S. Navrud, P.A.L.D. Nunes, M. Schaafsma, H. Vos, and A. Wagtendonk (2012), 'Using meta-analysis and GIS for value transfer and scaling up: Valuing climate change induced losses of European wetlands', *Environmental and Resource Economics*, **52**, 395–413.

Brown, T.C., J.C. Bergstrom, and J.B. Loomis (2007), 'Defining, valuing and providing ecosystem goods and services', *Natural Resources Journal*, **47** (2), 329–376.

Champ, P., K. Boyle, and T. Brown (eds) (2017), *A Primer on Nonmarket Valuation*, Netherlands: Springer Science and Business Media.

Chetty, R. (2009), 'Sufficient statistics for welfare analysis: A bridge between structural and reduced-form methods', *Annual Review of Economics*, **1**, 451–488.

Claassen, R., A. Cattaneo, and R. Johansson (2008), 'Cost-effective design of agri-environmental payment programs: U.S. experience in theory and practice', *Ecological Economics*, **65**, 737–752.

Daily, G.C. (1997), *Nature's Services*, Covelo, CA: Island Press.

Dale, V.H. and S. Polasky (2007), 'Measures of the effects of agricultural practices on ecosystem services', *Ecological Economics*, **64** (2), 286–296.

De Groot, R.S., M.A. Wilson, and R.M.J. Boumans (2002), 'A typology for the classification, description and valuation of ecosystem functions, goods and services', *Ecological Economics*, **41**, 393–408.

Drupp, M.A. (2018), 'Limits to substitution between ecosystem services and manufactured goods and implications for social discounting', *Environmental and Resource Economics*, **69** (1), 135-158.

Duke, J.M., S.J. Dundas, R.J. Johnston, and K.D. Messer (2014), 'Prioritizing payment for environmental services: Using nonmarket benefits and costs for optimal selection', *Ecological Economics*, **105**, 319–329.

Duke, J.M., S.J. Dundas, R.J. Johnston, and K.D. Messer (2015), 'The effect of spatial interdependencies on prioritization and payments for environmental services', *Land Use Policy*, **48**, 341–350.

Duran Vinent, O., R.J. Johnston, M. Kirwan, A. Leroux, and V. Martin (2019), 'Coastal dynamics and adaptation to uncertain sea level rise: Optimal portfolios for salt marsh migration', *Journal of Environmental Economics and Management*, **98**, 102262.

Faustmann, M. (1849), 'On the determination of the value which forest land and imma-ture stands pose for forestry', in M. Gane (ed.) (1968), *Martin Faustmann and the Evolution of Discounted Cash Flow*, Oxford: Oxford Institute.

Ferrini, S., M. Schaafsma, and I.J. Bateman (2015), 'Ecosystem services assessment and benefit transfer', in R.J. Johnston, J. Rolfe, R.S. Rosenberger and R. Brouwer (eds), *Benefit Transfer of Environmental and Resource Values: A Guide for Researchers and Practitioners*, Dordrecht, The Netherlands: Springer.

Fisher, B. and R.K. Turner (2008), 'Ecosystem services: Classification for valuation', *Biological Conservation*, **141** (5), 1167–1169.

Fisher, B., R.K. Turner, and P. Morling (2009), 'Defining and classifying ecosystem services for decision making', *Ecological Economics*, **68** (3), 643–653.

Fisher, B., K. Turner, M. Zylstra, R. Brouwer, R. de Groot, S. Farber, P. Ferraro, R. Green, D. Hadley, J. Harlow, P. Jefferiss, C. Kirkby, P. Morling, S. Mowatt, R. Naidoo, J. Paavola, B. Strassburg, D. Yu, and A. Balmford (2008), 'Ecosystem services and economic theory: Integration for policy relevant research', *Ecological Applications*, **18** (8), 2050–2067.

Freeman A.M., J.A. Herriges, and C.L. Kling (2014), *The Measurement of Environmental and Resource Values: Theory and Methods*, Washington, DC: Resources for the Future, 3rd edition.

Glenk, K., R.J. Johnston, J. Meyerhoff, and J. Sagebiel (2020), 'Spatial dimensions of stated preference valuation in environmental and resource economics: Methods, trends and challenges', *Environmental and Resource Economics*, **75** (2), 215–242.

Gómez-Baggethun, E., R. De Groot, P.L. Lomas, and C. Montes (2010), 'The history of ecosystem services in economic theory and practice: From early notions to markets and payment schemes', *Ecological Economics*, **69** (6), 1209–1218.

Gordon H.S. (1954), 'The economic theory of a common-property resource: The fishery', *Journal of Political Economy*, **62** (2), 124–142.

Guerry, A., S. Polasky, J. Lubchenco, R. Chaplin-Kramer, G.C. Daily, R. Griffin, M.H. Ruckelshaus, I.J. Bateman, A. Duraiappah, T. Elmqvist, M.W. Feldman, C. Folke, J. Hoekstra, P. Kareiva, B. Keeler, S. Li, E. McKenzie, Z. Ouyang, B. Reyers, T. Ricketts, J. Rockström, H. Tallis, and B. Vira (2015), 'Natural capital informing decisions: From promise to practice', *Proceedings of the National Academy of Sciences*, **112**, 7348–7355.

Haab, T.C. and K. McConnell (2002), *Valuing Environmental and Natural Resources: The Econometrics of Non-market Valuation*, Cheltenham, UK and Northampton, MA, USA: Edward Elgar Publishing.

Hanley, N. and E.B. Barbier (2009), *Pricing Nature: Cost Benefit Analysis and Environmental Policy*, Cheltenham, UK and Northampton, MA, USA: Edward Elgar Publishing.

Hanley, N. and M. Czajkowski (2019), 'The role of stated preference valuation methods in understanding choices and informing policy', *Review of Environmental Economics and Policy*, **13** (2), 248–266.

Hanley, N., S. Hynes, D. Patterson, and N. Jobstvogt (2015), 'Economic valuation of marine and coastal ecosystems: Is it currently fit for purpose?', *Journal of Ocean and Coastal Economics*, **2** (1), 1.

Hanley, N., F. Schläpfer, and J. Spurgeon (2003), 'Aggregating the benefits of envi-ronmental improvements: Distance–decay functions for use and non-use values', *Journal of Environmental Management*, **68**, 297–304.

Hartman, R. (1976), 'The harvesting decision when a standing forest has value', *Economic Inquiry*, **14**, 52–58.

Heberlein, T.A., M.A. Wilson, R.C. Bishop, and N.C. Schaeffer (2005), 'Rethinking the scope test as a criterion for validity in contingent valuation', *Journal of Environmental Economics and Management*, **50**, 1–22.

Holland, D.S., J. Sanchirico, R.J. Johnston, and D. Joglekar (2010), *Economic Analysis for Ecosystem Based Management: Applications to Marine and Coastal Environments*, Washington, DC: RFF Press.

Hotelling, H. (1947), Letter of June 18, 1947, to Newton B. Drury, included in 'The Economics of Public Recreation: An Economic Study of the Monetary Evaluation of Recreation in the National Parks', 1949, Mimeographed, Washington, DC: Land and Recreational Planning Division, National Parks Service.

Jack, B.K., C. Kousky, and K.R.E. Sims (2008), 'Designing payments for ecosystem services: Lessons from previous experience with incentive-based mechanisms', *Proceedings of the National Academy of Sciences*, **105**, 9465–9470.

Jakus, P.M. and W.D. Shaw (2003), 'Perceived hazard and product choice: an application to recreational site choice', *Journal of Risk and Uncertainty*, **26**, 77–92.

Johnston, R.J. and D.M. Bauer (2019), 'Using meta-analysis for large-scale ecosystem service valuation: progress, prospects and challenges', *Agricultural and Resource Economics Review*, https://doi.org/10.1017/age.2019.22.

Johnston, R.J. and R.S. Rosenberger (2010), 'Methods, trends and controversies in contemporary benefit transfer', *Journal of Economic Surveys*, **24** (3), 479–510.

Johnston, R.J. and M. Russell (2011), 'An operational structure for clarity in ecosystem service values', *Ecological Economics*, **70** (12), 2243–2249.

Johnston, R.J. and L.A. Wainger (2015), 'Benefit transfer for ecosystem service valuation: An introduction to theory and methods', in R.J. Johnston, J. Rolfe, R.S. Rosenberger, and R. Brouwer (eds), *Benefit Transfer of Environmental and Resource Values: A Guide for Researchers and Practitioners*, Dordrecht, The Netherlands: Springer, pp. 237–273.

Johnston, R.J., E.Y. Besedin, and B.M. Holland (2018a), 'Modeling distance decay within valuation meta-analysis', *Environmental and Resource Economics*, **72** (3), 657–690.

Johnston, R.J., E.Y. Besedin, and R. Stapler (2017a), 'Enhanced geospatial validity for meta-analysis and environmental benefit transfer: an application to water quality improvements', *Environmental and Resource Economics*, **68**, 343–375.

Johnston, R.J., K.J. Boyle, W. Adamowicz, J. Bennett, R. Brouwer, T.A. Cameron, W.M. Hanemann, N. Hanley, M. Ryan, R. Scarpa, R. Tourangeau, and C.A. Vossler (2017b), 'Contemporary guidance for stated preference studies', *Journal of the Association of Environmental and Resource Economists*, **4** (2), 319–405.

Johnston, R.J., G. Magnusson, M. Mazzotta, and J.J. Opaluch (2002), 'Combining economic and ecological indicators to prioritize salt marsh restoration actions', *American Journal of Agricultural Economics*, **84** (5), 1362–1370.

Johnston, R.J., J. Rolfe, R.S. Rosenberger, and R. Brouwer (eds) (2015a), *Benefit Transfer of Environmental and Resource Values: A Guide for Researchers and Practitioners*, Dordrecht, Netherlands: Springer.

Johnston, R.J., J. Rolfe, R.S. Rosenberger, and R. Brouwer (2015b), 'Introduction to benefit transfer methods', in R.J. Johnston, J. Rolfe, R.S. Rosenberger, and R. Brouwer (eds), *Benefit Transfer of Environmental and Resource Values: A Guide for Researchers and Practitioners*, Dordrecht, The Netherlands: Springer.

Johnston, R.J., J. Rolfe, and E. Zawojska (2018b), 'Benefit transfer of environmental and resource values: progress, prospects and challenges', *International Review of Environmental and Resource Economics*, **12** (2–3), 177–266.

Johnston, R.J., E.T. Schultz, K. Segerson, E.Y. Besedin, and M. Ramachandran (2012), 'Enhancing the content validity of stated preference valuation: The structure and function of ecological indicators', *Land Economics*, **88**, 102–120.

Johnston, R.J., E.T. Schultz, K. Segerson, E.Y. Besedin, and M. Ramachandran (2013), 'Stated preferences for intermediate versus final ecosystem services: Disentangling willingness to pay for omitted ecological outcomes', *Agricultural and Resource Economics Review*, **42** (1), 98–118.

Johnston, R.J., E.T. Schultz, K. Segerson, E.Y. Besedin, and M. Ramachandran (2017c), 'Biophysical causality and environmental preference elicitation: Evaluating the validity of welfare analysis over intermediate outcomes', *American Journal of Agricultural Economics*, **99** (1), 163–185.

Johnston, R.J., S.K. Swallow, D.M. Bauer, E. Uchida, and C.M. Anderson (2014). Connecting ecosystem services to land use: implications for valuation and policy, Chapter 8 in J.M. Duke and J. Wu (eds), *The Oxford Handbook of Land Economics*, Oxford University Press, pp. 196–225.

Just, R.E., D.L. Hueth, and A. Schmitz (2004), *The Welfare Economics of Public Policy: A Practical Approach to Project and Policy Evaluation*, Cheltenham, UK and Northampton, MA, USA: Edward Elgar Publishing.

Kanninen, B.J. (ed.) (2010), *Valuing Environmental Amenities Using Stated Choice Studies: A Common Sense Approach to Theory and Practice*, Dordrecht, Netherlands: Springer.

Landers, D.H. and A.M. Nahlik (2013), *Final Ecosystem Goods and Services Classification System (FEGS-CS)*, EPA/600/R-13/ORD-004914, Washington, DC: U.S. Environmental Protection Agency, Office of Research and Development.

Leroux, A.D., V.L. Martin, and Timo Goeschl (2009), 'Optimal conservation, extinction debt, and the augmented quasi-option value', *Journal of Environmental Economics and Management*, **58**, 43–57.

Lipton, D., D. Lew, K. Wallmo, P. Wiley, and A. Dvarskas (2014), 'The evolution of non-market valuation of U.S. coastal and marine resources', *Journal of Ocean and Coastal Economics*, **1**, 6.

Melstrom, R.T., F. Lupi, P.C. Esselman, and R.J. Stevenson (2015), 'Valuing recreational fishing quality at rivers and streams', *Water Resources Research*, **51**, 140–150, https://doi.org/10.1002/2014WR016152.

Millennium Ecosystem Assessment (MEA) (2005), *Ecosystems and Human Well-being: Synthesis*, Washington, DC: Island Press.

National Research Council (2005), *Valuing Ecosystem Services: Toward Better Environmental Decision-Making*, Washington, DC: The National Academies Press, https://doi.org/10.17226/11139.

Nelson, J.P. and P.E. Kennedy (2009), 'The use (and abuse) of meta-analysis in environmental and resource economics: an assessment', *Environmental and Resource Economics*, **42**, 345–377.

Nelson, E., G. Mendoza, J. Regetz, S. Polasky, H. Tallis, D.R. Cameron, K.M. Chan, G.C. Daily, J. Goldstein, P.M. Kareiva, E. Lonsdorf, R. Naidoo, T.H. Ricketts, and M.R. Shaw (2009), 'Modeling multiple ecosystem services, biodiversity conservation, commodity production, and trade-offs at landscape scales', *Frontiers in Ecology and Environment*, **7**, 4–11.

NESP (2016), *Federal Resource Management and Ecosystem Services Guidebook*, National Ecosystem Services Partnership, Durham, NC: Duke University, 2nd edition, https://nespguidebook.com.

Olander, L. and L. Maltby (2014), 'Mainstreaming ecosystem services into decision making', *Frontiers in Ecology and the Environment*, **12** (10), 539, https://doi.org/10.1890/1540-9295-12.10.539.

Olander, L.P., R.J. Johnston, H. Tallis, J. Kagan, L.A. Maguire, S. Polasky, D. Urban, J. Boyd, L. Wainger, and M. Palmer (2018), 'Benefit relevant indicators: Ecosystem services measures that link ecological and social outcomes', *Ecological Indicators*, **85**, 1262–1272.

Olander, L., S. Polasky, J.S. Kagan, R.J. Johnston, L. Wainger, D. Saah, L. Maguire, J. Boyd, and D. Yoskowitz (2017), 'So you want your research to be relevant? Building the bridge between ecosystem services research and practice', *Ecosystem Services*, **26**, 170–182.

Parsons, G.R. and A.B. Hauber (1998), 'Spatial boundaries and choice set definition in a random utility model of recreation demand', *Land Economics*, **74** (1), 32–48.

Pattanayak, S.K., S. Wunder, and P.J. Ferraro (2010), 'Show me the money: Do payments supply environmental services in developing countries?', *Review of Environmental Economics and Policy*, **4** (2), 254–274.

Plummer, M.L. (2009), 'Assessing benefit transfer for the valuation of ecosystem services', *Frontiers in Ecology and the Environment*, **7**, 38–45.

Polasky, S. and K. Segerson (2009), 'Integrating ecology and economics in the study of ecosystem services: Some lessons learned', *Annual Review of Resource Economics*, **1**, 409–434.

Polasky, S., E. Nelson, J. Camm, B. Csuti, P. Fackler, E. Lonsdorf, C. Montgomery, D. White, J. Arthur, B. Garber-Yonts, R. Haight, J. Kagan, A. Starfield, and C. Tobalske (2008), 'Where to put things? Spatial land management to sustain biodiversity and economic returns', *Biological Conservation*, **141** (6), 1505–1524.

Richardson, L., J. Loomis, T. Kroeger, and F. Casey (2015), 'The role of benefit transfer in ecosystem service valuation', *Ecological Economics*, **115**, 51–58.

Rolfe, J. and X. Wang (2011), 'Dealing with scale and scope issues in stated preference experiments', in J. Bennett (ed.), *The International Handbook on Non-Market Environmental Valuation*, Cheltenham, UK and Northampton, MA, USA: Edward Elgar Publishing.

Rosenberger, R.S. and J.B. Loomis (2017). 'Benefit transfer', in P.A. Champ, K.J. Boyle, and T.C. Brown (eds), *A Primer on Nonmarket Valuation*, 2nd edition, Dordrecht, The Netherlands: Springer.

Ruckelshaus, M., E. McKenzie, H. Tallis, A. Guerry, G. Daily, P. Kareiva, S. Polasky, T. Ricketts, N. Bhagabati, S.A. Wood, and J. Bernhardt (2015), 'Notes from the field: Lessons learned from using ecosystem services approaches to inform real-world decisions', *Ecological Economics*, **115**, 11–21.

Schaafsma, M. (2015), 'Spatial and geographical aspects of benefit transfer', in R.J. Johnston, J. Rolfe, R.S. Rosenberger, and R. Brouwer (eds), *Benefit Transfer of Environmental and Resource Values: A Guide for Researchers and Practitioners*, Dordrecht, The Netherlands: Springer.

Schaefer M.B. (1957), 'Some considerations of population dynamics and economics in relation to the management of marine fishes', *Journal of the Fisheries Research Board of Canada*, **14**, 669–681.

Schultz, E.T., R.J. Johnston, K. Segerson, and E.Y. Besedin (2012), 'Integrating ecology and economics for restoration: Using ecological indicators in valuation of ecosystem services', *Restoration Ecology*, **20**, 304–310.

Scott A. (1955), 'The fishery: The objectives of sole ownership', *Journal of Political Economy*, **63**, 116–124.

Silberberg, E. (1990), *The Structure and Function of Economics*, 2nd edition, New York, NY: McGraw Hill.

Simpson, R.D. (2014), 'Ecosystem services as substitute inputs: Basic results and important implications for conservation policy', *Ecological Economics*, **98**, 102–108.

Tallis, H. and S. Polasky (2009), 'Mapping and valuing ecosystem services as an approach for conservation and natural resource management', *Annals of the New York Academy of Sciences*, **1162**, 265–283.

Timmins, C. and W. Schlenker (2009), 'Reduced-form versus structural modeling in environmental and resource economics', *Annual Review of Resource Economics*, 1, 351–380.

Toman, M. (1998), 'Why not to calculate the value of the world's ecosystem services and natural capital', *Ecological Economics*, **25**, 57–60.

Turner, R.K. and G.C. Daily (2008), 'The ecosystem services framework and natural capital conservation', *Environmental and Resource Economics*, **39** (1), 25–35.

United States Environmental Protection Agency (U.S. EPA) (2015), *National Ecosystem Services Classification System (NESCS): Framework Design and Policy Application*, EPA-800-R-15-002, Washington, DC: United States Environmental Protection Agency.

Wainger, L. and M. Mazzotta (2011), 'Realizing the potential of ecosystem services: A framework for relating ecological changes to economic benefits', *Environmental Management*, **48** (4), 710–733.

Wainger, L.A., D.M. King, R.N. Mack, E.W. Price, and T. Maslin (2010), 'Can the concept of ecosystem services be practically applied to improve natural resource management decisions?', *Ecological Economics*, **69** (5), 978–987.

Warnell, K.J.D., M. Russell, C. Rhodes, K.J. Bagstad, L.P. Olander, D.J. Nowak, R. Poudel, P.D. Glynn, J.L. Hass, S. Hirabayashi, J.C. Ingram, J. Matuszak, K.L.L. Oleson, S.M. Posner, and F. Villa (2020), 'Testing ecosystem accounting in the United States: A case study for the Southeast', *Ecosystem Services*, **43**, 101099.

Whitehead, J.C., T.C. Haab, and J.C. Huang (2011), *Preference Data for Environmental Valuation: Combining Revealed and Stated Approaches*, London: Routledge.

Whitehead, J.C., S.K. Pattanayak, G.L. Van Houtven, and B.R. Gelso (2008), 'Combining revealed and stated preference data to estimate the nonmarket value of ecological services: An assessment of the state of the science', *Journal of Economic Surveys*, **22**, 872–908.

5. Incentives, institutions, and inequality: a pluralist approach to teaching environmental and natural resource economics

Kathleen Lawlor

5.1 BACKGROUND AND INTRODUCTION

Traditionally, introductory environmental and natural resource economics courses cover only the neoclassical approach to environmental[1] issues. While the neoclassical framework is certainly the most dominant economic approach for understanding environmental problems and policy solutions – both in the scholarly literature and in policy applications – there are other important schools of thought that warrant inclusion in an introductory environmental and natural resource economics course. Both political economy and new institutional economics provide important perspectives on environmental issues as well. The neoclassical approach focuses squarely on the importance of incentives for diagnosing and solving environmental problems. The political economy school, however, emphasizes the role of inequality in both shaping and determining environmental outcomes. The new institutionalists, on the other hand, pay particular attention to how formal institutions, such as property rights, and informal institutions, such as shared norms and values, affect communities' abilities to overcome collective action problems and sustainably manage the commons. While these three schools of thought offer meaningful critiques of each other, they also provide complementary lenses for understanding why environmental degradation occurs and analyzing corrective policy options.

For my undergraduate Environmental and Natural Resource Economics and Policy course I have developed a unique structure for presenting both the traditional and alternative theoretical frameworks in the field, which I call "the 3Is" – incentives, inequality, and institutions.[2] Orienting a class around the comparison of multiple perspectives for analyzing a problem can help students build critical thinking skills. Nosich (2012) argues that in order to use critical thinking skills within any discipline, we must first learn the discipline's most fundamental and powerful concepts, and then apply them to reasonably and reflectively ask and analyze the right questions. In my course, and in this chapter, I argue that the most fundamental and powerful concepts in Environmental and Natural Resource Economics can be distilled to these three theoretical explanations for why environmental degradation occurs and how it can be corrected: incentives, inequality, and institutional arrangements. My 300-level Economics course is required for Environmental Studies Policy and Management students and, as a result, the course is usually 90–95 percent Environmental Studies majors, and 5–10 percent Economics majors. I find that this is often Environmental Studies students' first encounter with theory and I enjoy hearing their diverse perspectives on which theory most resonates with them.

Teaching economics through the lens of pluralism can not only help build students' critical thinking skills, but it can also help students understand the complexity of applied policy analysis, which must balance competing interests and values. I argue that a pluralist approach is critical for understanding the policy applications of environmental and natural resource economics and has particular salience for assessing the effectiveness, efficiency, and equity of environmental policies. I also argue that analysis of environmental problems through the lens of pluralism is essential for advancing the discipline as well. Pluralist conversations lead to new critiques, new insights, and new policy solutions.

To provide focus for a course that covers both environmental economics *and* natural resource economics *and* applied policy analysis *and* introduces students to three divergent theoretical perspectives on environmental problems, I use carbon pollution and climate policy as a topical lens for the course. Climate change is, of course, a pollution problem and thus squarely sits within the space of environmental economics. But both its impacts and proposed policy solutions also encompass topics pertinent to natural resource economics. Calculating the social cost of carbon, for example, requires that non-market valuation techniques be used to understand the damages of climate change to numerous ecosystem services. And a key element of climate policy at multiple jurisdictional levels involves sustainable management of forests via incentives to reduce emissions from deforestation and forest degradation and enhance forest carbon stocks (policies and programs known as 'REDD+').

This chapter is organized as follows: In Section 5.2, I provide an overview of the three theoretical schools of thought covered in my course. Section 5.3 presents the course style and structure. Section 5.4 concludes.

5.2   THREE THEORETICAL PERSPECTIVES ON ENVIRONMENTAL PROBLEMS AND POLICY SOLUTIONS: INCENTIVES, INSTITUTIONS, AND INEQUALITY

5.2.1   Incentives: Neoclassical Framework

In the neoclassical framework, the primary source of environmental degradation (both pollution and unsustainable use of natural resources) is socially sub-optimal incentives caused by market failures, chief among them negative externalities and ambiguous property rights. Energy firms pollute the atmosphere with carbon, a familiar example goes, because the negative impacts of this pollution are borne by the public at large and firms (and energy users) do not take these social costs into account in their private profit-maximization (or utility-maximization) decision. Firms (and individuals) thus face an incentive to pollute. From the standpoint of Pigou (1920), negative externalities create these bad incentives. In Coase's (1960) view, ambiguous property rights to the air are responsible for creating these externalities and thus the incentive to pollute. The policy solution offered up by the neoclassicists is therefore to get firms and individuals to internalize the negative externality by putting a price on pollution so the social costs of pollution are factored into individuals' and firms' cost–benefit calculations. This pollution pricing could be achieved via a Pigouvian tax on emissions or via negotiation between the polluters and pollution victims (per Coase), assuming clean air/pollution rights can be established.[3]

Stavins (2011) notes that the unclear property rights problem identified by Coase is really a public goods problem, with pollution occurring as a result of the consumption good (e.g., clean air) being non-rival and non-excludable in consumption. The 'types of goods' framework, which delineates the differences between public goods, common-pool resources, private goods, and club goods, provides a clear theoretical framework for understanding why environmental degradation occurs and how sustainability problems might be corrected by changing the 'rules of the game', chiefly property rights. For example, by assigning property rights over timber harvesting, an institution can convert an unmanaged forest (a common-pool resource) that is rival and non-excludable in consumption from an open-access resource (non-excludable) to a resource that is managed more like a private good (rival and excludable in consumption).

The 'types of goods' framework is considered to be important foundational material in contemporary neoclassical presentations of environmental and natural resource economics, though its development represents contributions from Elinor Ostrom and the new institutionalist school of thought (see Ostrom and Ostrom 1977; Ostrom 1990; Ostrom et al. 1994). Ostrom (2003) describes how her work to clarify this framework builds on the work of Paul Samuelson (1954), Richard Musgrave (1959), and Mancur Olson (1965). The influences of Ostrom (and Coase, an important institutionalist and founder of the Law and Property Rights school) on the neoclassical school reflect the blurring of distinct boundaries between neoclassical and institutional economics. The 'types of goods' framework is discussed in detail in Section 5.2.3.

The neoclassical school's strengths include the straightforward policy prescriptions that flow from its diagnosis of environmental problems and the body of methods and tools the school provides to craft complementary analyses. The policy prescriptions are clear and widely used: incentivize individuals, firms, and governments to internalize externalities by pricing them via taxes; tradable emissions permits; individual transferable quotas; payments for ecosystem services; and tradable credits for wetlands, stream, and biodiversity loss/ mitigation. When the price of pollution or value of nature's services needs to be estimated for a cost–benefit analysis or to set a tax, the neoclassical school offers non-market valuation techniques, and, in the case of climate policy and a carbon tax, integrated assessment models and both positive and normative analysis of appropriate discount rates. All of these policies, methods, and tools of course provide ample material for courses on environmental and natural resource economics, as evidenced by their dominance in the field's textbooks.

5.2.2 Inequality: Political Economy Framework

An alternative diagnosis of environmental degradation and potential policy solutions comes from the field of political economy. This school of thought argues it is more than just bad incentives due to market failures that cause environmental degradation; rather, environmental degradation is driven by inequality, which allows the beneficiaries of such degradation to force the poor and less powerful to bear the costs. This view of environmental problems is articulated most elegantly by James K. Boyce in his 2002 book, *The Political Economy of the Environment*. Boyce's starting point is a critique of the Neoclassical view of environmental dilemmas. He observes that Neoclassical environmental economics has developed numerous sophisticated methods for figuring out the price of nature and its degradation, yet policy makers often fail to put a price on pollution or incorporate natural capital values into their decision-making. Boyce encourages us to ask *why* policy makers often fail to adopt the seemingly simple policy remedies offered by the neoclassical school. He argues that in order to understand these repeated failures, we must acknowledge that there are both winners and losers from environmental degradation and examine how wealth and power are distributed amongst resource users, as well as the causal effects of these factors on environmental outcomes.

Boyce's theoretical framework interrogates the notion of nameless and faceless externalities posed on others outside the market transaction and, effectively, asks us to consider the socioeconomic characteristics of both those imposing the external costs and those of the 'others' harmed by these externalities. His thesis is that environmental degradation occurs because the winners of environmental degradation are more powerful than the losers and the winners can therefore force the losers to bear these costs. An important conclusion of Boyce's work is that inequality is both a cause and consequence of environmental degradation. The policy solution offered by this theoretical framework is that a more equal distribution of wealth and power can thus be protective for the environment.

Boyce theorizes that greater inequalities of political power lead to more environmental degradation, while noting how this dynamic feedback loop between increasing inequality and increasing environmental degradation impacts and is impacted by individuals' valuation of costs and benefits and their rates of time preference. Boyce (2002, p. 39) observes that the willingness to pay valuation numbers used in cost–benefit analysis are shaped by one's ability to pay – and that the poor can be made poorer via degradation of their environment, further lowering their 'willingness to pay' for clean air and intact forests, for example. He also describes how inequality further shapes valuations of costs and benefits by influencing one's preferences (Boyce, 2002, p. 40). Citing Becker's (1983, p. 392) observation that '"preferences" can be manipulated and created through the information and misinformation provided by interested pressure groups', Boyce reminds us that powerful actors can withhold information about air pollution and its health impacts, and these information asymmetries can significantly affect our preferences, market behavior, and valuations.

In discussing how inequality can affect time preferences, Boyce (2002, pp. 42–44) turns the conventional wisdom that only the poor heavily discount the future, by theorizing that, under conditions of extreme wealth and power inequalities, the rich also have high time preference rates with respect to the environment. He acknowledges that the poor's struggle for survival often means they have strong preferences for immediate benefits, which can lead them to degrade their natural capital – in the case of subsistence farmers, for example – in an attempt to escape poverty, thereby deepening their poverty in a classic illustration of the 'poverty–environment' trap.[4] But Boyce also draws our attention to the political elite in a highly unequal society and their role in environmental degradation. He conjectures that where democracy is weak, these elites will lack legitimacy and therefore perceive their societal positions as insecure. This insecurity will lead them to regard their property rights over natural resources, for example, as fleeting, and encourage unsustainable levels of resource extraction.

The essence of Boyce's theory – that inequalities of wealth and power drive environmental degradation – is supported by a small body of empirical work and certainly merits further investigation and testing. In his chapter 'Rethinking the environmental Kuznets curve' with Mariano Torras, Boyce (2002, pp. 47–66) uses national-level data to test whether there are causal impacts of income inequality and power inequality on pollution and finds that greater inequality of power, as measured by degree of literacy and political and civil rights, leads to higher levels of pollution, particularly in low-income countries. Using data from the United States (US), Boyce (with Andrew R. Klemer, Paul H. Templet, and Cleve E. Willis) undertakes another test of his central hypothesis by using recursive modeling to investigate how variation in power distribution at the state-level affects states' adoption of environmental policy, and in turn, impacts on pollution and, ultimately, public health (Boyce, 2002, pp. 67–87). The analysis again confirms Boyce's hypothesis, finding that states with more equal distributions of power (an index variable based on per capita income, income inequality, race, and ethnicity) have stronger environmental policies, cleaner environments, and healthier populations.

Studies of natural resource degradation are more mixed in their support of Boyce's hypothesis. For example, Mikkelson et al. (2007) find that, both across countries and US states, biodiversity loss increases as a function of increasing income inequality. Yet, Alix-Garcia (2008) finds that inequality actually reduces deforestation in community forests (*ejidos*) in Mexico, due to a reduction of the poor's use of the forest commons in the more unequal communities. In their 2007 book *Inequality, Cooperation, and Environmental Sustainability*, Jean-Marie Baland et al. survey the literature and bring together several case studies that provide further empirical evidence and theoretical insight on this topic. This volume suggests that inequality can drive both degradation and protection of the local commons, with the key mechanism being how inequality affects collective action institutions. Similarly, in their examination of over 200 forest commons across six countries in South Asia, Latin America, and East Africa, Anderrson and Agrawal (2011) find that economic inequality is associated with worse outcomes for forests, but that this effect is moderated by the strength of local collective action institutions.

Boyce's theory and policy prescriptions are especially salient for analyses of the current climate crisis. A particularly vexing feature of climate change is that those countries who have contributed the least to the accumulation of greenhouse gases in the atmosphere are poised to experience (and are already experiencing) the most severe negative impacts of climate change. One wonders if the international community would have taken more aggressive action over the past 20 years to reduce greenhouse gas emissions if climate models suggested that the rich countries of the world, such as the United States and European nations, would experience the most negative impacts of climate change, rather than the poorer countries of the world, such as those in Africa and South Asia. This raises the question: if there were greater equality of wealth and power between nations, would emission levels be as high as they are today? And while Boyce's policy prescription – that a more equal distribution of wealth and power can be protective for the environment – might seem infeasible at the international level, within the United States, the idea bears striking similarity to many elements of the 'Green New Deal'. These connections to contemporary environmental issues facilitate incorporation of the political economy school into courses on environmental and natural resource economics.

5.2.3   Institutions: New Institutional Economics Framework

A third school of thought emphasizes the agency of communities to come together to overcome our environmental problems, provided the 'rules of the game' (institutional arrangements) appropriately match the relevant socio-ecological conditions. These 'rules of the game' include both formal institutions (e.g., laws, policies) and informal institutions (e.g., cultural norms). The work of Nobel Laureate Elinor Ostrom has defined this application of institutional economics to environmental problems. Her work on the potential of self-organized, community-based institutions to sustainably manage the commons continues to pose a strong counter-narrative to Hardin's (1968) characterization of all collective-action dilemmas as inevitable 'tragedies' and inspire ongoing empirical investigation of the topic (see, for example, Chhatre and Agrawal 2009; Porter-Bolland et al. 2012). In *Governing the Commons: The Evolution of Institutions for Collective Action* (1990), Ostrom presents a framework for identifying and understanding the institutional design principles that might lead to sustainable management of self-governed common-pool resources. Based on her analysis of case studies of jointly-used forests and grasslands in Japan and Switzerland; fisheries in Turkey, Canada, and Sri Lanka; irrigation systems in the Philippines, Sri Lanka, and Spain; and groundwater basins in California she identified eight 'design principles' associated with sustainable management of common-pool resources (see Table 5.1). She argued that further work should be done to test whether these design principles were consistently associated with positive outcomes in decentralized systems in order to develop a more nuanced theory of the conditions under which collective action for sustainable resource management takes place. The Ostrom design principles framework was expanded upon over the course of her career; notably in Dietz et al. (2003) and Ostrom (2009).

Other important contributions to environmental and natural resource economics come from Ostrom's work on 'types of goods'. As noted in Section 5.2.1, the 'types of goods' framework has come to be foundational theory in

Table 5.1   *The Ostrom 'design principles': characteristics associated*
with sustainability in self-governed, jointly-used
common-pool resource institutions[a]

(1)	Resource boundaries and resource use rights are clearly defined
(2)	Rules governing resource use are adapted to local socio-ecological conditions
(3)	Individuals affected by the resource use rules have the right to modify the rules
(4)	Resource use and rule compliance is monitored and the monitors are accountable to those that make the rules
(5)	Resource use rule violations are sanctioned, but small/initial infractions sanctioned less harshly than significant/repeated infractions
(6)	Local conflict–resolution mechanisms are easily accessed
(7)	External government officials recognize the rights of the resource users to self-governance
(8)	Where the resource is part of a larger socio-ecological system, institutions are vertically nested and mutually supporting

Source: [a]Adapted from Table 3.1 in Ostrom 1990, p. 90.

the neoclassical school, illustrating the influence of the new institutionalists on mainstream economic thought. Central to the 'types of goods' framework is an understanding of what it means for goods to be *rival* or *non-rival* (also referred to as *subtractable* or *non-subtractable*) and *excludable* or *non-excludable*. Where goods are rival, one person's consumption subtracts from another's possible consumption; with non-rival goods, one person's consumption does not diminish the amount available for others. If goods are excludable, it is feasible to prevent others from using them; where goods are non-excludable it is difficult to prevent consumption by others. By delineating the differences between goods that are rival/non-rival and excludable/non-excludable in consumption, the framework classifies goods into four different groups (see Table 5.2): (1) private goods (rival and excludable), (2) club goods (non-rival and excludable), (3) common-pool resources (rival and non-excludable), and (4) public goods (non-rival and non-excludable). Because their rivalrous and excludable nature provides strong incentives for enterprising individuals to produce and sell them, private goods generally encompass all goods and services commonly transacted in markets. Classic examples of public goods include national defense and sidewalks; because their non-rival and non-excludable nature means no one has an incentivize to produce them, public goods are chronically undersupplied (less than the socially optimal amount) in free market settings. Club goods (also known as *tool goods*) can be thought of as a type of public good only available to those within a group that has been given preferential access (e.g., library books are only available to those with a membership). The common-pool resources studied by Ostrom offer textbook examples of these rival, but non-excludable goods: fisheries, forests, meadows, and groundwater basins.

Explicit in Ostrom's (1990, pp. 2–5) critique of Hardin's (1968) depiction of all jointly-used resources as inevitable 'tragedies of the commons' is her observation that Hardin mischaracterized the collective-action dilemma herders grazing cattle on a shared commons faced as a Prisoner's Dilemma;[5] implicit in her critique is the notion that Hardin failed to distinguish between common-pool resources and public goods. Producing or sustaining a socially-optimal supply of both types of goods can be seen as problems of the *commons*, but, Ostrom notes (1990, pp. 30–33) there are important differences. The socially-optimal supply of both public goods and common-pool resources is challenged by the fact that the characteristics of both types of goods create incentives for resource beneficiaries to free-ride and not overcome the collective action dilemma. For public goods, the potential for free-riding weakens incentives to contribute to the good's production. For common-pool resources, incentives for free-riding can lead to overuse. However, the rivalrous nature of common-pool resources means that this resource depletion can trigger corrective action by incentivizing those that are using the resource and trying to sustain it to devise rules to constrain other's use. Ostrom notes:

> Thus, this distinction between a public good and a CPR [common-pool resource] is nontrivial. A person who contributes to the provision of a pure public good does not really care who else uses it, or when and where, so long as enough other individuals share the cost of provision. A person who contributes to the provisions of a CPR cares a great deal about how many others use it, and when and where, even if the others all contribute to its provision. (Ostrom 1990, p. 221, endnote 5)

And while the key distinction between common-pool resources and public goods is that the former are rival and the latter non-rival, there are degrees of difference in their excludability as well. While it is impossible to prevent others from breathing the public good of clean air in shared airshed, exclusion is not impossible with common-pool resources, but it is costly and therefore challenging (Ostrom, 1990, p. 30).

Stavins (2011) notes that common-pool resources are really only non-excludable if they are characterized by open-access regimes. This point highlights how the 'type of goods' framework helps us understand how the characteristics of resources can be changed from their natural, unmanaged state (e.g., an open-access forest) to a state more conducive for sustainability (e.g., a common-property regime) via the creation of institutions, which could include both formal institutions (written policies) and informal institutions (cultural norms). Table 5.2 uses the example of forests to illustrate how one resource can be conceptualized as each of the four types of goods once the institutional rules governing (or not) its use are specified. Table 5.2 also draws

Table 5.2   The role of institutions in shaping types of goods: the case of forests

	Excludable	Non-excludable
Rival	*Private goods* Timber from a common-property, individually-owned, or state-managed forest	*Common-pool resources* Timber from an open-access forest (governance is weak or non-existent)
Non-rival	*Toll goods* Hiking trails in a common-property, individually-owned, or state-managed forest	*Public goods* Carbon sequestration and avoided emissions from deforestation in open-access as well as governed forests

our attention to the link between externalities and public goods: the benefits from the production of a positive externality (planting trees to sequester carbon) and the elimination of a negative externality (stopping deforestation to reduce greenhouse gas emissions) are non-rival and non-excludable, and thus public goods.

Ostrom's work on polycentric institutions is another topic warranting inclusion in an introductory environmental and natural resource economics course, particularly one focused on climate policy. Ostrom (2012, p. 355) defines polycentric systems as those where 'multiple public and private organizations at multiple scales jointly affect collective benefits and costs'. Polycentric systems are composed of multiple institutions working to address the same social problem – such as public safety, water management, or climate change – but the institutions are not vertically nested and work independently of each other. As such, polycentric systems may be perceived as inefficient and ineffective due to their overlapping efforts and lack of coordination. In the context of climate change, conventional economic wisdom maintains that because reducing greenhouse gases are a global public good and leakage and free-riding would result from independent, uncoordinated efforts to reduce emissions at national or sub-national levels, collective action at the global level is the only way to effectively address the climate crisis. As a result, climate policy has been focused on achieving an international climate change agreement under the United Nations Framework Convention on Climate Change (UNFCCC) since 1992.

However, Ostrom (2012) argues, we should not necessarily dismiss a polycentric approach to fighting climate change – with multiple public jurisdictions, from municipalities to states to nations, along with private sector actors, making overlapping, uncoordinated efforts to reduce emissions – as chaotic, inefficient, or ineffective. Instead, she argues, polycentric approaches to the climate crisis have important advantages. First, when nested externalities (actions at one scale create costs or benefits for those at another scale) are present, polycentric approaches can effectively contribute to global emissions reduction. Second, undertaking emissions reductions efforts at sub-national and national levels is necessary for not only learning about what works, but also for building the trust that is necessary to commit to collective action at the international level. Finally, these independent actions can also inspire others to take actions, eventually leading to a coordinated international effort.

5.3   COURSE OVERVIEW

5.3.1   Seminar Style and Policy Orientation of Course

The University of North Carolina Asheville, where I teach this course, is a small, liberal arts school focused on undergraduate education. As such, our curriculum emphasizes critical thinking, interdisciplinarity, and social impact and our class sizes are small. My Environmental and Natural Resource Economics and Policy course is usually 18–22 students and run in the style of a seminar, with active student participation via Socratic-style questioning during lectures and many small-group and full-group discussions of assigned readings. As such, the structure and assignments of this course may only work well for a similarly-sized course. Because many of the assigned readings are academic journal articles and the assignments require independent research, the design of this course (see syllabus and reading list in Appendices I and II, respectively) could also work well for an introductory graduate-level course for policy-oriented students.

The course design is shaped not only by the small class size, but by the academic backgrounds of the students as well. The course is required for Environmental Studies Policy and Management students and, as a result, the class is usually composed almost exclusively of Environmental Studies majors, with only one or two Economics majors. This academic composition led me to orienting the course less around the quantitative applications of theory and problem sets, as may be typical in such a course, and more around understanding divergent theoretical lenses and conducting policy analysis. The course still covers core quantitative material, such as applying discount rates to conduct cost–benefit analysis of projects that include valuations of both market and non-market goods, but assignments and tests emphasize the importance of understanding a key policy implication of discounting – that projects with high upfront costs and benefits far in the future will look much worse than projects with immediate benefits and costs spread out over time when high discount rates are used rather than math problems.

The course is structured around three modules. First, we cover the three theoretical schools of thought: incentives, institutions, and inequality. This module also introduces the workings of cap-and-trade and emissions taxes – key policy instruments that we return to in layers of more nuanced detail throughout the course. The second module covers the tools and methods we use in the discipline to evaluate trade-offs. This module focuses on the tools and methods from the neoclassical school (cost–benefit analysis, discounting, non-market valuation methods), though we bring in insights from the political economy school on how the results of social cost–benefit analysis might mask significant heterogeneity in net benefits across populations and how one's economic position can affect their valuations of non-market goods and services. Module three turns to policy applications, where we closely examine the effectiveness, efficiency, and equity of specific policy instruments designed to sustainably manage natural resources and reduce pollution.

The '3E' framework of effectiveness, efficiency, and equity is widely used in applied policy analysis (see Angelsen and Wertz-Kanounnikoff (2008) and Stavins (2019) for two examples) and is one of the key analytical methods taught in this course. Students conduct semester-long research and produce policy briefs that analyze a contemporary environmental policy using these three criteria. This assignment necessitates that students integrate perspectives from the three theoretical schools with what they've learned about methods in order to conduct real-world policy analysis. Students apply what they've learned about non-market valuation and cost–benefit analysis to assess a policy's efficiency (whether the benefits outweigh the costs). Assessment of effectiveness and equity is informed by perspectives from the three theoretical schools. Analysis of whether a policy is likely to be effective in reducing environmental degradation might be informed by consideration of how well it is likely to change incentives or match institutional arrangements to local socio-ecological conditions. Early discussion of inequality and the political economy school in the course primes students to think critically about assessing whether an environmental policy's impacts are equitably distributed. Students are encouraged to think about equity both spatially (across different population sub-groups) and temporally (across generations) and to think about multiple dimensions of equity, including both equity of process and equity of outcomes.

5.3.2 Climate Policy Lens

To provide focus for a course that covers two sub-fields and three theoretical schools of thought, I use carbon pollution and climate policy as a lens. Climate change encompasses topics core to the teaching of both environmental economics, such as pollution control via Pigouvian taxes and tradable emissions permits, and natural resource economics, such as valuation of ecosystem services. Teaching students how economists estimate the monetary damages to society from each additional ton of carbon dioxide emissions – the social cost of carbon – brings together topics key to each respective sub-field: pricing pollution and calculating the socially optimal carbon tax, non-market valuation techniques for both use and non-use ecosystem services, and normative and positive debates around discount rates.

Climate change is of course a global issue, and international efforts to address the climate crisis figure prominently in my course. For example, we critically examine policies and measures designed to reduce emissions from deforestation and forest degradation and enhance forest carbon stocks (policies and programs known as 'REDD+'). REDD+ programs seek to make forests worth more standing than cut down, by paying those that would deforest or degrade them to instead sustain forests for their carbon sequestration services. REDD+ programs were originally conceived as carbon-offsetting programs between developed and developing countries, where the former would pay the latter to reduce projected levels of deforestation below an estimated reference scenario in order to offset their own greenhouse gas emissions. REDD+ has figured prominently in international climate talks and simultaneously advanced on the ground at the project and sub-national levels, with REDD+ carbon offsets linked to voluntary carbon markets, sub-national cap-and-trade systems, and bilateral and multilateral pay-for-performance initiatives.

Sustainable management of forests via REDD+ initiatives provides another clear linking ground for environmental and natural resource economics. Critical examination of REDD+ also invokes key questions rooted in both the '3Is' and '3Es' of the course: will REDD+ carbon payments be high enough to compete with the opportunity costs of leaving forests standing (e.g., agricultural profits) and actually be *effective* at changing deforestation agents' *incentives*? What risks (and opportunities) does REDD+ pose (offer) to indigenous peoples and will it promote *equity* or enhance *inequality*? If *institutional* arrangements around property rights and benefit distribution are weak or contested, can REDD+ still be an *efficient* means of reducing emissions or are marginal abatement costs likely to be higher than what models estimate due to these unaccounted transaction costs?

In this course we also hold mock international climate negotiations, using the World Climate game, developed by Climate Interactive.[6] The World Climate game is freely available and provides users with everything needed to simulate the annual Conference of the Parties (COPs) held each year under the United Nations Framework Convention on Climate Change, including briefing materials on the global climate crisis, country negotiating blocs' conditions and positions, and an emissions reduction scenarios simulator (called 'C-Roads'), which allows users to model the impacts of emissions reductions pledges on the climate in real-time. Engaging in these mock negotiations allows students to really understand why solving the climate crisis may be the most challenging collective action dilemma humanity has faced. And when students see how little power the developing countries have in these negotiations as compared with the United States, it becomes clear how issues of inequality are inextricably intertwined with environmental outcomes.

For the past four years, I have collaborated with an atmospheric science professor (Dr. Evan Couzo) to hold the climate talks, bringing together both his climate science class and my economics class. We have experimented with different formats for the talks and found that holding the mock negotiations during a two-and-a-half-hour block in the evening works best. The two-and-a-half-hour block allows for enough time to conduct two rounds of negotiations, with the second round providing the parties an opportunity to improve upon their climate outcome after using the C-Roads software to see the impact of their initial pledges on global average temperature. The extended block of time also allows space for each of the six country negotiating blocs (China, India, Other Developing Countries, the European Union, the United States, and Other Developed Countries) to give a small presentation on their position prior to the start of negotiations. Midway through the semester, we assign students to negotiating blocs to research and prepare a very brief (about five minutes) presentation on their bloc's key economic, energy, and climate adaptation issues as well as their climate policy positions around emissions reductions, REDD+, and finance for loss and damages and adaptation. Finally, the two-and-a-half-hour block also allows enough time for a potluck – another experiment in collective action!

5.4   CONCLUSION

This chapter presents a unique structure for applying a pluralist approach to the teaching of environmental and natural resource economics. I term this pluralist approach the '3Is': *incentives*, representing the neoclassical school; *institutions*, representing the new institutional economics school, with a focus on the work of Elinor Ostrom; and *inequality*, representing the political economy school, with a focus on the work of James K. Boyce. It is my contention that teaching economics through the lens of pluralism can help students build their critical thinking skills. The Association of American Colleges and Universities (AACU) defines critical thinking as 'a habit of mind characterized by the comprehensive exploration of issues, ideas, artifacts, and events before accepting or formulating an opinion or conclusion'. By introducing students to multiple theoretical approaches for diagnosing environmental problems and formulating policy solutions, the pluralist '3Is' approach helps students develop a habit of mind that is reflectively critical, inquiring what another perspective on the same issue might be. Linking the '3Is' to policy analysis via the '3Es' (effectiveness, efficiency, and equity) also helps students engage in comprehensive explorations of issues by emphasizing the following critical thinking skills: explaining issues, using evidence, formulating complex and imaginative questions, and developing logical and well-informed policy recommendations. The '3Es' policy brief assignment also helps students understand the complexity of applied policy analysis, which must balance competing interests and values. Finally, analysis of environmental problems through the lens of pluralism is essential for advancing the discipline as well. Pluralist conversations can lead to new critiques, new insights, and new policy solutions.

NOTES

1. In this chapter I often use the term 'environmental' to refer to both matters of pollution and natural resources and the term 'environmental economics' as shorthand for both environmental and natural resource economics.
2. In his 2010 paper 'The 3 REDD "I"s', Arild Angelsen uses a similar framework to describe what he believes is needed to make reduced emissions from deforestation and degradation (REDD) programs successful: information, incentives, and institutions.
3. The presence of clear property rights is only one assumption of the Coase Theorem. Other important, though often overlooked, assumptions of the Coase Theorem are that the number of negotiating parties is small, transaction costs are close to zero, there is equality of initial endowments between the parties, and that the negotiated pollution settlement has no wealth effects.
4. See Barbier (2010) for a review of the literature on poverty-environment traps and a theoretical model predicting their occurrence on less-favored lands when markets for land, off-farm labor, and credit are incomplete.
5. In collective-action dilemmas, cooperation is challenging but essential to avoid the worst outcome. These dilemmas arise where pursuing the rational choice at the individual level leads to a socially sub-optimal outcome that makes everyone worse off. Ostrom argues that Hardin was correct to observe that the herders faced a collective-action dilemma, but incorrect to characterize it as a Prisoner's Dilemma because the three key assumptions of the Prisoner's Dilemma did not apply. The game theory model of a Prisoner's Dilemma assumes (1) the actors cannot communicate, (2) the actors move simultaneously and thus aren't aware of the other's actions, and (3) the strategic interaction occurs only once. Because the herders could communicate, observe and respond to each other's actions, and are likely to have repeated interactions over time, Ostrom argues that the dire predictions of the Prisoner's Dilemma's don't hold and there is ample space for the herders to cooperate and devise sustainable solutions for managing the commons.
6. See https://www.climateinteractive.org/tools/world-climate-simulation/.

REFERENCES

Alix-Garcia, J. (2008), 'An exploration of the positive effect of inequality on common property forests', *Journal of Development Economics*, **87**: 92–105.
Anderrson, K. and A. Agrawal (2011), 'Inequalities, institutions, and forest commons', *Global Environmental Change*, **21**: 866–875.

Angelsen, A. (2010), 'The 3 REDD "I"'s', *Journal of Forest Economics*, **16** (4): 253–256.

Angelsen, A. and S. Wertz-Kanounnikoff (2008), 'What are the key design issues for REDD and the criteria for assessing options?', in A. Angelsen (ed.), *Moving Ahead with REDD: Issues, Options and Implications*, Bogor, Indonesia: Center for International Forestry Research (CIFOR), pp. 11–22.

Baland, J.-M., P. Bardhan, and S. Bowles (eds) (2007), *Inequality, Cooperation, and Environmental Sustainability*, Princeton, NJ, USA: Princeton University Press.

Barbier, E.B. (2010), 'Poverty, environment and development', *Environment and Development Economics*, **15**: 635–660.

Becker, G.S. (1983), 'A theory of competition among pressure groups for political influence', *Quarterly Journal of Economics*, **48** (3): 371–400.

Boyce, J.K. (2002), *The Political Economy of the Environment*, Cheltenham, UK and Northampton, MA, USA: Edward Elgar Publishing.

Chhatre, A. and A. Agrawal (2009), 'Trade-offs and synergies between carbon storage and livelihood benefits from forest commons', *Proceedings of the National Academy of Sciences* (PNAS), **106** (42): 17667–17670.

Coase, R. (1960), 'The problem of social cost', *Journal of Law and Economics*, **3** (10): 1–44.

Dietz, T., E. Ostrom, and P.C. Stern (2003), 'The struggle to govern the commons', *Science*, **302**: 1907–1912.

Hardin, G. (1968), 'The tragedy of the commons', *Science*, **168** (13 December).

Mikkelson, G.M., A. Gonzalez, and G.D. Peterson (2007), 'Economic inequality predicts biodiversity loss', *PLoS ONE*, **2** (5), e444.

Musgrave, R.A. (1959), *The Theory of Public Finance*, New York: McGraw-Hill.

Nosich, G.M. (2012), *Learning to Think Things Through: A Guide to Writing Across the Curriculum*, New York: Pearson.

Olson, M. (1965), *The Logic of Collective Action: Public Goods and the Theory of Groups*, Cambridge, MA: Harvard University Press.

Ostrom, E. (1990), *Governing the Commons: The Evolution of Institutions for Collective Action*, New York: Cambridge University Press.

Ostrom, E. (2003), 'How types of goods and property rights jointly affect collective action', *Journal of Theoretical Politics*, **15** (3): 239–270.

Ostrom, E. (2009), 'A general framework for analyzing sustainability of social-ecological systems', *Science*, **325**: 419–422.

Ostrom, E. (2012), 'Nested externalities and polycentric institutions: Must we wait for global solutions to climate change before taking action at other scales?', *Economic Theory*, **49**: 353–369.

Ostrom, V. and E. Ostrom (1977), 'A theory for institutional analysis of common pool problems', in Garrett Hardin and John Baden (eds), *Managing the Commons*, San Francisco, CA: W.H. Freeman, pp. 157–172.

Ostrom, E., R. Gardner, and J.M. Walker (1994), *Rules, Games, and Common-Pool Resources*, Ann Arbor, MI, USA: University of Michigan Press.

Pigou, A.C. (1920), *The Economics of Welfare*, London: Macmillan.

Porter-Bolland, L., E.A. Ellis, M.R. Guariguata, I. Ruiz-Mallen, S. Negrete-Yankelevich, and V. Reyes-Garcia (2012), 'Community managed forests and forest protected areas: An assessment of their conservation effectiveness across the tropics', *Forest Ecology and Management*, **268**: 6–17.

Samuelson, P.A. (1954), 'The pure theory of public expenditure', *Review of Economics and Statistics*, **36** (November): 387–389.

Stavins, R. (2011), 'The problem of the commons: Still unsettled after 100 years', *American Economic Review*, **101** (February): 81–108.

Stavins, R. (2019), 'The future of U.S. carbon-pricing policy: Normative assessment and positive prognosis', prepared for Environmental and Energy Policy and the Economy, National Bureau of Economic Research, National Press Club, Washington, D.C., 24 May.

APPENDIX I: SYLLABUS FOR A PLURALIST APPROACH TO TEACHING ENVIRONMENTAL AND NATURAL RESOURCE ECONOMICS (ECONOMICS 339)

Course Catalog Description: A pluralist examination of the causes of pollution and resource degradation as well as possible policy solutions through the theoretical lenses of neo-classical economics, institutional economics, and political economy. Critical attention is paid to how inequality, incentives, and institutional arrangements can drive environmental degradation. Topics include carbon pollution, air pollution, water pollution, as well as sustainable use of forests and other natural resources. Methods covered include non-market valuation, cost–benefit analysis, and applied policy analysis. Course considers various policy instruments including international climate agreements, carbon pricing, pollution taxes, cap-and-trade systems, and payments for ecosystem services.

[4 credit hour course; Two 100 minute meetings per week]

Professor: Dr. Kathleen Lawlor

Required Text: *Environmental Economics: A Very Short Introduction* by Stephen Smith (2011)

Additional Readings: Required readings will also include chapters from James K. Boyce's *Political Economy of the Environment* (Boyce 2002), Tom Tietenberg and Lynne Lewis' *Environmental and Natural Resource Economics* (Tietenberg & Lewis 2015), as well as academic journal articles and environmental policy briefs. All supplemental readings will be posted on Moodle.

Course Prerequisite: Introductory Economic Analysis (Econ 103)

This course is required for students in the Environmental Management & Policy concentration in Environmental Studies.

Course Description

Why is there environmental degradation and how do we fight it? What is the value of a clean environment to public health and economic well-being – and how can we quantify it? Are there trade-offs between economic development and environmental protection or can we have both? In this course we will develop analytical frameworks for unpacking these big-picture questions by covering key concepts from environmental and natural resource economics.

And to further explore the complexity of these questions, we will draw on three divergent schools of economic thought: neoclassical economics, political economy, and new institutional economics. Neoclassical approaches to environmental problems emphasize the importance of externalities and other market failures, whereas political economy approaches focus on the importance of inequality as a both a cause and consequence of environmental degradation. New institutional economics, on the other hand, pays particular attention to how formal institutions, such as property rights, and informal institutions, such as shared norms and values, affect communities' abilities to overcome collective action problems and sustainably manage the commons.

We will also learn the science and art of the dominant methods used in environmental and natural resource economics: cost–benefit analysis and non-market valuation techniques. Cost–benefit analysis is a tool widely used across many fields of economics and public policy. Non-market valuation allows us to assign a dollar value to the numerous ecosystem services nature contributes to well-being as well as the cost to human society of damaging clean air and water. Assigning these prices ensures that the value of nature is not considered to be zero in cost–benefit analyses. In addition to covering the theories and methods of environmental and natural resource economics, we will also learn how to conduct applied policy analysis, culminating in a thoroughly researched yet concise policy brief.

This course aims to introduce you to the most powerful and fundamental concepts of environmental and natural resource economics and build your critical thinking skills.[1] Throughout the semester we will focus on the most important environmental problem in the modern era: carbon pollution and climate change. Climate change encompasses issues specific to both environmental economics (the study of pollution control) and natural resource economics (the study of natural resource sustainability).

Student Learning Outcomes

By the end of this course you will be able to:

- Differentiate between private and public goods and identify opportunities for free-riding and collective action problems that can lead to environmental degradation
- Define and identify externalities and explain why privately and socially optimal outcomes will diverge in their presence
- Compare neoclassical, political economy, and new institutional economics approaches for understanding environmental problems
- Understand how economists evaluate trade-offs between the economy and the environment and explain how discount rates, valuation methods, meas-

urement of risk and uncertainty, and notions of justice influence results in cost–benefit analysis
• Understand contemporary problems in environmental policy from an economic perspective
• Apply the most powerful and fundamental concepts of environmental and natural resource economics to both (1) explain why pollution and resource degradation occurs and persists and (2) develop and analyze policies society can enact to fight such environmental degradation
• Analyze environmental issues from multiple perspectives by applying the 'effectiveness, efficiency, equity' (3 E) framework
• Research and write policy briefs that critically analyze environmental issues by (1) comprehensively explaining the key dilemma society faces, (2) identifying the key questions society needs to consider in order to develop solutions (recognizing trade-offs between objectives), (3) marshaling appropriate evidence to analyze competing interests, and (4) developing policy recommendations that logically follow from the analysis
• Demonstrate in-depth knowledge of international climate policy

Evaluation

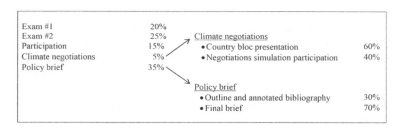

Exam #1 .... 20%
Exam #2 .... 25%
Participation 15%
Climate negotiations ... 5%
Policy brief 35%

Climate negotiations
• Country bloc presentation 60%
• Negotiations simulation participation ... 40%

Policy brief
• Outline and annotated bibliography ... 30%
• Final brief 70%

Participation

The structure of this course – a mixture of lectures, seminars, and student-led discussions – necessitates significant student participation and your thoughtful contributions to our collective learning process. Lectures on theory and methods require that you take excellent notes and diligently question the professor, seminar-style discussions necessitate that you come to class with the readings thoroughly digested, and the climate negotiations oblige you to become well-versed on the current state of international climate policy prior to our simulation.

Attendance at each class meeting is therefore required. However, I understand that illnesses and other unplanned events occasionally occur. To accommodate these unexcused absences, I have a 'two absences free' policy. Each unexcused absence after the first two will bring down your participation grade by 20 percentage points. [Absences due to documented family/medical emergency or University-sanctioned events are excused.] If, for some reason, you do end up missing class, please work with your classmates to find out what was covered and copy notes.

Expectations for seminar days

Many days we will hold seminar-style discussions of important academic journal articles. I strive to make these discussions as inclusive as possible and achieve participation rates of 100 percent. When all voices are heard, the learning value of these discussions is greatly enhanced. Therefore, for the dates marked as 'Seminar Day' on the syllabus, please come to class with the readings thoroughly digested and bring the articles with you. My expectations are that you have all done the readings and have something interesting to say about them, so you should expect that I may call on you to answer a specific question about the reading. To facilitate such high participation rates in our discussions, we will usually begin these days taking time to individually critically reflect and write on a handful of prompts and then sharing our thoughts in small groups before moving to full-class discussion.

Exams

Exams are an important incentive and learning device. They motivate us to review our notes, spend extra time on concepts we don't yet fully grasp, and ask our professors and fellow students questions about material that is unclear. We will be covering a lot of material in this course, while also independently researching a contemporary environmental topic and learning a new method of analysis and writing style (applied policy analysis for policy briefs). There is perhaps no better way to really learn material than through the process of creating a study guide that condenses and distills a course into its most important concepts and tools. You will therefore be permitted to bring one page of notes for Exam #1 and two pages of notes for Exam #2 (the final), which is cumulative. These note pages must be the product of your own work.

Climate negotiations

The greatest challenge to human prosperity in the modern era is global climate change. To explore the challenges and possibilities inherent in international climate policy, we will engage in a semester-long collaboration with a climate science class to simulate the experience of international climate policy negotiations. Together we will conduct mock international climate policy negotiations using Climate Interactive's World Climate simulation game and use the game's emissions reduction scenarios simulator (C-Roads) to model the impact of emissions reductions pledges on the climate in real-time.[2] Prior to the negotiations, you will be assigned to a country negotiating bloc and work with a small group of your peers to prepare a brief presentation on your negotiating bloc's key economic, energy, and climate adaptation issues as well as your climate policy position. These presentations will be delivered at the start of the climate negotiations meeting.

Policy brief

Being able to write well-researched and concise policy briefs is a critical skill for jobs in the environmental policy field. To ensure a diversity of topics and geographic regions are represented in this course, policy brief topics will be decided using 'tradable permits'. The assignment is composed of multiple milestones (see Table 5A.1). Printed copies of the policy brief assignments must be turned in during class on the day they are due.

NOTES

1.   There are multiple ways of defining 'critical thinking'. In this course, we will be applying the definition from the Association of American Colleges and Universities (AACU). AACU defines critical thinking as 'a habit of mind characterized by the comprehensive exploration of issues, ideas, artifacts, and events before accepting or formulating an opinion or conclusion'. We will therefore place emphasis on the following critical thinking skills: explaining issues, using evidence, formulating complex and imaginative questions, and developing logical and well-informed policy recommendations. Nosich (2012) argues that in order to use critical thinking skills within any discipline, we must first learn the discipline's most fundamental and powerful concepts, and then apply them to reasonably and reflectively ask and analyze the right questions. As such, this course's content focuses on the application of environmental and natural resource economics' most fundamental and powerful concepts to the analysis of the contemporary era's most important environmental problems.
2.   See https://www.climateinteractive.org/tools/world-climate-simulation/.

Table 5A.1   *Course schedule*

Day	Activity and Topics	Readings	Assignment Due
1	Policy Analysis Case: Washington State Carbon Tax		
Module 1: The 3Is of Environmental and Natural Resource Economics: Incentives, Institutions, and Inequality			
2	Introduction to Course		
3	Microeconomics Review		
4	*Incentives*: The Neoclassical Economic Approach to Understanding Environmental Problems and Policy Solutions	Intro & Ch 1 in Smith (2011), Hardin (1968)	Readings for discussion
5	*Incentives*: The Neoclassical Economic Approach to Understanding Environmental Problems and Policy Solutions	Ch 2 in Smith (2011)	
6	*Incentives*: Cap-and-Trade & Carbon Taxes	Ch 3 in Smith (2011)	
7	*Incentives*: Cap-and-Trade & Carbon Taxes	Ch 3 in Smith (2011)	
8	*Inequality*: The Political Economy Approach to Understanding Environmental Problems and Policy Solutions **[Seminar Day]**	Chs 1 & 4 in Boyce (2002)	Readings for discussion
9	*Inequality*: The Political Economy Approach to Understanding Environmental Problems and Policy Solutions **[Seminar Day]**	Chs 1 & 4 in Boyce (2002)	Readings for discussion
10	*Institutions*: Elinor Ostrom and the New Institutional Economics Approach **[Seminar Day]**	Ostrom et al. (1999), Dietz et al. (2003)	Readings for discussion
11	*Institutions*: Elinor Ostrom and the New Institutional Economics Approach **[Seminar Day]**	Ostrom (2009), Ostrom (2012)	Readings for discussion
Module 2: Evaluating Trade-offs			
12	Cost–Benefit Analysis	Ch 3 in Tietenberg & Lewis (2015)	
13	Cost–Benefit Analysis	Ch 3 in Tietenberg & Lewis (2015)	

Day	Activity and Topics	Readings	Assignment Due
14	Introduction to Policy Brief Project & Triple E Framework + Policy Analysis Case: Carbon Divestment		Initial selection of policy brief topics
15	Exam Review		Final selection of policy brief topics
16	EXAM #1		
17	**Guest Lecture**: The Clean Air Act & Climate Science *(Dr. Evan Couzo, Assistant Professor of STEM Education)*		
16	United Nations Framework Convention on Climate Change (UNFCCC): A Brief History		
17	Valuation Methods	Ch 4 in Tietenberg & Lewis (2015)	
18	Valuation Methods + Introduction to Country Bloc Teams	Ch 4 in Smith (2011) + Blomquist (2014)	
19	Discussion of Valuation Studies **[Seminar Day]**	Carson et al. (2003), Kramer & Mercer (1997)	Readings for discussion
20	The Social Cost of Carbon	Ch 5 in Smith (2011), CarbonBrief (2017), Howard (2014) *pp. 1–11	
Module 3: Carbon Pricing and Policy Design in Practice			
21	Reduced Emissions from Deforestation and Degradation (REDD+)	Chs 2–4 in Angelsen (2008)	Outline & Annotated Bibliography
22	Discussion of Offsets and REDD+ **[Seminar Day]**	Ghazoul et al. (2010), Ickowitz et al. (2017), Surui Project Design Document (2012) *pp. 1–30 only	Readings for discussion
23	*** *Policy Brief Meetings* *** Climate Negotiations *** 2.5 hour meeting in evening***		Country bloc presentations

Day	Activity and Topics	Readings	Assignment Due
24	Climate Negotiations debrief + Comparing Carbon Taxes, Cap-and-Trade, and Carbon Dividends	Stavins (2019)	
25	Comparing Carbon Taxes, Cap-and-Trade, and Carbon Dividends	Boyce (2013)	
26	Discussion of Carbon Pricing Instruments [**Seminar Day**]	Pastor et al. (2013), Boyce (2018), Kirchner et al. (2019)	Readings for discussion
27	Discussion of Carbon Pricing Instruments [**Seminar Day**]	Klenert et al. (2018), Jenkins (2019), Ch 9 in Boyce (2002)	Readings for discussion
28	Exam Review		Final Policy Brief
29	**EXAM #2 (Cumulative Final)**		

APPENDIX II: READING LIST FOR A PLURALIST APPROACH TO TEACHING ENVIRONMENTAL AND NATURAL RESOURCE ECONOMICS (ECONOMICS 339)

Module 1: Introduction to the 3Is of Environmental Economics: Incentives, Institutions, and Inequality

Incentives: The Neo-Classical Economic Approach to Understanding Environmental Problems and Policy Solutions

Smith, S. (2011), 'The economy and the environment', Chapter 1 in *Environmental Economics: A Very Short Introduction*, Oxford, UK: Oxford University Press, pp. 1–13.
Smith, S. (2011), 'The economic theory of efficient pollution control', Chapter 2 in *Environmental Economics: A Very Short Introduction*, Oxford, UK: Oxford University Press, pp. 14–37.
Hardin, G. (1968), 'The tragedy of the commons', *Science*, **162**: 1243–1248.

Incentives: Cap-and-Trade & Carbon Taxes

Smith, S. (2011), 'Environmental policy: instrument choice', Chapter 3 in *Environmental Economics: A Very Short Introduction*, Oxford, UK: Oxford University Press, pp. 38–69.

Inequality: The Political Economy Approach to Understanding Environmental Problems and Policy Solutions

Boyce, J.K. (2002), 'Stealing the commons', Chapter 1 in *The Political Economy of the Environment*, Cheltenham, UK and Northampton, MA, USA: Edward Elgar Publishing, pp. 1–11.
Boyce, J.K. (2002), 'Inequality as a cause of environmental degradation', Chapter 4 in *The Political Economy of the Environment*, Cheltenham, UK and Northampton, MA, USA: Edward Elgar Publishing, pp. 33–46.

Institutions: Elinor Ostrom and the New Institutional Economics Approach

Ostrom, E., J. Burger, C.B. Field, R.B. Norgaard, and D. Policansky (1999), 'Revisiting the commons: Local lessons, global challenges', *Science*, **284**: 278–282.
Dietz, T., E. Ostrom, and P.C. Stern (2003), 'The struggle to govern the commons', *Science*, **302**: 1907–1912.
Ostrom, E. (2009), 'A general framework for analyzing sustainability of social-ecological systems', *Science*, **325**: 419–422.
Ostrom, E. (2012), 'Nested externalities and polycentric institutions: Must we wait for global solutions to climate change before taking action at other scales?', *Economic Theory*, **49**: 353–369.

Module 2: Evaluating Trade-offs

Cost–Benefit Analysis

Tietenberg, T. and L. Lewis (2015), 'Evaluating trade-offs: benefit-cost analysis and other decision-making metrics', Chapter 3 in *Environmental and Natural Resource Economics* (10th edition), New York: Pearson, pp. 46–72.

Valuation Methods

Tietenberg, T. and L. Lewis (2015), 'Valuing the environment: Methods', Chapter 4 in *Environmental and Natural Resource Economics* (10th edition), New York: Pearson, pp. 73–104.

Smith, S. (2011), 'Economic information and values in environmental policy decisions', Chapter 4 in *Environmental Economics: A Very Short Introduction*, Oxford, UK: Oxford University Press, pp. 70–92.

Blomquist, G. (2014), 'Value of a statistical life', in T.C. Haab and J.C. Whitehead (eds), *Environmental and Natural Resource Economics: An Encyclopedia*, Santa Barbara, CA, USA: Greenwood, pp. 330–333.

Carson, R.T., R.C. Mitchell, M. Hanemann, R.J. Kopp, S. Presser, and P.A. Ruud (2003), 'Contingent valuation and lost passive use: Damages from the Exxon Valdez oil spill', *Environmental and Resource Economics*, **25**: 257–286.

Kramer, R.A. and D.E. Mercer (1997), 'Valuing a global environmental good: U.S. residents willingness to pay to protect tropical rain forests', *Land Economics*, **73** (2): 196–210.

The Social Cost of Carbon

Smith, S. (2011), 'The economics of climate change', Chapter 5 in *Environmental Economics: A Very Short Introduction*, Oxford, UK: Oxford University Press, pp. 93–128.

CarbonBrief (2017), 'Q&A: The social cost of carbon', *CarbonBrief Explainers*, 14 February 2017. Accessed 11 March 2020 at https://www.carbonbrief.org/qa-social-cost-carbon.

Howard, P. (2014), *Omitted Damages: What's Missing from the Social Cost of Carbon*, Washington, D.C. and New York: Environmental Defense Fund, Natural Resources Defense Council, and Institute for Policy Integrity.

Module 3: Carbon Pricing and Policy Design in Practice

Reduced Emissions from Deforestation and Degradation (REDD+)

Angelsen, A. and S. Wertz-Kanounnikoff (2008), 'What are the key design issues for REDD and the criteria for assessing options?', Chapter 2 in A. Angelsen (ed.), *Moving Ahead with REDD: Issues, Options and Implications*, Bogor, Indonesia: Center for International Forestry Research (CIFOR), pp. 11–22.

Lubowski, R. (2008), 'What are the costs and potentials of REDD?', Chapter 3 in A. Angelsen (ed.), *Moving Ahead with REDD: Issues, Options and Implications*, Bogor, Indonesia: Center for International Forestry Research (CIFOR), pp. 23–30.

Angelsen, A., C. Streck, L. Peskett, J. Brown, and C. Luttrell (2008), 'What is the right scale for REDD?', Chapter 4 in A. Angelsen (ed.), *Moving Ahead with REDD: Issues, Options and Implications*, Bogor, Indonesia: Center for International Forestry Research (CIFOR), pp. 31–40.

Ghazoul, J., R.A. Butler, J. Mateo-Vega, and L.P. Koh (2010), 'REDD: A reckoning of environment and development implications', *Trends in Ecology and Evolution*, **25** (7): 396–402.

Ickowitz, A., E. Sills, and C. de Sassi (2017), 'Estimating smallholder opportunity costs of REDD+: A pantropical analysis from households to carbon and back', *World Development*, **95**: 15–26.

Surui Forest Carbon Project (2012), Surui Project Design Document, Version 1.2, 02 February, 2012.

Comparing Carbon Taxes, Cap-and-Trade, and Carbon Dividends

Stavins, R. (2019), 'The future of U.S. carbon-pricing policy: Normative assessment and positive prognosis', prepared for Environmental and Energy Policy and the Economy, National Bureau of Economic Research, National Press Club, Washington, D.C., 24 May 2019.

Boyce, J.K. (2013), 'Cap and dividend: Carbon revenue as common wealth', in *Economics, the Environment and Our Common Wealth*, Cheltenham, UK and Northampton, MA, USA: Edward Elgar Publishing, pp. 73–91.

Carbon Pricing Instruments

Pastor, M., R. Morello-Frosch, J. Sadd, and J. Scoggins (2013), 'Risky business: Cap-and-trade, public health, and environmental justice', in C.G. Boone and M. Fragkias (eds), *Urbanization and Sustainability: Linking Urban Ecology, Environmental Justice and Global Environmental Change, Human–Environment Interactions 3*, DOI 10.1007/978-94-007-5666-3_6, Dordrecht: Springer Science+Business Media, pp. 75–94.

Boyce, J.K. (2018), 'Carbon pricing: Effectiveness and equity', *Ecological Economics*, **150**: 52–61.

Kirchner, M., J. Schmidt, and S. Wehrle (2019), 'Exploiting Synergy of Carbon Pricing and Other Policy Instruments for Deep Decarbonization', *Joule*, **3** (4): 891–893.

Klenert, D., L. Mattauch, E. Combet, O. Edenhofer, C. Hepburn, R. Rafaty, and N. Stern (2018), 'Making carbon pricing work for citizens', *Nature Climate Change*, **8**: 669–677.

Jenkins, J.D. (2019), *Why Carbon Pricing Falls Short And What to Do About It*, University of Pennsylvania: Kleinman Center for Energy Policy.

Boyce, J.K. (2002), 'Democratizing environmental ownership', Chapter 9 in *The Political Economy of the Environment*, Cheltenham, UK and Northampton, MA, USA: Edward Elgar Publishing, pp. 125–138.

6. Principles for teaching the principles of environmental and resource economics

Tim Haab

THE BACKSTORY

Where to start? That's not a rhetorical question, or a placeholder acknowledging my writer's block for starting this chapter. No, 'Where to start?' is a question I regularly ask myself as I prepare to teach a principles-level environmental and resource economics class. Because for much of my career I have taught classes on environmental and resource economics to non-economics majors, I often find myself trying to walk a fine line between teaching an environmental/resource class with economic principles sprinkled in or teaching a principles of economics class with sprinkles of environmental/resource topics.

In conversations with colleagues around the world who teach similar classes, I have plenty of anecdotal evidence that I am not alone in walking this fine line. Over the past two decades, I have taught a principles of environmental and resource economics class to undergraduates over a dozen times. At Ohio State, this class is cross-listed between applied economics and the school of environment and natural resources. Students enroll in and attend the same class, but they enroll under different 'section' numbers. The typical student enrolling in the applied economics section is taking the class as a major elective, and often has little interest in environmental topics—these are primarily agribusiness/agricultural economics students to whom we try to teach a little economics along the way through electives. The typical student enrolling in the other section are environmental science or resource management students, with a passion for saving the environment, and to the extent they care about economics, they want to blame economics (and economists) for any environmental problems.

Of course, this an overly stereotypical characterization of the students in the class,[1] but it's a fair description for talking about the question: 'Where to start?' If we emphasize environmental applications, we lose the students who want to learn the principles of economics, and if we teach a straight principles of economics class—but relabel the axes on our supply and demand graphs for environmental applications—then we lose the interest of the environmental students. At times it seems like a no-win situation: student grades (which I tend to focus too little attention on), and my teaching evaluations (which I tend to focus too much attention on) suffer.

Early in my offerings of the class I found very little balance between economic and environmental topics. Evidence abounded with my teaching evaluations differing by over a point—on a five point scale—between the two sections. Which section 'liked' the class more hinged on whether I tried to teach an economics class with environmental applications or an environmental class with economic applications. It wasn't until the fourth or fifth offering of the class that I realized I needed to take a different approach to teaching the class, and it all came down to the realization that environmental/resource studies and economics are not two different fields, but rather they are the same field intricately intertwined so that the lessons of one are not separable from the lessons of the other. With this realization came a complete redesign of my introduction to the principles of environmental and resource economics.

This redesign wasn't an attempt to please students so I could get better teaching evaluations—that turned out to be a side-benefit. Rather, the redesign fell out of my realization that environmental and resource economics is not just the principles of economics applied to environmental and resource topics. If the fields of economics and environmental/resource science are inextricably tangled, then there must be a set of principles that weave the two fields into an untangled tapestry worth looking at from multiple sides. I'm not sure that metaphor worked, but you get the point—you can't study economics without considering the environment, and you can't study the environment without considering economics.

- *Imagine if* we taught all students from the beginning of any principles of economics class that markets are only fully efficient if all costs and benefits of production and consumption, including any costs or benefits borne by those who are not buyers and sellers in the market, are fully captured in the market and reflected in the price of marketed goods.
- *Imagine if* we taught all students from the beginning of any principles of economics class that unregulated markets are only efficient if there are no external costs and benefits, no market power, and full information.
- *Imagine if* we taught all students from the beginning of any principles of economics class that markets that fail to capture the full range of costs and benefits and are subject to manipulation are not 'free' unless an outside agent acts on behalf of society. That agent is the government. So somewhat

ironically, it may very well be the case that a market requires government intervention to be 'free'.

- *Imagine if* we taught all students from the beginning of any principles of economics class that markets are not built to price goods and services that are valued but not traded in markets—and that we need tools and methods for pricing these unpriced goods and services.
- *Imagine if* we taught all students from the beginning of any principles of economics class that efficiency doesn't have to be predicated on the particular goal of maximizing total economic productivity. The social goal may be total economic productivity, or it may be any one of a million other distributions of social well-being. No matter the goal, economics provides a valuable set of tools for understanding how to achieve those goals using the least amount of society's resources—and thereby freeing those resources for other uses (or nonuses).

Well, in my opinion, we don't have to imagine this, because these imagined principles of economics are the very principles we have learned from the study of environmental and natural resource economics.

We just need to make sure we are introducing the principles from the beginning of our classes.

- *Imagine if* all students learn the principles of environmental and natural resource economics instead of the principles of economics.

Let us not just imagine.

So how, then, do I introduce the principles of environmental and resource economics without focusing solely on one or the other field? Rather than take 10,000 words to give you an outline of an introduction with talking points and more of me just talking at you, I'm going to take a different approach in the rest of this chapter.

Over the years—a lot of years—my frequent co-author, co-blogger, and former colleague, John Whitehead and I have tossed around the idea of writing a principles of environmental and resource economics book. In various fits and starts we have put together proposals, drafted outlines, drafted chapters, and then procrastinated until the project dies on the shelf. Eventually one or the other of us will resurrect the idea and try to get it started again, until we realize the amount of work it will take and move on to lower hanging fruits. Nonetheless, we have put together enough pieces over the years to get to where I have various drafts of introductions sitting in files. The remainder of this chapter is that introduction.[2] Throughout the chapter I will provide some brief 'author's notes' explaining how I think the principles of economics and environmental economics are fundamentally related. This chapter illustrates how I think about the inextricable links between the study of economics and the study of the environment, and it ends with a rather striking realization (for me at least): we have been teaching the principles of economics incorrectly. Without the principles of environmental and resource economics, the principles of economics are incomplete, and the consequences of failing to recognize this have resulted in misled students, poor decision making, bad policies, and catastrophic outcomes.

Author's note: Using environmental issues to motivate the study of economics sets a tone that the two topics are inextricably linked.

INTRODUCTION TO THE (UNWRITTEN, BUT ASPIRATIONAL) PRINCIPLES OF ENVIRONMENTAL AND RESOURCE ECONOMICS

What Types of Questions Do Environmental and Natural Resource Economists Think About?

Natural resource damages

On April 20, 2010, the Deepwater Horizon oil drilling rig in the Gulf of Mexico, owned by Transocean and contracted to drill for oil by BP, suffered a catastrophic explosion. On April 22, the Deepwater Horizon sank 5,000 feet into the depths of the Gulf of Mexico. Eleven of the 126 workers aboard the Deepwater Horizon died. The explosion and resulting sinking of the oil rig caused the piping in the drilled well to break near the marine floor. Over the next 87 days, oil from the severed pipes flowed freely into the Gulf of Mexico. By the time the well was capped on July 15, 2010, the U.S. government estimated that over 4.9 million barrels of oil had flowed into the Gulf of Mexico. Authorities believe the Deepwater Horizon oil spill to be the largest marine oil spill ever.

With immediate and ongoing impacts to marine and coastal plants and corals, marine mammals, fish, the food chain, recreation and tourism, how do we calculate the natural resource damages of the Deepwater Horizon oil spill? How can we use these damage estimates to prevent another large oil spill?

Air quality

Sulfur dioxide, an air pollutant that comes mainly from burning coal in power plants to produce electricity, can cause breathing problems in children and the elderly, is a main ingredient in acid rain that can damage plants, animals and property, and can lead to haze and smog decreasing visibility in cities and natural areas. According to the U.S. Environmental Protection Agency, between 1980 and 2015, national sulfur dioxide concentrations in the U.S. decreased by 84 percent and are now below national standards. Much of the decrease in sulfur dioxide levels is credited to an economics-based policy known as cap and trade. The decrease in sulfur dioxide levels is viewed as one of the most successful uses of economics in solving an environmental problem.

How can economics be used to solve environmental problems? What are the advantages and disadvantages of using economics to solve environmental problems as opposed to other types of policies? Can lessons from the sulfur dioxide cap-and-trade program be used to solve other environmental problems like climate change?

Climate change

The 1980s, 1990s, 2000s, and 2010s were the warmest four global decades on record. Between 1880 and 2012, according to the Intergovernmental Panel on Climate Change (IPCC),[3] global surface temperatures rose 0.85 degrees Celsius (1.53 degrees Fahrenheit). One consequence of increasing global temperatures is increasing sea levels due to increased ice melt. The IPCC reports that between 1901 and 2010 the average sea level has risen by 0.19 meters. The IPCC concludes that a large portion of the change in global temperatures is 'extremely likely' to have been caused by factors under human control: carbon dioxide, methane and nitrous oxide emissions caused by economic and population growth.

If economic factors are at least partially responsible for rising global temperatures and the resulting impacts, what economic policies can be implemented to reduce the potential economic impacts of climate change? How can we measure the benefits and costs of preventing climate change? Are the potential damages from failing to prevent climate change worth avoiding?

Fisheries collapse

Atlantic Cod were a large part of the culture, economy and diet of eastern Canada and New England from the time Europeans settled in North America in the 1600s. By the early 1970s, over 800,000 tons of cod were caught each year by commercial fishers for economic gain. In 1992, that catch had fallen to zero, and the governments of Canada and the United States issued a ban on catching North Atlantic Cod in hopes of saving the fish stock. It is now feared that the Atlantic Cod fish stock may never recover.

If the Atlantic Cod fishery collapsed due to the pursuit of economic gain, could a better understanding of economics have prevented the collapse? Could anything have been done to prevent it?

Deforestation

The World Wildlife Fund estimates that between 46 and 58 thousand square miles of forest are lost every year to pressures from economic development. That's an area roughly the size of the state of North Carolina lost, resulting in decreased biodiversity, decreased recreational and tourism opportunities and increased greenhouse gas emissions.

If the pressures of economic development are causing the problem, can better economics solve it?

Energy

According to BP, there are currently 1,697,590,000,000 barrels of oil proven to be in the ground around the world. At the current estimated extraction rate of oil, 91,670,300 barrels per day, there are enough proved reserves of oil to last another 50.7 years.

Will we run out of oil? Will we find more oil? Can we (and should we) switch to other kinds of energy, like natural gas, wind, or solar? If we run out of oil, then what? What will happen to the price of oil and oil-related products as oil becomes more and more scarce? Will we have reached our limits?

Author's note: Now that the reader has an idea of the types of questions economists ask about environmental issues, a new approach to the principles of economics can be introduced that uses the human–natural ecosystem as the foundation for deriving the principles of economics.

The Economics of Environmental and Natural Resources

These are just a sample of the types of questions that environmental and resource economists attempt to address. The range of questions and topics that environmental and resource economics addresses is practically endless. Many economists view environmental and resource economics as a small subfield of the broad field of economics. We have a different view: economics without consideration of the limits of the world's environmental and natural resources is incomplete. The natural world provides the foundation upon which economies are built and human well-being is defined. The basics of economics lie within a broader ecosystem. In many cases, environmental and natural resource problems are caused by a failure to understand the role nature must play in basic economics. The tools of economics can be used to not only inform, but in many cases solve, problems caused by incomplete understanding of economics. Our goal is to provide the reader with the tools needed to understand the value of economics in solving and avoiding environmental and natural resource disasters.

Nature and People

Let's start with a thought experiment. Shipwrecked and stranded on a deserted island, you and two friends have some questions to answer. Can you survive?

If you can survive, how? Will you have enough food? Can you build shelter to protect you from the heat, or the weather? Who is best at building shelter? Who is best at growing food? Should you each plan to survive on your own, or can you do better by working together? If you go it alone, will your success come at the expense of your friends? Should you have rules between you that tell you what you can and can't do? If you can at least survive, are there better ways to organize yourself to make everyone better off? If someone is made better off, does that mean someone else is made worse off? If you must live off the land, will you eventually run out of land to use? Can you keep living well long into the future, or are the bounties of the island guaranteed to eventually run out? Can you and your friends coexist on the island for the long term without ruining the island, each other, or both?

While overly simple, what we just described are many of the questions that the field of environmental and natural resource economics tries to answer, but on a much larger scale, the world. We can think of ourselves as living on a large island (Earth) with friends (a lot of them and growing) and trying to figure out how best to exist, survive, and even thrive for the long term without ruining the very set of resources that allow us to exist for ourselves, each other, and the future.

Perhaps the easiest way to think of Earth is to think of it as an *ecosystem*. An ecosystem is a group of interacting living things and their natural environment. *Ecology* is the study of the interaction among living things and their natural environment. Ecology is a broad term and encompasses all living things and all environments. Obviously, humans are a subset of all living things. *Economics* is the study of how humans interact with each other and their natural environment for their own and each other's well-being. In this sense, an *economy* can be thought of as the human ecosystem: humans interacting with each other and their natural environment.

Using these definitions, environmental and natural resource economics is the study of the human ecosystem: how do people interact with each other and their natural environment and to what ends? In most cases, living things aim to survive long enough to reproduce. Little attention is paid to understanding how well-off such living beings are: when was the last time you asked about the well-being of the fly living in your house versus the fly living in the African safari? Do you care? Or perhaps more important, does the fly care? But humans aim to thrive. Each decision a person makes is aimed at improving his or her own condition.

Author's note: In the standard economic treatment of scarcity, time is used as the primary limiting factor for economic decisions. Using resource constraints to motivate scarcity provides a more 'natural' connection between the absolute laws of the physical sciences, and the absolute constraints imposed by the physical environment leading to the human laws of supply and demand.

Scarce Resources and Human Well-being

Economists call human well-being utility. *Utility* is the happiness or satisfaction you get from doing something. If you eat more, your utility goes up. If you get a nicer car, your utility goes up. If someone kicks you in the shin, your utility goes down. We assume that most people like it when their utility goes up, so any reasonable person's goal is to maximize their own utility. Whether it is to produce more, or consume more, or work more, or play more, people are constantly making decisions trying to increase their utility. But increasing utility requires more stuff and unfortunately the physical part of the human ecosystem has limits. To produce more, or consume more, or do more, requires more and more stuff: building more houses requires cutting down more trees; eating more food requires farming more land; producing more energy requires more room for waste disposal. Since each of these resources are limited, it is not possible to do everything and constantly make everyone better off.

We call these limits *scarcity*. Scarcity drives decisions. If there were no scarcity, everyone could have everything they want, and everyone could keep increasing their utility. But because everything is scarce, people must make decisions. When you make a decision, you are giving something up: you are giving up the opportunity to do the alternative. When you go to class, you are giving up the opportunity to sleep in. When you buy a new shirt, you are giving up the opportunity to buy ice cream. Every decision involves giving up something to get something else (otherwise it wouldn't be a decision). That thing you give up to get what you want is called an *opportunity cost*. All decisions are costly. In order to buy a new car you have to give up eating at restaurants as much. To get more food you might have to buy a smaller house. To get more electricity you might have to dig deeper into mountains to get more coal. To commute further to work you might have to emit more pollution from your car. In economics there is an expression attributed to Nobel-prize-winning economist Milton Friedman, 'There's no such thing as a free lunch.' This means that no matter what decision is being made, there is a trade-off between the benefit of making the decision and the opportunity cost of the alternative; and all decisions have costs.

BOX 6.1   UNDERSTANDING OPPORTUNITY COSTS

Think About It: Suppose you find a surprise $10 in your infrequently worn pants pocket.

- Utility: Are you better or worse off than you were before?
- Scarcity: List five possible things you might spend $10 on. Why can't you have all of these?
- Trade-Offs: If you had to choose, which of your five things would you pick? Why?
- Opportunity Cost: What was the second best alternative on your list?

A real world example of opportunity costs:
The following e-mail showed up in Tim's inbox from his alma-mater, University of Maryland, Baltimore County (UMBC).

> It's that time of year again! Our fiscal year is winding down and we need your help in meeting our giving goals for the end of it. For just $10 each month, you can help us maintain UMBC's status as a world-class leader in research, discovery, and undergraduate education:
> - For the cost of a movie ticket, you could help send a student to an out-of-state research conference.
> - For the cost of two soy lattes, you could help support one of our many need- and merit-based scholarships for undergraduates.
> - For the cost of half a tank of gas, you could help update our classrooms with state-of-the-art equipment.
> - For the cost of a dozen donuts, you could help fund undergraduate research grants and student initiatives.

What should Tim choose?
    Why do we care so much about the costs of decisions? The most straight-forward answer is that we care about the costs of decisions because the costs represent how much of our scarce resources we are using. If our goal is to maximize our well-being, and we do assume that is our goal, then in making any decision, we want to make sure we are getting what we want at the lowest cost. Why? Because then we have the maximum amount leftover to get more stuff.
    If we give you $10 to spend and you want a candy bar, are you more likely to buy the candy bar from the store that charges you $1.00 for the candy bar, or the store that charges you $1.50 (assuming that the two stores are the same in every other detail)? Unless you are odd, of course you would choose the $1.00 candy bar. Why? The easy answer is because it is cheaper. But what does it really mean for something to be cheaper? It means that to get that candy bar you must give up less of other stuff. You now have more money to spend

to get more stuff. And if you keep making decisions so that you are always getting what you want by giving up the least you can to get it, then you will be maximizing your utility.

Summing up what we have talked about so far: people want and consume stuff so they can maximize their own utility. Resources are scarce, so people face trade-offs in deciding what to make and consume. To get the most of their scarce resources, people will make the decision that uses the least amount of their scarce resources to get what they want, and in doing so people maximize their own utility.

Author's note: Once scarcity is defined based on absolute natural and physical constraints, it becomes obvious that we need to figure out a way to allocate these scarce resources to meet society's wants and needs. Connecting physical scarcity to the allocation problem creates the connection we need to understand why economics and the study of environmental and natural resources cannot be separated.

The Allocation Problem

With a limited amount of stuff to go around, how should we decide who gets what, when and how? We call this the *allocation* problem: if there is a limited amount of stuff to go around (scarce resources) and everyone is better off with more stuff (utility), what is the best way to divide society's scarce resources to maximize society's well-being, today, tomorrow and into the future?

At its heart, economics tries to solve the allocation problem. In most principles of economics textbooks, the definition of economics is something along the lines of:

Economics is the study of the allocation of society's scarce resources.[4]

With 7.5 billion people on earth, all competing over a scarce set of resources, how do we best decide who gets what, when they get it and how it is made?

This is a complicated question. The question becomes even more complicated when the natural environment is recognized as being one of the scarce resources. A definition of environmental and natural resource economics would be something like:

Economics is the study of the allocation of society's scarce environmental and natural resources.

What is the best way to divide society's scarce environmental and natural resources to maximize society's well-being, today, tomorrow and into the future?

Albert Einstein, who we have been told was a smart guy, is quoted as having said: 'Everything should be made as simple as possible, but not simpler.' So, rather than try to figure out how to answer the complicated allocation question for everyone all at once, we will make the allocation problem simpler using a *model*. A model is a simpler representation of a complicated situation. A model is a picture of reality with the irrelevant details stripped away. Think of a model as a map. In drawing a map from one place to another, you can strip (assume) away a lot of the detail and focus on the most direct path from one point to the next. If you put your Google Maps app on satellite view, you will get a lot of detail of your route. You can see all of the buildings, trees, and parking lots along the way. But if the goal is to get from one place to another, all of those details are unnecessary. The realistic satellite view is too complicated. If instead you switch Google Maps to the default view, you get a much cleaner picture of the route, without the unnecessary details. Finding the best solution can be made simpler by assuming away details that are not related to the problem. An *assumption* is a way to make a complicated problem simpler by stripping away unnecessary details.

BOX 6.2   UNDERSTANDING MODELS

Think About It: Suppose you want to give the President walking directions from his residence in the White House to the Environmental Protection Agency Headquarters in the Ronald Reagan Building. Below is a picture of two maps of the area. The map on the left is the satellite view of the area from Google Maps, and the map on the right is the default view of the area from Google Maps. Both maps can be considered 'models' of the area.

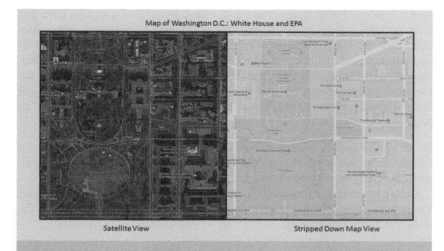

Figure 6.1   How detailed do models need to be?

Questions:

- Which of these two maps is a more realistic model of the area?
- Which of these two maps is a more useful model for giving the President directions from the White House to the EPA in the Ronald Reagan Building?

Models

Economists use models to make simple pictures of complicated questions. To see how models work, let's go back to the allocation problem: if there is a limited amount of stuff to go around (scarce resources) and everyone is better off with more stuff (utility), what is the best way to divide society's scarce resources to maximize society's well-being, today, tomorrow and into the future?

To provide a realistic answer to this question we would need to think about how 7.5 billion people decide what to buy, when to buy it and how to make the money to pay for it. We would also need to know who is going to make what the people want, where they are going to get the stuff to make it with, how to get it from where they make it to where it's needed, and how much to charge for it. Like we said, it's complicated. So let's try to simplify things by making some assumptions.

Author's note: Due to space constraints I have eliminated a section here that gives a fairly typical textbook explanation of how we can use representative consumers and representative producers to model economic interactions. Below, the chapter picks back up by introducing resource ownership. Harkening back to scarcity being defined based on natural constraints, the focus on resource ownership and the potential for externalities creates a much richer introduction to markets and the standard circular flow model of an economy.

In our simple model, producers take labor, capital and natural resources and convert them into goods that consumers want and bads that consumers do not want, but need to go somewhere.

Before building our resource allocation model, we need to know something about who owns which resources (after all, the producers have to get the resources from somewhere).

Resource Ownership Assumptions: Labor, capital, and some natural resources are owned by consumers. Some natural resources are unowned.

At first this might seem like an odd assumption, but in most modern economies, most resources for production are owned by the consumer. Labor is straightforward—if producers want to produce they must either use their own labor (and since producers are also consumers they are using a consumer's labor), or the producer must hire labor from other consumers. You work because someone is willing to pay for your labor.

Ownership of capital is a bit trickier. Capital is the equipment necessary to produce—machinery, supplies, buildings, anything that is used to produce something else. But consumers don't really own machinery. So how can we assume that consumers own capital? To get capital, producers need funding. They get this funding from investments from consumers. Consumers lend funds to producers (either by holding savings in banks, or through more direct investments like buying stock). Producers use these funds to buy capital for production. Because we are concerned here with studying the allocation of resources, and not with studying finance or investment, we simplify by assuming the direct ownership of capital by consumers.

In most introductory economics texts, natural resources are lumped together into a single resource called land, and it is assumed that consumers own all land as well. As we will see later, this leads to a fundamental flaw in the basic economic models; many resources included in the broad land category are in fact unowned or at least viewed as unowned by consumers and producers. Who owns the air you breathe? Who owns the water in the oceans, lakes, rivers and streams? Who owns the forest? Who owns the trees of green? Who owns the beauty of a sunset or the vistas at the Grand Canyon? Who owns the fishes in the deep blue sea?

While it is true that some natural resources are owned by consumers—for example, land on which our houses are built and the land that is farmed—some natural resources are unowned—like clean air—and some are owned on behalf of everyone by the government (which doesn't yet exist in our simple model, but will become important shortly)—like national parks. For now we assume that some natural resources are owned by consumers, and some are not owned by anyone.

Author's note: Weaving all of these pieces together, consumers, producers, scarcity, markets, and natural resource constraints provides the foundation to lay out a model of economic activity that I think resonates with both students of economics and students of the natural sciences. Linking human and physical systems explicitly from the beginning helps to avoid the common criticism that the environment is a special case, or an afterthought to most economists. It also makes it explicit that to have efficient markets, or efficient allocations of resources, we must think about environmental and natural resources issues from the beginning and introduce a role for government and institutions from the start. By linking the physical and human models from the start, it becomes clear that efficient markets, while desirable, are in fact a special case.

Markets

Now we have enough pieces to put together a model to begin to answer the allocation question. The model we will first lay out is called a *circular* model of an economy. Most introductory economics texts have a version of a circular model, but the environmental and natural resource economics circular model is a little more complicated, but we think much more realistic.

Based on the allocation question, we are trying to figure out how to allocate society's scarce resources so consumers can maximize their utility. We have assumed that consumers own most of the resources. Consumers are willing to give up some of their resources in exchange for goods and services made by producers. For example, consumers are willing to work in exchange for *wages* that might be used to buy goods and services. Consumers are willing to lend money to producers (by saving) in return for *interest*. Producers use these savings to buy capital. Consumers are willing to lease their owned land, a natural resource, to producers in exchange for *rent*.

Producers are willing to exchange goods and services for other productive resources. When a producer sells a good, they receive payments in exchange. The total payment received for goods and services sold by a producer is *revenue*. The producer uses revenue to pay wages, interest and rent on resources (labor, capital, natural resources) from consumers. These expenses are called *costs*.

Both consumers and producers will 'use' unowned natural resources when they are available. When a commuter drives to work in his or her gas-guzzling car, they have to get rid of their exhaust somewhere. The commuter chooses, whether they realize it or not, to get rid of their exhaust in the free trash can called the air. A nuclear power plant owner uses water from the local waterways to generate electricity. The water is drawn from a local waterway, run close to a nuclear reactor where it heats to the point of boiling. The steam from the boiling water turns a turbine that produces electricity. The heated water is then released back into local water bodies causing increases in water temperatures that may be detrimental to aquatic life.

We call any way in which consumers and producers trade resources a *market*. A market is any situation or mechanism that promotes trade between two people or groups of people. A store is a market. Amazon.com is a market. The drug deal on the street corner is a (black) market. Any situation where two or more people exchange things is a market.

The market where consumers provide resources to producers is the *input market*. The resources consumers supply to the input market are *inputs*. Consumers *supply* inputs to the input market and producers *demand* inputs from the input market.

The market where producers provide goods and services to consumers is the *output market*. The goods and services producers supply to the output market are *outputs*. Producers *supply* outputs to the output market and consumers *demand* outputs from the output market.

Although markets do not exist for unowned natural resources, consumers and producers both demand and supply natural goods (and bads). These *nonmarket* goods and services play a large part in the remainder of this book. Consumers demand air to breathe, sunshine, scenic beauty and a place to dispose of waste, like automobile emissions, from nature, and nature is willing to supply these services to consumers. Producers demand water for production, raw materials, and a place to dispose of waste, and nature supplies them.

Author's note: While not necessary for the flow of this explanation, I find it useful in class to take a slight detour at this point and have a discussion of the role of money in allocating resources.

SIDEBAR: It's about at this point that readers might start to wonder about money. So far, we have talked about exchange of resources for goods and services but have made little mention of the role money plays. This might seem odd when talking about economic models and the economy, but the reality is most economic studies have little to do with money. To the non-economist, the value of a $5 bill is five dollars. To an economist, a $5 bill represents the value of goods and services that are being exchanged, and the value of goods and services being foregone when that $5 bill is used to buy goods and services.

Any market transaction is an exchange of goods. When you buy a pizza, you are not just paying $9.99 for the pizza, but you are giving up the opportunity to purchase $9.99 worth of something else. What that something else is worth depends on your preferences. One person might be willing to give up $9.99 to purchase a pizza, foregoing the chance to buy two cheeseburgers for the same price. But another person might not make the exchange because the chance to buy two cheeseburgers might be too high a price to pay for pizza. Even though the cheeseburgers are the same price for both people, and the same amount of money would be exchanged in both cases, the opportunity costs of buying the pizza are different for each person. What determines value is each person's willingness to exchange different amounts of goods and services.

If money is not valuable in itself, what then is money? Money is a unit of account, a store of value and a medium of exchange. Being a unit of account, money allows us to have a common denominator when talking about what something is worth. Money being a store of value allows us to trade our labor for money and then buy things when we want them. Money being a medium of exchange allows us to avoid bartering goods for goods.

Money is a convenience. It is the lubricant that makes market exchanges easier. For markets to work, consumers and producers must be able to negotiate exchanges with each other. I'll give Joe a pizza, but he has to give me four gallons of gas for my car. I'll give Joan a pizza, but she will have to give me two baseballs for my kid's baseball team. Market exchanges negotiated this way will get complicated. Instead, money makes these exchanges much easier. Joe will pay $9.99 for a pizza if the pizza is worth at least $9.99 of other stuff to Joe. I'll take $9.99 for the pizza if the pizza is worth less to me than $9.99 worth of other stuff. Both Joe and I gain from this exchange. Money just made it easier. END OF SIDEBAR

An Ecological–Human Interaction Model

Putting our model together, we end up with a closed system in which nature and people interact in markets and outside of markets to allocate resources to meet the needs of society and maximize utility. This model is admittedly human centered, and ultimately, we will be measuring utility from a human perspective. To the extent that other disciplines approach the question of well-being differently, the economists' answer to the allocation question is one piece of a complex puzzle of environmental and natural resource allocation to ensure prolonged human well-being.

The ecological–economic circular model is a closed system where resources flow from consumers and nature to producers and back to consumers and nature in a different form. Input and output markets act as a means of facilitating exchanges between consumers and producers, and nature acts as a supplier of resources for consumption and production and the recipient of byproducts of the consumption and production process.

In this simple model the government plays no role, and this is how the circular model is often presented. However, we believe that studying the interplay between the economy and nature without the government is a gross oversimplification of reality that renders the circular model unhelpful in answering the allocation question. Instead, we believe the government plays three important roles in allocating scarce resources: (1) the government must establish the rules by which players in the economy must play; (2) the government steps in to markets with policies and regulations to ensure that markets are operating the way that they are supposed to work; and (3) the government must ensure that the allocation of resources is fair. The first two roles for government fall squarely within the purview of economics with role 2 being front and center. The third objective, fairness, is difficult and is often punted by economists (who are we to define what is fair?). However, recognizing how resources are divided among people, and the impacts of that distribution on social well-being is important in understanding economic systems. Throughout my teaching of environmental and natural resource economics I weave in issues of fairness and equity occasionally and discuss the inherent difficulties with defining and measuring fairness within an economic system.

The government interacts in our circular model through the interaction of consumers and producers in the input and output markets. The government collects taxes from consumers (income taxes) and producers (business taxes) to supply goods and services that markets either don't supply (public goods) or supply incompletely (called market failures).

While not providing any direct answers to the allocation problem, the ecological–human circular model provides a roadmap for the rest of the book.

WRAPPING UP: IMAGINE IF...

Well, there's the simplest way I have figured out to introduce the principles of environmental and natural resource economics. As most of you have realized, there is really nothing new here. But setting up the problem as one in which nature, the economy, and the government are all part of the same ecosystem, we can begin to question how we teach not only the principles of environmental and resource economics, but how we teach the principles of economics.

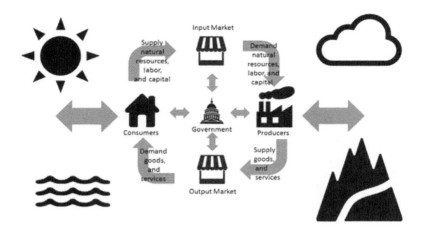

Figure 6.2   An economic–ecological circular model

NOTES

1. A running joke in the class is that I can tell which student is enrolled in which section of the class by whether they are wearing a John Deere hat or Birkenstocks.
2. …and yes, I recognize that if John or I ever get motivated enough to write the full book, we'll now need to either self-plagiarize this chapter, or write a whole new one.
3. See   http://www.ipcc.ch/pdf/assessment-report/ar5/syr/AR5_SYR_FINAL_SPM .pdf.
4. For example, in his well-known *Principles of Economics* textbook, Greg Mankiw says economics is 'the study of how society manages its scarce resources'. Another popular principles of economics textbook by McConnell et al. (2021) says economics is the '…social science concerned with how individuals, institutions, and society make optimal (best) choices under conditions of scarcity'.

REFERENCES

Mankiw, N.G. (2021), *Principles of Economics* (9th ed.), CENGAGE Learning Custom Publishing.
McConnell, C.R., Brue, S.L., and Flynn, S.M. (2021), *Economics* (22nd ed.), Boston: McGraw-Hill Irwin.

PART II

Pedagogy

7. Teaching environmental justice with data-driven projects

Amy Henderson

ENVIRONMENTAL JUSTICE IN THE ECONOMICS CURRICULUM

When a predominantly black community in Warren County, North Carolina was chosen to receive 60,000 tons of soil contaminated with cancer-causing PCBs the modern environmental justice movement was born. The Warren County Citizens Concerned (WCCC) group protested the site location, which did not meet existing Environmental Protection Agency (EPA) standards for either distance above the water table or soil type, decrying the selection as environmental racism.[1] After four years of legal challenges, contaminated soil began to be delivered to the new landfill in September 1982. Trucks hauling the soil were initially blocked by protesters laying in the road, leading to numerous arrests including that of District of Columbia Delegate to Congress Walter E. Fauntroy.

Upon Delegate Fauntroy's return to Washington, he and Congressman James J. Florio (NJ) requested that the US General Accounting Office (GAO) conduct a formal investigation into the location of hazardous waste facilities in southeastern states. The GAO's 1983 report found that three of the four (offsite) hazardous waste landfills in EPA Region IV[2] were located in predominantly black communities, and that all four landfills were located in high-poverty areas (US GAO, 1983). Though the authors of the GAO report were careful to characterize the limitations of their study, the findings were widely viewed as evidence of environmental racism, further empowering a movement begun through grass-roots activism.

Following the GAO report, a broad and diverse literature investigating the issue developed. Academic studies in fields spanning the disciplines of economics, law, sociology, geography, and public policy, found that low-income and nonwhite households were disproportionately subjected to a wide range of environmental harms.[3] Characterizing the diverse literature investigating the correlations between environmental quality and race and income, Spencer

Banzhaf stated: "In short, the correlation qualifies as a 'stylized fact' as much as anything in social science" (Banzhaf, 2012, p. 1) Yet environmental justice often is not taught in environmental economics courses. Indeed, some texts don't even cover it.[4] Of course class time is a scarce resource, and instructors must make difficult decisions regarding topics to cover. This chapter makes the case that incorporating an environmental justice module in the environmental economics course is a good use of that limited time, as doing so can help students connect environmental policy with people's lived experiences, acquaint students with some of the skills needed for consequential research, and contribute to mastery of higher-order proficiencies.

Contribution to Learning Outcomes: Building Research Skills

Economics department program learning outcomes often map closely to Hansen's proficiencies (HP), which follow a learning hierarchy progressing from basic cognitive tasks through higher-order intellectual functions (Hansen, 2001; Myers, Nelson and Stratton, 2011).[5] Though lower-level learning outcomes such as accessing and displaying command of existing knowledge may be readily achieved and documented, guiding students towards mastery of higher-level proficiencies has proven more challenging.[6] Key characteristics of the environmental justice literature make it well situated to enhance mastery of the higher-order proficiencies *interpret and manipulate economic data* (HP4) and *apply existing knowledge* (HP5), which will, in turn, better prepare students to *create new knowledge* (HP6).

Despite numerous exhortations for economists to use more active, collaborative, and experiential teaching methods,[7] we continue to lag behind other disciplines in employing these approaches.[8] Furthermore, though there is widespread agreement in other STEM fields regarding the benefits of consequential research experiences for undergraduates, it largely remains an experience reserved for only the top students in economics (Siegfried et al., 1991; Fenn et al., 2010), despite evidence that the greatest benefits may accrue to those in the bottom third of the critical thinking distribution (Seifert et al., 2014).[9] Given that consequential research opportunities are not made widely available to economics undergraduates, it is likely that economics faculty perceive the benefit/cost ratio to be lower than that experienced by our colleagues in other disciplines.[10]

A critical factor influencing the cost of mentoring an undergraduate researcher is the amount of supplemental skill development that must be provided. Perhaps the lack of meaningful research opportunities for undergraduates in economics is attributable in part to our failure to foster development of the proficiencies necessary to successfully undertake such work. For example, a student lacking adequate data-handling and analysis skills (HP4) would be prohibitively costly to mentor through a research project that would produce results meaningful to an outside audience. To remedy this deficiency DeLoach and colleagues (2012) have argued in favor of methodically incorporating building blocks of the research process into the curriculum at all levels, a sentiment echoed in Wagner's (2015) model of a four-year research plan.[11]

Providing students with the opportunity to work with relevant data to answer meaningful questions is an example of incorporating such research building-blocks into field-level courses like Environmental and Natural Resource Economics. When students have access to real data pertaining to issues that interest them they become intrinsically motivated to improve their data-handling and analysis skills in order to unlock the answers the data hold (Henderson, 2016). Environmental justice is ideal for this purpose on two fronts: (1) many students find social justice issues deeply engaging, and (2) there is a rich array of publicly available environmental data sets with which students can engage (see Data Resources Appendix for examples). In order to test for the existence of an environmental justice problem, demographic data are required as well, requiring students to become familiar with the mechanics of accessing some of the staple datasets relied upon by economists. Additionally, many environmental data sets include location information, making them well-suited for use with geographic information systems (GIS), an increasingly important tool for many economists.

Environmental justice topics are also appealing to students because the literature is still relatively young, with many open questions. Thus, even if one hews to the restrictive definition of undergraduate research, making a contribution to the literature is not outside the realm of possibility. Finally, at a time when the profession is grappling with its poor track record of attracting and retaining female and minority students, engagement with the environmental justice literature can make these students feel more welcome in the discipline in at least two ways. First, several landmark articles in the field have been authored by women, providing an important model for students.[12] Second, active learning and "connected knowing," which stems from linking classroom learning to tangible social outcomes, have been shown to be especially powerful in increasing motivation and learning outcomes for women and racial or ethnic minorities (Bartlett, 1996; Bayer and Rouse, 2016).

The next section provides flexible frameworks for designing data-driven environmental justice modules based on differing course levels and goals. The subsequent section provides a guide to the mechanisms underlying disparities. This material can help students link economic theory with observed outcomes and can be implemented in conjunction with a data-based module. Alternatively, it can be used on its own to further learning outcomes when course structure precludes quantitative work.

DATA-BASED ENVIRONMENTAL JUSTICE PROJECTS

Environmental Economics and Natural Resource Economics courses are usually upper-level courses in an economics curriculum, but course subject matter and prerequisites vary widely. In some schools, there may be a single course covering both environmental and natural resource topics that carries minimal prerequisites, while other schools offer a rich array of narrowly focused courses, such as energy economics, with rigorous prerequisites. The foundation which students bring to a course will naturally affect the type of data-based exercises that can be successfully implemented; tailoring exercises to make them accessible to students at different levels can ensure that all students benefit from engagement with elements of the quantitative research process.

In addition to variations in student preparation instructor backgrounds also vary, with different areas of specialization, research focus, and tools employed in their research. The alternative frameworks presented below consider this heterogeneity as well, offering suggestions for exercises that fall squarely within the wheelhouse of mainstream economics instructors, as well as geographic information system (GIS)-based exercises for the growing number of environmental economists who use this tool in their research.

Two project frameworks are presented below, one which is primarily statistics-based, and one which utilizes GIS. Each project can be modified based on course goals and students' prior experiences. Suggestions for companion readings accompany each project.

Statistical Case Study: The Negative Externalities of Industrial Hog Production

This research project, which uses simple linear regression, enables students to determine whether the negative effects from industrial hog production have a disproportionate impact on poor or minority communities, thereby enhancing data handling and analysis skills (HP4). The exercise can be used successfully with students who have limited prior statistical experience and can also be extended to further enhance research competencies of more advanced students.

Before embarking on the project, it is important to acquaint students with two legal theories of discrimination: disparate impact and disparate treatment. When thinking about discrimination, one might picture a scenario with a bad actor: the landlord who will not rent to nonwhite households, or the employer who will not promote women into positions of authority. This conception of discrimination is consistent with the legal theory of *disparate treatment*: the intentional disadvantaging of a protected group because of their protected status. However, this is not the only model of discrimination. The theory of *disparate impact* discrimination looks solely at outcomes, without consideration of intent. The distinction between these two theories of discrimination is useful when thinking about environmental justice issues. The EPA, informed by a Supreme Court ruling, has determined that disparate impact is a valid theory of discrimination when evaluating environmental justice concerns (Plan EJ 2014, 2011, p. 3). Thus, if low-income or nonwhite households bear a disproportionate share of our nation's environmental burdens that is unjust, regardless of the mechanism(s) by which those burdens arise.

The early environmental justice literature focused on the disparate impact question using simple statistical techniques. In addition to the GAO report discussed above, early studies often cited as evidence of environmental racism include Bullard (1983) and a 1987 report by the Commission for Racial Justice of the United Church of Christ (CRJ), an organization that had been deeply involved in the protests against the Warren County landfill siting. Bullard's analysis of the relationship between solid waste facility locations and the ethnicity of surrounding neighborhoods was a case-study focused on Houston, TX (Bullard, 1983); though Bullard's study has been widely cited in the academic literature, the limited geographic area under analysis restrained its political impact. Conversely, the 1987 CRJ report was a nationwide study of the location of hazardous waste facilities and the demographic characteristics of surrounding neighborhoods, which echoed the findings of the regional 1983 GAO report while extending them to the nation as a whole (Commission for Racial Justice, 1987). These findings provided empirical support for the growing environmental justice movement, and pressure mounted for government action.

Students who have experience with more sophisticated analyses may want to know why additional explanatory variables are not being included in the regression. Explaining the distinction between the two theories of discrimination will clarify the utility of the simple linear regression in this case. The section "Understanding the Mechanisms Underlying Disparities" explores the role of multiple regression analysis in determining how some groups come to bear a disproportionate share of the nation's environmental burdens.

This project studies the distributional impacts of well-documented negative externalities associated with industrial swine production, including negative human health effects for workers and nearby residents (Schwartz et al., 1992; Thu et al., 1997; Swinker, 1998; Kravchenko et al., 2018). Many students are not familiar with concentrated animal feeding operations (CAFOs) and retain a story-book image of bucolic farms with rolling green pastures. Images of swine CAFOs, manure lagoon pits, field spraying of liquid waste, and devastation caused by lagoon spills have a salient effect on students and motivate engagement with data. Eastern North Carolina is among the top hog producers in the United States. It is particularly noteworthy for the degree of industry concentration, the average number of hogs per farm, and the population density in areas with hog CAFOs.[13] These factors combine to create significant impacts on neighboring residents.[14]

Data handling and statistical analysis
The distribution of environmental burdens attributable to the presence of Swine CAFOs in Eastern North Carolina is well suited to statistical analysis because North Carolina's Department of Environmental Quality makes detailed information on permitted swine facilities publicly available in spreadsheet form (see Data Resources Appendix). The permitted-facilities list covers all animal feeding operations in North Carolina with at least 250 swine, 100 confined cattle, 75 horses, 1,000 sheep, or 30,000 poultry. The spreadsheet is well organized and formatted, and it is easy to select facilities by regulated operation to focus on swine facilities. Among the variables included in the dataset are regulated operation, regulated activity, allowable count (i.e., number of permitted animals), number of (liquid manure) lagoons, and location information (longitude and latitude). To facilitate project implementation a dataset which combines swine CAFO data with tract-level ACS data is available from the author at https://sites.google.com/smcm.edu/ejchapter. The dataset is provided in Excel format, and includes a data dictionary tab defining all variables.

Testing for a disparate impact requires only simple linear regression, which can be made accessible to all students. Using linear regression, students can investigate whether the location of hog CAFOs in Eastern North Carolina imposes a disparate impact on poor or minority communities. For example, the total number of permitted swine within a census tract can be used as a proxy for environmental burden (the dependent variable), and demographic variables such as the percentage of tract residents who identify as minority can be used as the test variable. This type of basic correlation analysis is consistent with both the early environmental justice literature and recent work which focuses on the disparate impact question (Mikati et al., 2018).

Instructors can adjust the level and scope of the work in accordance with student competencies, available course time, and expected out-of-class workload. For students with limited statistical experience, instructors could focus on explaining the difference between simple and multivariate regression (disparate impact verses disparate treatment in this context), reading a data dictionary, how indicator variables are constructed, running a simple linear regression in Excel, interpreting the coefficient of interest, and assessing statistical significance. Using an indicator variable – such as whether the tract is majority minority – as the test variable can simplify interpretation.

Instructors should remind students when interpreting the results that a finding indicating an environmental justice concern does not necessarily mean that hog production facilities are intentionally placed in poor or minority communities in order to harm those communities. The concept of disparate impact simply means that the location of the facilities leads to more of the negative effects impacting poor and/or minority communities than other communities. To test for disparate treatment – intentional negative impact on poor and/or minority communities – it would be necessary to control for all objective factors explaining the location of industrial hog farms.

An Excel-based linear regression exercise, including interpretation prompts, is available at the companion website given above; the file is in Word format so it may be easily adapted. As written, the exercise is well scaffolded with both text and screenshots, so it could be assigned as a homework exercise in courses with a statistical prerequisite. The following excerpt from the exercise, which introduces the dependent and independent variables used to determine whether the location of industrial hog farms has a disparate impact on lower-income residents, demonstrates in-exercise instruction:

> The variable "TotalCount" is our dependent variable, indicating the total number of hogs allowed on hog farms in that census tract. We can consider this a proxy variable for the negative environmental effects caused by concentrated, industrial hog production, as these effects are increasing with the number of swine. The POVP50 variable is an indicator variable which identifies census tracts in which the percent of people whose incomes fall below the poverty line exceeds the median for North Carolina. In North Carolina the median census tract has 15.1 percent of individuals living below the poverty line. We will use these two variables to determine whether the location of hog production facilities has a disparate impact on low-income individuals.

Following this text, the exercise walks students through the steps necessary to run a regression in Excel using these two variables; annotated screenshots facilitate successful student engagement.

Students are then prompted to engage with their results through a series of questions. Ultimately students are asked to conduct additional tests without new scaffolding.

Digging deeper: extensions
Database development is a key building block for quantitative research, and a competency that many students – even those who have taken a statistics course – struggle with. A group activity to work on identifying variables necessary to test for the existence of an environmental justice problem related to industrial hog production can contribute to the development of this competency. This activity is best implemented after students have read one of the background articles described below, but before the instructor has provided the dataset. Students should be asked to specify the dependent variable (or alter-

native dependent variables) and the independent variables. More advanced students can be asked to identify the unit of analysis; this may require some scaffolding on the part of the instructor as database conceptualization is often challenging for students. Students could also be asked to conduct a search to identify possible sources for the variables they have specified.

Identifying the correct population for analysis is another crucial research skill. Post-analysis the instructor could lead a discussion based on the question: "Is it appropriate to include all populated North Carolina census tracts in this analysis?" If students have read the Wing et al. (2000) article (discussed below), they should have a solid starting point for this discussion. Issues to be discussed can include: whether it is appropriate to include census tracts in which industrial hog production is not feasible, such as urban and mountainous areas; whether excluding certain areas is problematic when conducting a disparate impact test; how exclusion of urban areas could be expected to affect results; how exclusion of mountainous areas could be expected to affect results; which of the two effects could be expected to dominate if both are excluded.

Readings
"North Carolina's Hog Waste Problem has a Long History. Why Wasn't it Solved in Time for Hurricane Florence?" is a 2018 *Pacific Standard* article (Moon, 2018) which can be used to motivate student interest in the topic, an approach which is especially useful if the instructor does not want to lose in-class time to providing background information. The online version of the article includes links to a wide range of supporting material including data, scholarly articles, legislative records, and other popular press pieces. "Environmental Injustice in North Carolina's Hog Industry," published in *Environmental Health Perspectives*, is a scholarly article that tests for disparate impacts of hog CAFO externalities on poor and minority populations in Eastern North Carolina (Wing et al., 2000). Using block-group level data, Wing and colleagues find that poor minority communities are disproportionately affected. Instructors could assign this article either before or after the statistical exercise, depending on whether they wish to allow students to engage with the data without preconception of what the data will show, or want to use Wing et al. (2000) as a model for the statistical assignment.

"CAFOs and Environmental Justice: The Case of North Carolina" (Nicole, 2013) is a 2013 news piece in *Environmental Health Perspectives* that can serve both roles if instructors only want to assign one article. Using images, descriptive prose, and first-hand accounts, the article motivates the issue well. Additionally, the article summarizes scholarly work from a number of sources and includes a callout box with Wing and colleagues' findings.

Geographic Information System: Visualizing Data

This project empowers students to explore the spatial distribution of TRI facility locations relative to economic and demographic patterns, providing an opportunity to connect classroom learning to tangible social outcomes. It also contributes to the development of research competencies by familiarizing students with TRI and ACS datasets, as well as GIS software.

As the environmental justice literature evolved, it moved beyond hazardous waste facility locations to study the distributional effects of other environmental hazards. This evolution was supported by the development of a new database, the Toxics Release Inventory (TRI), which was established by law to track the manufacture and use of chemicals that can have significant adverse human-health or environmental impacts. Establishment of the TRI was motivated by the Union Carbide disaster in Bhopal, India, in 1984, which has been called the world's worst industrial accident (Diamond, 1985). Months after the catastrophe in Bhopal where thousands were killed, a similar, though less deadly, toxic gas leak occurred at a Union Carbide plant in West Virginia (Franklin, 1985), solidifying support for government action. In 1986 the Emergency Planning and Community Right-to-Know Act (EPCRA) was passed; Section 313 of the Act mandated the establishment of the TRI. TRI data on hundreds of toxic chemicals became available in 1988, and researchers eagerly seized the opportunity to incorporate these data into their analyses. TRI data are publicly available and readily accessible for student use. These important data do have limitations which should be discussed with students, particularly the fact that they are self-reported.

Geographic information system (GIS) software is an increasingly important tool for environmental and natural resource economists. GIS-based exercises can be a great leveler in a mixed-audience course, as economics students often will not have previously used GIS. For instructors who use GIS software in their own research, it allows an instructor to engage students with environmental data in a visual way that can be empowering to those with limited quantitative skills. It also provides an opportunity to familiarize students with not only this important research tool but also the mechanics of accessing key economic data sources such as the American Community Survey (ACS), both of which are building blocks for future consequential research.

Assigning students to groups that are balanced, based on students' prior course work and self-reported proficiencies, can further level the playing field and lead to more productive engagement with data in mixed-skill classrooms. Student surveys can be conducted using Google Forms, which organizes collected data into a spreadsheet. In this format, the survey data can be fed into a freely available Excel spreadsheet macro, created by Malcolm K. Sparrow at the Harvard Kennedy School, to create balanced groups.[15] One note of caution, work by Jensen and Owen (2001) found that group work is beneficial to women only if the group is not dominated by men. Given the underrepresentation of women in economics generally, instructors may find that balancing on gender leaves women isolated within male-dominated groups. In such a case, research shows it is preferable to cluster on gender, while balancing on other (skill) variables. Similarly, where possible, it is beneficial not to isolate students of any minority within a group.

Reading

Instructors teaching Environmental Economics to students with varying disciplinary backgrounds may not make extensive use of scholarly articles. However, the disciplinary diversity of the environmental justice literature makes it possible to find an article that all students can engage with productively. Older environmental justice articles are particularly accessible. An article such as "Coming to the Nuisance or Going to the Barrios – A Longitudinal Analysis of Environmental Justice Claims," by Vicki Been and Francis Gupta (1997), published in *Ecology Law Quarterly*, is accessible to all audiences and addresses one of the important mechanisms that may contribute to disparate impacts.

"Is Environmental Justice Good for White Folks? Industrial Air Toxics Exposure in Urban America," published in *Social Science Quarterly* by economists Michael Ash and colleagues (2013), is fairly reader-friendly and is well-written. This article, which uses the EPA's Risk-Screening Environmental Indicators (RSEI) microdata, can pair well with a GIS assignment using Toxic Release Inventory (TRI) data, as the RSEI are based in part on TRI data. Ash and colleagues' results show that urban areas with greater disparities in the distribution of environmental health risk produce higher average health risks for all residents. This finding indicates that everyone has a stake in achieving environmental justice, and may make students eager to explore the data for their own geographic area.

Scaffolded GIS exercise

Using GIS, students can visually explore the spatial distribution of TRI facility locations relative to economic and demographic patterns. The length and complexity of the GIS exercise can be adapted based on factors such as the amount of class time to be devoted to the exercise, students' access to computers outside of the classroom, and the average proficiency level of the cohort. Using an open-access GIS package such as QGIS increases flexibility, as students are not tied to a lab with licensed software. Installation is somewhat time-consuming, however, and students with a Chromebook will not be able to install the software on their personal computers. In-class labs requiring students to run QGIS on their personal computers should have a pre-lab component including installation of QGIS and download of relevant ACS data. A scaffolded guide for these pre-lab activities is available from the author at https://sites.google.com/smcm.edu/ejchapter. The guide directs students to download Maryland ACS data. Instructors may wish to tailor the geographic area under analysis to an area of greater interest to their student population in order to increase students' internal motivation.

The American Community Survey (ACS) provides detailed data on a wide range of economic and demographic variables. Many of these variables are available in a geodatabase file which can be readily imported into a GIS package. The data tables are distinct from the geography, so variables of interest will need to be joined. Providing step-by-step documentation for this process is key to successful engagement with the data. Having students work through each step themselves will prepare them for future projects employing these important economic data. Alternatively, to conserve time, the instructor could perform this work and save the resulting shapefile for students to access directly.

Preparing the TRI data for analysis requires a bit more effort. When the facility-level data are downloaded as a .csv file considerable reformatting is required before the data can be imported into GIS. Additionally, some facilities lack longitude and latitude data; obtaining and entering these values increases the data preparation burden. Teaching these data-cleaning steps would confer useful data-handling competencies; however, time constraints may make doing so cost-prohibitive. In field-level courses I perform these tasks in advance; students are provided with a cleaned file of TRI facility data for our state.[16]

Whether students engage with the project outside of class or have an instructor-led experience during class meeting time, providing students with an exercise packet that provides both text instruction and screenshots supports student learning and transfer of skills to future research endeavors. A detailed exercise packet is available from the author at https://sites.google.com/smcm.edu/ejchapter. The file is in Word format and can be modified to suit course objectives. The exercise guides students through the basics of building a map with the relevant data, including: setting the coordinate reference system; adding the ACS data as a vector layer; and importing spreadsheet (TRI) data. The exercise also teaches students how to make sense of data in GIS, including: viewing underlying data in the attribute table; joining data and geography layers; visualizing data using symbology, including graduated symbology with data transformations; making selections based on an expression; studying clustering through nearest neighbor analysis; and more. The project, as written, is lengthier than can be completed in a standard class period. I often limit the number of steps I assign but provide the entire packet for students who want to further develop these competencies.

Data visualization alternatives

Instructors who are not proficient in GIS but are interested in using data visualization in the classroom have several options. QGIS is a free and open-source GIS package. The QGIS Project (QGIS.org) provides extensive documentation and well-scaffolded training materials. It is feasible to learn enough using these materials to run meaningful classroom exercises. Combining these resources with the provided exercise packet can speed adoption.

Alternatively, many of the benefits of a GIS-based exercise can be realized by using an interactive online mapping system. The EPA provides two such tools, one of which, EJscreen, is specifically dedicated to environmental justice issues. On this site students can explore the relationship between various demographics and the spatial distribution of environmental hazards. Users can focus on a geographic area of interest and add features like hazardous waste or TRI facility locations from a wide range of available map "layers." The EPA has also constructed EJ Indexes for 11 key environmental hazards. These indexes combine demographic information with environmental hazard data in a unified indicator which can be mapped using EJscreen. The tool is reasonably user-friendly and can be used to enhance students' understanding of environmental justice concerns. Within the tool students can also search for maps created by other users. To do so, under the add maps menu, select "search for maps" and then "search geoplatform." If instructors have assigned the Ash et al. (2013) article, students may be interested in visualizing RSEI data. Conducting a geoplatform search for "RSEI" will return many interesting maps which allow students to visually explore the relationship between the distribution of environmentally induced health risks and population demographics.

To derive some of the same research-competency development outcomes discussed above, instructors could have students explore demographics and TRI facility locations in EJscreen, then visit the ACS and TRI sites to familiarize themselves with the data available from these sources.

UNDERSTANDING THE MECHANISMS UNDERLYING DISPARITIES

Theories of Discrimination

The distinction between disparate impact and disparate treatment theories of discrimination has often been a point of confusion in the literature. For example, both the GAO (1983) and UCC (1987) reports studied the correlation between the location of hazardous waste facilities and the characteristics of surrounding communities as of the (then) most recent census. Neither report considered the characteristics of the surrounding communities at the time the facilities were sited. Some researchers argued that this was a significant flaw in study design because if the surrounding communities became predominantly minority or low-income *after* facility siting there would be no evidence of an environmental justice problem.[17]

As studies grew more sophisticated, moving beyond simple correlations to multiple regression analysis, findings became mixed (Anderton et al., 1994), and some questioned whether the widespread acceptance of the conclusion that poor and minority communities tend to bear a disproportionate share of the nation's environmental burdens was warranted (Bowen, 2002). Researchers who found that race was not significant once other controls were included in the analysis typically characterized their findings as inconsistent with an environmental justice problem, yet this assessment of the evidence fails to distinguish between the existence of a disproportionate burden and the mechanism by which that burden was generated.

Is there any reason, then, to conduct more sophisticated analyses which control for objective factors related to firm siting decisions such as wage rates, access to transportation, and land costs? Or to study neighboring populations at the time of the siting decision, rather than conduct a cross-sectional analysis based on current locations and demographics? The answer is a resounding yes, to these and many other research questions. Such analyses are essential because if we do not understand the mechanism(s) by which disproportionate burdens arise, policies to correct the injustice may be ineffective or even counterproductive.

Hamilton (1995) was the first to clearly articulate a distinction between (1) finding that a disadvantaged group bears a disproportionate share of an environmental burden, and (2) determining why that disproportionate burden arises. Hamilton's analysis of capacity expansion at hazardous waste facilities found a disparate impact on nonwhite communities, a finding he characterized as consistent with environmental racism. He then tested three competing theories that might explain the mechanism by which the disparate impact could have arisen: (1) pure discrimination; (2) Coasian bargaining; (3) collective action. Hamilton ruled out pure discrimination, finding that variations in collective action across communities contributed to the observed disparities. This model, of clearly identifying the research question(s) being tested at each stage of the analysis, has not always been adhered to in environmental justice studies but recent work by Banzhaf and colleagues calls on researchers to take just such an approach (Banzhaf, 2012; Banzhaf et al., 2019).

Economic reasoning provides a foundation for categorizing and testing mechanisms which could lead to inequitable outcomes. Since Hamilton (1995), researchers have grouped these mechanisms under a variety of organizing structures. Instructors may find it helpful to broadly classify them into demand-side and supply-side models. Doing so reinforces for students the connection between the economic way of thinking and the mechanisms being evaluated, providing an opportunity to *connect and apply existing knowledge* (HP5).

Location Theory

On the supply side, the theory of the firm informs our analysis. We assume that firms are profit maximizers, and, all else equal, lower costs lead to higher profits. This suggests several mechanisms by which a disproportionate share of pollution could fall on nonwhite and poor communities. Consider the firm's decision of where to operate a new (polluting) facility. Location theory identifies key factors firms consider when comparing alternative venues for a new plant, such as land, labor, energy, and transportation costs. Firms also take into account the anticipated total tax burden at competing sites and may be attracted to areas where industry is already established, providing agglomeration economies. Two factors suggested by location theory, manufacturing intensity (or percentage of land zoned for industry) and percentage of employment in manufacturing, have been included in a number of environmental justice studies. These variables, along with population density, are commonly found to be statistically significant, whether in explaining noxious firms' location decisions (Boer et al., 1997) or the distribution of air toxics exposures (Arora and Cason, 1999; Morello-Frosch et al., 2001; Ash et al., 2013). Wolverton's 2009 study of TRI facilities' location decisions in Texas controlled for typical factors suggested by location theory and found that input costs were critically important in explaining plant siting decisions, as was the presence of a pre-existing TRI facility. Thus while Wolverton (2009) identified a contemporaneous disparate impact of polluting activity on minority and low-income populations in Texas, she found that race was not a determining factor in the siting decisions of polluting facilities.

Consumer Choice

The theory of consumer choice guides our analysis on the demand side. Assuming that environmental quality is a normal good, those with higher incomes will choose to purchase more of it, leaving those with lower incomes in more polluted areas. This, of course, does not mean that lower-income groups want to live in more polluted environments, but rather, that given the constraints faced, they may prioritize other consumption goods over environmental quality. In other words, even if all income groups are willing to trade some current consumption for reduced exposure to toxics, given diminishing marginal utility of consumption goods, higher-income groups will be more willing to trade off additional consumption in order to "buy" more environmental quality than will lower-income groups. This is a chance to reinforce the concept of opportunity cost with students – for lower income households the marginal utility of an additional unit of consumption is higher, and thus the opportunity cost of "buying" better environmental quality is higher. Therefore, in the presence of full information, housing prices will tend to be lower near polluting facilities, making them attractive to households who may be priced out of communities with a lower environmental burden.

Students will likely be able to identify firms' location decisions as a supply-side factor. Even prior to the environmental and/or natural resource course they will likely have encountered the idea of externalities, and the associated notion that productive activities often generate pollution as a by-product. It may be more challenging for students to identify a demand-side mechanism by which a disparate impact could arise.

After the instructor introduces the concept of environmental justice, the history of the movement and governmental responses, and the disparate impact and disparate treatment theories of discrimination, providing students an opportunity to brainstorm potential mechanisms by which disparities could arise can be a productive exercise. For next-level analysis, ask students to link each mechanism to a related economic theory. Because demand-side factors are less likely to spontaneously occur to students than supply-side factors, asking them to categorize the mechanisms in this way can provide useful scaffolding. For groups that require additional scaffolding, a worksheet could be provided that identifies relevant theories and asks them to detail the means by which the theory would apply.

A number of studies have sought to determine whether (1) polluting facilities were originally sited in communities that were disproportionately low-income or minority, or (2) communities hosting polluting facilities became disproportionately low-income or minority in response to the siting of the facility, a hypothesis often referred to as "coming to the nuisance." As Been noted as early as 1995, this distinction is critically important for policy reasons; if areas surrounding toxic facilities see a large influx of minority or low-income residents after siting, changes to siting procedures could consume considerable resources to no purpose. Though results are not uniform, the literature has not found strong support for this hypothesis (Been, 1995; Been and Gupta, 1997; Pastor et al., 2001; Gamper-Rabindran and Timmins, 2011; Depro et al., 2015).

Collective Action

The theory of collective action (Olson, 1965) helps us to understand why individual demand for a public good like environmental quality will typically not lead to adequate provision. Since the benefits of a public good cannot be withheld from those who failed to contribute to its provision there is a strong incentive to "free ride" on the efforts of others to provide the good. Action is costly, and most residents hope someone else will shoulder that burden. If the ability to overcome the challenges to achieving collective action differs across populations in a way that is related to race it could lead to a disproportionate environmental burden. Subsequent to Hamilton's (1995) finding that communities with greater potential for collective action were less likely to see hazardous waste capacity expanded, many studies have similarly included variables attempting to control for a community's capacity for collective action. Most commonly, researchers have followed Hamilton and used some measure of voter participation rates. Other variables meant to proxy a community's ability to engage in successful collective action include the percent of registered voters and homeownership. Despite Hamilton's early finding in support of the collective action hypothesis, the literature remains unsettled in this area as well, with some studies finding that voter turnout is not explanatory (Boer et al., 1997; Arora and Cason, 1999). Gray and Shadbegian found that pulp and paper mills "in areas with politically active populations that are also environmentally conscious emit less pollution," but this is a narrow finding that depends heavily on the "environmentally conscious" variable (Gray and Shadbegian, 2004, p. 532).[18] The collective action proxy variable, percent homeownership, used by Morello-Frosch et al. (2001) in their study of the distribution of environmental health risk in Southern California, was statistically significant and of the expected sign in some specifications, but became insignificant once land use controls were included in the model. Curiously, Naidu et al. (2013) found that voter turnout was *positively* related to environmental health risk in Ohio.

The potential for collective action may not be captured well by voter participation rates or other commonly used proxy variables, further complicating assessment of whether problems of collective action contribute to disproportionate environmental burdens. A related literature, which has been explored by economists, political scientists, and sociologists, investigates the relationship between racial and ethnic diversity and the provision of public goods. There is a sizable body of literature which indicates that public goods provision is lower in communities with more racial heterogeneity (for example, Alesina et al., 1999; Stichnoth and Van der Straeten, 2013), or where there is greater between-group inequality (Baldwin and Huber, 2010). Similarly, some environmental justice analyses find that environmental health risks are higher in more segregated urban areas (Morello-Frosch and Jesdale, 2005) and that urban areas with greater disparities in the distribution of environmental health risks produce higher average health risks for all residents (Ash and Fetter, 2004; Ash et al., 2013). Taken together these literatures provide some support for the collective action hypothesis.

Pure Discrimination

The theory of pure discrimination is generally unappealing to economists. On the producer side, it requires that firms sacrifice higher profits in order to indulge their taste for discrimination (Becker, 1957). Testing the theory of pure discrimination (disparate treatment) is essentially an indirect test. Take the case of discrimination on the basis of race. If a disparate impact is found to exist, then alternative theories for how that disparate outcome could have arisen are tested. If race remains a statistically significant explanatory variable after relevant objective factors have been controlled for then the results can be characterized as consistent with disparate treatment. In some instances, researchers have found that no race effect remains once other relevant factors have been controlled for (Wolverton, 2009), while in others a race effect persists even after controlling for economic factors such as income, percentage of land zoned for industrial use, percentage of residents employed in manufacturing, and population density (Sadd et al., 1999). Because no study can claim to control for all potential objective explanatory factors, such results can only be characterized as consistent with a disparate treatment theory. Further complicating any generalization of findings regarding disparate treatment is the growing body of evidence that the mechanisms underlying disproportionate environmental burdens may differ significantly by region (Arora and Cason, 1999; Zwickl et al., 2014), indicating that disparate treatment could be a plausible hypothesis in some geographic areas, while being ruled out in others.[19]

GOVERNMENT RESPONSES

The mechanisms by which minority and low-income groups have come to bear a disproportionate share of the nation's environmental burden have not been clearly identified, but the literature establishing that such disparities exist is clear. Starting in 1990 the federal government began to respond incrementally to the mounting evidence that minority and low-income communities bore a disproportionate share of the nation's environmental burden. The establishment of the Environmental Equity Working Group by the George H.W. Bush administration in 1990 was the first of many steps on a rocky path towards integrating environmental justice concerns into administrative rulemaking and enforcement actions. In 1992 the Working Group issued a report which found that "[r]acial minority and low-income populations experience higher than average exposures to selected air pollutants, hazardous waste facilities, contaminated fish and agricultural pesticides in the workplace" (EPA, 1992, p. 3).

Commitment towards achieving environmental justice was solidified in 1994 when President William J. Clinton issued Executive Order 12898, which required federal agencies to incorporate environmental justice considerations into their mission by "identifying and addressing, as appropriate, dispropor-tionately high and adverse human health or environmental effects of [their] programs, policies, and activities on minority populations and low-income populations". The order also established an Interagency Working Group to coordinate environmental justice efforts across agencies. Yet, despite these and subsequent efforts, a 2005 GAO report found that insufficient attention was being paid to ensuring that minority and low-income populations would not bear a disproportionate share of the negative impacts from pollution during the rulemaking process (GAO, 2005).

Efforts by the Barack H. Obama administration to improve attention to environmental justice considerations across Federal agencies were launched in 2010 when *Plan EJ 2014* was announced by the EPA (subsequently pub-lished September 2011). *Plan EJ 2014* articulated cross-agency goals for the consistent incorporation of environmental justice concerns in rulemaking and enforcement, as well as goals for tool development (EPA, 2011). 2010 also saw the reconvening of the Interagency Working Group (IWG) on Environmental Justice – the first meeting of the group in ten years – which led to the 2011 signing of a memorandum of understanding by 17 of the IWG Federal agencies. Formal guidance was issued on when and how to incorporate environmental justice concerns into the rulemaking process; the EPA identifies five rules that have since been issued which considered environmental justice.[20] The *EJ 2020 Action Agenda*, designed to build upon *Plan EJ 2014*, was published in 2016; it echoed earlier goals and established new goals regarding progress on specific problem areas, including lead disparities, drinking water, air quality, and hazardous waste sites (EPA, 2016).

NOTES

1. See McGurty (2000) for a detailed history of the incident. As a nice example for students, Hampson (2010), a senior thesis, was cited in Banzhaf et al. (2019) as a source for a detailed description; showing students that undergraduate research can be cited in a peer-reviewed publication helps demonstrate the value of such work.
2. The eight states in EPA region IV were: Alabama, Florida, Georgia, Kentucky, Mississippi, North Carolina, South Carolina, and Tennessee. The Warren County landfill was one of the four considered, as its siting was what prompted the inquiry.
3. In addition to the studies mentioned above, for evidence of disproportionate impact on nonwhite communities see, for example, Been (1995), Hamilton (1995), Been and Gupta (1997), Boer et al. (1997), Ringquist (1997), Arora and Cason (1999) and Baden and Coursey (2002) (Hispanic only).
4. Many standard texts, such as Callan and Thomas's (2009) *Environmental Economics and Management*, provide cursory coverage of environmental justice as an equity consideration, while others, such as Kolstad's (2011) *Environmental*

Economics, appear to skip it entirely. Instructors adopting Tietenberg and Lewis's (2016) *Environmental and Natural Resource Economics* will find thorough environmental justice coverage, with a dedicated chapter on the topic.

5. Hansen's proficiencies require that students be able to: (1) access existing knowledge; (2) display command of existing knowledge; (3) interpret existing knowledge; (4) interpret and manipulate economic data; (5) apply existing knowledge; and (6) create new knowledge (Hansen, 2001).

6. These concerns are not confined to the faculty. Hansen (2001) and Henderson (2016) present anecdotal evidence that senior economics majors are themselves doubtful that they have mastered the advanced proficiencies.

7. See, for example, Becker (1997), Salemi (2002), Hawtry (2007) and Allgood et al. (2015).

8. Comparing undergraduate faculty as a whole to economics faculty in particular reveals a stark contrast in teaching methods, with economics faculty spending far more of their time lecturing and much less time on cooperative learning activities (Watts and Schaur, 2011; Eagan et al., 2014).

9. This may also be due in part to the restrictive way undergraduate research has typically been defined, rather than embracing a broader definition of "creating new knowledge" such as those reflected in Hansen (2001) and Henderson (2016, 2018).

10. Economists may also be more sensitive to cost effectiveness than faculty in other disciplines. Goffe and Kauper (2014) found that even faculty who believe alternative methods are superior to lecture fail to adopt them because lecture is viewed as more cost effective. Furthermore, benefits may be higher for faculty in the natural and physical sciences where research with undergraduate collaborators is often publishable, and their programs may explicitly reward publication with students in the tenure and promotion process. Costs may also be lower where it is easier to integrate undergraduate students into an existing lab with an established structure – a situation far more common in the natural and physical sciences.

11. Also advocating to close the skills gap, Cebula (2017) has urged requiring all economics students to take an econometrics course by the end of their junior year to facilitate consequential research during the senior year.

12. Note that I say "an important model for students," not "female students." It is critically important that female students see female economists as contributors to the discipline – too often the papers assigned in economics courses have uniformly male authors. Yet if we are to change the culture of the profession to one that is more welcoming to women it is equally important that male students see women as consequential contributors to economic discourse.

13. While population density is much lower in top NC hog-producing counties like Sampson ($67/mile^2$) and Duplin (73) than the average for the state (208), it is considerably higher than in Iowa's top-producing counties, Sioux (45), Washington (39), and Plymouth (29). Iowa is the nation's top pork producer.

14. Additionally, much of Eastern North Carolina is comprised of low-lying flood plain. It is a vulnerable ecosystem with three major river basins draining into productive estuaries. The Cape Fear Riverkeeper organization has characterized their river basin as containing more factory farms (including cattle and poultry) than nearly any other place on the planet.

15. The GRumbler macro is available for download at https://sites.hks.harvard.edu/fs/msparrow/GRumbler--main.html.

16. The exercise packet includes a detailed description of the data-preparation work that has been done so students who wish to pursue future work with TRI data have guidance.
17. An example of this reasoning can be found in Gray et al. (2010), who state that a failure to control for household consideration of pollution level when deciding where to live can lead to false conclusions regarding the existence of EJ concerns. "Thus we could observe a positive correlation between poverty and environmental risk which would appear to support EJ concerns, but which reflects the opposite direction of causation – the poor 'moving towards' higher-pollution (and low-rent) neighborhoods" (Gray et al., 2010, p. 6) This argument confuses the reason for the disparate impact with the existence of the disproportionate burden.
18. Additionally the significance of voter turnout is heavily dependent on model specification.
19. For example, several studies focused on Southern California have found a significant relationship between race and toxic exposure even after controlling for other causal factors such as income, land use, labor force, and population density (Boer et al., 1997; Sadd et al., 1999; Morello-Frosch et al., 2001), and Arora and Cason (1999) found that even after controlling for both economic and collective action factors race was a significant determinant of toxic releases in the non-urban South.
20. The "Rules that have considered Environmental Justice" since the work under *Plan EJ 2014* include: Definition of Solid Waste (2015), Mercury and Air Toxics Standard (2011), National Ambient Air Quality Standard (2012), Petroleum Refinery Residual Risk and Technology Review (2014), and Worker Protection Standard (2014). https://www.epa.gov/environmentaljustice/plan-ej-2014-incor porating-environmental-justice-rulemaking (accessed May 9, 2019).

REFERENCES

Alesina, A., Baqir, R. and Easterly, W. (1999), 'Public Goods and Ethnic Divisions', *Quarterly Journal of Economics*, **114** (4): 1243–1284.
Allgood, S., Walstad, W. B. and Siegfried, J. J. (2015), 'Research on Teaching Economics to Undergraduates', *Journal of Economic Literature*, **53** (2): 285–325.
Anderton, D. L. et al. (1994), 'Environmental Equity: The Demographics of Dumping', *Demography*, **31** (2): 229–248.
Arora, S. and Cason, T. N. (1999), 'Do Community Characteristics Influence Environmental Outcomes? Evidence from the Toxics Release Inventory', *Southern Economic Journal*, **65** (4): 691–716.
Ash, M. and Fetter, T. R. (2004), 'Who Lives on the Wrong Side of The Environmental Tracks? Evidence from the EPA's Risk-Screening Environmental Indicators Model', *Social Science Quarterly*, **85** (2): 441–462.
Ash, M., Boyce, J., Chang, G. and Scharber, H. (2013), 'Is Environmental Justice Good for White Folks? Industrial Air Toxics Exposure in Urban America', *Social Science Quarterly*, **94** (3): 616–636.
Baden, B. M. and Coursey, D. L. (2002), 'The Locality of Waste Sites within the City of Chicago: A Demographic, Social, and Economic Analysis', *Resource and Energy Economics*, **24** (1–2): 53–93.
Baldwin, K. and Huber, J. D. (2010), 'Economic versus Cultural Differences: Forms of Ethnic Diversity and Public Goods Provision', *American Political Science Review*, **104** (4): 644–662.

Banzhaf, S. (2012), 'The Political Economy of Environmental Justice: An Introduction', in Banzhaf, H. S. (ed.), *The Political Economy of Environmental Justice*. Stanford: Stanford University Press, pp. 1–20.

Banzhaf, S., Ma, L. and Timmins, C. (2019), 'Environmental Justice: The Economics of Race, Place, and Pollution', *Journal of Economic Perspectives*, **33** (1): 185–208.

Bartlett, R. L. (1996), 'Discovering Diversity in Introductory Economics', *Journal of Economic Perspectives*, **10** (2): 141–153.

Bayer, A. and Rouse, C. E. (2016), 'Diversity in the Economics Profession: A New Attack on an Old Problem', *Journal of Economic Perspectives*, **30** (4): 221–242.

Becker, G. S. (1957), *The Economics of Discrimination*. University of Chicago Press.

Becker, W. E. (1997), 'Teaching Economics to Undergraduates', *Journal of Economic Literature*, **35** (3): 1347–1373.

Been, V. (1995), 'Analyzing Evidence of Environmental Justice', *Journal of Land Use and Environmental Law*, **11** (1): 1–36.

Been, V. and Gupta, F. (1997), 'Coming to the Nuisance or Going to the Barrios – A Longitudinal Analysis of Environmental Justice Claims', *Ecology Law Quarterly*, **24** (1): 1–56.

Boer, J. T. et al. (1997), 'Is there Environmental Racism? The Demographics of Hazardous Waste in Los Angeles County', *Social Science Quarterly*, **78** (4): 793–810.

Bowen, W. (2002), 'An Analytical Review of Environmental Justice Research: What Do We Really Know?', *Environmental Management*, **29** (1): 3–15.

Bullard, R. D. (1983), 'Solid Waste Sites and the Black Houston Community', *Sociological Inquiry*, **53** (2/3): 273–288.

Callan, S. J. and Thomas, J. M. (2009), *Environmental Economics and Management: Theory, Policy and Applications*. Cengage Learning.

Cebula, R. J. (2017), 'High-Impact Teaching in Economics: A Flexible Paradigm Utilizing Introductory Econometrics for Promoting Undergraduate Research and Publishing', *American Economist*, **52** (2): 247–257.

Commission for Racial Justice (CRJ) (1987), *Toxic Wastes and Race in the United States: A National Report on the Racial and Socio-Economic Characteristics of Communities with Hazardous Waste Sites*. New York: United Church of Christ. Available at: https://www.nrc.gov/docs/ML1310/ML13109A339.pdf.

DeLoach, S. B., Perry-Sizemore, E. and Borg, M. O. (2012), 'Creating Quality Undergraduate Research Programs in Economics: How, When, Where (and Why)', *The American Economist*, **57** (1): 96–110.

Depro, B., Timmins, C. and Neil, M. O. (2015), 'White Flight and Coming to the Nuisance: Can Residential Mobility Explain Environmental Injustice?', *Journal of the Association of Environmental and Resource Economists*, **2** (3): 439–467.

Diamond, S. (1985), 'The Bhopal Disaster: How it Happened', *New York Times*, 28 January, p. 1. Available at: https://www.nytimes.com/1985/01/28/world/the-bhopal-disaster-how-it-happened.html.

Eagan, M. K. et al. (2014), Undergraduate Teaching Faculty: The 2013–2014 HERI Faculty Survey, Education Research, Los Angeles.

EPA (2011), *Plan EJ 2014* (EJ 2014). Washington, DC: US Environmental Protection Agency. Available at: https://nepis.epa.gov/Exe/ZyPDF.cgi/P100DFCQ.PDF?Dockey=P100DFCQ.PDF.

EPA (1992), *Environmental Equity Reducing Risk for All Communities*. EPA-230-R-92-008. Wsahington, DC: US Environmental Protection Agency

EPA (2016), *EJ 2020 Action Agenda: The U.S. EPA's Environmental Justice Strategic Plan for 2016–2020* (EJ 2020). Washington, DC: US Environmental Protection Agency. Available at: https://www.epa.gov/sites/production/files/2016-05/documents/052216_ej_2020_strategic_plan_final_0.pdf.

Fenn, A. J., Johnson, D. K. N., Smith, M. G. and Stimpert, J. L. (2010), 'Doing Publishable Research with Undergraduate Students', *Journal of Economic Education*, **41** (3): 259–274.

Franklin, B. A. (1985), 'Toxic Cloud Leaks at Carbide Plant in West Virginia', *New York Times*, 12 August, p. 1. Available at: https://www.nytimes.com/1985/08/12/us/toxic-cloud-leaks-at-carbide-plant-in-west-virginia.html.

Gamper-Rabindran, S. and Timmins, C. (2011), 'Hazardous Waste Cleanup, Neighborhood Gentrification, and Environmental Justice: Evidence from Restricted Access Census Block Data', *American Economic Review: Papers and Proceedings*, **101** (3): 620–624.

GAO (1983), 'Siting of Hazardous Waste Landfills and their Correlation with Racial and Economic Status of Surrounding Communities', US Department of Energy, Office of Scientific and Technical Information, June 1983, GAO/RCED-83-168. Full details available at https://www.osti.gov/biblio/5606995-siting-hazardous-waste-landfills-correlation-racial-economic-status-surrounding-communities.

GAO (2005), 'EPA Should Devote More Attention to Environmental Justice When Developing Clean Air Rules'. Available at: https://www.gao.gov/assets/250/247171.pdf.

Goffe, W. L. and Kauper, D. (2014), 'A Survey of Principles Instructors: Why Lecture Prevails', *Journal of Economic Education*, **45** (4): 360–375.

Gray, W. B. and Shadbegian, R. J. (2004), '"Optimal" pollution abatement – whose benefits matter, and how much?', *Journal of Environmental Management*, **47**: 510–534.

Gray, W. B., Shadbegian, R. J. and Wolverton, A. (2010), 'Environmental Justice: Do Poor and Minority Populations Face More Hazards?' Working Paper 10–10, Washington, DC. Available at: https://www.epa.gov/sites/production/files/2014-12/documents/environmental_justice_do_poor_and_minority_populations_face_more_hazards.pdf.

Hamilton, J. T. (1995), 'Testing for Environmental Racism: Prejudice, Profits, Political Power?', *Journal of Policy Analysis and Management*, **14** (1): 107–132.

Hampson, C. (2010), 'Warren County and Environmental Justice: A Community Fighting Back', Senior Thesis, University of North Carolina at Asheville.

Hansen, W. L. (2001), 'Expected Proficiencies for Undergraduate Economics Majors', *Journal of Economic Education*, **32** (3): 231–242.

Hawtry, K. (2007), 'Using Experiential Learning Techniques', *Journal of Economic Education*, **38** (2), 143–152.

Henderson, A. (2016), 'Growing by Getting Their Hands Dirty: Meaningful Research Transforms Students', *Journal of Economic Education*, **47** (3): 241–257.

Henderson, A. (2018), 'Leveraging the Power of Experiential Learning to Achieve Higher-Order Proficiencies', *Journal of Economic Education*, **49** (1): 59–71.

Jensen, E. J. and Owen, A. L. (2001), 'Pedagogy, Gender, and Interest in Economics', *Journal of Economic Education*, **32** (4): 323–343.

Kolstad, C. D. (2011), *Environmental Economics*. Oxford University Press.

Kravchenko, J. et al. (2018), 'Mortality and Health Outcomes in North Carolina Communities Located in Close Proximity to Hog Concentrated Animal Feeding Operations', *North Carolina Medical Journal*, **79** (5): 278–288.

McGurty, E. M. (2000), 'Warren County, NC, and the Emergence of the Environmental Justice Movement: Unlikely Coalitions and Shared Meanings in Local Collective Action', *Society & Natural Resources*, **13** (4): 373–387.

Mikati, I. et al. (2018), 'Disparities in Distribution of Particulate Matter Emission Sources by Race and Poverty Status', *American Journal of Public Health*, **108** (4): 480–486.

Moon, E. (2018), 'North Carolina's Hog Waste Problem has a Long History. Why Wasn't it Solved in Time for Hurricane Florence?', *Pacific Standard*, 16 September. Available at: https://psmag.com/environment/why-wasnt-north-carolinas-hog-waste -problem-solved-before-hurricane-florence.

Morello-Frosch, R. and Jesdale, B. M. (2005), 'Separate and Unequal: Residential Segregation and Estimated Cancer Risks Associated with Ambient Air Toxics in US Metropolitan Areas', *Environmental Health Perspectives*, **114** (3): 386–393.

Morello-Frosch, R., Pastor, M. and Sadd, J. (2001), 'Environmental Justice and Southern California's "Riskscape": The Distribution of Air Toxics Exposures and Health Risks Among Diverse Communities', *Urban Affairs Review*, **36** (4): 551–578.

Myers, S. C., Nelson, M. A. and Stratton, R. W. (2011), 'Assessment of the Undergraduate Economics Major: A National Survey', *Journal of Economic Education*, **42** (2): 195–199.

Naidu, S. C., Manolakos, P. T. and Hopkins, T. E. (2013), 'Environmental Justice in Ohio', *Review of Radical Political Economics*, **45** (3): 384–399.

Nicole, W. (2013), 'CAFOs and Environmental Justice: The Case of North Carolina', *Environmental Health Perspectives*, **121** (6): 182–190.

Olson, M. (1965), *The Logic of Collective Action*. Cambridge, MA: Harvard University Press.

Pastor, M., Sadd, J. and Hipp, J. (2001), 'Which Came First? Toxic Facilities, Minority Move-in, and Environmental Justice', *Journal of Urban Affairs*, **23** (1): 1–21.

Ringquist, E. J. (1997), 'Equity and the Distribution of Environmental Risk', *Social Science Quarterly*, **78** (4): 811–829.

Sadd, J. L. et al. (1999), '"Every Breath You Take...": the Demographics of Toxic Air Releases in Southern California', *Economic Development Quarterly*, **13** (2): 107–123.

Salemi, M. K. (2002), 'An Illustrated Case for Active Learning', *Southern Economic Journal*, **68** (3): 721–731.

Schwartz, D. A. et al. (1992), 'Airway Injury in Swine Confinement Workers', *Annals of Internal Medicine*, Am Coll Physicians, **116** (8): 630–635.

Seifert, T. A. et al. (2014), 'The Conditional Nature of High Impact/Good Practices on Student Learning Outcomes', *Journal of Higher Education*, **85** (4): 531–564.

Siegfried, J. J. et al. (1991), 'The Economics Major: Can and Should We Do Better than a B–?', *AEA Papers and Proceedings*, **81** (2): 20–25.

Stichnoth, H. and Van der Straeten, K. (2013), 'Ethnic Diversity, Public Spending, and Individual Support for the Welfare State: A Review of the Empirical Literature', *Journal of Economic Surveys*, **27** (2): 364–389.

Swinker, M. (1998), 'Human Health Effects of Hog Waste', *North Carolina Medical Journal*, **59** (1): 16–18.

Thu, K. et al. (1997), 'A Control Study of the Physical and Mental Health of Residents Living Near a Large-Scale Swine Operation', *Journal of Agricultural Safety and Health*, **3** (1): 13–26.

Tietenberg, T. H. and Lewis, L. (2016), *Environmental and Natural Resource Economics*. Routledge.

UCC (1987), 'Toxic Wastes and Race in the United States: A National Report on the Racial and Socio-Economic Characteristics of Communities with Hazardous Waste Sites', Commission for Racial Justice, United Church of Christ (UCC). An image of the archived paper can be found here: http://uccfiles.com/pdf/ToxicWastes&Race .pdf.

US General Accounting Office (1983), Siting of Hazardous Waste Landfills and Their Correlation With Racial and Economic Status of Surrounding Communities. Available at: https://www.gao.gov/products/RCED-83-168.

Wagner, J. (2015), 'A Framework for Undergraduate Research in Economics', *Southern Economic Journal*, **82** (2): 668–672.

Watts, M. and Schaur, G. (2011), 'Teaching and Assessment Methods in Undergraduate Economics: A Fourth National Quinquennial Survey', *Journal of Economic Education*, **42** (3): 294–309.

Wing, S., Cole, D. and Grant, G. (2000), 'Environmental Injustice in North Carolina's Hog Industry', *Environmental Health Perspectives*, **108** (3): 225–231.

Wolverton, A. (2009), 'Effects of Socio-economic and Input-related Factors on Polluting Plants' Location Decisions', *BE Journal of Economic Analysis & Policy*, **9** (1): 1935–1982.

Zwickl, K., Ash, M. and Boyce, J. K. (2014), 'Regional Variation in Environmental Inequality: Industrial Air Toxics Exposure in U.S. cities', *Ecological Economics*, **107**, 494–509.

DATA RESOURCES APPENDIX

US EPA Toxics Release Inventory Data
https://enviro.epa.gov/triexplorer/tri_release.chemical
Available as a csv or Excel file; be sure to check box for longitude/latitude data if using with GIS.

Canadian National Pollutant Release Inventory
https://open.canada.ca/data/en/dataset/40e01423-7728-429c-ac9d
-2954385ccdfb
Available in CSV format for years 1994 to latest release year; includes geocoding data.

American Community Survey (ACS) Data for GIS
https://www.census.gov/geographies/mapping-files/time-series/geo/tiger-data
.html
Available with select economic and demographic data in geodatabase format; block group or tract level.

North Carolina List of Permitted Animal Facilities
https://deq.nc.gov/about/divisions/water-resources/water-resources-permits/
wastewater-branch/animal-feeding-operation-permits/animal-facility-map
Available as an Excel file; current year permit data; includes geocoding data.

US Power Plant Emissions (eGRID)
https://www.epa.gov/energy/emissions-generation-resource-integrated
-database-egrid
Available as an Excel spreadsheet; includes geocoding data.

California Solid Waste Facilities List
https://www2.calrecycle.ca.gov/SolidWaste/Site/Search
Available as a three-sheet Excel file or a flat text file to use in GIS applications; highly detailed dataset.

EJSCREEN Interactive Mapping Tool from the Environmental Protection Agency
https://ejscreen.epa.gov/mapper/

Risk Screening Environmental Indicators (RSEI) from the Environmental Protection Agency
General information:
https://www.epa.gov/rsei/rsei-geographic-microdata-rsei-gm
Microdata access and documentation:
https://www.epa.gov/rsei/ways-get-rsei-results#microdata

8. A small collection of pen-and-paper classroom experiments for teaching environmental economics classes

Stephan Kroll

INTRODUCTION

The times when undergraduate economics classes were solely taught in a chalk-and-talk kind of way are fortunately over. Over the last 20 to 30 years, teaching economics classes interactively, which often means with experiments, has become *en vogue*. Many Principles textbooks have experiments built into their online learning management systems; websites for teaching experiments, such as Veconlab or EconPort, have grown in popularity; commercial experiment providers such as Aplia or MobLab have increased their portfolio substantially; and some instructors even program their own experiments on platforms like z-Tree or oTree, which are usually used to program experiments for research, not teaching, purposes.

The motivation underlying this trend is obvious. There is some truth to the saying "I see I forget, I hear I remember, I do I understand." For example, economics instructors can show a supply–demand graph and explain the predictions stemming from it dozens of times in a Principles class, to little avail. And yet, when students participate as buyers or sellers in an experimental market they quickly realize that this market magically converges to its equilibrium, and that they are not able to charge or pay a price different from the equilibrium price, which at the onset of the experiment nobody (other than the instructor) even knew. This way these students get a much better understanding of the power of that supply–demand model and of what "converging to the equilibrium" and "price-taking" really mean.

In large Principles classes with 150+ students, using internet-based experiments makes a lot of sense. An online market with 40+ buyers and 40+ sellers converges within seconds to its equilibrium; how well online market experiments work has recently been documented by Lin et al. (2020). In addition, software for online experiments usually produces an overview of the data the moment the experiment ends.

However, there is something to be said for the use of pen-and-paper experiments in smaller classes. The flexibility, the more personal connection between instructor and participants and among participants, the excitement and laughter in the room while the experiment is going on—an in-classroom experiment definitely adds something to the learning experience an online-based experiment cannot.

Of course, in-classroom pen-and-paper based experiments are tough or impossible to administer in large classes. For some experiments (public good experiments, for example), an i-clicker or other remote student response systems can also be employed in large classes, but for other experiments (market experiments, for example) they cannot be used or at least not as easily. Fortunately, the size of environmental economics classes at most institutions (at least the ones I have taught at in the U.S., Germany, and Vietnam) are reasonably small—10 to 20 students at a liberal arts school in the U.S., 20 to 50 at large public schools in the U.S. and Germany, and 80 to 100 at a university in Hanoi, which for some of the experiments I broke up into several sections.

In this chapter I am presenting "how-to" guides for two main sets of experiments (market experiments and public good experiments) and one smaller single experiment (WTP vs WTA valuation experiment), followed by a brief summary of two other papers about experiments I use extensively in my environmental and natural resource (ENR) economics classes (opportunity cost experiment and labeling experiment). This selection is very personal and certainly not exhaustive; it is entirely based on the experiments I am using in my own ENR classes.

The electronic appendix to this chapter contains supplementary material, such as instructions, subject decision sheets, Excel sheets, and in some cases homework assignments for all five experiments (https://osf.io/dujas/).

Instructors considering using classroom experiments in their ENR classes might ask themselves, and this chapter's author, a few important questions before taking the plunge: (a) Do I have to put a lot of effort into these experiments, and are they worth the effort? (b) How should I incentivize students' participation and seriousness? (c) Will I (always) get the results that are consistent with what I am about to teach? And (d) what if pen-and-paper is not possible because of something like, well, a pandemic?

General Level of Effort Instructors Need to Make

Obviously I do think the experiments I am presenting here are worth the effort, but they are certainly not effortless. If an instructor lectures on a specific topic for the umpteenth time, there is a good chance the marginal cost of preparing that lecture is close to zero. Preparing a pen-and-paper experiment, even when done many times before, is never entirely costless—each time, copies have to be made, instructions have to be distributed before class (handing them out at the beginning of class is an option too, but that might take away time from the actual experiment), and experimental data have to be collated, entered in an Excel sheet and organized for the following lecture and/or related assignment. Then there is the cost of losing control a bit—an instructor usually knows what happens during class when lecturing by advancing and discussing slides, but when conducting an experiment one has to be prepared for surprises and for explaining or discussing the reasons why something might, or might not, have happened the way it did or should have. They also eat up time that cannot be used for a new topic. And, while conducting particularly the market experiment can be exhilarating and fun for the instructor, it can also be exhausting (which I personally do not mind/notice), much more so than hitting the "Next" button in a slide show.

But I think conducting classroom experiments are worth the effort—many students understand certain topics more intuitively, an occasional experiment instead of (or together with) a lecture breaks up the routine of the semester, and instructors can always refer back to them when discussing related topics later on. And, no small feat, students usually love the experiments; some of my students have written in their end-of-semester evaluations that the experiments were the highlight of the class, which might be more a reflection of my other teaching than of the experiments, but still...

Incentivizing Classroom Experiments

An important question is how to incentivize classroom experiments. Using money awards, tied to the performance of subjects, is the preferred *modus operandi* in research experiments, but in classroom experiments instructors usually refrain from paying out money to all participants, for obvious budgetary reasons. I personally have used three different major options: small amounts of extra-credit points, odds for winning a single prize, or not incentivizing the experiment at all.

The advantage of using small amounts of extra-credit points is that students often take those very seriously and that there is a certain wiggle room on how much these extra credits are really worth; instructors can indicate that they keep track of these points, that they normalize them at the end of the semester, and that these points might make a difference for the final grade (I usually announce that they could make a difference if students are right on the cusp to a higher grade so that more points would be better than less in order to make a difference). That level of vagueness would not pass the smell-test with journal reviewers of experimental research papers, but in teaching experiments it is allowed and okay. The disadvantage is that instructors do need to keep a running tab of the results, plus I often have had to respond to a flurry of student inquiries at the end of the semester about whether these students did not deserve a higher grade in the class, given that they received so many points in experiments X, Y and Z. Like with other aspects of teaching, instructors need to set the expectations early and clearly.

Alternatively, instructors could provide a small but not insignificant financial or physical prize (like a mug, chocolate, T-shirt, etc.) that only one or very few subjects would win. This is a good incentive as well, but it is a bit more complicated than it sounds. This prize should not be automatically awarded to the person or group with the highest amount of points, because that would distort the incentives in the experiment. The point of a market experiment or a public good game is not to "beat" the other students but to get as many points as possible—30 points when other students have 40 points should be better than 25 points when others have 20 points. But an award system that awards the group with the highest amount of points would incentivize behavior that could lead students to prefer the latter outcome with 25 points over the former with 30 points. What to do about it? One way is to treat the points as probabilities that might not add up to 100 (this method was, to my knowledge, first proposed by Roth and Malouf, 1979).

An example illustrates: imagine an experiment with two participants and a maximum possible combined payoff (= social optimum) of 100 points (if the actual maximum combined payoff is different from 100 then after the experiment it should be normalized to 100). The points the two participants achieve in the experiment will be their "raffle tickets" to win the prize. If they do not achieve the social optimum, however, then there is a certain probability that neither one will win the prize. In the first of the two examples above, the player with 30 points will have raffle tickets 1–30, the player with 40 points will have tickets 31–70, and tickets 71–100 are not going to either player, which means the prize is not awarded if one of those tickets is "drawn." In the second example, the player with 25 points would have a higher likelihood of winning the prize than the player with 20 points, but, consistent with the incentive system the experiment is trying to imitate, combined they would have a lower likelihood compared to the 30–40 case.

An instruction sheet and simple Excel file for this method is provided in the online appendix for this chapter. The advantages of the method are that instructors do not have to worry (and argue with students) about extra-credit points, and that, even though a prize is needed, this prize is relatively cheap; I personally do not mind paying out of pocket for chocolate or similar items worth $20–50 or asking the department chair or dean for financial support, but of course I do understand that some instructors might feel differently.

The disadvantage is that it adds another layer of complexity and that the explanations of this mechanism might distract students from what is really important.

A third alternative is… no incentive at all. Particularly when I conduct a classroom experiment at relatively short notice or when I am asked to give a guest lecture, I sometimes just tell students "to get as many points as possible," and the majority of students is trying to do exactly that. There is always the unavoidable "who won?"—"you are all winners" dialog at the end of an experiment, which indicates that the incentives for some students ("beating others") are not consistent with what they are supposed to be ("getting as many points as possible, even if others get even more"), but in market experiments behavior does not seem to be impacted too much by which incentive system is chosen; it might have a bigger impact in public good games.

Are Results from Classroom Experiments (Always) Consistent with Teaching Objectives?

The short answer is "no." The longer answer is "not always, but even when they are not, they still provide fodder for thoughts and discussions." The market experiment described below will usually have prices and quantities reasonably close to the market equilibrium, particularly in the treatment most relevant for ENR classes, the one with externalities and without polices addressing those externalities. In the public good experiments, almost every result is instructive; usually there is a mix of free-riders, (conditional) cooperators and others among students in classroom experiments, just like in research experiments (and in real life). In the WTA–WTP experiment, it is really the set-up and its discussion that are pedagogically important, almost independent of what subjects do. The opportunity cost experiment always works like clockwork, and the labeling experiment usually does as well.

Can These Experiments Be Used Even in Remote Classroom Settings?

In 2020, the year I am writing these lines, instructors at many universities around the globe were not able to teach in a regular classroom or, when teaching in a classroom, were not able to hand out material or let students work in group settings due to social distancing requirements. Even in non-pandemic times, some instructors are teaching ENR classes for their university's online programs and thus not in a classroom. Can they conduct the experiments presented in this chapter even if face-to-face interactions are difficult or not possible?

It depends. The market experiment for one is very interactive, and while I could imagine a real-time back-and-forth on, for example, a discussion board within a learning management system platform like Canvas or Moodle or the chat room of Zoom or Teams, such interaction seems cumbersome, time-intensive and daunting (I have not tried it). Since the main advantage of the pen-and-paper experiment, the ability of generating instant and spontaneous discussions in a classroom, would be diminished greatly anyway, it might be easier to use commercial or non-commercial providers such as Veconlab or MobLab instead.

The other experiments presented here, however, are less interactive, and could be conducted as one-shot games even in an online environment. The decision sheets students have to fill out could be assigned as homework, and instructors would have time to evaluate them and calculate results before the next online class meeting or video recording they prepare in an asynchronous setting.

Further Reading

For those instructors interested in using other experiments in their (not only ENR) classes, the book by Charles Holt (2019) has to be the first stop. A lot of the chapters in Holt's book, now in its second edition, are based on peer-reviewed articles he has published since the late 1980s; a quick Google Scholar search for "Charles Holt classroom" will unearth many of these papers. The book also lists recommendations on some of the topics mentioned above. Prof. Holt also developed the Veconlab website (http://veconlab.econ.virginia.edu/admin.htm) with a plethora of available online experiments; it can be used to accompany Holt (2019) or as a stand-alone.

EconPort (https://econport.org/) is an "economics digital library specializing in content that emphasizes the use of experiments in teaching and research" and also provides, like Veconlab, a menu of experiments instructors can conduct online.

Of course, economic experiments are not only used for pedagogical purposes. Important research questions in environmental and resource economics have been addressed in peer-reviewed experimental research papers and book collections. These questions concern, for example, the impact and acceptability of environmental policies, the functioning of institutions like cap-and-trade markets and green taxes, the precision of valuation methods, and the validity of theoretical models on regulation and compliance, all topics covered in many ENR classes. Hundreds of academic articles by environmental and resource economists using experimental methods can be found in most major ENR journals such as the *Journal of Environmental Economics and Management* and *Environmental and Resource Economics*, but also in journals for experimental economists, such as *Experimental Economics* and *Journal of the Economic Science Association*. While those papers do not always lend themselves directly to classroom experiments, their methodology and results are easier to understand for most students once these students have participated in the experiments described in this book chapter. Books and special journal issues dedicated solely to experiments for environmental and resource economists include Cherry et al. (2007), Messer and Murphy (2010), List and Price (2013), and Kroll and Suter (2017).

SUPPLY–DEMAND MARKET EXPERIMENTS WITHOUT AND WITH EXTERNALITIES AND (PIGOUVIAN-LIKE) TAXATION

This market game is based on Holt's (1996) description of a supply–demand classroom experiment, which in turn is modelled after Smith (1962) and Chamberlain (1948). The basic motivation of all three of these papers is to demonstrate how (well) equilibrium predictions fare in a simple supply–demand market experiment with a relatively small number of traders.

Following Holt's design, the basic version of the experiment divides subjects into two groups, buyers with resale values that form a market demand curve and sellers with marginal production costs that form a market supply curve. Market participants interact with each other in "double oral auctions"—buyers post bids, improve/increase other buyers' bids or accept sellers' asks; sellers post asks, improve/decrease other sellers' asks or accept bidders' bids.

The main insights students should get from Holt's original experiment are that the market converges to its equilibrium even though all traders see only their own values or costs and are not aware of others' values and costs and therefore of the equilibrium price. As an additional bonus, instructors can also impose taxes and price ceilings and/or floors to the market to demonstrate what impact those have on the market outcome. The addition of a tax is particularly powerful since the experiment demonstrates nicely how, with non-perfectly-inelastic supply and demand curves, the equilibrium price does not change by the amount of the tax, a concept that many students and non-economists have a tough time to grasp.

Instructors of environmental economics classes should add an additional component that Holt did not include in his description—external costs. These external costs are deductions in earnings that each trade causes to all other traders in the market, and they stand in, of course, for negative externalities from pollution. Unless corrective policies are implemented, the market will disregard the externalities and still converge to its original equilibrium, as shown experimentally first by Plott (1983). Instructors can use this outcome to highlight Plott's main insight: "Theory asserts that the market [with externalities] will behave as if there are not externalities at all. Policy makers untrained in the finer aspects of economic theory have no trouble in rejecting this line of reasoning in favour of models more compatible with their intuitions."

BOX 8.1   BASIC DESIGN OF MARKET EXPERIMENTS

General Overview of Experiment

The class is divided into ten (or eight, in classes with 9–20 students) groups, of which five are on one side of the room ("buyer groups") and five are on the other side of the room ("seller groups"). One student or a TA is needed to record prices on the board behind the instructor. Buyers have three units with decreasing resale value they like to buy; they make bids or accept asks. Sellers have three units with increasing costs they like to sell; they make asks or accept bids. Units not bought or sold have no value or costs. Note that within a period all buyers have different resale values and all sellers have different cost numbers. The overall supply and demand curves, however, do not change—the five sets of resale values are just shuffled in each period among all buyers, and the five sets of cost numbers are shuffled among all sellers. Supply and demand schedules are shown in Table 8.1.

Table 8.1   Supply and demand schedules for market experiment

Price (in tokens)	Quantity Demanded	Quantity Supplied
100	2	15
90	4	15
80	5	15
70	8	13
60	11	11
50	13	8
40	15	5
30	15	4
20	15	2

There are no externalities in the first three or four periods. Then each trade causes a cost of 2.5 tokens each for the other eight traders, which results in an overall externality of 20 per trade. Finally, in the periods with externalities and a tax, this tax is equal to 20 tokens (in the experiment I usually do not return the tax revenues to the market but instructors should discuss what options there are for the revenue recycling).

Set-up

- When students enter the classroom, have them sit in ten rows, with five rows on each side of the class, facing the front of the classroom. A reverse "V" shape is advantageous so that you can easily see and point at the inside student (the trader) of each group. Each group should have about the same size.
- Each group's trader is on the inside, but remind groups that they can change their traders after the instructions are read or after each period.
- Hand out instructions (if not already posted or handed out before class) to each student.
- Hand out record sheets, one for each group. All buyer (B) sheets on one side and all seller (S) sheets on the other side, with sheets B1 and S1 to the groups in the first row and sheets B5 and S5 to the groups in the last row.
- If more than ten students are present then choose one student or, if available, the class's teaching assistant, to help you with recording bids, asks and prices. (I usually choose the last student who came to class to be the helper.)
- Read the instructions out loud.
- Stress to students that only the trader can act on behalf of their groups, that those traders have to raise their hands and that they can only make bids and asks or accept offers of other groups, when you explicitly point at them. After a period or two, when everybody is on board, you might sometimes see ten hands up at the same time and you choose between them according to a uniform distribution.
- The instructions mention that each period stops after three minutes but usually I go until a lull in the action indicates that all trades that are possible are made, which in early periods takes more than three minutes, but in later periods takes less.
- After I call on traders, I always repeat their bid or ask ("Buyer B2 bids 45") so that the record keeper behind me can more easily write down the correct numbers. Once an offer is accepted, the record keeper writes down the price of that trade and erases all bids and asks.
- As seen in the table above, the equilibrium number in the periods without policies is 11 (for ten groups) so expect about nine to 11 trades in one period.
- Once prices are reasonably close to the equilibrium, usually after three or four periods, introduce an externality: each trade (in a market with

ten traders) results in a cost of 2.5 tokens for everybody else for a total external cost of 20.

- After one or two periods with only the externality, introduce a tax (on sellers) of 20 tokens for each trade they make.
- At the end of each period, ask trading groups to record their gains from each trade they conducted, the externalities imposed on them from other trades (by counting the total number of trades and subtracting the ones they were involved in) and, if they are sellers in a period with taxation, the total amount of tax they have to pay. Also, in order to entice traders make a trade when they are indifferent, in each period each group receives one token for each trade they make.
- Time permitting, I sometimes end a class with a single market where traders of all buyer and seller groups stand across from each other and trade without my guidance. That period goes lightning fast and is a fun way of ending class that participants as well as spectators enjoy.

What to Expect

The ten sets of resale values and cost numbers generate a predicted equilibrium price of 60 tokens and equilibrium quantity of 11 trades (note that in a market with ten groups, buyers would like to buy and sellers would like to sell up to 15 units each, so in equilibrium only four trades are "missing"). The first period usually goes slow, the quantity might be low, and the prices might or might not be close to 60. Shortly after, however, the market moves fast, quantity of trades is close to equilibrium and so are, at least on average, equilibrium prices. In line with predictions and similar to what Plott (1983) observed, the equilibrium is a good predictor even in the periods with externalities. Once the tax is introduced, trading goes down and prices increase by about half of the tax (market supply and demand curves used in this experiment are equally elastic in the relevant price range).

Table 8.2 below shows the results when I conducted this experiment with four distinct groups at Foreign Trade University in Hanoi in December 2019. I taught two classes with about 100 students each (students were business and economics students with very good understanding of the English language), and I split each class into two groups that came at different times. Each of the ten groups in each session consisted of four or five students. Due to time constraints I could do only four periods for two groups and five periods for the other two groups; usually I try to do at least seven periods.

Table 8.2　　*Exemplary results in market experiment*

Period	Treatment	Equilibrium Price	Equilibrium Quantity	Socially Optimal Quantity	Gr. 1 Av Price/ Quantity	Gr. 2 Av Price/ Quantity	Gr. 3 Av Price/ Quantity	Gr. 4 Av Price/ Quantity	Overall Av Price/ Quantity
1	No Ext.	60	11	11	62.4/8	57.0/8	59.8/8	57.2/9	59.0/8.25
2	No Ext.	60	11	11	61.0/8	66.0/9	58.5/11	56.3/9	60.3/9.25
3	No Ext.	60	11	11	–	56.3/9	59.7/10	–	58.1/9.5
3/4	Ext./ No Policy	60	11	7	56.6/10	56.3/10	59.1/12	60.5/11	58.2/10.75
4/5	Ext./Tax	70	7	7	71.5/6	68.2/6	66.7/7	64.6/7	67.6/6.5

The main results are as expected: all average market prices were reasonably close to the equilibrium price, even though the prices in the markets with taxation were mostly below the predicted price; another period would probably have been helpful. The quantity of trades gradually increased in the periods without taxation. Not shown here, but obvious: total economic surplus went up from period 4/5. Instructors might want to highlight that the tax revenues have to be included in the calculations of total surplus (see the Excel sheet in the electronic appendix).

Further Readings

Chamberlain (1948) claimed, and observed, that equilibrium price predictions do not fare well in small markets, when the outcomes of trades were not publicly observable. Famously, Vernon Smith was unsatisfied with the market set-up in Chamberlain's classroom experiment (in which Smith participated) and designed a much more centralized market with widely observable prices, a metaphor for many real-world market institutions. He reports in Smith (1962) that such markets result in predicted equilibrium outcomes and efficiency. Holt (1996) then adjusted Smith's design so it can be used as a teaching tool to make students understand what "such markets result in predicted equilibrium outcomes" actually means.

Plott (1983) introduces externalities into an experimental market and compares market behavior (and efficiency) across four different treatments: no policy, tax, standard and licenses, which we now call tradable permits. In today's world with "z-Tree" (Fischbacher, 2007), "oTree" (Chen et al., 2016) and other software for computerized research experiments, Plott's experiment feels archaic with prices written on a chalkboard and only eight independent sessions, two for each treatment. But the writing is superb, the results are crisp and convincing, and when students in my classes read this paper as an assignment they appreciate the problem externalities pose after they have participated in the classroom experiment themselves. Even though I do not include standards and tradable permits in a classroom experiment, the discussion of Plott's results across all treatments is still instructive.

The Electronic Appendix for this Experiment Contains:

- Instructions
- Ten sets of record sheets (five for buyers, five for sellers)
- Excel sheet with overview
- Example of homework assignment
- PowerPoint slides for Plott (1983) paper

PUBLIC-GOOD EXPERIMENTS: SUMMATION, BEST-SHOT, WEAKEST-LINK, CONDITIONAL COOPERATORS, THRESHOLD PUBLIC GOOD

Fundamentally, many environmental and common-resource problems can be modelled either as markets with externalities or as public good problems (see Cherry et al., 2013, for an experimental comparison of the two). In public good (PG) games, individual contributions can stand in for pollution mitigation or resource use restraint decisions. The summation PG game (where the size of the PG is determined by the sum of individual contributions) describes, for example, the incentives in a climate change mitigation situation well; it is one of the most researched games in experimental economics, with literally thousands of published studies.

The basic summation public good game provides valuable insights for students of all levels and majors and can generate lively discussions in the classroom. The simplicity of the basic variation is powerful, and the main results—students' contributions to the public good are less than the social optimum but often higher than what traditional economic theory predicts—are observed with astonishing regularity. Teaching students the incentive structure of a summation public good and the motivation of why people do not contribute to a public good, but not teaching them to be free riders themselves is a fine line. As one student once said in my Principles class after participating in a public good experiment, seeing the results and listening to the discussion about it: "this game really opened my eyes—now I understand why people do not contribute to a public good. But I don't like it."

BOX 8.2   BASIC DESIGN OF PUBLIC GOOD EXPERIMENTS

In addition to the summation public-good experiment, I propose to conduct at least a subset of several other public-good experiments with different incentive structures: the conditional cooperation, threshold, best-shot, and weakest-link public good experiments. In the next section I briefly explain the motivation behind all five games.

Motivation

Summation public good game
The summation PG game stands for most pollution or common resource problems: it is in everybody's individual interest to free-ride on others' (mitigation/refraining) efforts, but the social optimum occurs when everybody mitigates. Climate change, overfishing, urban pollution are just a few examples that can fundamentally be modelled as summation public goods.

Summation public good game with conditional cooperation
While many, albeit not all, subjects in classroom PG games contribute nothing to a public good like a "class account," their motivation is not straightforward to disentangle: some might be just the proverbial free riders who always contribute the minimum independent from what others do, but some would be willing to contribute if they only knew that enough others contribute as well. When observing a zero contribution in a traditional summation public good game one cannot distinguish the motive of greed (by the free riders) from fear (by people who are willing to contribute if they only knew that others did too), even though that distinction might be important for policy recommendations for (environmental) public good situations. Ostrom (2000) discussed how collective action for ENR and ENR-like problems are impacted by the existence of social preferences. Fischbacher et al. (2001) designed an easy way to unscramble the motives greed and fear by using a "strategy method"—a table where subjects indicate how much they would contribute if they knew with certainty how much others contributed. They observed, and so have many researchers using their method since their paper was published, that 40–60 percent of subjects can be identified as conditional cooperators—subjects willing to match contributions by others. One can easily see/teach how important conditional cooperation is in the governance of environmental goods, such as the climate commons (for reviews see for example, Ostrom 2010, and Carrattini et al., 2019).

Summation public good game with threshold

The summation public good game has traditionally been used to model climate change interactions, particularly between countries (e.g., Barrett, 1994, 2007). Recently emphasis has shifted, because climate scientists are making a stronger case that in addition to the damage from a gradual climate change there is also the chance of a catastrophic outcome if a certain temperature threshold is surpassed. While mentioning the word "catastrophic" usually does not cause celebrations among observers, the idea of a threshold does offer, at least theoretically, a silver lining. In game-theoretical lingo, it can turn the social dilemma of a regular summation PG with just one free-riding equilibrium into a coordination game with two equilibria that can be rank-ordered—the free-riding equilibrium and the "catastrophe avoidance equilibrium." In the latter, if everybody else is willing to contribute to avoid the catastrophe then I am willing to do my part too, not because I am a conditional cooperator or due to some other social preferences, but just because it is in my own (monetary) interest to be the pivotal contributor. The good news then is that such a threshold can provide a coordination device, and at least in laboratory studies (Barrett and Dannenberg, 2012; Brown and Kroll, 2017) equilibrium play is observed frequently. Instructors can point out that the 1.5–2°C goal in the Paris Climate Agreement is consistent with this idea.

The bad news is that high levels of uncertainty about the threshold or of heterogeneity among the players can remove this coordination device, which means that the game becomes just a basic social dilemma again, with only a free-riding equilibrium (Barrett and Dannenberg, 2012). Instructors can change the payoff functions of the experiment to reflect this problem.

Best shot and weakest link public goods

While the above-mentioned games are all variations of the summation public good game, instructors might find it important to point out that the quantity (size) of an environmental good provided is not always determined solely by the sum of individual contributions. Sandler (1997) and Barrett (2007) discuss in their books how (environmental) clean-up decisions are basically best-shot games, where the highest level of effort instead of the sum determines the size of the public good, while avoiding a pollution problem in the first place can often be modelled by a weakest-link game, where the lowest effort determines the size of the public good (the seminal paper on this distinction is Hirshleifer, 1983).

These are not innocuous changes from the summation public good with only one equilibrium—both aggregation technologies, best shot and weakest link, turn the public good game into coordination games with several equilibria. In the best-shot game, all equilibria involve one player contributing while the others can free-ride on the first player's contribution. In each of these equilibria all players are better off compared to the situation with nobody contributing (which in this game is not an equilibrium anymore), but the lone contributor does not gain as much from their own contribution as everybody else, which could complicate coordination.

In the weakest-link game, all equilibria are symmetric in contributions and can be rank-ordered. All players prefer the equilibrium with the highest possible contributions. But that is also the riskiest equilibrium—if there is any doubt that maybe one of the other players will not make a contribution, then it is in the interest of any individual player not to make a high contribution either, since this would be wasted. One could argue that two neighborhoods, cities or countries with two very different levels of pollution are stuck in two different equilibria.

Set-up

The set-up for these experiments is very easy, except for the conditional cooperation experiment. After reading the instructions, students receive decision sheets for all PG games. The instructor has to make two design choices: group size (usually four in one group vs. the entire class) and length (one-shot vs. multiple-shot). The electronic appendix contains material for all different combinations.

The decision sheets ask students for their contributions (out of 10 "tokens"); for example, for the summation game (without threshold) it looks like this:

Game 1: Your Payoff $= 0.5 * sum(x_1, x_2, x_3, x_4) + (10 - x_j)$ (what you keep for yourself)

Your contribution x_j (out of 10): _____

You keep $(10 - x_j)$: _____

BOX 8.3   FORMULAS FOR PUBLIC GOOD GAMES

Once all students have filled out their decision sheets, the instructor collects them and then, either during a break in class or between classes, enters the contributions in the Excel sheet. Instructors who like to play each game repeatedly probably should, depending on the class size, ask students or TAs to help with the data entries to keep things going.

The most complex PG experiment to conduct is the conditional cooperation PG experiment, since explaining how the strategy sheet works takes an additional step. As in the paper that used this method first (Fischbacher et al., 2001), students are not just making unconditional decisions as in those other four experiments but they also fill out a strategy sheet with conditional contributions—how much would you contribute if you knew with certainty that the others contributed on average amount x? In the Instructions, I use Figure 8.1 to help students visualize what is going on (coauthors and I have also used this graphic in research papers on conditional cooperation).

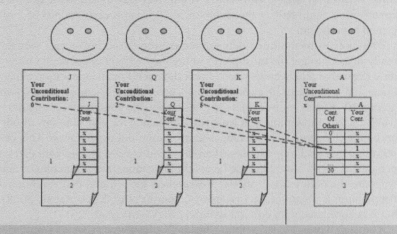

Figure 8.1   Graphic for conditional cooperation instructions

Four students (J, Q, K and A) all write down their unconditional contributions and fill out the table with conditional contributions. Then for one randomly selected student (A in this case), the table is "payoff-relevant" while for the other three students the unconditional contributions are payoff-relevant; the Excel sheet makes the random selection. This distinction is of course only relevant for calculating the payoffs; to highlight the point of the experiment, everybody's table is interesting (and the unconditional contributions are less so). Fischbacher et al. (2001) and subsequent papers using their methodology only reported the entries in the table.

To calculate the payoffs in the example (which the Excel sheet will do for the instructor), note that J, Q and K chose 0, 2 and 5 as their unconditional contributions, which results in a (rounded) average of 2. Student A specified that they would contribute 1 token if the others contribute on average 2. That means the total contributions to the public good are 0, 2, 5 and 1, for a total of 8, so everybody's payoff is 10 minus their respective contribution, plus one half of the sum of contributions, which is 4.

What to Expect

In the summation PG games, one can expect many free riders who contribute 0, particularly in ENR classes for economics and business majors, which is consistent with the provocative title of the classic paper by Marwell and Ames (1981) ("Economists free ride, does anyone else?"). However, free riding is far from ubiquitous; quite a few students will contribute at least some fraction of their endowments. Many seem to "hedge their bets" by contributing about half of the endowment, at least in early rounds of a repeated experiment.

The motives of the free riders are not entirely clear, however—are they really just out to get the most points or are they willing to cooperate if they only knew that others cooperated? Enter the conditional cooperation experiment and its strategy sheet. Many papers on conditional cooperation report around 30–40 percent free riders and 40–60 percent conditional cooperators (subjects that are willing to at least partially match the contributions of others). I have observed similar ranges in my classroom experiments. This observation can lead to great classroom discussions—are people with certain personality types more likely to be conditional cooperators than others, and what are the policy implications? Researchers have found that conditional cooperation is ubiquitous across many countries (e.g., Kocher et al., 2008), but it is correlated with cultural worldviews (Cherry et al., 2017).

The summation PG game with threshold offers two types of equilibria, the free-riding equilibrium and the catastrophe-avoidance equilibrium. With certain thresholds, I often observe contributions consistent with the latter. Sometimes the threshold is missed by a small amount, but the outcomes in those cases, while not an equilibrium, are still on aggregate better than the free-riding equilibrium.

Finally, equilibrium outcomes and coordination are rarely observed in best-shot and weakest-link public goods, at least in the first round. If instructors conduct several rounds of these experiments, they can add communication and/or transfer payments, which usually help with coordination. Low levels of contribution in either game will certainly generate some discussion of how we can get to a (better) equilibrium.

Further Readings

Sandler's (1997) and Barrett's (2007) books discuss the relevance of different "aggregation technologies," the ways individual contributions are aggregated into a public good; both focus on environmental problems. Barrett (2016) provides a clean overview of different public good games, and how they apply to international environmental cooperation. Fischbacher et al.

(2001) is the brief seminal paper that introduced the conditional cooperation method; as of the time of writing this chapter, the paper has been cited around 3000 times, according to Google Scholar. While most papers using the same method have been able to replicate the original findings, Burton-Chellew et al. (2016), however, report evidence that at least some conditional cooperators found with the strategy method are cooperating because of confusion and not because of social preferences.

The Electronic Appendix Contains:

* Instructions for all five PG games
* Decision sheets
* Excel sheet for calculations
* PowerPoint slides
* Homework assignments

WTP V WTA: AUCTION VALUATION EXPERIMENT

Instructors of many environmental economics classes cover the question of what is the appropriate measure of the value of an environmental good—the (marginal) willingness to pay (WTP or MWTP) for an improvement in environmental quality or the (marginal) willingness to accept (WTA or MWTA) for a decline in environmental quality?

Standard microeconomic theory predicts that, given small income effects, willingness-to-pay and willingness-to-accept measures should be approximately equal for most combinations of goods if the goods are close substitutes, which market goods and money usually are (Willig, 1976; Randall and Stoll, 1980). Environmental improvements or decreases in health risks as one good and money as a second good, however, are not close substitutes. Hanemann (1991) provides an exposition of why the divergence of WTA and WTP occurs for imperfect substitutes and non-marginal changes, and how this divergence depends on the degree of substitution. In fact, WTA measures have been found to exceed WTP measures significantly in CV studies (Horowitz and McConnell, 2002) and laboratory markets (Knetsch and Sinden, 1984).

Shogren et al. (1994) provide empirical evidence in support of Hanemann's insights. They observe that in laboratory markets WTA and WTP for a change in the size of a candy bar (a market good) converge to each other and converge to the actual outside market price. But for changes in the health risk from food poisoning, a good not tradable in a market, WTA exceeds WTP consistently and significantly, and the two measures do not converge. Highlighting this finding in a lecture is then a good segue into a discussion about which measure should be used to value environmental goods in which situations.

Many undergraduate and graduate textbooks dedicate several pages to this exact question, and they usually cite the above-mentioned papers (for example, Hanley et al., 2007, 2019; Kolstad, 2010; Goodstein and Polasky, 2017; at a more technical level for graduate students, Phaneuf and Requate, 2017). Some of them (for example, Kolstad, 2010, and Goodstein and Polasky, 2017) even dedicate a textbox to a discussion of the Shogren et al. paper and its results.

However, students might have trouble seeing how Shogren et al. elicited the WTA and WTP measures for different goods, particularly for a change in health risk. Kolstad (2010, p. 147), for example, just states that "students were asked WTP and WTA questions." Astute economics students might ask themselves what incentives these students had to tell their values truthfully anyway. Going through an actual experimental exercise will help them understand the incentive-compatibility of the auction Shogren et al. used and highlight the difference between WTA and WTP. (As an aside, students will also be able to understand the underlying logic of experimental auctions as method to elicit values in general; see Lusk and Shogren (2007) as the standard guide to this method applied in economics and marketing).

BOX 8.4   BASIC DESIGN OF WTP–WTA EXPERIMENT

Overview of Experiment

Shogren et al. (1994) used a 2 × 2 experimental design, with WTP v WTA as "between-subjects" treatment variable and "candy bars v sandwiches" as "within-subjects" treatment variable: half of their subjects participated in WTP experiments where they had to indicate their willingness to pay for an upgrade from a small candy bar to a larger candy bar and for an upgrade from a regular sandwich to a more stringently screened and thus safer sandwich. The other half were endowed with large candy bars and safer sandwiches and were then asked for their WTA for a downgrade. Note that the words "upgrade" and "downgrade" were avoided in their instructions and that the subjects had to eat the sandwiches before leaving the experiment.

Obviously, a WTP–WTA experiment has to be organized in a simpler fashion in the classroom, and students can hardly be forced to eat a food item in the way Shogren et al.'s subjects were. But a simpler design will help get the main points across and prepare students for the reading of Shogren et al. and other WTP–WTA papers. Fundamentally the experiment can be conducted either in an abstract way (which is easier to do in the classroom) or with actual goods similar to the way Shogren et al. conducted theirs (just not decreases in health risk) or both, which is what I usually do.

In the abstract classroom experiment, students get sheets with two distinct integer numbers between 1 and 100. In the WTP experiment they are told that the lower number is their "endowment"—the number they receive if they do not win the auction—and the higher number is the number they receive if they win the auction (in the WTA experiment, the roles of the numbers are reversed). Then the instructor asks the students to fill out their decision sheet, indicating how many points they are willing to "pay" to receive the upgrade (WTA: how many points they would like to receive in order to accept the lower number). Finally, the instructor enters the WTP bids (or WTA asks) in an Excel sheet, which automatically sorts them from highest to lowest, calculates the fifth-highest bid (or fifth-lowest ask), and highlights the four winning entries who have to pay the fifth-highest amount (or receive the fifth-lowest amount in the WTA treatment). If the instructor offers extra-credit points as incentive, then the students with the four highest bids in the WTP treatment receive their higher number on their sheets minus the fifth-highest bid while the remaining students receive the lower number on their sheets. In the WTA treatment, the students with the four lowest asks receive their lower number plus the fifth-lowest ask, while everybody else receives their higher number.

After (or in lieu of) the abstract experiment, instructors can conduct similar auctions with actual goods if they are willing and able to provide these goods. They can either endow all subjects with a good of a certain size and elicit bids for upgrades (asks for downgrades), or they endow all students with nothing in the WTP treatment and with the actual good in the WTA treatment where the winners will not receive a good (just their compensation). Small and large candy bars of the same kind, or older-looking and fresher apples could be candidates for pairs of items; chocolate, fruits, university gear, etc., could be candidates for single items. Note that a fifth-price WTP auction for a single item means an instructor needs to provide four units of the item, but a fifth-price WTA auction implies all but four of the students that are participating in this auction will receive the item; only the four winners will not.

Discussion

This experiment is a good exercise in preparation of the Shogren et al. (1994) paper, which in turn leads to a discussion of the appropriateness of WTA vs WTP. My preferred way of conducting this experiment is to do auctions for the abstract good first, with half of the class being in the WTA treatment and the other half in the WTP treatment, followed by the auctions for an actual good (not an upgrade).

Usually I conduct the first auction (abstract good) for extra-credit points and without explanations of why it is in everybody's interest to bid (WTP) or ask for (WTA) their true value differences. Next I reveal the winning bids/asks and the price the winners have to pay/receive; bids and asks are often all over the place, and only few students reveal their true value differences. I then use examples from class to show the weak dominance of "truth-telling" and go into a spiel on how these auctions can be used to elicit people's true values in economics and marketing, *á la* Lusk and Shogren (2007). Then I conduct the auctions for real items (usually chocolate bars) and real money. Bids and asks in these auctions are usually relatively reasonable. In the following class, after assigning the Shogren et al. paper as reading, I talk about the paper and the relevance of the difference between WTP and WTA for environmental goods.

The Electronic Appendix Contains:

- Instructions for abstract and real good valuations
- Subject decision sheets
- Homework example
- PP slides for class

SUMMARY OF PAPERS WITH OTHER CLASSROOM EXPERIMENTS

In this section I briefly overview two other papers and the classroom experiments I employ in my ENR classes; I basically use them exactly the way they are described in the original papers.

Opportunity Costs and Emissions Permit Markets

When the EU decided to sell permits in its new CO_2 trading system in the early 2000s, the uproar by utilities and industry was large enough to reverse the decision so that permits were basically handed out for free (Kanter, 2008), similarly to SO_2 permits in the US in the 1990s. For utilities this had two effects—getting these permits was a big windfall gain, but using them still involved opportunity costs since permits could be sold instead of used. In a move that did not surprise economists, but shocked policy makers and the general public, utilities accepted the windfall gains from the "free" permits without hesitation but increased their electricity prices nevertheless as if they had had to pay for the permits in first place.

Holt et al. (2010) designed a little classroom experiment that helps explain why utilities made their output pricing decisions with free permits the same way they would have had they had to pay for permits; this paper is a side product from the bigger research program on auctions for emission permits (see, for example, Burtraw et al., 2009, and Wråke et al., 2010). The experiment also illustrates nicely the size of the windfall gain, and it visualizes that the efficiency effect of the grandfathering-vs-auctioning-of-permits decision is relatively small (zero in the experiment), while the distributional effect can be large. Finally, in classes with non-economics majors it is also a great tool to teach the concept of opportunity costs.

Their experiment is simple and can be implemented in a class of any size between 10 and 60 (I have also used it in my classes at the Foreign Trade University in Vietnam with about 100 students, but it becomes more complicated in large class settings). Students get a decision sheet which they use to decide how many units of a final product to produce. The production of this final product needs two inputs—"fuel" with an increasing marginal cost and permits; prices for output and permits as well as fuel costs are fixed. Half of the students need to buy a permit for each unit of output they produce, while the other half has enough permits to cover the production of all possible output units, and they can sell the permits they do not use in case the output price is not high enough. This is not an interactive experiment; it is rather just a calculation exercise at the end of which all students should have made the same output decision, independent of how they received the permits originally.

Because of its simplicity I conduct this experiment without any incentives at all; the majority of students is usually motivated by just getting the answers right. At the beginning of the exercise I hand out the decision sheets and instructions, read the instructions aloud, and then every couple of minutes change the output prices in three different periods (which results in a different number of permits demanded in each period). Once most students have filled in their sheets, I go over the correct numbers and show an Excel sheet that highlights why the decisions by both groups are the same, but also how the windfall gain for those who received their permits for free is reflected in the higher "earnings"—the difference in earnings is exactly equal to the number of permits given for free times the (fixed) permit price, independent of how

Table 8.3a   Decision sheet when permits cost $3 each

		Period 1		
(1) Capacity unit	(2) Price (at which product can be sold)	(3) Fuel cost	(4) Permits used (1 permit needed for each capacity unit operated)	(5) Price − fuel costs − permit costs (0 if no permit used)
1st	$	$1	0 or 1	
2nd	$	$3	0 or 1	
3rd	$	$5	0 or 1	

Sum of price–cost difference for units operated:_____

Total earnings for the production period:_____

Table 8.3b   Decision sheet when permits are given free of charge

		Period 1		
(1) Capacity unit	(2) Price (at which product can be sold)	(3) Fuel cost	(4) Permits used (1 permit needed for each capacity unit operated)	(5) Price − fuel costs (0 if no permit used)
1st	$	$1	0 or 1	
2nd	$	$3	0 or 1	
3rd	$	$5	0 or 1	

Sum of price–cost difference for units operated:_____

Earnings on unused permits sold at $3 each:_____

Total earnings for the production period:_____

many permits are actually being used. In lower-level classes I also show how one can derive a supply curve for the final product by looking at the production decisions given the three different output prices.

To illustrate, I post here the two decision sheets for one period as Tables 8.3a and 8.3b. The electronic appendix for this experiment contains the instructions, the two full decision sheets, the Excel sheet, and a list of simple homework questions.

Asymmetric Information (Market for Lemons)

This experiment deals with the lemons problem, and I employ it sometimes in an ENR class to illustrate the need for harmonized and credible third-party eco-labels. The paper from which this experiment is taken, Holt and Sherman

(1999), is motivated by the lemons problem for experience goods, goods that suffer *ex ante* from an information asymmetry between sellers and buyers, which is resolved *ex post* with the consumption of this good. With a couple of small twists, however, it can also be used for credence goods, goods that suffer even *ex post* from information asymmetries, such as environmental goods like "dolphin-safe tuna" or "organically-produced food" (for a recent discussion of credence good labeling for environmental goods, see Sheldon, 2017). It is one of the most entertaining and discussion-inspiring classroom experiments I use, and sometimes I conduct it at that point in a semester when I notice that the energy in the classroom is gradually decreasing.

In the basic set-up several sellers set a price and a "quality grade" (1, 2 or 3), which are posted on a board; a good of a higher grade is costlier to produce for the seller but has a higher value for the buyer. Buyers are then asked sequentially, which seller's offer they would like to accept. Since the maximum quantity buyers demand is less than what sellers are able to produce, there is pressure on sellers to charge prices for each grade that are not much higher than the sellers' marginal costs. Sellers have two units to sell, with the second unit having a slightly higher marginal cost than the first one; and buyers like to buy one unit. I usually assign three or four students to one seller group, and two students to one buyer group.

Figure 8.2 shows demand and supply curves for all three grades (in this case with five sellers who would like to sell ten units and seven buyers; these numbers can be changed to three or four sellers and four to six buyers). As

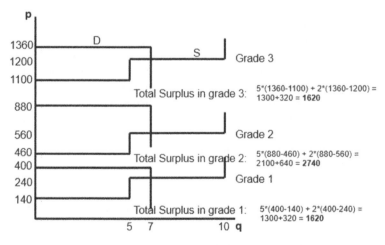

Figure 8.2   Demand and supply curves in the lemons market experiment

can be seen, the socially optimal grade is grade 2, since it generates the largest total surplus as measured by the difference between buyers' values and sellers' costs. In the first part of the experiment, when buyers can observe grades and prices, grade 2 is also the equilibrium grade. While in that part sellers engage in a cut-throat competition, buyers have to do only simple computations to see which seller's good is the most lucrative for them.

Once the market is reasonably close to its equilibrium combination of grade and prices, usually around period 4, the instructor makes a small but impactful change—sellers still choose price and grade on their record sheets, which are collected, but now only prices are written on the board. Buyers do not know which grade they are buying (they can choose not to buy anything). The result from this change is predictable—most sellers either choose prices that are consistent with the lowest grade (which buyers can then accept risk-free) or prices that are consistent with higher grades, but they actually choose grade 1. If buyers purchase the latter, they make a loss.

Because this experiment is primarily about experience goods, the grades of each sold unit are announced at the end of each period. Not surprisingly, after a few periods the sellers offer only goods with low grades and low prices. This works like clockwork, and often I stop right there even in an environmental economics class since this result provides already enough material for discussion about the value of labels. If the market already collapses like that when consumers learn the quality after each round, most students can imagine how bad the market functions when consumers can*not* learn the quality after each round; who knows if a dolphin-safe tuna really is dolphin-safe.

A couple of extensions are possible: the obvious one is turning the experience good into a credence good by not announcing any grades until the very end of the experiment. While the results would be straightforward, such a treatment could also trigger discussion about whether consumers will ever learn the quality of a credence good without labeling. As a next extension instructors could then allow sellers to create their own labeling scheme—sellers can come up with a costly but credible labeling scheme themselves.

The electronic appendix for this experiment contains instructions, decision sheets, an Excel sheet, PowerPoint slides and examples of homework assignments, all for the experiment with experience goods.

REFERENCES

Barrett, S. (1994), 'Self-enforcing international environmental agreements', *Oxford Economic Papers*, **46**, 878–894.
Barrett, S. (2007), *Why Cooperate? The Incentives to Supply Global Public Goods*, Oxford, UK: Oxford University Press.

Barrett, S. (2016), 'Coordination vs. voluntarism and enforcement in sustaining international environmental cooperation', *Proceedings of the National Academy of Sciences*, **113** (51), 14515–14522.

Barrett, S. and A. Dannenberg (2012), 'Climate negotiations under scientific uncertainty', *Proceedings of the National Academy of Sciences*, **109** (43), 17372–17376.

Brown, T. and S. Kroll (2017), 'Avoiding an uncertain catastrophe: climate change mitigation under risk and wealth heterogeneity', *Climatic Change*, **141** (2), 155–166.

Burton-Chellew, M.A., C. El Mouden and S.A. West (2016), 'Conditional cooperation and confusion in public-goods experiments', *Proceedings of the National Academy of Sciences*, **113** (5), 1291–1296.

Burtraw, D., J. Goeree, C.A. Holt, E. Myers, K. Palmer and W. Shobe (2009), 'Collusion in auctions for emission permits: an experimental analysis', *Journal of Policy Analysis and Management*, **28** (4), 672–691.

Carrattini, S., S. Levin and A.Tavoni (2019), 'Cooperation in the climate commons', *Review of Environmental Economics and Policy*, **13** (2), 227–247.

Chamberlain, E.H. (1948), 'An experimental imperfect market', *Journal of Political Economy*, **56** (2), 95–108.

Chen, D., M. Schonger and C. Wickens (2016), 'OTree—an open-source platform for laboratory, online, and field experiments', *Journal of Behavioral and Experimental Finance*, **9**, 88–97.

Cherry, T.L., S. Kroll and J.F. Shogren (2007). *Environmental Economics, Experimental Methods*, Oxfordshire, UK: Routledge Publishing.

Cherry, T.L., D.M. McEvoy and H. Sælen (2017), 'Conditional cooperation and cultural worldviews', *Economics Letters*, **158**, 51–53.

Cherry, T.L., S. Kallbekken, S. Kroll and D.M. McEvoy (2013), 'Cooperation in and out of markets: an experimental comparison of public good games and markets with externalities', *Economics Letters*, **120** (1), 93–96.

Fischbacher, U. (2007), 'Z-tree: Zurich toolbox for ready-made economic experiments', *Experimental Economics*, **10** (2), 171–178.

Fischbacher, U., S. Gächter and E. Fehr (2001), 'Are people conditionally cooperative? Evidence from a public goods experiment', *Economics Letters*, **71** (3), 397–404.

Goodstein, E.S. and S. Polasky (2017), *Economics and the Environment* (8th ed.), Hoboken, NJ, USA: Wiley Publishing.

Hanemann, W.M. (1991), 'Willingness to pay and willingness to accept: how much can they differ?', *American Economic Review*, **81** (3), 635–647.

Hanley, N., J.F. Shogren and B. White (2007), *Environmental Economics: In Theory and Practice* (2nd ed.), London, UK: Red Globe Press.

Hanley, N., J.F. Shogren and B. White (2019), *Introduction to Environmental Economics* (3rd edn), Oxford, UK: Oxford University Press.

Hirshleifer, J. (1983), 'From weakest-link to best-shot: the voluntary provision of public goods', *Public Choice*, **41**, 371–386.

Holt, C.A. (1996), 'Classroom games: trading in a pit market', *Journal of Economic Perspectives*, **10** (1), 193–203.

Holt, C.A. (2019), *Markets, Games, and Strategic Behavior* (2nd edn), Princeton, NJ, USA: Princeton University Press.

Holt, C. and R. Sherman (1999), 'Classroom games: a market for lemons', *Journal of Economic Perspectives*, **13** (1), 205–214.

Holt, C., E. Myers, M. Wråke, S. Mandell and D. Burtraw (2010), 'Teaching opportunity cost in an emissions permit experiment', *International Review of Economic Education*, **9** (2), 34–42.

Horowitz, J.K. and K.E. McConnell (2002), 'A review of WTA/WTP studies', *Journal of Environmental Economics and Management*, **44** (3), 426–447.

Kanter, J. (2008), 'EU carbon trading systems brings windfall for some, with little benefit to climate', *New York Times*, December 9, 2008, https://www.nytimes.com/2008/12/09/business/worldbusiness/09iht-windfall.4.18536167.html.

Knetsch, J.L. and J.A. Sinden (1984), 'Willingness to pay and compensation demanded: experimental evidence of an unexpected disparity in measures of value', *Quarterly Journal of Economics*, **99** (3), 507–521.

Kocher, M., T.L. Cherry, S. Kroll, R.J. Netzer and M. Sutter (2008), 'Conditional cooperation on three continents', *Economics Letters*, **101** (3), 175–178.

Kolstad, C.D. (2010), *Environmental Economics* (2nd edn), Oxford, UK: Oxford University Press.

Kroll, S. and J. Suter (2017), 'Introduction to the special issue: experiments on environmental and natural resource policies', *Strategic Behavior and the Environment*, **7** (1–2), 1–7.

Lin, P.-H., A.L. Brown, T. Imai, J.T. Wang, S.W. Wang and C.F. Camerer (2020), 'Evidence of general economic principles of bargaining and trade from 2,000 classroom experiments', *Nature Human Behavior*, **4**, 917–927.

List, J.A. and M.K. Price (eds) (2013), *Handbook on Experimental Economics and the Environment*, Cheltenham, UK and Northampton, MA, USA: Edward Elgar Publishing.

Lusk, J.L. and J.F. Shogren (2007), *Experimental Auctions: Methods and Applications in Economic and Marketing Research*, Cambridge, UK: Cambridge University Press.

Marwell, G. and R. Ames (1981), 'Economists free ride, does anybody else? Experiments on the provision of public goods', *Journal of Public Economics*, **15**, 295–310.

Messer, K.D., and J.J. Murphy (2010), 'Foreword: special issue on experimental methods in environmental, natural resource, and agricultural economics', *Agricultural and Resource Economics Review*, **39** (2), iii–vi.

Ostrom, E. (2000), 'Collective action and the evolution of social norms', *Journal of Economic Perspectives*, **143**, 137–158.

Ostrom, E. (2010), 'Polycentric systems for coping with collective action and global environmental change', *Global Environmental Change*, **20**, 550–557.

Phaneuf, D.J. and T. Requate (2017), *A Course in Environmental Economics: Theory, Policy, and Practice*, Cambridge, UK: Cambridge University Press.

Plott, C.R. (1983), 'Externalities and corrective policies in experimental markets', *Economic Journal*, **93** (369), 106–127.

Randall, A. and J.R. Stoll (1980), 'Consumer's surplus in commodity space', *American Economic Review*, **71** (3), 449–457.

Roth, A.E. and M.W.K. Malouf (1979), 'Game-theoretic models and the role of information in bargaining', *Psychological Review*, **86**, 574–594.

Sandler, T. (1997), *Global Challenges: An Approach to Environmental, Political and Economic Problems*, Cambridge, UK: Cambridge University Press.

Sheldon, I.M. (2017), 'Certification mechanisms for credence attributes of foods: does it matter who provides diagnosis?', *Annual Review of Resource Economics*, **9**, 33–51.

Shogren, J.F., S.Y. Shin, D.J. Hayes, and J.B. Kliebenstein (1994), 'Resolving differences in willingness to pay and willingness to accept', *American Economic Review*, **84** (1), 255–270.

Smith, V.L. (1962), 'An experimental study of competitive market behavior', *Journal of Political Economy*, **70**, 111–137.

Willig, R. (1976), 'Consumer's surplus without apology', *American Economic Review*, **66** (4), 589–597.

Wråke, M., E. Myers, D. Burtraw, S. Mandell and C. Holt (2010), 'Opportunity cost for free allocations of emissions permits: an experimental analysis', *Environmental and Resource Economics*, **46**, 331–336.

9. Teaching environmental and natural resource economics with research projects

John C. Whitehead

For many years I taught environmental and resource economics in the traditional lecture format. As I gained experience conducting research and, sometimes, applying research results in a policy context I began to realize that the relationships among economic outcomes and exogenous factors that we draw shifting lines for and the little number examples we provide are based on years and years of my own and others' empirical research. I began trying to integrate research projects into my courses in an attempt to get students to realize this as well and, hopefully, gain a deeper understanding of the theoretical relationships. There is a large literature on the benefits of undergraduate research as an activity undertaken outside the classroom (DeLoach et al. 2012; Henderson 2016; Hoyt and McGoldrick 2017a, 2017b). Many of the activities described in this literature are geared towards advanced students or as a semester-long activity. The activities described in this chapter can be implemented as a smaller component of a course and are appropriate for the average student (Henderson and Kose 2019).

At Appalachian State University in North Carolina we teach two environmental and resource economics courses. The lower level course has no prerequisite and draws students from across campus. These may be students taking the course as a general education elective or those who are majoring in environmental economics, environmental geology or sustainable development. Sustainable business minors are also required to take the course. This course ranges from 30 to 75 students. The second course is dual listed at the senior and graduate levels. Appalachian State does not have a graduate program in economics, the graduate students are typically from the sustainable MBA concentration, public administration or data analytics programs. This course has a prerequisite of microeconomics principles or the lower level environmental and resource economics course. Students enrolled in the upper level course have a wide range of empirical backgrounds from little or no training in statistics to those having taken graduate level cross-section and/or time-series regression courses. We also teach a third course on benefit–cost analysis in which environmental policy is the primary application. This is also dual listed for economics seniors and the same diverse group of graduate students. The latter two courses range in size from 10 to 25 students. I have also taught more than a dozen independent studies courses where students completed a research project and presented the results at undergraduate research conferences. This chapter is drawn from that experience.

In each of these contexts I have developed research assignments and activities that can be undertaken by students with little or no statistical background. Several of the research projects can be completed with graphical methods. Each of the assignments can also be extended to more advanced statistical techniques. In this chapter we limit the empirical analysis to ordinary least squares regression, but instructors of economics graduate courses can easily adapt these to more advanced techniques.

The conduct of research at the undergraduate level is more effective if the results are presented in written or oral form. The problem is that it is difficult to assign term paper-length writing assignments in large classes due to the burden of grading the papers. It is also difficult to teach writing in these classes in addition to teaching environmental and resource economics principles. As an alternative, I have assigned abstracts as the writing component of the project (Marshall and Underwood 2019). Students are asked to write abstracts that would be appropriate for submission to be reviewed for potential presentation at an undergraduate research conference. A short abstract (200 words) is assigned in the lower level course and a longer abstract (750–1000 words) is assigned in the upper level course. I use the guides for writing abstracts from Appalachian State's Office of Student Research. In the smaller upper level classes I have also assigned research papers of research note or policy brief length (1000–2500 words). Of course, longer term papers may be the norm at other institutions.

In the lower level courses I devote about one class period to describing the assignment. This is broken up into two half-class periods. The first half-class period describes the data and analysis. Students conduct the analysis and turn in their answers as a graded assignment. The second half-class period discusses how to write the abstract and the context for a research abstract. This semester (Fall 2020) I have a 39 student section of the lower level course. Students will be given the choice of working on a contingent valuation method willingness to pay estimation project or one of the several Veconlab experiments conducted during the semester (with the students as the subjects). Both of these are described below. Students can choose to work alone or in pairs.

These research activities are based on currently available data that have been used in published research, available on the Internet or can be collected by students in classroom experiments or with convenience samples.[1] Many of the activities can be motivated by the idea of a replication study (Hamersmesh 2007; Duvendack et al. 2017). A replication study in economics can take two forms. The most straightforward is when an independent researcher uses data from a published study and attempts to reproduce the results of the study using identical (or simpler or more advanced) statistical methods. The second type is when a researcher collects similar data to determine if the results hold up in different circumstances or time periods. The exercises described in this chapter can follow either type of replication study.

A broad range of topics are covered related to valuation of public goods, environmental policy, and natural resource economics. For valuation topics we use data that can be collected as course projects or available from published studies. We rely mostly on laboratory experimental methods for applications in environmental policy. For natural resource topics we rely on data borrowed from other researchers or laboratory experiments. Experimental data can also be collected as an in-class student experience (Holt 2003) and then re-purposed for the research project. In the rest of this chapter I describe research activities that I have implemented in some detail and then cover some others that I have considered more briefly. For each example, I work through the analysis to illustrate the range of effort that can be expected of students.

VALUATION OF PUBLIC GOODS

The allocation of public goods is a foundational topic taught in environmental and resource economics courses. A classroom exercise or problem set typically presents students with an individual demand curve for some measure of environmental quality or quantity (Q), $WTP = a - bQ$, where WTP is the marginal willingness to pay for Q. Individual demand is aggregated over n households and compared to a marginal cost function to find the optimal amount of environmental quality or quantity. Students typically find this to be an abstract problem. The typical instructor response is to explain how economists estimate WTP with revealed and stated preference methods. Then instructors might show the students some WTP from the empirical literature and explain how these estimates can be applied to value nonmarket environmental goods. This still may leave students perplexed about the details behind the estimates.

Contingent Valuation Method

One of the more accessible stated preference approaches is the contingent valuation method (CVM). The CVM is a survey approach to environmental valuation in which respondents are asked questions that reveal their value for changes in public goods. At a minimum, a CVM survey describes a public good to be valued, describes the proposed change in the good, describes a payment vehicle (e.g., a tax) describes a policy implementation rule (e.g., referendum voting) and asks a dichotomous choice question such as: "Would you vote in favor of a policy that would provide ΔQ at a cost of $\$A$?"

To make valuation of public goods more concrete it is useful to have students calculate their own willingness to pay estimate. Students could be instructed to conduct a literature review to find published studies that contain the necessary information (a frequency table with the percentage of votes in favor of a policy presented at each policy cost amount). Or, students could conduct their own CVM survey and data collection on-campus or in the community (Dickinson and Whitehead 2015; Henderson 2016).

With the dichotomous choice form of the CVM, survey respondents are asked whether they would be willing to pay a specific amount of money (A) for a change in the level of environmental quality or quantity (ΔQ). It is useful at this point to illustrate to students that total willingness to pay is the area underneath the marginal willingness to pay function. The typical empirical result is that the probability of a yes response falls as the amount of money increases. Given this sort of data, most undergraduate students can estimate willingness to pay with two nonparametric willingness to pay estimators known as the Turnbull (Haab and McConnell 1997) and Kriström (1990) estimators.

To illustrate these estimators, the dichotomous choice CVM data is graphed in probability and dollar amount space (see Figure 9.1). The Turnbull estimator is a lower bound on *WTP* in which a respondent's *WTP* is assumed to be equal to the sum of rectangles formed by the probability of a yes response (on the vertical axis) and the change in the dollar amount presented to respondents. The Kriström estimator is equal to the Turnbull plus the triangles above the rectangles. The triangle to the right of the highest bid can be found using the slope between the two highest bids. The triangle at the top of the survival curve can be found by assuming that 100 percent of respondents would agree to pay $0.

The data can be gathered by a literature search conducted by students and/ or the instructor could provide the research articles to students. An example of the necessary information is presented in Table 9.1. The numbers in Table 9.1 come from Carson et al. (2003) which is a study of the willingness to pay to avoid another Exxon Valdez type oil spill and one of the first to present the Turnbull estimate. Many dichotomous choice contingent valuation studies do not present this frequency table so students may need to spend some effort on this task if the articles are not provided to them (a short list of articles and data sets are provided in Appendix A on the companion website, https://osf.io/ dujas/).

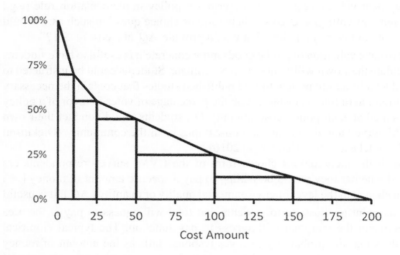

Figure 9.1   *Turnbull and Kriström survival curves*

Table 9.1   *Turnbull and Kriström estimators with dichotomous choice CVM data*

Cost amount	Yes response	Turnbull rectangles	Kriström triangles
$0	100%		
$10	67.42%	$6.74	$1.63
$30	51.69%	$10.34	$1.57
$60	50.59%	$15.18	$0.17
$120	34.24%	$20.54	$4.91
$246	0%		$21.57
		$\sum = \$52.80$	$\sum = 29.85$

The Turnbull willingness to pay estimate is: $WTP = 0.6742 \times 10 + 0.5169 \times (30 - 10) + 0.5059 \times (60 - 30) + 0.3424 \times (120 - 60) = \$52.80$. The Turnbull estimate presented in Carson et al. (2003) is $53.60 which is due to the use of a follow up "double bounded" valuation question. A simple replication exercise is to estimate the Kriström willingness to pay estimate. The replication question is "How does WTP change if a different estimation approach is used?"[2] To motivate this in a more practical sense, the instructor can describe to students the practice of sensitivity analysis in benefit–cost analysis. For example, suppose the aggregate benefit associated with a household *WTP* value is not greater than the cost. Since the Turnbull is the lower bound estimate, would this result change with an estimate that is higher? The triangles in the Kriström estimator sum to $29.85 with $246 used as the cost amount that drives the yes probability to zero (this is found with the slope between the two highest cost amounts presented in the survey). The Kriström *WTP* is equal to $82.64 which can be used to motivate the importance of replication in economics. Most of the difference in the Turnbull and Kriström estimators is due to the truncation at the highest cost amount, which is a typical practice.

There are several potential extensions to this assignment for instructors who would like to move beyond the geometric estimation of willingness to pay. Instructors who would like to use actual data and more advanced statistics can estimate the model with ordinary least squares regression (i.e., the linear probability model).[3] The result of this regression analysis is $\Pr(yes) = 0.657 - 0.00268 \times Cost$. The willingness to pay estimate is the area of the triangle below the regression line equal to $80.56, which is similar to the Kriström estimate. The estimate of the cost amount that drives the probability of a "yes" response to zero is $245. In a benefit–cost analysis, instructors could point out that the parametric estimate might be the best-case analysis and sensitivity analysis would be used with the lower bound Turnbull.

A more advanced assignment would ask students to test the CVM data for scope effects (i.e., "more is better"). This would involve data from an article that estimates more than one willingness to pay amount with differences being an increase in the environmental quantity or quality. Several examples of articles with readily available data and the simple calculations necessary to estimate the scope effect can be found in Whitehead (2016). Data from the Deepwater Horizon CVM study is described in Appendix B and located in the companion website (Bishop et al. 2017).

If the class project involves data collection and the students are faced with the small sample problem it might be best to ask a "payment card" question. With a payment card question, respondents are asked directly how much they are willing to pay and offered a number of suggestions. For example: "What is the maximum tax amount that you would be willing to pay to achieve ΔQ?" with $5, $10, $15, $20, $25, and so on listed for respondents to choose from. Willingness to pay can be estimated with measures of central tendency (e.g., mean, median), where the midpoint method is used to convert interval to continuous data, instead of nonparametric and parametric estimators.

Travel Cost Method

The travel cost method (TCM) is an approach to measure the value of recreation trips. It is often used to estimate the benefits of public recreational areas (e.g., parks) and recreational activities (e.g., fishing, hiking). There are several forms of the TCM but the single-site TCM is the most straightforward to teach. With this version, a recreation demand curve is the relationship between recreation trips to a site and the travel costs required to get there. The travel cost is an increasing function of distance traveled. In Figure 9.2 the recreation demand curve is illustrated with $n = 53$ visitors to Wrightsville Beach, NC. This basic empirical relationship is robust with revealed preference data and sure not to disappoint students (who can be disappointed when they collect data and find that the expected statistical relationships are just not there). In the rest of this section we describe several data collection and estimation activities that begin with the graphical "eyeball test" and moves on to simple regression.

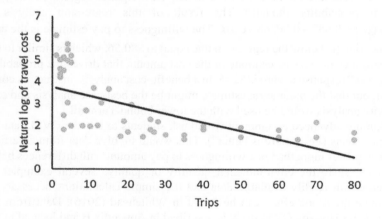

Figure 9.2   Travel cost demand scatter plot and demand curve

There are several approaches that can be used to estimate a travel cost demand curve. One of these does not involve travel costs at all but adapts insights from early versions of the CVM called contingent behavior (another stated preference approach). Contingent behavior scenarios pose hypothetical questions and ask about changes in behavior in these different situations. In this approach data can be gathered in two or three scenarios. The first is the status quo, the second is a scenario with improved or worsening quality (to shift the demand curve) and the third scenario involves some sort of increased cost of access.

A winter sports (i.e., skiing) questionnaire is provided in Appendix B in the companion website. Respondents are first asked for their revealed preference trips to three local ski areas the sum of which is x_1. Second, they are asked how many trips they would take with a higher access cost (x_2). Third, they are asked stated preference questions about how many trips they would take in a climate change scenario (x_3, rising temperatures and reduced snowfall). Three versions of the survey were used which presented increased cost as $25, $10,or $50. Each student in this large class of about 75 students was asked to conduct at least five interviews (these could be in-person or paper and pencil). Some asked friends while some conducted intercept interviews at the student union and other locations on campus. In a sample of $n = 37$ the mean trips over the three questions were $\bar{x}_1 = 7.81$, $\bar{x}_2 = 5.68$ and $\bar{x}_3 = 4.11$.[4] Implicitly the average cost of a trip is the sum of the travel cost and the entrance fee. For this exercise it is not necessary to know the magnitude of the baseline cost.

A graphical representation of these data provides some visual guidance for the subsequent analysis. In Figure 9.3 the three data points are illustrated with large dots. The squares are choke prices estimated with linear interpolation. To provide statistical rigor to the analysis, students can be taught the paired sample t-test. In this test the differences in a variable over a single observation are determined (e.g., $d = x_1 - x_2$) and the t-test for the difference is a test for differences in the two trip measures $(t = \bar{d} / \sqrt{\sigma / n})$. This test is easily conducted with the data analysis add-in in MS Excel. With these data there are statistically significant differences between baseline trips and the trips with the cost increase $(t = 5.32)$ and between baseline trips and trips with the quality change $(t = 9.66)$.

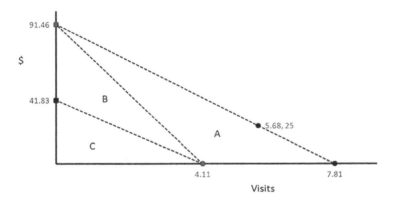

Figure 9.3   *Recreation demand curves estimated from three mean visit estimates*

Considering just the change in trips with the quality change, this can be used in a benefit transfer exercise. Students could be asked to conduct a literature search for a journal article that estimates the value of a recreation trip that is suitable for their local case study. Or, students could be pointed to a comprehensive source that compiles estimates of the value of a range of activities (e.g., Rosenberger and Loomis 2001).[5] The mean of the consumer surplus per trip of downhill skiing from Rosenberger and Loomis (2001) is $28 ($1996). The value of the reduced number of trips (i.e., cost) would be $104 = \$28 \times (7.81 - 4.11)$ per person. Aggregate benefits would be equal to the product of $104 and the relevant population (estimation of which is also an interesting student exercise).

Students could also be asked to estimate a linear recreation demand curve with these three sample means, estimate consumer surplus and conduct welfare analysis. Only basic geometry is needed. Using the formulas in MS Excel for the slope and intercept, the baseline inverse demand curve is $P = 91.46 - 11.71 \times Visits$.[6] The total consumer surplus is $357 = 0.5 \times 91.46 \times 7.81$ (Area A + B + C in Figure 9.2). Consumer surplus per trip is $46 = \$357 \div 7.81$.

Assuming that the choke price stays constant, the demand curve with the quality change is $P = 91.46 - 22.25 \times Visits$. Instructors can explain that estimates like these are used to present stylized demand models in textbooks. The total consumer surplus is $188 = 0.5 \times 91.46 \times 4.11$ (Area B + C in Figure 9.2) and the consumer surplus per trip is $46 = \$188 \div 4.11$. The value of the reduced number of trips (i.e., cost of climate change) would be $170 = \$46 \times (7.81 - 4.11)$. Assuming a parallel shift of demand, the inverse demand curve with the quality change is $P = 48.13 - 11.71 \times Visits$. The total consumer surplus is $98.91 = 0.5 \times 48.13 \times 4.11$ (Area C in Figure 9.3) and the consumer surplus per trip is $24 = \$99 \div 4.11$. A useful discussion can be had around which assumption about the choke price is most appropriate (does the consumer surplus per trip stay constant after a quality change?) or if both estimates should be used in sensitivity analysis. In other words, which estimate is closest to the benefit transfer estimate from Rosenberger and Loomis (2001)?

More advanced projects can collect similar data in the community. In an ongoing project one of my benefit–cost analysis classes collected visitor email addresses at the then under construction Rocky Knob Mountain Bike Park. The survey asked for current visits with the existing 2.8 miles of trail and visits with a completely developed park with 8 miles of trail. The means of the trips and round-trip travel cost ($0.25 per mile) variables are $\overline{Trips} = 48.61$ and $\overline{TC} = 10.05$. A simple regression model estimated on these data is $Trips = 56.42 - 0.78 \times TC$ (see Figure 9.4). Evaluating the linear demand model at the means, the consumer surplus over the mean number of trips is

$1767 = 0.5 \times 48.61 \times 72.67$, and the consumer surplus per trip is $36 = \$1767 \div 48.61$. Instructors should be sure to note how simple regression estimates like these compare to consumer surplus per trip estimates in the economics literature (e.g., Rosenberger and Loomis, 2001).

SUMMARY OUTPUT

Regression Statistics	
Multiple R	0.312
R Square	0.097
Adjusted R Square	0.081
Standard Error	49.836
Observations	57

ANOVA

	df	SS	MS	F	Significance F
Regression	1	14741.08	14741.08	5.94	0.02
Residual	55	136600.43	2483.64		
Total	56	151341.51			

	Coefficients	Standard Error	t Stat	P-value	Lower 95%	Upper 95%
Intercept	56.42	7.34	7.69	0.000	41.71	71.12
TC	-0.78	0.32	-2.44	0.018	-1.41	-0.14

Figure 9.4   MS Excel regression output with Rocky Knob data (dependent variable is visits)

Over the years, these data supported several student research papers in environmental, senior seminar, and independent study classes. In 2014 we surveyed Rocky Knob visitors to see how many visits they made to the completed park to see if the trips they said they would take were similar to the trips they actually took. This resulted in an independent study and a published article (Atkinson and Whitehead 2015). During the summer of 2019 an independent study student collected email addresses on site and an internet survey collected data on visits and travel costs. These data resulted in a revealed preference consumer surplus per trip estimate, and combined with actual visits, allowed the conduct of an ex-post benefit–cost analysis. More extensive community-based research projects such as this can provide much raw data for students over time (Henderson 2016).[7]

Yet, sometimes the outcomes of these are not always as hoped. In Whitehead et al. (2016) we conduct a benefit–cost analysis using data from a student project that collected email addresses for an Internet survey. The Internet survey asked questions about recreation visits under different cost and greenway extension scenarios. Given the nature of the recreation area, a local park without an access fee, there was limited variation in travel costs so the contingent behavior scenarios included changes in travel time (due to traffic, etc.). Even then, multiple regression analysis does not lead to a statistically significant coefficient on the travel cost coefficient. Additional effort was required in order to develop a fixed effects panel data model that solved the problem. I was lucky that the independent study student was statistically advanced and not discouraged by the limitations of ordinary least squares.

Extensions

More advanced students can be encouraged to use data from published articles to replicate results using the level of statistics that they are comfortable with (there is nothing wrong with simple regression models in terms of teaching economics). Primary CVM and TCM data is available for download in Whitehead (2015). More and more journals are requiring that data be shared for replication purposes. Instructors and students should check the journal websites for available data sets.

Collecting primary data has been revolutionized by the Internet to where it is affordable and quick. An MTurk survey could cost as little as $100 (MTurk workers will complete a survey for $0.75 or less) and produce useable data within a week. Students have also been collecting data on social media. A tweet could generate a usable convenience sample. A $100 advertisement on Facebook might generate a sample of the general population of $n = 100$ in a week. Marketing firms that maintain panels for business and academic research can be used if the research budget is more substantial (say $1500 minimum for $n = 400$). These samples are generally better than MTurk or Facebook. And if you spend that much money the research may be publishable so survey design might be the instructor's role with the class serving as a focus group. And make sure you have checked with your Internal Review Board (IRB) for human subjects' approval if these student projects will be used beyond the classroom.

Another nonmarket valuation method is hedonic pricing where housing prices are correlated with environmental amenities. In the past I've had a capstone student explore the effect of Blue Ridge Mountain views on property values in Blowing Rock, NC. Using data collected from the MLS (in a small sample of $n = 100$), a view might add $200,000 to a $400,000 house. In an independent study, another student estimated the effect of hemlock woolly adelgid damage (Sullivan and Whitehead 2017) on local property values with data from the county tax assessor. This study found that there was no effect for locals but second homes were bought at a discount. Other students have used the data from Bin et al. (2011) and Schwarz et al. (2017) to estimate the impact of sea level rise and brownfields on household prices in various projects. These data are very useful in demonstrating the basic empirical relationship that environmental amenities affect behavior in markets, But, developing these more complex valuation models and willingness to pay estimates is likely too difficult for undergraduates.

ENVIRONMENTAL POLICY

Many students come to the environmental and resource economics course as non-majors with only one microeconomics course or even no economics background. This can make teaching incentive-based environmental policy instruments a challenge (even students who have an economics background may find it challenging). Incentive-based policies include pollution taxes and tradeable pollution permits (i.e., cap-and-trade). With a pollution tax, buyers or sellers face a per unit charge on an economic activity that generates a negative externality. With a tradeable pollution permit, a cap on the total amount of emissions is set.

Experimental economics is a good way to help develop a better understanding of many of these basic concepts. Experiments can be conducted in the classroom with paper and pencil (see Kroll, Chapter 8 in this volume) or using simple props such as playing cards (Holt 1996; Anderson and Stafford 2000). Many of these classroom games can be expanded to collect experimental economics data that can be used in a research context. I have been using the Veconlab suite of online experiments extensively over the years for teaching purposes (Holt 2003).[8]

These experiments are highly useful in an environmental and resource economics course without a microeconomics prerequisite. The challenge in these courses is always whether and/or how to teach supply and demand as background for market-based environmental policy (Caviglia-Harris 2003; Lewis 2011). The first two Veconlab experiments described below help teach demand and supply relationships by putting students in the roles of buyers and sellers. In the demand experiment a pollution tax can be imposed. The supply experiment illustrates the similarities between cap-and-trade and a pollution tax. These experiments can then be followed by the call market experiment which implements a uniform price double auction. It helps if students are taught some auction theory before placing them in this experiment. One version of the call market allows imposition of a tax which produces a result illustrating a tax on pollution.

Output Tax

The most basic environmental policy taught in microeconomics and environmental economics courses is the Pigouvian output tax. The tax charged to the producer shifts the supply curve upwards, since it increases the cost of production, and price rises and output falls. Thus, the negative pollution externality is internalized into the market.

The Veconlab "demand" experiment is one of the simpler experiments in the suite and is useful for introducing students to the software. In the demand experiment, students are provided with marginal values for a product and choose how much to purchase (between 0 and 3 units). The preset marginal values are $18, $12, and $6 for consumption of units 1, 2 and 3. Random prices are presented and students choose whether to purchase the unit or not. During the experiment students can be presented with a tax on their purchase (obviously, instructors should make clear that the product generates pollution). The preset tax is $4.

In an experiment conducted with a large class ($n = 64$) asynchronously, the preset experiment was used. The data can be analyzed by students in a number of ways. First the eyeball test can be applied by finding the average consumption in each round and plotting this by round. In Figure 9.5 it is clear that consumption falls with the tax. The solid lines are the means of consumption during the treatments. The dots are the means within each round (this graph is produced using MS Excel and the raw data). Veconlab generates a step function demand graph during and after the experiment which can be used for debriefing without, in my experience, detracting from the research experience of producing the time series chart. In rounds 1–10 average consumption is 1.67. In rounds 11–20 average consumption falls to 1.46. The cyclical pattern of consumption across rounds in Figure 9.5 remains a mystery.

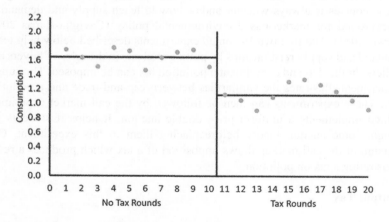

Figure 9.5   Results from the Veconlab "demand" experiment

Tests can also be conducted to determine if there are statistically significant differences across treatment (and if the treatment means are statistically different from the predictions, but this is more advanced). Students without a statistics background can be taught these tests (motivated by the research theme of the project). Assuming independence across treatments and rounds, the difference in means test is

$$t = \frac{\overline{x}_1 - \overline{x}_2}{\sqrt{\frac{s_1^2}{n_1} + \frac{s_2^2}{n_2}}},$$

where $\overline{x}$ are the means, s^2 is the sample variance and n is the sample size for treatments 1 and 2. The result of this test using the MS Excel data analysis plug-in is

$$t = 9.41 = \frac{1.65 - 1.12}{\sqrt{\frac{1.05}{640} + \frac{0.97}{640}}}$$

which is statistically significant at the $p = 0.01$ level (students might also be instructed in the rudiments of hypothesis testing).

Finally, advanced students can use these data in regression analysis. Ordinary least squares is sufficient to generate the basic result that the tax reduces consumption (with the assumption that each observation is independent). The estimated regression model is

$$Quantity = 3.12 - 0.14 \times Price - 0.51 \times Tax; R^2 = 0.57,$$

where Tax is equal to 1 for rounds 11 to 20. All of the t-statistics on the coefficient estimates are greater than 13 (in absolute value). Advanced students can use panel data regression methods to better test the hypothesis that the tax reduces consumption. With clustered standard errors the t-statistics are all greater than 10 (in absolute value). Of course, students without a statistics background can fit a similar model (with split samples) with the slope and intercept functions in MS Excel.

Pollution Permits

Holt et al. (2010) describes a pollution permits game that is useful for teaching opportunity costs. There are two versions of the opportunity cost experiment on the Veconlab online experimental software. The version used by Holt et al. (2010) and Wråke et al. (2010) is the "opportunity cost" experiment in the micro principles menu. Another version of this experiment is called "production cost" and is found in the "markets" menu of experiments. The production cost experiment allows the random assignment of price and cost parameters. Both can be conducted asynchronously or during class time.

In both versions of the experiment, research subjects decide whether to produce a unit of a product $(y = 1)$ or not produce $(y = 0)$. The payoff to producing a product is if the output price is greater than the sum of a fuel input cost and the cost of a required emissions allowance. In the more simple opportunity cost version of the experiment, the output price is randomly drawn from a uniform distribution: $p \sim U[1,9]$ with prices displayed in \$0.50 increments. There are three production decisions in each of 16 rounds. The fuel input costs are increasing with each unit of output: $c_1 = 1$, $c_2 = 3$, and $c_3 = 5$.

There are 16 rounds with treatment 1 in rounds 1–8 and treatment 2 in rounds 9–16. In treatment 1 two "free" emissions allowances are provided. If the free emissions allowance is not used then it can be sold in an allowance market. If the research subject wants to produce the third unit s/he must purchase an allowance from the market. In treatment 2 there are no free allowances. If the subject wants to produce a unit, then an allowance must be purchased from the market. The cost of an emissions allowance is a constant \$3.

In the "grandfathered" permits rounds (1–8) the cost of the first two allowances is implicit (i.e., an opportunity cost) and the cost of the third allowance is explicit. In rounds 9–16 the cost of each allowance is explicit. In each round the decision of whether to produce is:

$$Prob(y = 1) = Prob(p - c_x - 3 > 0), x = 1, 2, 3.$$

The teaching moment comes when the graphical results are revealed and students realize that the permit price in rounds 1–8 is an opportunity cost and should be treated as a real cost.

Since the experiment is asynchronous it can be assigned to be completed outside the classroom. I have used this assignment to provide data for differences in proportions test, to illustrate the research process and provide data for the research abstract assignment in both environmental courses, a business statistics course, and a managerial economics course for MBA students. In this chapter we'll use data from a recent class where 35 students completed the assignment.

For courses where teaching the statistical test is not feasible the "eyeball test" is often sufficient for a research project. Figure 9.6 shows that experimental subjects are over-producing in the first eight rounds due to a lack of recognition of the opportunity cost of the grandfathered permits. For students with a statistics background the difference in means test is

$$t = 4.74 = \frac{1.75 - 1.36}{\sqrt{\dfrac{0.86}{280} + \dfrac{1.00}{280}}}$$

(assuming independence across treatments and rounds), which is statistically significant at the p = 0.01 level in two-tailed test.

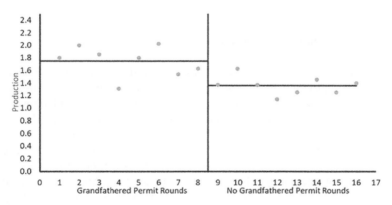

Figure 9.6   Results from the Veconlab "supply" experiment

More advanced students can use these data in regression analyses to conduct similar tests. At the most basic level these data provide information for estimation of a supply curve, $Q = f(P, D)$, where Q is quantity sold, P is output price, and D is a dummy variable for the tax treatment (rounds 9–16). Considering each round as an observation the sample size is $n = 560$.[9] The estimated regression model is:

$$Q = 0.561 + 0.241 \times P - 0.386 \times D; R^2 = 0.35$$

where each of the coefficients is statistically different from zero ($p < 0.05$). These results are as expected considering the typical mistake of ignoring the opportunity cost of grandfathered permits. As the price increases quantity sold increases and production is lower when permits are not grandfathered. Environmental economics students often suggest that free allocation of permits may lead to overproduction, but experience in this game, data analysis, and writing an abstract may convince them otherwise.

In all of these examples a single experiment can generate enough data for research projects for a large class. The instructor can randomly select a fraction of the full data set for individual students or each student can be assigned a single period in the non-treatment and treatment rounds (e.g., round 1 and round 11, round 1 and round 12, etc.). More advanced students can replicate the hypothesis tests of Wråke et al. (2010), who compares production with predictions for three hypotheses (including the effects of relative earnings). See Appendix B in the companion website for this analysis with the student experimental data.

Regional Greenhouse Gas Initiative

The Regional Greenhouse Gas Initiative (RGGI) is the first mandatory cap-and-trade program to address climate change in the United States (see http://www.rggi.org). The primary market is a permit auction and allowances (i.e., CO_2 permits) can then be sold in a secondary market. The Veconlab production cost experiment described above is one of several experiments designed to support the design of the RGGI market (Holt et al. 2007). The Veconlab "emissions permits auctions" experiments can be used to generate auction data under a variety of conditions. This experiment is useful to demonstrate that auctioned permits work just like a tax. A number of different types of analyses can be supported with different versions of this experiment. For example, Burtraw et al. (2011) conducts price discovery experiments over different auction mechanisms. Burtraw et al. (2009) allow for collusion in experimental auctions and allows students to gain a better understanding of market power. Goeree et al. (2010) extend the supply and opportunity cost experiment so that permit holders can participate in a secondary market. Students can gain a better understanding of how "free" grandfathered permits have an opportunity cost.

Murray and Maniloff (2015) analyze the factors that have affected emissions under RGGI. To support this analysis, they develop a demand and supply model for the primary (auction) and secondary markets. This model is used to inform an empirical analysis of the factors that affect CO_2 emissions. Students can use these data to compare emissions means before and after the implementation of RGGI, and conduct correlation analysis between emissions and other important variables. The more advanced students can conduct simple and multiple regression analysis to replicate the results.

RGGI conducts quarterly auctions and there are currently $n = 48$ auction clearing prices (https://www.rggi.org/Auctions/Auction-Results/Prices -Volumes). Following the theory in Murray and Maniloff (2015), students can examine the correlation of these prices with macroeconomic variables.

Public Goods

Many environmental goods and services have public characteristics and therefore many environmental issues are not immune to the free-rider problem. Experimental economics has a vast literature on the voluntary provision of public goods. This research is very informative for discussion of international environmental agreements such as the Montreal Protocol, the Kyoto Protocol and the Paris Climate Agreement. There are several ways to implement a public goods game during a semester-length course, from playing with a deck of cards (Holt and Laury 1997) to laboratory experiments (Hasson et al. 2010). All of these types of classroom experiments can provide data for a student project. These data, in general, can be analyzed sufficiently with the "eyeball" test as in Figures 9.4 and 9.5. The Veconlab "public goods" experiment can be used to demonstrate the basic free riding result (Chaudhuri and Paichayontyijit 2017). A typical series of rounds that have incentives to cheat on a voluntary agreement ultimately lead to declining contributions. Subsequent treatments can be used to illustrate how punishment (e.g., a tariff) can be used to enforce the international agreement.

NATURAL RESOURCE ECONOMICS

The two most basic natural resource economics models that are taught in undergraduate courses are the depletable resource model and the common pool resource model applied to the fishery. The major theoretical result from the depletable resource model is Hotelling's Rule – depletable resource prices should rise at the rate of interest over time, absent changes in supply and demand conditions. A large amount of research finds that Hotelling's Rule does not hold, largely because of market failures and changes in supply and demand conditions (Livernois 2009).

For a depletable resource project the student should take advantage of the data resources of the Energy Information Administration (EIA, http://www .eia.gov). The EIA has time series of prices for oil, natural gas, and other resources. Students should be instructed to be careful to download a series that has been inflation adjusted or to make these calculations themselves.

Students can first be shown the smooth Hotelling price path and then a graph of actual prices like Figure 9.7. A simple research project in this case is purely descriptive. The student assignment is to explain the events that have led to price fluctuations over time.

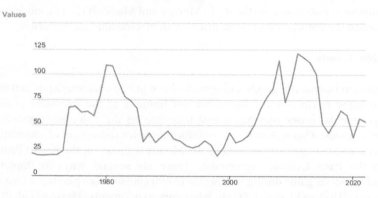

Figure 9.7   EIA short-term energy outlook, annual average imported crude oil price, July 2020

Students could use the data from Lee et al. (2006) and conduct a time-series analysis of prices for 11 depletable natural resources. Simple trend models can be fit with MS Excel to determine the growth rate. More ambitious students can attempt to add data to extend these time-series, if possible.

A recent issue of the *Energy Economics Journal* (August 2019) was devoted to replications. All of the papers in this issue of the journal provide the data used for the replication. A course with a focus on energy economics would find this special issue very useful. One of these papers examines the supply and demand shocks that affect oil prices (Kim and Vera 2019).

Common Pool Resources

The "tragedy of the commons" is one of the better-known natural resource models. Many students enter the classroom with some familiarity with it, perhaps by being exposed to Garrett Hardin's classic 1968 *Science* article on the topic in an environmental science or some other course (Hardin 1968). While there are plenty of stories (e.g., buffalo) and anecdotes, an empirically demonstrated tragedy is difficult to find. In the context of an unregulated commercial fishery, landings (i.e., catch or yield) first increase with effort and then, as the stock size falls, begin to decrease with additional effort. There is limited data on this relationship because commercial fishing activity has become heavily regulated and effort data (e.g., net "soak time," traps or trips) is difficult to gather and/or confidential.

However, the state of Maine has published lobster data that contains annual landings and the number of lobster traps, a well-defined unit of fishing effort.[10] The time period is from 1880 to 2019. The ordinary least squares regression model over 45 years from 1931 to 1975 is:

$$Pounds = 1.86 + 41.28 \times Traps - 19.89 \times Traps^2; R^2 = 0.71.$$

Each of the regression coefficients is statistically different from zero. When displayed graphically, the quadratic model illustrates the relationship that appears in almost every economics textbook (Figure 9.8). Instructors often fabricate parameters for the quadratic model when developing examples and problem sets. This model could be used instead and data could be simulated from these parameters for simple research projects. Students could also be encouraged to investigate different time periods, include price effects (measuring the total revenue curve), and other variables (water temperature). Students could interpret the economic significance of the parameters (i.e., marginal product). Simpler analyses could use the average product (pounds ÷ traps) and compare means over different time periods.

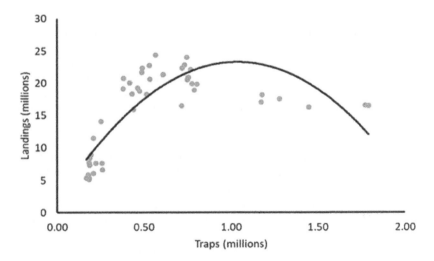

Figure 9.8   Maine lobster catch and effort (1931–1975)

An excellent case study on the commons problem is the golden crab fishery in Florida (Crosson et al. 2013). Annual landings and effort data for a short time-series are described in Crosson (2010). Monthly data is available and is useful for analyzing the landings/effort model in a fishery that is not overfished (i.e., the catch/effort function is not hill shaped).[11] Alternative measures of effort and time-periods associated with the discussion in Crosson et al. (2013) can be explored with regression analysis.

Veconlab also has a common pool resource experiment that is set up with a quadratic benefit function and a linear cost function. Participants tend to choose extraction rates based on their private benefits and costs which creates a negative externality. A second treatment can be used to increase the cost of extraction (e.g., a tax). The resulting data can be used to support an "eyeball test" of the pattern of responses (with less extraction and a more efficient outcome with the tax), differences in means, correlation and regression analyses as described above for the other Veconlab experiments.

One of the solutions offered by economists to the overfishing problem is creating markets for the rights to fish. This policy has various names such as individual transferable quotas (ITQs) or catch shares. ITQs have several purported beneficial outcomes such as price stability, increased safety and longer seasons. Brinson and Thunberg (2016) survey a number of ITQ programs in the U.S. and assess them empirically against the benefits described in the fishery management plan that led to their implementation. A spreadsheet data file provided in the companion website to the book contains the raw material to allow students to conduct their own replication tests of Brinson and Thunberg (2016). For example, the 95 percent confidence interval around the mean pre-ITQ Gulf of Mexico red snapper ex-vessel price is $3.66 and $4.10 ($n = 7$). These prices do not contain the benchmark, pre-ITQ price of $3.48 lending support to the notion that ITQs lead to higher prices by spreading catch over the season. There are a number of other tests that can be supported by these data.

The Florida Fish and Wildlife Conservation Commission provides a data download query webpage that allows for monthly landings (in pounds) and average price by species (make sure to adjust these prices for inflation).[12] Data such as these can be used to estimate the effect of landings on ex-vessel price. This allows for a more direct and rigorous test of the potential effect of an ITQ on red snapper ex-vessel price. The expectation is that in an unregulated fishery the race for fish will lead boats to bring fish to market as quickly as possible and this supply increase will decrease the price. With an ITQ, firms own their own quota and can smooth the catch across the season and avoid price crashes. A difference in means test and a simple regression of price on landings will provide an estimate of this effect. In the seven years before ITQs (2000–2006), the red snapper average monthly price was $3.33. In the seven years after ITQs (2007–2013), the red snapper average monthly price was $3.74. The difference in means is statistically significant ($t = 11.37$). In a price response regression over the pre-ITQ months, the coefficient on landings is negative and statistically significant. In the same regression but with post-ITQ data, the coefficient on landings is statistically significant but much smaller (i.e., monthly landings have a much smaller effect). While there are other explanations and more analysis is required, this result suggests that ITQs have had the intended price effect for red snapper in Florida.[13]

Finally, for courses that contain a water allocation component, Veconlab contains a "Tragedy of the Common Canal" experiment (Holt et al. 2012). The experiment provides for a number of treatments for the allocation of a water resource between upstream and downstream users: Coasian bargaining, auctions and fees. In my implementation of this experiment in the MBA class I found that Coasian bargaining increased efficiency from 80 percent to 88 percent and a uniform price auction increased efficiency from 78 percent to almost 98 percent (Figure 9.9). Again, the "eyeball test" can be used by students without any statistical background and the data can support statistical analyses.

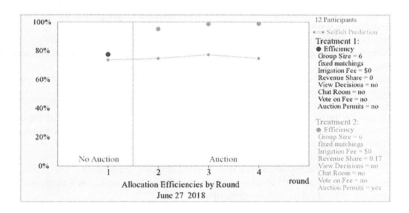

Figure 9.9   *Tragedy of the Common Canal Veconlab results graph*

CONCLUSIONS

In even the best taught lecture courses, students are often left wondering how economics is actually done. Elegant theories are presented and mastered but oftentimes the "what's next?" question is left unanswered. In this chapter

I have described a number of low opportunity cost research activities that may help to solidify several concepts in environmental and resource economics. The focus of this chapter is on in-class activities and small projects but each of these research approaches can be used for an out-of-the-classroom undergraduate research experience, independent study or practicum courses. All of these activities and projects have been field tested in my courses to varying degrees with perceived outcomes ranging from "not a total disaster" to "I should receive a teaching award for this." At the least, students will get a glimpse of the research process and, in my experience, this can lead to further student research which has known benefits.

NOTES

1. All of the data used or mentioned in this chapter is available at this book's companion website: https://doi.org/10.17605/OSF.IO/DUJAS.
2. See Whitehead (2017) for an example of a replication of the Kriström estimator.
3. Data can be reconstructed from frequency tables in journal articles if the sub-sample sizes are included. See Appendix A in the companion website for a short list of articles.
4. If the data collection effort is too great then simulated data can be generated in MS Excel as I've done here (since I can not find the full data set that was created by my students). In this example the means were based on a single student spreadsheet with $n = 5$ observations and 37 random numbers were pulled from a uniform distribution with $\bar{x} \pm 2$ as the endpoints for the three values.
5. See http://recvaluation.forestry.oregonstate.edu for the updated database.
6. Note that the slope and intercept MS Excel functions can be used instead of simple regression.
7. See Whitehead et al. (2014) for a non-environmental example of this type of community-based research project.
8. See http://Veconlab.econ.virginia.edu.
9. Of course, more rigorous analysis would account for the panel nature of the data.
10. Thanks to Lynne Lewis for the pointer to https://www.maine.gov/dmr/commercial -fishing/landings/index.html
11. Thanks to Scott Crosson for providing these data.
12. See https://public.myfwc.com/FWRI/PFDM/ReportCreator.aspx
13. See also Sun et al. (2019) who analyze the bluefin tuna sushi auction market and provide monthly data in their appendix.

REFERENCES

Anderson, L.R. and S.L. Stafford (2000), 'Choosing winners and losers in a classroom permit trading game', *Southern Economic Journal*, **67** (1): 212–219.

Atkinson, K. and J.C. Whitehead (2015), 'Predictive validity of stated preference data: Evidence from mountain bike park visits before and after trail system expansion', *Applied Economics Letters*, **22** (9): 730–733.

Bin, O., B. Poulter, C.F. Dumas, and J.C. Whitehead, (2011), 'Measuring the impact of sea-level rise on coastal real estate: A hedonic property model approach', *Journal of Regional Science*, **51** (4): 751–767.

Bishop, R.C., K.J. Boyle, R.T. Carson, D. Chapman, W.M. Hanemann, B. Kanninen, R.J. Kopp J.A. Krosnick, J. List, N. Meade, R. Paterson, S. Presser, V.K. Smith, R. Tourangeau, M. Welsh, J.M. Wooldridge, M. DeBell, C. Donovan, M. Konopka, and N. Scherer (2017), 'Putting a value on injuries to natural assets: The BP oil spill', *Science*, **356** (6335): 253–254.

Brinson, A.A. and E.M. Thunberg (2016), 'Performance of federally managed catch share fisheries in the United States', *Fisheries Research*, **179**: 213–223.

Burtraw, D., J. Goeree, C.A. Holt, E. Myers, K. Palmer, and W. Shobe (2009), 'Collusion in auctions for emission permits: An experimental analysis', *Journal of Policy Analysis and Management*, **28** (4): 672–691.

Burtraw, D., J. Goeree, C. Holt, E. Myers, K. Palmer, and W. Shobe (2011), 'Price discovery in emissions permit auctions', in R.M. Isaac and D.A. Norton (eds), *Experiments on Energy, the Environment, and Sustainability* (Research in Experimental Economics, Vol. 14), Emerald Group Publishing Limited, Bingley, pp. 11–36.

Carson, R.T., R.C. Mitchell, M. Hanemann, R.J. Kopp, S. Presser, and P.A. Ruud (2003), 'Contingent valuation and lost passive use: Damages from the Exxon Valdez oil spill', *Environmental and Resource Economics*, **25** (3): 257–286.

Caviglia-Harris, J.L.(2003), 'Introducing undergraduates to economics in an interdisciplinary setting', *Journal of Economic Education*, **34** (3): 195–203.

Chaudhuri, A. and T. Paichayontvijit (2017), 'On the long-run efficacy of punishments and recommendations in a laboratory public goods game', *Scientific Reports*, **7** (1): 1–8.

Crosson, S. (2010), 'Trends in the South Atlantic golden crab fishery', NOAA Technical Memorandum NMFS-SEFSC-608.

Crosson, S., T. Yandle, and B. Stoffle (2013), 'Renegotiating property rights in the Florida golden crab fishery', *International Journal of the Commons*, **7** (2): 521–548.

DeLoach, S.B., E. Perry-Sizemore, and M.O. Borg (2012), 'Creating quality undergraduate research programs in economics: How, when, where (and why)', *American Economist*, **57** (1): 96–110.

Dickinson, D.L. and J.C. Whitehead (2015), 'Dubious and dubiouser: Contingent valuation and the time of day', *Economic Inquiry*, **53** (2): 1396–1400.

Duvendack, M., R. Palmer-Jones, and W.R. Reed (2017), 'What is meant by "replication" and why does it encounter resistance in economics?' *American Economic Review*, 107 (5): 46–51.

Goeree, J.K., K. Palmer, C.A. Holt, W. Shobe, and D. Burtraw (2010), 'An experimental study of auctions versus grandfathering to assign pollution permits', *Journal of the European Economic Association*, **8** (2–3): 514–525.

Haab, T.C. and K.E. McConnell (1997), 'Referendum models and negative willingness to pay: Alternative solutions', *Journal of Environmental Economics and Management*, **32** (2): 251–270.

Hamermesh, D.S. (2007), 'Replication in economics', *Canadian Journal of Economics*, **40** (3): 715–733.

Hardin, G. (1968), 'The tragedy of the commons', *Science*, **162** (3859): 1243–1248.

Hasson, R., Å. Löfgren, and M. Visser (2010), 'Climate change in a public goods game: Investment decision in mitigation versus adaptation', *Ecological Economics*, **70** (2): 331–338.

Henderson, A. (2016), 'Growing by getting their hands dirty: Meaningful research transforms students', *Journal of Economic Education*, **47** (3): 241–257.

Henderson, A.B. and E. Kose (2019), 'The role of course-based undergraduate research experiences in extending transformative learning to all students', *Journal of Transformative Learning*, **5** (2).

Holt, C.A. (1996), 'Classroom games: Trading in a pit market', *Journal of Economic Perspectives*, **10** (1): 193–203.

Holt, C.A. (2003), 'Economic science: An experimental approach for teaching and research', *Southern Economic Journal*, **69** (4): 755–771.

Holt, C.A. and S.K. Laury (1997), 'Classroom games: Voluntary provision of a public good', *Journal of Economic Perspectives*, **11** (4): 209–215.

Holt, C.A., C.A. Johnson, C.A. Mallow, and S.P. Sullivan (2012), 'Water externalities: Tragedy of the common canal', *Southern Economic Journal*, **78** (4): 1142–1162.

Holt, C., E. Myers, M. Wråke, S. Mandell, and D. Burtraw (2010), 'Teaching opportunity cost in an emissions permit experiment', *International Review of Economics Education*, **9** (2): 34–42.

Holt, C.A., W. Shobe, D. Burtraw, K. Palmer, and J.K. Goeree (2007), *Auction Design for Selling CO2 Emission Allowances Under the Regional Greenhouse Gas Initiative*, Final Report to the New York State Energy Research Development Authority, October 26.

Hoyt, G.M. and K. McGoldrick (2017a), 'Promoting undergraduate research in economics', *American Economic Review*, **107** (5): 655–659.

Hoyt, G.M. and K. McGoldrick (2017b), 'Models of undergraduate research in economics: Advice from eight exemplary programs', *Journal of Economic Education*, **48** (4): 288–289.

Kim, G. and D. Vera (2019), 'Recent drivers of the real oil price: Revisiting and extending Kilian's (2009) findings', *Energy Economics*, **82**: 201–210.

Kriström, B. (1990), 'A non-parametric approach to the estimation of welfare measures in discrete response valuation studies', *Land Economics*, **66** (2): 135–139.

Lee, J., J.A. List, and M.C. Strazicich (2006), 'Non-renewable resource prices: Deterministic or stochastic trends?', *Journal of Environmental Economics and Management*, **51** (3): 354–370.

Lewis, L.Y. (2011), 'Environmental and natural resource economics: Teaching the non-major and major simultaneously', in G. Hoyt and K. McGoldrick (eds), *International Handbook on Teaching and Learning Economics*, Cheltenham, UK and Northampton, MA, USA: Edward Elgar Publishing.

Livernois, J. (2009), 'On the empirical significance of the Hotelling rule', *Review of Environmental Economics and Policy*, **3** (1): 22–41.

Marshall, E.C. and A. Underwood (2019), 'Writing in the discipline and reproducible methods: A process-oriented approach to teaching empirical undergraduate economics research', *Journal of Economic Education*, **50** (1): 17–32.

Murray, B.C. and P.T. Maniloff (2015), 'Why have greenhouse emissions in RGGI states declined? An econometric attribution to economic, energy market, and policy factors', *Energy Economics*, **51**: 581–589.

Rosenberger, R.S. and J.B. Loomis (2001), *Benefit Transfer of Outdoor Recreation Use Values: A Technical Document Supporting the Forest Service Strategic Plan* (2000 revision). Gen. Tech. Rep. RMRS-GTR-72. Fort Collins, CO: U.S. Department of Agriculture, Forest Service, Rocky Mountain Research Station.

Schwarz, P.M., G.L. Gill, A. Hanning, and C.A. Cox (2017), 'Estimating the effects of brownfields and brownfield remediation on property values in a new south city', *Contemporary Economic Policy*, **35** (1): 143–164.

Sullivan, B.J. and J.C. Whitehead (2017), 'The effect of evergreen loss on property values in Watauga County, NC', *Proceedings of the 4th Appalachian Research in Business Symposium*, Appalachian State University, March.

Sun, C.-H., F.-S. Chiang, D. Squires, A. Rogers, and M.-S. Jan (2019), 'More landings for higher profit? Inverse demand analysis of the bluefin tuna auction price in Japan and economic incentives in global bluefin tuna fisheries management', *PloS One*, **14** (8): e0221147.

Whitehead, J.C. (2015), 'Albemarle–Pamlico Sounds revealed and stated preference data', *Data in Brief*, **3**: 90–94.

Whitehead, J.C. (2016), 'Plausible responsiveness to scope in contingent valuation', *Ecological Economics*, **128**: 17–22.

Whitehead, J.C. (2017), 'Who knows what willingness to pay lurks in the hearts of men? A Rejoinder to Egan, Corrigan, and Dwyer', *Econ Journal Watch*, **14** (3): 346–361.

Whitehead, J., J. Lehman, and M. Weddell (2016), 'A benefit–cost analysis of the Middle Fork Greenway Trail', Working Paper (16-01. Department of Economics, Appalachian State University, Boone, NC.

Whitehead, J.C., D.S. Noonan, and E. Marquardt (2014), 'Criterion and predictive validity of revealed and stated preference data: The case of "Mountain Home Music" concert demand', *Economics and Business Letters*, **3**: 87–95.

Wråke, M., E. Myers, D. Burtraw, S. Mandell, and C. Holt (2010), 'Opportunity cost for free allocations of emissions permits: An experimental analysis', *Environmental and Resource Economics*, **46** (3): 331–336.

10. Teaching natural resource economics using policy briefs: ethics in pedagogy and practice

Leah Greden Mathews

INTRODUCTION

Though my training is primarily in environmental economics, one of the courses I was explicitly hired to teach was Natural Resource Economics. I have taught the course 23 times in the last 22 years and have enjoyed my primary audience, environmental studies students with a concentration in policy and management, more than I might have expected at the outset. While the course readings, activities, and assignments have shifted over the years, there have been two elements that have remained constant in each offering: an explicit policy focus in readings and discussion, and a major writing assignment that contributes a significant portion of the student's course grade.

Why the policy focus? I am an applied environmental economist by training and my initial interest in the discipline came through its pragmatism. Economics is everywhere, and can—and should, in my opinion—be used to improve decision making, whether it be individual, government, business, or community decisions. Thus, a focus on the policy implications of economics suits my training and dispositions; it also clearly (if implicitly) implies a professional responsibility or ethic. Given that environmental studies students with a concentration in policy and management take Natural Resource Economics (ECON 345), the policy focus was also a direct effort to help my students unlearn the perceptions they often bring to class: that economics (and some economists) is (are) evil, and capitalism is the root of all environmental and natural resource destruction. By helping my students understand that economics can help us make better decisions, and in fact can yield improved outcomes for natural resource management and sustainability, I hoped to win them over a bit.

And why require these students to write a policy document, instead of just relying on the reading and discussion of policy memos? The answer is fourfold. First, writing is an important skill for students to acquire and hone in college, for both personal (improves learning, communication) and professional reasons. As a first generation college student myself, I feel a significant personal commitment to ensure that my students are gaining skills and knowledge that will both enhance their learning and serve them as lifelong learners and professionals, regardless of which path they choose in life. Writing is one of those skills. Second, I teach at a small public liberal arts university and teaching writing is an important component of our shared pedagogy. A third reason I require a major writing assignment in ECON 345 is that while many faculty require research papers on campus, very few introduce students to other forms of professional writing such as a policy brief. Finally, the act of policy writing requires students to put themselves in the position of decision makers; this requires a level of professional empathy that is integral to developing a sense of proper professional conduct. Thus, I have identified a bit of a pedagogical niche: an economist who teaches a form of applied, professional writing to an audience of primarily non-majors.

LITERATURE REVIEW

Writing skills have long been identified as important for undergraduate learning and skill development. In his seminal book *Engaging Ideas: The Professor's Guide to Integrating Writing, Critical Thinking and Active Learning in the Classroom*, Bean (1996) notes that "writing is both a process of doing critical thinking and a product of communicating the results of critical thinking" (p. 4). Grauerholz (1999) is one of many teacher-scholars who provides an example of how to manage a writing-intensive course, noting that any course can benefit from the inclusion of writing assignments as long as they are specifically tailored to the learning goals and objectives of the course. Shaw (1999) points out that, "for the vast majority of students, whereas the substance of courses may become lost, outdated, or updated over time, reading, presentation, and writing skills will remain beneficial for a lifetime" (p. 157).

Similarly, the need for writing in economics classrooms has long been identified. Siegfried et al's 1991 review and assessment of the undergraduate economics curriculum argued for student opportunities to practice their economics skills and to "do economics." Among their recommendations was the encouragement of opportunities to develop skills through writing, noting that "writing clearly is the acid test for thinking like an economist" (p. 211). Cohen and Spencer (1993) report on the value of converting a "traditional" economics course to one that incorporates writing, noting a dramatic improvement in student writing, thinking, and arguing skills, commenting that the "modest effort" associated with incorporating writing was clearly outweighed by the benefits to students in their experience.

Simpson and Carroll (1999) report on a survey of Davidson College Department of Economics alumni designed to assess the value of different types of undergraduate writing experiences in the process of gaining skills in thinking like economists and professional preparation. Alumni respondents reported that evaluations of class readings and short papers were the most effective writing assignments in terms of preparation for their future careers, thus reinforcing the idea of tailoring writing assignments for specific student learning outcomes. McGoldrick's 2008 survey of undergraduate economics programs found that despite the labor-intensive nature of writing assignments, a majority of responding departments (70 percent) included a writing component in their curriculum (McGoldrick, 2008), suggesting an infusion of writing opportunities for undergraduate economics majors. Though most of the writing assigned in economics courses are most certainly research papers, case studies, and other economics-oriented writing forms, some instructors such as Goma (2014) argue that creative writing may also serve as an important tool for learning economics.

In the context of teaching natural resource economics, the contribution of the current chapter is two-fold. First, it provides detailed documentation on how one can teach both writing process and form in an applied, policy-oriented course. Second, it highlights the many ways that teaching policy is, in fact, an exercise in introducing ethics across the curriculum.

BACKGROUND: THE NATURAL RESOURCE ECONOMICS CLASS

I am privileged to teach in an economics department at a small university of approximately 3200 students with a large environmental studies program major. Because of the popularity of the Environmental Studies (ENVR) program, perennially one of the three most popular majors on campus, our department has for decades offered two separate courses, Environmental Economics & Policy and Natural Resource Economics. The courses have historically been populated by ENVR majors with a Policy & Management concentration since it was required for over two decades that they complete both these courses (along with Principles of Microeconomics and Principles of Macroeconomics). Over the years, we've added a Land Economics course, The Economics of Food, and, on occasion, I have the delight of teaching Economics of Waste. This means that in the Natural Resource Economics class, I have been able to focus on natural resource sustainability and resource management, leading students to understand the different realities and management implications for depletable, renewable, rechargeable, and recyclable resources. I typically book-end the course with discussions of sustainability writ large, and in the core of the course, I focus on resources by type, covering models of resource depletion, price paths, and policy implications. In any given year, I am sure to cover minerals, forests, water, and energy and assign Tietenberg and Lewis (2018) as the primary text supplemented by journal articles and case studies. The course has a prerequisite of Principles of Microeconomics though a significant majority of the students in the course are non-majors.

Student evaluation is multi-faceted, with two exams (each worth 20 percent of the course grade), classroom performance (15 percent), a Community Connections Assignment (10 percent), and policy brief (35 percent) comprising the assignments. Class size has varied from 11 (in years when multiple sections were offered and/or our university capped enrollment for writing-intensive courses) to 26. Most students in this junior-level course are either juniors or seniors. I tend to avoid using prepared slides, preferring instead a conversational approach to the material, adding outlines, graphs, and other important class details on the board as we flow through the day's topic. This allows me to build in a multi-directional information flow in the class, where student participation is highly encouraged and valued at any stage of their understanding of the material.

METHOD: THE POLICY BRIEF ASSIGNMENT

The Policy Brief (PB) assignment is introduced on the first day of class so that students may set their expectations for this course as a "writing" class. Their assignment is to: "Write a policy brief identifying how economics can be used to address a natural resource issue, problem, or concern." To ensure an economic (as opposed to political or other) lens is used I add: "Economics should be used to identify causes of and/or solutions to the problem as well as convey a welfare analysis of how involved parties will be affected by the policy solution you propose."

The primary output is a short policy brief, an "action memo" that is directed to a specific audience. The PB assignment assists students in achieving key course objectives and learning outcomes including the ability to:

(1)   identify and understand the principle concepts of microeconomic theory and analysis as they relate to natural resource economics,
(2)   apply the basic tools of economic analysis to natural resource issues,
(3)   discuss the strengths and limitations of the use of economics as a tool for natural resource decision making,
(4)   write a policy brief related to an issue or problem in natural resource economics and understand the importance of good communication in policy making.

Over the many years of teaching the course, the set of scaffolded assignments associated with the policy brief have shifted somewhat based on student feedback, my perceptions of whether the activities aligned well with desired student learning outcomes, and input from staff at the university's Writing Center. The assignments, which build on each other and class activities, have stabilized in the last five years to include:

- Multiple writing workshops, in and outside of class.
- Peer review of preliminary assignments.
- A proposal identifying the issue to be addressed and preliminary thoughts on the economic frame for how the issue/problem/concern has developed and can be resolved or improved.
- Two drafts of the policy brief (the first, peer reviewed in class, the second, instructor reviewed).
- Final policy brief.
- A short, lively presentation at our class "policy slam" during finals week.

In early years, the memo was to be no more than eight pages in length, though over time I came to realize that length was inappropriately long for this assignment. Some students had difficulty separating the writing of a policy brief or memo from a research paper, and I am committed to helping students learn how to improve both the support for and concision of their claims, and also offer models that may be useful for their post-graduation professional writing. Currently, the body of the policy brief must be no more than three pages; additional pages are required for a cover letter addressed to their audience, an Executive Summary, and References.

As with economists' choice of research questions, individual beliefs are important in the process students engage in during policy brief topic selection. Which natural resource management issues concern the student enough to learn about them? Which problems have presented researchers with incentive to study and add to the empirical literature demonstrating the need for improved policy? At the foundation of these issues is an ethical framework and belief together with a moral commitment to make at least some level of effort in addressing the problem. Motivating factors may include a concern for distributive or procedural justice, or, frequently in the case of natural resource and environmental concerns, a concern for intergenerational equity or fairness in resolving natural resource damage claims. When students identify a problem they believe is important, they seek opportunities where their voice may have an influence.

Further, in crafting their policy action statement the student author of the policy brief must recommend a *specific* action. This recommended path of action is based on either implicit or explicit values of the policy maker or advisor. I require students to document a rigorous defense of their policy using scientific evidence of the need for action and economic studies documenting the benefit of their recommended approach over its alternatives, and to include a brief welfare analysis.

The assignment requires students to direct their policy brief to an individual they believe should take action to support their recommended policy. Thus, they are asking their audience to make a choice, to take a stand, to forego some other action in order to see the policy move forward. This requires the expenditure of political and social capital, as well as financial resources, and requires trade-offs: something will not get done if the student's recommended policy is implemented, which illustrates a common saying among economists that "there is no such thing as a free lunch." In the brief I require students to outline a welfare analysis identifying the winners and losers that will arise from the policy change; inherent in this calculus is the sense that the winners' benefits will outweigh the losers' costs. The ethics of the recommendation are thus implicit in the methods I prescribe in the assignment.

The final element of the assignment in which ethics are prevalent comes into play if students choose to pursue a community-engaged topic. In these instances, it is required that students adopt a sincere responsiveness to community "clients" by adopting a practice of first listening to the needs, desires, and constraints of the community partner before formulating ideas about which action should be prescribed or pursued. Seeking to genuinely work *with* and *in* the community requires maintaining open lines of communication, staying open to nonlinear paths and less-than-tidy outcomes, and crafting final products that are both desired by and useful for community organizations. Effectively, students who engage in community-based policy projects receive additional instruction, nurturing, and practice in developing research and professional ethics that supplement those offered to the students more generally throughout the assignment.

For community-based projects, students must meet community partners where they are, in terms of understanding disciplinary nuance and potential policy outcomes. They must include information that can help their community partner/audience make the case for the policy, even if it isn't obvious that it is aligned with the student's personal position. After all, the community partner is driving the policy request in this instance, not the student. While the student should engage in meaningful dialogue with the partner about policy options (including its costs, benefits, winners, losers, and unforeseen or spillover outcomes), in community-engaged assignments, the student should not impose their beliefs or values on the community partner, offering ideas instead of directives.

In all instances, I require students to write specifically to their audience, adopting language and format that will be understandable and most useful to them. They must find a way for the action they wish to propose to resonate with those who may not naturally agree with them or who may hold different values. Finding points of contact and being able to communicate with those who hold opposing views is an important skill that I wish my students to develop through this assignment. Thus, my own personal set of research and professional ethics are also implicit in my assignment.

Writing Workshops

Because of my commitment to process, and the difficulty that many people have with writing, early on I adopted the use of writing workshops as a tool to help students explore ideas and "try them on" in their writing, to gain experience with the many elements necessary in the writing process including peer review, and to reflect on the various stages of their own writing process. At each offering, I explicitly request both formal (via course evaluation tools) and informal feedback on which elements of the PB assignment work for students and which don't; a significant majority of students have expressed explicit endorsement of and support for continuing the writing workshops. Through this lagged feedback mechanism, I have developed a series of five writing workshops that I now consistently use throughout the semester. The workshops take place in class or as independent workshops and/or out-of-class assignments, depending on the class schedule, inclement weather (e.g., snow days), and if there are days when I need to miss class due to a conference or other commitment. In either case, a structured workshop is offered; the only difference is whether I am guiding students or they are self-directed.

The first workshop is geared toward topic brainstorming and refinement to help students move toward their first assignment, a proposal. Following written feedback on proposals, we have a second workshop to help students incorporate the feedback they received on the proposal and move toward creating an outline for their PB and writing the first draft. The third workshop is typically a peer review of the first drafts. The fourth workshop uses a short role-playing exercise completed in pairs, where students play each other's devil's advocate; this exercise assists students in refining the voice, concepts, and approach they will use to convince their skeptical audience that they should take the action they are recommending in their PB. The fifth workshop varies somewhat based on the class schedule and student progress to date. Sometimes it is used for individual consultations to get final questions answered or to run ideas by me they have developed in response to comments on their drafts; other times, it is more directed work such as refining the Executive Summary, choosing the right title, and/or framing the cover letter to their audience.

Each workshop begins with a call for five minutes during which students center themselves on the task at hand. I invite students to take out a piece of paper or their computer and jot down whatever is in their heads at the moment (a grocery or to-do list, what they will say when they call grandma and tell her they're not coming for Thanksgiving dinner, the reason why they think this exercise is silly, and so on)—just to clear their head. If they would find more benefit from meditation or some other activity they have identified as helpful for centering and focus, I invite them to choose that instead. Each workshop typically involves some personal reflection on the writing process such as a status or progress check, asking themselves to articulate how they feel about their progress so far, crafting a list of required actions and/or a "backwards plan" to get them to the next assignment. If the workshop is completed in class, we talk as a group about what was helpful about the day's activities. Workshops end with a reminder of next steps as well as tips and suggestions collected from students in past semesters on how best to move through the series of scaffolded assignments.

A significant benefit of the workshops is that they tend to diffuse anxiety about writing, or about policy writing, and/or about writing about topics in economics. Most of my students have not written a piece of policy writing, and/or have not written "an economics paper," so there is an understandable amount of anxiety. An additional benefit is that the final products tend to be fairly well-written; in those semesters when we have fewer than five workshops, it tends to show up in the quality of the final products. Of course, the workshop format is also conducive to helping students to learn how to learn to write as it provides an opportunity for reflection on their own writing process as well as a low-stakes mechanism for experimenting with practices that may or may not work for them.

Support for Students' Writing Process

I populate the course Moodle[1] page with model assignments, including at least one full set of assignments (proposal to final draft). This can ease anxiety for students who may have never written a piece of policy writing; in addition, it serves to demonstrate the feasibility of taking a fairly rough idea and shaping it into something that is authoritatively written and convincing to one's audience, all in the span of one semester. Along with the sample "template" assignments used with the permission of former students, I also include a sample of "real world" policy briefs, including one contributed by a former student whose artifact was written during his time in local government.

Additional support for students' writing process comes in the form of style notes, tips from past students, and the occasional visit by Writing Center staff who have presented workshops on writing to a specific audience and alternate formats for policy briefs. These activities are all designed to support writing as a *process* rather than a one-time activity, which is consistent with our department objective of exposing students to alternate forms of writing and the importance of developing life skills that will be practical in graduate school, the world of work, and/or our students' personal lives.

Students are required to turn in all previous assignments that contain peer or instructor comments with each consecutive assignment which serves at least three objectives. First, it reminds me of the student's evolution in the assignment. On occasion, an early idea will resurface two assignments later and provide a "feather in the cap" of the policy brief in the form of a particularly strong claim or mechanism for appealing to their audience. Second, it provides me the opportunity to revisit the earlier feedback that I and others have provided, which can streamline the process of getting my multi-tasked brain back into their topic while facilitating the current set of comments. And third and perhaps most importantly, students are able to see their own progress which is an important tool for learning. If they feel stuck, they may review earlier assignments to be reminded of their motivation and passion for the topic, which also helps reinforce the role of reflection in the writing process.

Though many students are less than excited about the focus on writing in the course, a significant majority recognize the benefit it brings to their lives. In fact, many students comment that they receive more writing instruction and feedback, as well as space to reflect on their own process, in my class than in any other they take on campus.

Instructor Feedback

I provide feedback to each student at each stage of the writing process in order to ensure students are heading in the right direction and are using their scarce time resources effectively. This continual feedback also nudges (most) students to superior final products, which makes final grading more straightforward and pleasurable. Most of the comments I provide are content-oriented; I resist the urge to edit student writing line by line as it can be both time-consuming and frustrating. Instead, if I notice grammar, flow, or stylistic challenges with a piece of writing, I may mark one or two sentences and invite students (on their own, with a peer, or in a Writing Center appointment) to revise the remainder of their assignment with that feedback in mind. In addition to specific assignment and content-related items, I provide a quick summary statement of one or two sentences or a bullet list that outlines the priorities I suggest for their writing process at that stage. For longer assignments such as full memo drafts, I toggle between hand-written comments on shorter assignments and audio feedback, recorded on my iPhone and delivered to them via email and/or Moodle. Unexpected benefits of using audio comments include students being able to hear the intonation in my voice which provides more information than words alone; in addition, many students indicate they prefer the audio, which makes sense given differential learning styles (e.g., visual vs. auditory) and the tech-orientation of many students.

Final Presentations: From PowerPoint to Policy Slam

Just as writing competency is an important skill for student development, so is oral competency. And though students have opportunities through the writing workshops to gain valuable experience sharing their ideas orally at various stages in their evolution, it is also important for them to have the chance to share the ideas in their final policy brief, including welfare implications, with their peers. When I started teaching the class, I explored various options for the final presentations. For a while, it was de rigueur for faculty to assign PowerPoint presentations as it was a relatively new communication tool and an important one for students to learn. However, after a few semesters of watching students (and me) get bored watching several presentations on multiple consecutive class days, my excitement faded. For many years, we then moved to a roundtable discussion format, and there were a few years where the topics aligned to allow for themed panel-style events. All served the purpose of providing students a chance to share their ideas and get practice on a short (less than five minute) non-technical presentation. These short presentations have also been an appropriate way to add closure for individual students and the class as a whole.

That said, I felt that at least some (and in some semesters, many) students found each of these final presentation options (PowerPoint, roundtable discussion, panels) rather rote and uninteresting to prepare and deliver. I cannot recall the exact origin of my idea to adopt the policy slam format, but I believe it was after reading or hearing a story on a "science slam" event (http://scienceslam .net/). In any case, a few years ago I introduced the policy slam and I do not anticipate changing it; in fact, I have since adopted it in other classes as well.

The policy slam prompt asks students to prepare a short (1.5–2 minute), fun, upbeat, non-technical "slam-style" presentation of their policy brief topic. This is designed to serve the same function as a Toastmasters-style "elevator speech" or "lightening rounds" at professional meetings but also enables students' creativity and out-of-the-box thinking on how to convey the key points of their policy to unfamiliar audiences. Students are evaluated on how effectively they communicate their policy motivation, proposal, and the welfare analysis of the action they recommend (winners, losers, support, and opposition).

The assignment has been a roaring success (both figuratively and literally), with students showing up in costume to deliver poems they have written, performing original songs that would resonate with their intended audience(s), designing interactive and call-and-response activities, puppet shows, and other creative forms in addition to original policy poems delivered slam-style. There is always laughter, loud clapping, and a high amount of energy in the room. Students explore their creative side—sometimes willingly, as in the case of the extroverts, artistic types, and/or experienced poetry slam performers, and sometimes less than willingly, as in the case of an otherwise introverted student who asked to *please* present first because they didn't feel comfortable sitting around in a bee costume waiting their turn to perform their poem on the importance of ecosystem service valuation. Because we do the policy slam during our final exam period, we have created joyful but distracting noise externalities for students completing exams in adjacent classrooms. On more than one occasion, I have been asked by other instructors to share my secret sauce for fun during finals week—a week that is typically more dour.

In addition, the evolution of final presentation to a policy slam requires that students successfully and creatively convey their policy to a general audience, further demonstrating my belief in the importance of research accessibility and literacy.

LESSONS LEARNED

Reflections on the Assignment

The policy brief assignment is both a good fit for our campus, providing a relatively unique applied-writing experience that is distinct from undergraduate research (to which they are exposed in many other courses), as well as personally for me, given my professional commitment to providing exposure to skills and experiences useful to students, while also serving to enhance course relevance to our discipline and community. The fact that the assignment is difficult to plagiarize given the scaffolded set of assignments and workshops is an added bonus.

I have observed that the policy briefs written on community-based topics as opposed to national or international-level problems have been the most compelling, in terms of final product quality and useful insights. This could be due to strong students selecting local topics, the relative accessibility of local experts who can provide essential background materials and insights, or some other factors. As a result of this observation, in recent years I have strongly encouraged students to consider a local natural resource issue for the focus of their policy brief. On occasion, I have worked with community partners to facilitate student engagement with the issue and various community representatives working on the problem. For example, when the Asheville Design Center and the Center for Craft were brainstorming ways to address problems of stormwater runoff, walkability, and urban greenspace in downtown Asheville, students were provided with a tour of the space in question and access to representatives of the nonprofits and affected property owners, as well as the opportunity to volunteer and showcase their ideas for addressing some of the space's natural resource challenges at a community event. This opportunity for community engagement fits with our campus mission, student interests, as well as my pedagogical focus on economic literacy and responsibility to disseminate results to relevant constituencies. Though not all students jumped on this community-engaged and supported opportunity, those that did were able to engage with students and faculty in other disciplines thus enabling real-time critique of some of their narrowly economic policy solutions. In addition, they were able to utilize knowledge accumulated via community interactions to enhance their policy proposals for dealing with stormwater runoff, urban greenspace design, and other natural resource issues embedded in the design. Joyfully, sometimes these community interactions lead to unanticipated, spillover outcomes for students including internship and job opportunities and professional contacts useful for mentoring and network-building.

In order to ensure final product usefulness for community partners, I have allowed some flexibility with the final format of the policy brief. If a student's community partner would find more value in a well-researched and documented one-pager, infographic, or news brief-style artifact, I allow for those substitutions. Calling upon our university's Writing Center staff, in recent years I have incorporated a staff-led workshop on writing and preparing these alternative formats. The hyper-focus on tailoring to one's audience in terms of language, content, and format is useful for all students, regardless of whether they are working with a community partner. And though some students submit their final products to community partners for use in "the real world," I secretly wish that all students had the interest and stamina to polish their final policy brief and submit it to their selected audience to enhance the realism of the assignment.

Changes in Campus Support for Writing: Implications

As with most campuses, curriculum revision can affect how and what we teach. Though I have always required a piece of policy writing in Natural Resource Economics, it was during the period when our campus adopted a requirement that students enroll in writing-intensive (WI) courses both in and outside the major that I was able to refine the policy brief assignment and workshops more intentionally. During this era, faculty development workshops were regularly offered and I took full advantage of the opportunity to engage with Writing Center staff to learn how to teach writing, how to become more efficient with grading writing assignments by using rubrics and resisting the urge to edit papers, and other refinements. An added bonus was that when my course was designated writing-intensive, my department was able to restrict enrollment in the course to accommodate the fact that teaching writing can be quite time-intensive. During this era, my sections were typically 16–18 students which enabled me to complete two rounds of instructor review for each draft. While definitely time-consuming, I found I enjoyed the opportunity to help shape students' ideas more fully and provide detailed feedback on how to do so. Regretfully but not surprisingly, our campus has since abandoned the explicit WI requirement assuming that we are, in fact, already teaching writing within our majors and that students are exposed to various types of writing instruction through their general education course fulfillment.

This change has had real implications for my pedagogy. The removal of the WI designation and other department resource constraints led to larger class sizes, thus increasing the time and effort cost of teaching writing with the same intensity as I had been doing in the past. Though I attempted to continue my practice of reviewing two drafts from each student, it became impossible to achieve given the resource constraints I faced. I thus switched from a format of two rounds of instructor review plus one round of peer review to two rounds of peer review and one instructor review, with the opportunity for students to request a second round of instructor review and/or meet with me individually to discuss their revision process. Though some of the final products are still stellar, my perception is that there has been a decline in the quality of products since eliminating the second round of instructor review. In my judgement, fewer final products are ready for submission to a student's chosen audience or could (should) be used as writing samples for professional purposes (graduate school, job application). Of course, there may be other reasons for observing this change. It may be that the elimination of the WI designation sends a signal to students that writing is not worth (as much of) their time and they may be less invested in making the effort to learn to write well. In either case, it has been a bit discouraging to see the change in the quality of some final products given my pedagogical and professional ethics. The allocation of additional campus resources to fund teaching assistants and Writing Center staff, and/ or additional rounds of peer review, may help mitigate the effects of scarce faculty time available to review and grade writing assignments, especially for faculty with large classes.

THE MOST SIGNIFICANT LESSON LEARNED: ETHICS IMPLICIT IN TEACHING PHILOSOPHY AND PEDAGOGY

Like most economists, I haven't explicitly taught, addressed, or (in most semesters) even named the ethics prevalent in the content and pedagogy of my courses. Though our discipline was essentially founded by a moral philosopher (Adam Smith), and there have been articulate presentations of the philosophy and ethics inherent in our discipline (Robinson, 1964; Sen, 1987), most academic economists reject the idea that explicitly addressing ethics is necessary in our classrooms.

As Pernecky (2003) notes:

> While many professors consider ethics as integral to their disciplines, most economists tend to see it as tangential, or even foreign to their subject. Indeed, economists learn this early on; most introductory economics textbooks completely dichotomize the normative, "un-testable" world inhabited by ethicists, from the positive, empirically-grounded realm of economics (p. 11).

Indeed, we tend to defer to the positivity of our methods and statements, and attempt to leave the normative or subjective statements at the door. Virtually all introductory textbooks reify this distinction for students, and often we confidently present our field as one void of emotion and values, as if we are market "engineers" or mere analysts of its outcomes. We take pride in our ability to predict market outcomes and conduct welfare analysis, and are confident suggesting mechanistic policy solutions to resolve the problems that arise, for example, in situations of market failures such as air and water pollution externalities.

Ironically, engineering programs include an explicit ethics requirement for accreditation purposes, yet our discipline has nothing similar. The American Economics Association (AEA) recently (April 2018) adopted a code of professional conduct yet there is no requirement for teaching ethics to undergraduates. In fact, though there are resources for detecting plagiarism and promoting academic honesty, there is no mention of ethics in the AEA Resources for Economists internet page under Teaching Resources. Recent sessions at the 2019 Allied Social Sciences Association (ASSA) meeting have addressed ethical research or professional practices (Josephson et al., 2018; Gunderson, 2019; Lybbert, 2019; Smale and Josephson, 2019), and critiques of our discipline's ethics and our teaching of its ideology abound (McCloskey, 1996; Di Ruzza and Halevi, 2004; Feiner, 2004; Wilbur, 2004; Dent and Parnell, 2015).

Clearly, though, the positive vs. normative distinction that we default to in our teaching is a false dichotomy. It is never the case that we're talking only about either facts or values/emotions; our epistemologies rely on both fact and value. This is especially true when we are talking about policy matters, an arena that is essentially based upon the notion that behavior change should (must) occur, or where bad behavior (e.g., pollution) must be limited. In the case of my classroom assignment (an "action brief" intended to spur someone to action), I ask students to identify a situation where economics can help improve natural resource management or outcomes which implies a belief that the current path is not correct, or could be improved in some way. Ethics are clearly implicit in this approach.

Thus, it should not be surprising that ethics are embedded everywhere in my policy brief assignment. As previously mentioned, ethics, or at the very least value judgments, are implicit in: (1) my decision to ask students to take on the role of policy makers; (2) in student decisions about the topic on which to direct their policy; (3) student judgements about a specific policy to recommend and their rationale for doing so; and (4) the research and professional ethics associated with the format and style of the assignment and final deliverable itself. However, because these ethical elements have up to now been implicit rather than explicit, I have not asked students to specifically name the ethical motivations or implications of their policy recommendation.

There are several motivations for economists to include ethics more explicitly in the classroom. In addition to our field originating in moral philosophy (e.g., see Adam Smith's book entitled *The Theory of Moral Sentiments*; Smith, 2002), the inclusion of applied ethics is useful for several important student learning outcomes and for student development. Teacher-scholars have documented the benefit of teaching ethics for developing critical thinking skills (Card, 2002; al Hashimi et al., 2016) and increased student engagement (Stutz, 2011; Beever, 2016). The use of "everyday ethics" in the classroom may contribute to students' moral development as well. As Fried (2009) states, "Ethical issues arise in the context of economics courses all the time … This presents teaching opportunities to sensitize students to the difference between right and wrong in a particular context that matters to them" (p. 28). Though not all economists may feel responsible for the moral development of their students, it is essential to facilitate students' ability to connect economics with their everyday lives which may be accomplished through the incorporation of ethics. In addition, courses with a policy focus require students to recognize the boundaries or limitations of the more mechanistic elements of economic analysis. The explicit incorporation of ethics into teaching economics can provide a framework for this discussion.

Barrera (2003) provides perhaps the most convincing argument for incorporating moral philosophy and applied ethics into the economics curriculum, noting that it complements economics students' "technical skills by situating allocative efficiency within the full spectrum of alternative evaluative criteria for market outcomes" (p. 43). He further states:

> The purpose of studying ethical theory in an economics curriculum is neither to diminish nor discredit the analytical power of neoclassical economics; it is to situate the latter within a larger framework that puts theory in a much better position to serve policy. Technical proficiency is a must for our majors, and such rigor should not in any way be compromised when incorporating ethical theory in their economic education. However, they should also be deft in recognizing why, when and how

to supplement neoclassical analytical results with non-economic insights. Moral philosophy has much to contribute in developing such acuity in our economics majors. (pp. 53–54)

Several economists have documented their use of ethics in economics classrooms. Pernecky (2003) describes his response to a requirement for university-wide teaching of normative ethics by adopting an ethical lens to study income distribution, the environment, private property rights, and other topics in his course on Economic Justice. Fried (2009) outlines the ethics embedded in several courses in the Union College Economics curriculum, while Davis (2009) describes his use of ethical criteria to evaluate market outcomes as a supplement to traditional coverage in his teaching a course on The Economics of Sin. He observes, "The intersection of economics and ethics is potentially huge. Not only did the field of economics grow out of Adam Smith's interest in ethical problems, but every price change raises ethical issues to the degree that it affects the wellbeing of both producers and consumers" (p. 51).

DISCUSSION AND IMPLICATIONS

Thus, ethics are embedded everywhere in my policy brief assignment, even though I have not explicitly told my students of this reality. Reflecting on and articulating the ethical practices embedded in the course, it has become clear that there is tremendous value to naming these practices. Not only is casually ignoring the ethics implied by my pedagogy a dishonest practice—albeit one that most economists follow every day—but it is also a less effective strategy for helping my students learn and apply economics.

Because economists rely on values in our methods and approaches, we need to think about all the places we are relying on our personal and professional values in order to fully convey the secrets, wisdom, and limitations of our discipline. Some of these values are moral judgements. A moral judgement is a statement grounded in reason; that is, we have a logical reason to say this or that; it is not something that one merely "feels." When one looks at a situation and has reason to believe one option is superior to another based on reason, we are using values to make the judgement (Albertzart, 2013). In a nutshell, this reasoned approach is what policy analysts follow when they recommend policy, and it is also the approach I ask my students to take in the policy brief assignment.

Cost–benefit type analyses can be done strictly based on monetary outcomes but they can also be done in terms of other kinds of effects, effects that recognize people's abilities to flourish. Recognizing what it takes for people to flourish in a capability sense (Nussbaum and Sen, 1993), is much more than wealth in a financial sense. It is tied to social, cultural, political and other capitals, and to relationships and interactions. Cultures encourage some discourses over others. In the disciplinary culture of economics, we favor the myth of the "rational" actor in part because it is familiar to us from our training as "good" economists and also because it helps our quantitative models run. These values are the foundation of economics. The values and the ethics implied by them get passed on to our students, and the cycle continues.

And yet, many of my students are keen to criticize the standard neoclassical models. They sense the irrationality of actors, the political and social influence of institutions, and other elements that disrupt the tidy neoclassical interpretation of the world.

Similarly, when we teach about standing in cost–benefit analysis (Zerbe, 2018), valuing statistical lives (Robinson, 2018), or distributional accounting (Krutilla, 2018), an implied ethics is invoked. Wilbur (2004) outlines three ways in which ethics are important in our discipline:

> 1. Economists have ethical values that help shape the way they do economics. 2. Economic actors have ethical values that help shape their behaviors. 3. Economic institutions and policies impact people differentially and thus ethical evaluations must supplement economic evaluations. (pp. 156–7)

He continues: "Economics would be greatly enriched if it recognized that there is no alternative to working from a world view. Making explicit the ethical values embodied in that world view would help keep economics more honest and useful" (p. 157).

In terms of my own pedagogy, it is now clear to me that I should talk about ethics and make more explicit where in the class content and in the policy brief assignment ethics appear. Though sustainability concerns certainly need to clearly articulate ethics (though apparently frequently do not, per Parmentier and Moore, 2016), it is also ethics specific to the economics discipline (the disciplinary ethics Wilbur describes) and codes of professional conduct (professional ethics) that are being invoked. In making these changes, students will have the opportunity to: (1) learn about our disciplinary values and ethics; (2) acquire critical thinking skills through naming points of view and clearly articulating the strengths and weaknesses of those views (Card, 2002; al Hashimi et al., 2016); (3) become better students of economics, recognizing disciplinary strengths and weaknesses, where our field touches others, and where we have to work cross-disciplinarily, how to think critically; and (4) enhance skills that promote lifelong learning through exposure to the moral aspects of everyday living, or "everyday ethics." In addition, this work serves as a model for how to engage appropriately in the policy world—with transparency and honesty—

something that is becoming ever more relevant and that I believe is important for economics faculty to model.

Though I am not personally ready to begin offering a distinct course on Economics and Ethics as suggested by Barrera (2003), there are several straightforward mechanisms for incorporating moral philosophy and ethics more explicitly in natural resource and environmental economics classrooms. One is the adoption of additional contemplative practices (Barbezat and Bush, 2014) which can help students deepen their understanding of course material and increase their creativity and insight. Card (2002) notes that "ethics is a process of thinking, not a set of established answers" (p. 20) and suggests the use of case studies to help nudge students to become better ethical thinkers. Beever (2016) advocates that case studies be augmented with narratives of stakeholder accounts, as opposed to mere recording of facts, to assist students in understanding situational complexity and motivations for action. The case outlined in Monteith (2007) serves this purpose as it documents the challenges and ethical dimensions of applied natural resources and environmental research, which I imagine can be useful for initiating a discussion of professional and research ethics. When discussing case studies that lack stakeholder accounts, it would be straightforward to ask students mid-discussion to role play potential stakeholder motivations and positions, which would prime them for thinking about their own motivations and positions and also potentially enliven the discussion. In addition, short, occasional insertions of "ethics minutes" (Davis, 2009) can also nudge thinking and smooth the path for clear articulation of ethical practices, as could the discussion of issues associated with the ethics of data presentation, analysis, and interpretation (Ghaly, 2009), especially for faculty whose teaching is more quantitative in orientation.

Slight tweaks to some of my current class activities can also serve to make ethics more explicit for my students. For example, the role-playing workshop could require that when students take on their role of adversary to the policy idea, they clearly articulate the moral or ethical source of their beliefs and criticisms. The policy brief proposal could be required to include a statement of the student author's ethical beliefs as they articulate the motivation for policy action and outline the specific action they believe should be undertaken. Though I may not feel confident helping students navigate the nuances of all of these discussions, I am certain I could identify a philosophy colleague who would be willing to come to class to help get us started.

CONCLUSION

Those making policy need to articulate the values that they use to make recommendations in order to be fully aware of, and transparent about, what is being recommended. What is the policy maker committed to? What are policy makers (or analysts or consultants) recommending *others* commit themselves to? When we recommend a policy, or ask our students to recommend a policy, we are recommending the values implicit in the policy. Naming these values and the implicit ethical choices that are required by the policy, is an important form of critical analysis that should be incorporated in our pedagogy. A welfare analysis that many of us require is a fine start to this process but this should be enhanced with more clear articulation of the ethics underlying the policy in order to ensure full transparency.

I see this transparency as a necessary element for gaining a deep understanding of our disciplinary values, perspectives, and methods. Naming is an important element of this process. To ensure we don't mislead students or build in the wrong values, we need to be more explicit.

Adam Smith's "invisible hand" is an example of how easy it is to mislead students into a misrepresentation of his original ideas, which were much more complex and nuanced than the free market capitalist interpretation that predominates. Our economics textbooks tend to oversimplify things to make material accessible to students. Faculty workloads make it difficult for us to take the time to read, reflect and synthesize the material required to make explicit that which is implicit in our disciplinary dogma. In addition, the likely predominant belief that ethics is not an economic concern means it is unlikely for teachers to weigh their own time and energy commitments in favor of doing this work. As a result, many of us don't do this work meaningfully in our courses, including me.

Though my Natural Resource Economics policy brief assignment has evolved over time, it has always been covered in ethics. It thus provides an example of how one may embed both ethics and writing across the curriculum in an economics course.

The process of reflecting on the policy brief writing assignment has enabled me to both articulate the ethics implied in my teaching practice, and renew my commitment to professional honesty and transparency. It is clear that while policy writing is useful for skill development, acknowledging and using ethics is required in order to most fully engage students in policy discussions.

ACKNOWLEDGEMENTS

Dr. Melissa Burchard and Dr. Amy Lanou provided useful queries that helped articulate my goal for the chapter; Dr. Burchard's explicit invitation to consider using ethics as a frame and pointing out that I am really a moralist at heart was especially formative. Various Writing Center Directors including Dr. Mary Alm and Jessica Pisano are gratefully acknowledged as they helped refine assignments and in-class writing workshops over the years; similarly, a multitude of anonymous student Writing Consultants at UNC Asheville's Writing

Center have helped improve my students' process and products. I appreciate the hundreds of students who have completed this assignment, demonstrating grit and creativity and trust in the process, many of whom provided useful feedback to improve the experience of future students. To Dr. Rick Chess, who helped name some of my writing assignments as contemplative approaches to writing and learning; I will always be grateful for that sidewalk conversation years ago. The University of North Carolina Asheville's Interdisciplinary Distinguished Professor of the Mountain South fund provided the time for me to write this piece as well as funding to support my able student research assistants, Renee Ambroso and Audrey Thomas.

NOTE

1.   Moodle is an online learning platform designed to provide educators and their students with personalized learning environments. Through Moodle, educators can post documents, assignments, and online forums pertaining to their course.

REFERENCES

Albertzart, M. (2013), 'Principle-Based Moral Judgement,' *Ethical Theory and Moral Practice*, **16**(2), 339–354. Retrieved from http://www.jstor.org.proxy177.nclive.org/stable/24478801.

al Hashimi, S., M. Sheen, J. Essary and M. Humeidan (2016), 'Integrating Ethics Training into an Undergraduate Research Program: Applying the Triplex Model,' *Teaching Ethics*, **16**(2), 243–250. https://doi.org/10.5840/tej2016113037.

Barbezat, D. P. and M. Bush (2014), *Contemplative Practices in Higher Education: Powerful Methods to Transform Teaching and Learning*, San Francisco: Jossey-Bass.

Barrera, A. F. (2003), 'A Case for Incorporating Moral Philosophy in an Economics Curriculum,' *Teaching Ethics*, **3**(2), 41–58. https://doi.org/DOI: 10.5840/tej2003323.

Bean, J. C. (1996), *The Professor's Guide to Integrating Writing, Critical Thinking and Active Learning in the Classroom*, San Francisco: Jossey-Bass.

Beever, J. (2016), 'Teaching Ethics Ecologically,' *Teaching Ethics*, **16**(2), 195–206. https://doi.org/10.5840/tej20161213.

Card, R. F. (2002), 'Using Case Studies to Develop Critical Thinking Skills in Ethics Courses,' *Teaching Ethics*, **3**(1), 19–27. https://doi.org/DOI: 10.5840/tej20023112.

Cohen, A. J. and J. Spencer (1993), 'Using Writing Across the Curriculum in Economics: Is Taking the Plunge Worth It?,' *Journal of Economic Education*, **24**(3), 219–230.

Davis, L. (2009), 'Teaching the Economics of Sin,' *Teaching Ethics*, **9**(2), 51–58. https://doi.org/DOI: 10.5840/tej2009924.

Dent, E. B. and J. A. Parnell (2015), 'Reconciling Economics and Ethics in Business Ethics Education: The Case of Objectivism,' *The Journal of Ayn Rand Studies*, **15**(2), 131–156. https://doi.org/10.5325/jaynrandstud.15.2.0131.

Di Ruzza, R. and J. Halevi (2004), 'How to Look at Economics Critically: Some Suggestions,' *A Guide to What's Wrong with Economics*, London: Anthem Press, pp. 133–143.

Feiner, S. (2004), 'There Are None So Blind...,' *A Guide to What's Wrong with Economics*, London: Anthem Press, pp. 176–184.

Fried, H. (2009), 'The Michael S. Rapaport Initiative to Introduce Ethics Into the Economics Curriculum at Union College,' *Teaching Ethics*, **9**(2), 25–50.

Ghaly, A. (2009), 'Ethics Across the Curriculum and Geographic Information Systems,' *Teaching Ethics*, **9**(2), 59–64. https://doi.org/DOI: 10.5840/tej2009925.

Goma, O. D. (2014), 'Creative Writing in Economics,' *College Teaching*, **49**(4). https://doi-org.proxy177.nclive.org/10.1080/87567555.2001.10844598.

Grauerholz, L. (1999), 'Creating and Teaching Writing-Intensive Courses,' *Teaching Sociology*, **27**(4).

Gunderson, C. (2019), 'A Discussion of Ethical Issues Pertaining to Media Relations for Agricultural Economists,' presented at the American Economic Association Annual Meeting, Atlanta.

Josephson, A., W. A. Masters and J. D. Michler (2018), 'Beyond the IRB: Towards a Typology of Research Ethics in Applied Economics,' presented at the American Economic Association Annual Meeting, Atlanta.

Krutilla, K. (2018), 'Distributional Accounting in Benefit–Cost Analysis,' *Teaching Benefit-Cost Analysis*, Cheltenham, UK and Northampton, MA, USA: Edward Elgar Publishing, pp. 208–222.

Lybbert, T. (2019), 'Ethics in Econometrics,' presented at the American Economic Association Annual Meeting, Atlanta.

McCloskey, D. (1996), 'Missing Ethics in Economics,' in A. Klamer (ed.), *The Value of Culture: On the Relationship between Economics and Arts*, Amsterdam: Amsterdam University Press, pp. 187–202.

McGoldrick, K. M. (2008), 'Writing Requirements and Economic Research Opportunities in the Undergraduate Curriculum: Results from a Survey of Departmental Practices,' *The Journal of Economic Education*, **39**(9), 287–296.

Monteith, D. (2007), 'Ethics, Management, and Research in Glacier Bay, Alaska,' *Teaching Ethics*, **8**(1), 67–80. https://doi.org/DOI: 10.5840/tej2007815.

Nussbaum, M. and A. Sen (eds) (1993), *The Quality of Life*, Oxford: Clarendon Press.

Parmentier, M. J. and S. Moore (2016), 'The Camels are Unsustainable: Using Study Abroad as a Pedagogical Tool for Teaching Ethics and Sustainable Development,' *Teaching Ethics*, **16**(2), 207–221. https://doi.org/10.5840/tej2016113038.

Pernecky, M. (2003), 'Faculty Development for Teaching Ethics Across the Curriculum: The Case of an Economic Justice Course,' *Teaching Ethics*, **4**(1), 11–23. https://doi.org/DOI: 10.5840/tej20034112.

Robinson, J. (1964), *Economic Philosophy*, Penguin Books.

Robinson, L. (2018), 'Valuing Statistical Lives,' in *Teaching Benefit-Cost Analysis*, Cheltenham, UK and Northampton, MA, USA: Edward Elgar Publishing, pp. 105–113.

Sen, A. (1987), *On Ethics and Economics*, Oxford: Blackwell Publishing.

Shaw, V. N. (1999), 'Reading, Presentation, and Writing Skills in Content Courses,' *College Teaching*, **47**(4), 153–157. http://www.jstor.org/stable/27558968.

Siegfried, J. J., R. L. Bartlett, W. L. Hansen, A. C. Kelley, D. N. McCloskey, and T. H. Tietenberg (1991), 'The Status and Prospects of the Economics Major,' *The Journal of Economic Education*, **22**(3), 197–224. https://doi.org/10.2307/1183106.

Simpson, M. S. and S. E. Carroll (1999), 'Assignments for a Writing-Intensive Economics Course,' *Journal of Economic Education*, **30**(4), 402–410.

Smale, M. and A. Josephson (2019), 'What Do You Mean by "Informed Consent"? Household Survey Ethics in Development Research,' presented at the American Economic Association Annual Meeting, Atlanta.

Smith, A. (2002), *Adam Smith: The Theory of Moral Sentiments*, in K. Haakonssen (ed.), Cambridge Texts in the History of Philosophy, Cambridge: Cambridge University Press. https://doi.org/10.1017/CBO9780511800153.

Stutz, J. (2011), 'Integrating Applied Ethics into a College-Level Non-Majors Biology Course,' *Teaching Ethics*, **11**(2), 47–56. https://doi.org/10.5840/tej20111126.

Tietenberg, T. H. and L. Lewis (2018), *Environmental and Natural Resource Economics*, New York: Routledge.

Wilbur, C. (2004), Teaching Economics as if Ethics Mattered,' in *A Guide to What's Wrong with Economics*, London: Anthem Press, pp. 147–157.

Zerbe, R. O. (2018), 'The Concept of Standing in Benefit–Cost Analysis,' in *Teaching Benefit–Cost Analysis*, Cheltenham, UK and Northampton, MA, USA: Edward Elgar Publishing, pp. 58–68.

11. Using technology to teach sustainability with applications to conservation biology and ecosystem service management

Shana M. McDermott

11.1 INTRODUCTION

Environmental policy does not exist in an economic vacuum. Creating sustainable guidelines requires multiple, coordinated responses across individuals and disciplines. While the need for collaboration is not a new concept, it is becoming more widely accepted and attempted in all forms of public policy. The EPA, for example, embraces cooperative federalism by working with local states and governments when setting environmental policy (EPA, 2020). Even health policy recommendations from WHO and CDC stress the importance of joint efforts as exhibited by the One Health Approach (WHO, 2017; CDC, 2020). The One Health Approach is an international, interdisciplinary collaborative effort to limit the emergence of infectious diseases. Needless to say, it is becoming more important and common to consider a wide range of specialists and stakeholders when generating public policy. This is why it is beneficial to highlight the collaborative nature of sustainable environmental policy early in a student's academic career, and preferably, immediately in your environmental or ecological economics course.

Admittedly, collaboration is tough. Managing efforts across individuals and fields present numerous challenges, and the struggles are well-documented (Fish, 1989; Golde and Gallagher, 1999; Nowacek, 2009). Thankfully, different technologies exist to facilitate larger group efforts. Introducing these technologies through small tweaks and engaging extensions to commonly covered environmental economics topics, like the environmental Kuznets curve, Pigouvian taxes, and climate change, can help students better understand how to work in tandem with others to inform policy. Additionally, students (and teachers alike) increasingly experience the world through screens, which is why introducing a channel for collaboration is essential when preparing students for the future.

The channels considered here ask students to engage with their natural environment through either data collection applications or virtual simulations. Several of the suggestions allow students to collect and contribute their observations to larger interdisciplinary citizen science datasets, which is a sustainable effort by itself. In other words, you can create assignments that accomplish multiple goals by using the student's scarce time and effort as efficiently and productively as possible.[1]

It's important to note that this chapter is not intended as a comprehensive lesson plan for how to teach sustainability concepts. Instead, the cases below provide motivating material and experiential nature-based applications that can be *incorporated at any point in a semester with minimal time and effort.* Use what resonates with your class content, adapt it as necessary, and leave behind what doesn't. Using one or several of these applications in class will help students

1. retain environmental policy and sustainability foundation concepts,[2]
2. manage their own environment and health using accessible and sustainable outlets,[3] and
3. participate in future sustainability behaviors beyond your course.[4]

As Marian Wright Edelman once said "education is improving the lives of others and for leaving your community and world better than when you found it" (Edelman, 1992).

Finally, use the suggestions below as inspiration for exploring newer technologies created after the publication of this book or for applications related to topics beyond this chapter.

11.2   INTEGRATION OF ECONOMICS AND CONSERVATION BIOLOGY: BIODIVERSITY AND INVASIVE SPECIES

11.2.1   Environmental Kuznets Curve, Biodiversity, and iNaturalist

One objective of sustainable development is to ensure that future generations have access to the same or better ecosystem services than are available today. And biodiversity, or the variability of living organisms within an ecosystem,[5] is a crucial input to ecosystem services, including food security (Pimental et al., 1997; Young, 1999; Thrupp, 2000; Toledo and Burlingame, 2006), pharmaceutical production (Pimental et al., 1997; Erwin et al., 2010), and bioremediation of chemical pollution (Abatenh et al., 2017). Studies also show that biodiverse ecosystems produce more resilient environments, and consequently economies, that can better withstand and recover from a variety of disasters (Di Falco and Chavas, 2008; Schippers et al., 2015). However, the topic of biodiversity doesn't always make it into an environmental economics course, until now.

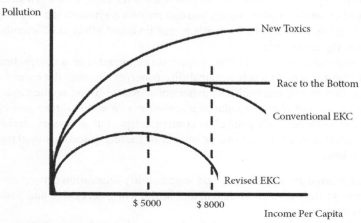

Source: Dasgupta et al. (2002).

Figure 11.1   Visualization of different observed and hypothesized EKC relationships

Introducing a small extension to the commonly covered environmental Kuznets curve (EKC) provides an opportunity for more in-depth discussion and analysis related to biodiversity. Most environmental economics textbooks present the traditional inverted U-shaped EKC relationship between pollution or environmental degradation and economic growth. Yet many studies have critiqued and reanalyzed this relationship, as illustrated in Figure 11.1. More recently, Strong et al. (2011) estimate the EKC relationship by using biodiversity as a measure of environmental quality (or degradation). In particular, they find a combination relationship of those presented in Figure 11.1 or a "lazy S-curve." I use this result from Strong et al. (2011), Figure 11.2, as a stepping-stone for a richer discussion about biodiversity that can be as short or as long as time permits.

When time is limited, merely defining biodiversity, introducing its relationship to ecosystem services (see above), and discussing Strong et al.'s (2011) result is a fruitful use of class time.

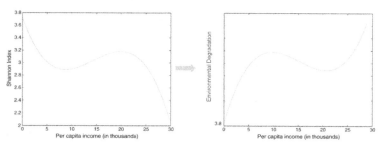

Note: A falling Shannon index implies lower levels of biodiversity or increasing environmental degradation, whereas an increasing Shannon index relates to a reduction in environmental degradation.
Source: Adapted from Strong et al. (2011).

Figure 11.2   An illustration of how biodiversity fits the traditional EKC relationship with environmental degradation on the y-axis

When time allows, it is worth digging deeper into how to calculate biodiversity and then ask students to apply it to their own neighborhoods. There are several ways and debates on how to calculate biodiversity.[6] Since I often refer to biodiversity as a proxy for the health of an ecosystem, I prefer to use the Shannon entropy function (*SE*), which factors in both the number of species (or richness) and the evenness of individual species, where

$$SE = -\sum_{i=1}^{N} p_i \ln p_i$$

and p_i = the proportion of individuals found in the ith species and estimated using $\frac{n_i}{N}$.[7]

Interpreting Shannon entropy values is relatively straightforward. Larger *SE* values correspond to higher levels of diversity (more even distribution of species) and, consequently, a healthier ecosystem; max *SE* equals $-\ln\left(\frac{1}{\#\,species\,categories}\right)$. Lower Shannon entropy values coincide with less diverse or unbalanced ecosystems;[8] the lowest *SE* equals zero.

Table 11.1 provides *SE* calculations for two sample ecosystems. Even though the total number of species observed are identical across the two ecosystems, Ecosystem 1 is more diverse because of the even distribution across

Table 11.1   Shannon entropy calculation example

Species Name	# Observed	P_i	$-P_i ln P_i$
ECOSYSTEM 1			
Species 1	20	0.25	0.35
Species 2	20	0.25	0.35
Species 3	20	0.25	0.35
Species 4	20	0.25	0.35
Total	80		**H = 1.40**
ECOSYSTEM 2			
Species 1	70	0.88	0.12
Species 2	3	0.04	0.12
Species 3	2	0.03	0.09
Species 4	5	0.06	0.17
Total	80		**H = 0.51**

species types. Ecosystem 2 has a lower Shannon value, and a lower level of biodiversity, because of the dominance of Species 1.

Once the students have a basic understanding of how to calculate and interpret Shannon values, I then ask them either on homework or for a larger research project, to go outside and derive their own measures of biodiversity using the app iNaturalist. iNaturalist is a popular nature app that allows an individual to both identify species names (and characteristics) and record observations for use in bigger citizen science projects (e.g., documenting endangered species and helping jurisdictions prioritize conservation efforts (iNaturalist Press, 2020)).[9] To learn more about how to get started with iNaturalist check out their getting started and teacher guides (iNaturalist Intro, 2020; iNaturalist TG, 2020).

Here are several extended examples of how to incorporate iNaturalist and biodiversity measures:

- Homework application: Ask students to record 100 (or any number, just make it realistic) observations from two geographic locations (e.g., park, campus, neighborhood, etc.), preferably from one relatively developed area and one place that is considered more "natural." Ask the students to compare and contrast the Shannon values they observe and to explain the difference between the two locations. Most likely, students will find higher *SE* values from the natural areas relative to highly developed sites, which provides a helpful link to the Strong et al. (2011) article. Ask them to compare and contrast their findings to Strong et al.'s (2011) results.

- Extension: Use in conjunction with EDDMapS App (discussed below) to help restrict observations to native species only.
- Semester Research Projects or Senior Thesis using unique observations gathered with the help of iNaturalist or publicly available records/data available on the app and website:
  - Create a simplified EKC for a location(s) of their choice breaking down the geographic areas by neighborhoods, cities, counties, etc.
  - Allow for different measures of development when generating the EKC. For example, ask students to determine how biodiversity varies by zoning classification (i.e., which type of zoning district puts more pressure on biodiversity and by how much?), noise level, or light pollution level.
  - Combine biodiversity measures and other publically available datasets like the American Time Use survey (ATUS, 2020) or the Behavioral Risk Factor Surveillance System (BRFSS, 2020). For example, ask students to examine how biodiversity impacts the amount of time spent outdoors or affects stated levels of happiness.
    - Extensions vary. For instance, students could "back-of-the-envelope" calculate how the trade-offs of labor/leisure or happiness may affect health and healthcare costs.

11.2.2 Invasive Species and EDDMapS

Invasive alien species (IAS) are one of the main drivers of biodiversity loss worldwide and result in significant environmental and economic losses (Pimental et al., 2005; Charles and Dukes, 2008). IAS makes a great case study for an environmental economics course because

1. Human disturbances, such as deforestation and land degradation, are associated with making habits more vulnerable to non-native species (Kolar and Lodge, 2001; Daehler, 2003; Leishman and Thomson, 2005; Jauni et al., 2015).
2. Economic activity like trade and transportation introduce non-native species into novel environments (Levine and D'Antonio, 2003; Essl et al., 2005; Westphal et al., 2008; Hulme, 2009; Seebens et al., 2013).

There are several ways to incorporate the discussion of IAS into traditional environmental economics coursework.

When time is limited, an easy way to introduce IAS is as an example within a broader (nonmarket) valuation discussion. For this option, I reference McIntosh et al. (2010), who estimate the willingness to pay to delay aquatic invasive species introduction into United States' waterways. When introducing this paper, I first show pictures of different aquatic species from around the country, each with an increasingly more disturbing appearance. For example, I begin with zebra mussels covering a shopping cart, a video of an Asian carp breaking a woman's jaw as it jumps into her boat (yes, this video is as painful to watch as it sounds), and end with a picture of Pacu or the "ball-cutter" fish (I don't think an explanation is required). At the end of the day, it doesn't matter what pictures are used as long as you have fun with the presentation – you're simply trying to get the students engaged and curious about IAS. As one can imagine, the "ball-cutter" fish always receives a tremendously cringe-worthy reaction from the students. Then, once students have seen a small sampling of aquatic IAS, I ask, "How much would you be willing to pay in the form of a one-time payment to delay low to high impacts from aquatic invasive species for one year?" We then compare the class average to McIntosh et al.'s result of $48 per person annually. When the $48 is aggregated, it amounts to $4 billion, which is far more than the Federal government currently spends for all IAS at $394 million annually. Therefore, the Federal government under-regulates IAS relative to what is optimal. Using this paper aids in the discussion of IAS, nonmarket valuation techniques, and evaluating environmental policy.

When time allows, I like to introduce the EDDMapS app. EDDMapS, initially launched by the Center for Invasive Species and Ecosystem Health at the University of Georgia, is an app used for documenting the location and distribution of invasive species and native pests throughout the United States and Canada. Students can contribute pictures and GPS coordinates of IAS observations through the online form or the smartphone app and add to the almost 5 million available records as of July 2020 (EDDMapS, 2020). Students can then use either their observations or the broader distribution maps available on the website for simple homework assignments or more extensive research projects.

- Homework application:
  - Have the students record a predetermined number of well-known IAS in their area, evaluate their location (i.e., are the IAS consistently found in a particular area?), and discuss possible reasons for their spread. For example, if observations are near the road or along the edge of a trail, then some type of human transmission is likely to blame.
  - Have students research one or multiple IAS at the local or state level, conduct research on how it was introduced/spreads, and propose a miti-gating policy. For example, if the IAS mainly spread through firewood, then policy could include banning the movement of firewood or issuing a Pigouvian tax per log bundle calculated at the expected damage per bundle.
- Semester Research Projects or Senior Thesis using EDDMapS data.

- • Expand the homework applications into a longer research project.
- • Policy memo:
  - • Ask the students to write a policy memo where they propose a biosecurity measure to prevent the introduction, spread, or establishment of IAS (see firewood example above). I enjoy using policy memos in my environmental economic courses because they are relatively short papers, usually a maximum of two pages single-spaced, that force students to break down complex issues to be suitable for a "lay" audience. Additionally, students often find this assignment useful, and many have gone on to use their memos in job applications when a writing sample is required.

11.3 ENVIRONMENTAL POLICY: PIGOUVIAN TAX AND LITTERATI

Litter is a frequent topic in my courses, especially when discussing environmental sustainability in the news. Because even though visible litter has decreased by over 60 percent in the past 40 years, there are still over 51 billion pieces of trash discarded along roads annually (MSW Consultants, 2009). Annual litter cleanup spending costs the U.S. more than $11.5 million, damage wildlife, human health, municipal infrastructure, and reduces property values (Mrosovsky, 2009; MSW Consultants, 2009; Williams et al., 2013). Traditional methods for mitigating litter and its impacts include fines and slogans (e.g., slam dunk the junk, be part of the solution, not the pollution) (NCLS, 2020), which have proven mildly successful (TX DOT, 2013; Zeitlin, 2019). Reducing litter further is a challenge because of its non-point source nature, unless, of course, you are taking a class in environmental economics that introduces market instruments and Pigouvian taxes. Pigouvian taxes provide a way to target high-frequency litter offenders before they become trash (e.g., tobacco and packaging products).

One of the worst offenders is plastic, a result of the 340 percent per capita increase in plastic packaging over the past 40 years (MSW Consultants, 2009). This is why I like to use plastic, specifically plastic bags, to motivate the concept of Pigouvian taxes. Many major countries and cities have already successfully implemented plastic bag taxes for reducing plastic use and, consequently, pollution (Zeitlin, 2019). One of the most successful stories is Ireland's tax, established in 2002, that reduced plastic bag consumption by 94 percent (Rosenthal, 2008). After just four months of a similar €0.10/bag fee in Portugal, the use of single-use plastic bags dropped 74 percent, and consumption of reusable plastic bags dropped 61 percent (Martinho et al., 2017). Within the United States, Chicago has seen a 28 percent decrease in plastic bag use since 2017 (Giangreco, 2019) and Washington D.C., a 75 percent decrease of plastic bag removal from the Potomac River (Zeitlin, 2019).

If the data is available, then Pigouvian taxes can address many litter sources, not just plastic bags. Enter Litterati.[10] Litterati is an App where users identify, map, and (hopefully) discard litter around the world. Most famously, the Litterati technology helped San Francisco combat cigarette litter. By using the Litterati technology, San Francisco policymakers identified and mapped 5,000 pieces of improperly discarded trash, showing exactly how much cigarette butts contribute to litter in the city. The city used this data to double the existing cigarette sales tax in the form of a Pigouvian charge, raising over $4 million in annual tax revenue (Kirschner, 2020).

If the San Francisco example isn't enough to inspire students to use the app independently, then here are some quick and more advanced methods of incorporating Litterati into an environmental economics class.

When time is limited,

- Homework Option 1 or extra credit: Simply ask the students to document and discard a certain number of pieces of trash as a problem on homework or for extra credit.[11] This is a great assignment, especially at the end of the semester, when everyone is stressed and wants an excuse to get outside. Although this assignment may not seem like economics, the students are helping solve the public good problem of litter pollution (i.e., third-party intervention is one solution for this market failure).
- Homework Option 2: Ask students to examine the Litterati data for a specific geographic area (e.g., their hometown, neighborhood surrounding the university, etc.) and determine the biggest litter offender. Have them follow up with a reasonable Pigouvian tax (or deposit-refund system) for that item (e.g., expected damage per unit or reference a similar established fee used elsewhere).

When time allows,

- Policy memo: Expand Homework Option 2 from above into a policy memo, making sure the students address the memo to the relevant town, county, state, or federal representative (i.e., decide the geographic scale for the tax).
- Semester Research Projects or Senior Thesis Option 1: Use the Litterati data to calculate the worst litter offenders and develop an appropriate policy for them. To aid in this assignment, have the students document the type and amount of each piece of litter within a specific geographic area. See Table 11.2 for an example. Once they have their table created, have

them calculate a Herfindahl-Hirschman Index (HHI_{Litter}) for litter concentration where

$$HHI_{Litter} = \sum_{i=1}^{N} s_i^2$$

and s_i equals the percentage share of each unique source of litter.

Table 11.2   Sample litter collection data

Litter type	# Observed	s_i
Cigarette butt	100	26%
Plastic bottle	250	66%
Tire	10	3%
Styrofoam cup	20	5%
Total	380	100%

Using HHI_{Litter} will help students quantify the concentration of litter. Students can then propose a policy using the HHI_{Litter} as motivation; it's easier to address highly concentrated litter rather than a diverse range of litter (or numerous sources). For example, an HHI_{Litter} closer to 10,000 indicates a dominant litter source that may respond well to a Pigouvian tax(es), while an HHI_{Litter} closer to 0 represents many different sources that require more creativity and policy options.

- Semester Research Projects or Senior Thesis Option 2: Use the Litterati app to calculate HHI_{Litter} across different geographic areas and combine with data on miles driven on nearby roadways, population, dominant industry type, etc., to see how different variables affect litter concentration and source.

11.4   SUSTAINABLE BEHAVIOR – OROECO AND JOULEBUG

> Let everyone sweep in front of his own door, and the whole world will be clean –
> Johann Wolfgang von Goethe

Ensuring individuals cooperate to achieve collective sustainable actions may require policy intervention like Pigouvian taxes above, but individual pro-environmental behavior is also important. Voluntary sustainable behavior requires getting individuals to concern themselves with the long-term interest of the collective and the environment (Schwartz, 1977; Frick et al., 2004). Studies show that pro-environmental habits are more likely to form when an individual has an awareness of the problem[12] (Hunecke et al., 2001; Nordlund and Garvill, 2003; Bamberg and Möser, 2007; Barr, 2007; Wittenberg et al., 2018) and understands the effectiveness of their own behavior[13] (Harland et al., 2007; Wittenberg et al., 2018). Two popular apps exist to develop problem awareness and knowledge on the effectiveness of actions, Oroeco and Joulebug.

Oroeco, created in partnership with UC Berkley's CoolClimate research group, tracks student's behavior to calculate carbon footprints and provides personalized tips to simultaneously save money and reduce pollution (Oroeco, 2020). It also, conveniently for class, allows for competitions among individuals and collaborations for larger class projects. JouleBug provides nearly identical features to Oroeco but tracks a broader range of sustainable behavior, not just those related to GHG emissions and climate change (JouleBug, 2020). Both apps help teach problem awareness (climate change and resource use issues) and the effectiveness of their actions (in terms of reduced carbon footprint and money saved on their bills).

What's more, these apps are easily tailored to any length of time or class size. Allow students to track their behavior for a week or a semester. Have students compete over sustainable behavior individually (smaller class size) or in groups (larger class size). Regardless of your desired approach, I provide a sample assignment for homework or extra credit that could quickly turn into a larger semester-long research project.

When time is limited, ask students to use the app for two weeks or less.

- Homework or extra credit: Simply choose an amount of time for the students to observe and log their behavior (e.g., one week, two weeks, etc.). Once established, ask students to compete to see whose climate impacts and actions are the most sustainable (could make the outcome a function of pollution reduced and money saved).

When time allows, give students upwards of an entire semester to track their behavior.

- Homework or extra credit: See above, except extend the length of time students use the app.
- Semester Research Projects or Senior Thesis: Expand the homework assignment above and ask students to research the trade-offs they made

while using the app. Consider asking them to dive deeper into the social cost of carbon if using Oroeco.

11.5 TAKEAWAYS

The applications and examples discussed in this chapter introduce quick and easy ways to create experiential learning opportunities for commonly covered sustainability topics. Additionally, the first three technologies presented, iNaturalist, EDDMapS, and Litterati, teach the importance of collaboration; they aggregate single observations to improve either biodiversity, invasive species, or litter mapping to inform natural resource policy. The last two apps, Oroeco and Joulebug, teach students how to value and incorporate sustainable behavior at home and beyond. All of these tools give students the chance to work with updated sustainability data, along with real opportunities to improve the world around them. Importantly, studies show that students are more likely to continue their sustainable behavior into the future when exposed to nature, which is encouraged by the use of these assignments (Bratman et al., 2012; Collado and Evans, 2019; Whitburn et al., 2019).

While certainly not an exhaustive list of available applications, the examples included in this chapter are the most reputable, freely available, and widely accessible (both geographically and electronically) options I have found to date. However, there are several other tools worth briefly considering:

- OpenTreeMap, produced by the USDA, takes user observations to calculate the value of urban tree ecosystem services and other urban forestry analyses. Unfortunately, the app does require a substantial fee if you were to use it for class. However, there are several public urban area "OpenTree tree maps" available for select markets, which calculate in detail numerous ecosystem service benefits. It appears urban areas are regularly becoming more available, so consider checking for updates periodically.
- Video games, of which there are several. One of the best examples is Cities: Skylines – Natural Disasters, a simulation-based video game that forces students to confront the challenging trade-offs of urban and infrastructure decision making in the face of sustainable development (Livingston, 2016). Cities: Skylines has been used by real cities worldwide to help plan urban infrastructure projects (Donnelly, 2016; Wakefield, 2017). One caveat worth mentioning is that this video game does require a beefy computer processor and graphics card, making the game inaccessible for some students. Alternatively, a similar goal can be achieved by using the freely available SimCity BuildIt game for phones or tablets because it allows for pollution from development (i.e., forcing students to confront trade-offs

from economic growth). See how big your students' cities can grow and ask them to describe the trade-offs they face along the way.[14]

Finally, remember that new technology is created and published daily. Use the tools from throughout the chapter to inspire you to look for other available applications related to sustainability or other environmental economics topics, such as areas covered throughout this textbook. Happy teaching!

NOTES

1. Because what kind of economics chapter would this be if it didn't encourage efficiency throughout.
2. Many of the examples in this chapter provide students with experiential learning opportunities. Studies consistently show that students who "learn by doing" retain more material and are better able to connect textbook theories to real-world scenarios (Benek-Rivera and Mathews, 2004; Hackathorn et al., 2011; Dadach, 2013; Hao et al., 2020).
3. Many of the experiential applications included in this chapter require students to get outside and to observe their natural environment, which may help improve student's physical and mental well-being. As I've experienced first-hand, this will result in more attentive and interested students during class. No, I'm not making this up. Spending time outside is increasingly linked to better education and health outcomes (Berman et al., 2008; Van den Berg et al., 2015; Aerts et al., 2018; Twohig-Bennett and Jones, 2018). Additionally, Richard Louv, author of *Last Child in the Woods*, coined the term "nature-deficit disorder," which refers to behavioral problems resulting from individuals spending less time outdoors (Louv, 2008). Nature-deficit disorder leads to individuals having limited connection with their immediate natural surroundings, potentially contributing to obesity, attention disorders, and depression. Furthermore, given college students' increasingly busier schedule (GenZ, 2020), it has become challenging to get students outside. Not surprising, anxiety and depression are surging among college students (ADAA, 2007; Huckins et al., 2020). The applications contained within the chapter give students "permission" to get outside, which should result in positive results both for you as the instructor, but also for the students' well-being.
4. Experiences in nature are positively related to pro-environmental attitudes and behaviors (Rosa and Collado, 2019). For example, interacting with nature increases willingness to conserve biodiversity and willingness to pay for the conservation of urban green spaces (Lo and Jim, 2010; Soga et al., 2016).
5. The definition of biodiversity seems to vary both within and across disciplines (Holt, 2006). This could provide for fruitful discussion if time allows.
6. Biodiversity is generally calculated using either the Shannon function or the Simpson Index (Keylock, 2005), although there are other measures as well, such as through Deng entropy (Deng, 2016). A quick comparison of the two most common measures shows that the Shannon function is strongly influenced by species richness and by rare species while the Simpson index gives more weight to evenness and common species. Generally speaking, the Shannon index estimates the actual *state* of the environment because it depends more on species richness and less abundant species. On the other hand, the Simpson index highlights the

trend of ecosystem diversity because it counts more on dominant species and is not affected by less abundant elements.

7. The Shannon index assumes species are sampled randomly from an infinite population.

8. Of course, this doesn't necessarily account for invasive alien species, which is another topic mentioned below that could certainly be combined with this discussion.

9. An additional benefit beyond class is that all observations are available for anyone who uses the app. Here are some additional ideas with that in mind. Collect data for larger local projects: have the students collect observations that will help scientists gauge patterns of global change in natural ecosystems and wildlife (City of Surrey, 2020; Harvey, 2020). Alternatively, set up your own challenge in the iNaturalist app and have your class add to a larger set of observations (iNaturalist TG, 2020).

10. An alternative technology, if you live near the coast, is the Clean Swell app technology created by the Ocean Conservancy. Similar in nature to Litterati, Clean Swell lets users record the type and location of trash on beaches with the larger goal of keeping beaches, waterways, and the ocean free of land pollution.

11. It should be obvious that when you document a piece of litter you also discard it, but sometimes it's necessary to state the obvious. However, touching trash during a pandemic (looking at you, COVID-19) is discouraged.

12. For example, having a knowledge of how recycling affects resource use, or consumer actions release GHG's that lead to climate change.

13. For example, using a reusable water bottle saves around 1,460 plastic bottles annually (4 bottles a day*365 days/year = 1,460 bottles).

14. In the past, I've had students compete to see who can make a city with the highest population, weighted by average resident happiness (a function of pollution). The winning student(s) receives bonus points on homework or exams.

REFERENCES

Abatenh, E., Gizaw, B., Tsegaye, Z., & Wassie, M. (2017). The role of microorganisms in bioremediation – A review. *Open Journal of Environmental Biology*, **2**(1), 030–046.

Aerts, R., Honnay, O., & Van Nieuwenhuyse, A. (2018). Biodiversity and human health: Mechanisms and evidence of the positive health effects of diversity in nature and green spaces. *British Medical Bulletin*, **127**(1), 5–22.

ADAA (2007), *Anxiety Disorders on Campus: The Growing Need for College Mental Health Services*, accessed 3 August 2020 at https://adaa.org/sites/default/files/FINALCollegeReport.pdf.https://adaa.org/sites/default/files/FINALCollegeReport .pdf.

ATUS (2020), *American Time Use Survey*, accessed 5 August 2020 at https://www.bls .gov/tus/.

Bamberg, S., & Möser, G. (2007). Twenty years after Hines, Hungerford, and Tomera: A new meta-analysis of psycho-social determinants of pro-environmental behaviour. *Journal of Environmental Psychology*, **27**(1), 14–25.

Barr, S. (2007). Factors influencing environmental attitudes and behaviors: A UK case study of household waste management. *Environment and Behavior*, **39**(4), 435–473.

Benek-Rivera, J., & Mathews, V. E. (2004). Active learning with jeopardy: Students ask the questions. *Journal of Management Education*, **28**(1), 104–118.

Berman, M. G., Jonides, J., & Kaplan, S. (2008). The cognitive benefits of interacting with nature. *Psychological Science*, **19**(12), 1207–1212.

Bratman, G. N., Hamilton, J. P., & Daily, G. C. (2012). The impacts of nature experience on human cognitive function and mental health. *Annals of the New York Academy of Sciences*, **1249**(1), 118–136.

BRFSS (2020). Behavioral Risk Factor Surveillance System, accessed 6 August 2020 at https://www.cdc.gov/brfss/index.html.

CDC (2020). *One Health*, accessed 2 August 2020 at https://www.cdc.gov/onehealth/index.html.

Charles, H., & Dukes, J. S. (2008). Impacts of invasive species on ecosystem services. In *Biological Invasions* (pp. 217–237). Springer, Berlin, Heidelberg.

City of Surrey (2020). *City Nature Challenge 2020*, accessed 2 August 2020 at https://www.surrey.ca/vision-goals/biodiversity-conservation-strategy/citizen-science.

Collado, S., & Evans, G. W. (2019). Outcome expectancy: A key factor to understanding childhood exposure to nature and children's pro-environmental behavior. *Journal of Environmental Psychology*, **61**, 30–36.

Dadach, Z. E. (2013). Quantifying the effects of an active learning strategy on the motivation of students. *International Journal of Engineering Education*, **29**(4), 1–10.

Daehler, C. C. (2003). Performance comparisons of co-occurring native and alien invasive plants: implications for conservation and restoration. *Annual Review of Ecology, Evolution, and Systematics*, **34**(1), 183–211.

Dasgupta, S., Laplante, B., Wang, H., & Wheeler, D. (2002). Confronting the environmental Kuznets curve. *Journal of Economic Perspectives*, **16**(1), 147–168.

Deng, Y. (2016). Deng entropy. *Chaos, Solitons & Fractals*, **91**, 549–553.

Di Falco, S., & Chavas, J. P. (2008). Rainfall shocks, resilience, and the effects of crop biodiversity on agroecosystem productivity. *Land Economics*, **84**(1), 83–96.

Donnelly, J (2016). Cities: Skylines used by Swedish city planners to design new city district. *PC GAMER*. Accessed 2 August 2020 at https://www.pcgamer.com/cities-skylines-used-by-swedish-city-planners-to-design-new-city-district/.

EDDMapS (2020). About, accessed 2 August 2020 at https://www.eddmaps.org/about/.

Edelman, M. W. (1992). *The Measure of Our Success: A Letter to My Children and Yours*. Beacon Press.

EPA (2020). *Cooperative Federalism at EPA*, accessed 2 August 2020 at https://archive.epa.gov/epa/newsreleases/epa-advances-cooperative-federalism-through-designation-process-sulfur-dioxide-and.html.

Erwin, P. M., López-Legentil, S., & Schuhmann, P. W. (2010). The pharmaceutical value of marine biodiversity for anti-cancer drug discovery. *Ecological Economics*, **70**(2), 445–451.

Essl, F., Dullinger, S., Rabitsch, W., Hulme, P.E., Hülber, K., Jarošík, V., Kleinbauer, I., Krausmann, F., Kühn, I., Nentwig, W., & Vilà, M. (2011). Socioeconomic legacy yields an invasion debt. *Proceedings of the National Academy of Sciences*, **108**(1), 203–207.

Fish, S. (1989). Being interdisciplinary is so very hard to do. *Profession*, 15–22.

Frick, J., Kaiser, F. G., & Wilson, M. (2004). Environmental knowledge and conservation behavior: Exploring prevalence and structure in a representative sample. *Personality and Individual Differences*, **37**(8), 1597–1613.

GenZ (2020). *The Key to GenZ Marketing*, accessed 3 August 2020 at https://www.quad.com/resources/realism-the-key-to-gen-z-marketing/.

Giangreco, Leigh (2019). How behavioral science solved Chicago's plastic bag problem. *Politico*. Accessed 2 August 2020, https://www.politico.com/news/magazine/2019/11/21/plastic-bag-environment-policy-067879.

Golde, C. M., & Gallagher, H. A. (1999). The challenges of conducting interdisciplinary research in traditional doctoral programs. *Ecosystems*, 281–285.

Hackathorn, J., Solomon, E. D., Blankmeyer, K. L., Tennial, R. E., & Garczynski, A. M. (2011). Learning by doing: An empirical study of active teaching techniques. *Journal of Effective Teaching*, **11**(2), 40–54.

Hao, Q., Barnes, B., & Jing, M. (2020). Quantifying the effects of active learning environments: Separating physical learning classrooms from pedagogical approaches. *Learning Environments Research*, **24**, 109–122.

Harland, P., Staats, H., & Wilke, H. A. (2007). Situational and personality factors as direct or personal norm mediated predictors of pro-environmental behavior: Questions derived from norm-activation theory. *Basic and Applied Social Psychology*, **29**(4), 323–334.

Harvey, F. (2020). Be a citizen scientist: Track plastic waste, spot a spider monkey or beat coronavirus. *The Guardian*. Accessed 2 August 2020 at https://www.theguardian.com/environment/2020/apr/18/be-a-citizen-scientist-track-plastic-waste-spot-a-spider-monkey-or-beat-coronavirus.

Holt, A. (2006). Biodiversity definitions vary within the discipline, *Nature*, **444**(7116), 146–146.

Huckins, J. F., DaSilva, A. W., Wang, W., Hedlund, E., Rogers, C., Nepal, S. K., ... & Wagner, D. D. (2020). Mental health and behavior of college students during the early phases of the COVID-19 pandemic: Longitudinal smartphone and ecological momentary assessment study. *Journal of Medical Internet Research*, **22**(6), e20185.

Hulme, P. E. (2009). Trade, transport and trouble: Managing invasive species pathways in an era of globalization. *Journal of Applied Ecology*, **46**(1), 10–18.

Hunecke, M., Blöbaum, A., Matthies, E., & Höger, R. (2001). Responsibility and environment: Ecological norm orientation and external factors in the domain of travel mode choice behavior. *Environment and Behavior*, **33**(6), 830–852.

iNaturalist Intro (2020). Accessed 2 August 2020 at https://www.inaturalist.org/pages/getting+started.

iNaturalist Press (2020). Accessed 2 August 2020 at https://www.inaturalist.org/pages/press.

iNaturalist TG (2020). Teachers Guide. Accessed 2 August 2020 at https://www.inaturalist.org/pages/teacher's+guide.

Jauni, M., Gripenberg, S., & Ramula, S. (2015). Non-native plant species benefit from disturbance: A meta-analysis. *Oikos*, **124**(2), 122–129.

JouleBug (2020), *JouleBug*, accessed 8 August 2020 at https://joulebug.com/.

Keylock, C. J. (2005). Simpson diversity and the Shannon–Wiener index as special cases of a generalized entropy. *Oikos*, **109**(1), 203–207.

Kirschner, Jeff (2020), City of SF leverages Litterati to earn $4 in yearly tax revenue from tobacco industry. Accessed 2 August 2020 at https://www.litterati.org/stories/san-francisco-leverages-litterati-to-generate-4m.

Kolar, C. S., & Lodge, D. M. (2001). Progress in invasion biology: predicting invaders. *Trends in Ecology & Evolution*, **16**(4), 199–204.

Leishman, M. R., & Thomson, V. P. (2005). Experimental evidence for the effects of additional water, nutrients and physical disturbance on invasive plants in low fertility Hawkesbury Sandstone soils, Sydney, Australia. *Journal of Ecology*, **93**(1), 38–49.

Levine, J. M., & D'Antonio, C. M. (2003). Forecasting biological invasions with increasing international trade. *Conservation Biology*, **17**(1), 322–326.

Livingston, C. (2016). Natural disasters lets you destroy your cities: Skylines cities, but also save them. *PC GAMER*. Accessed 2 August 2020 at https://www.pcgamer.com/natural-disasters-lets-you-destroy-your-cities-skylines-cities-but-also-save-them/.

Lo, A. Y., & Jim, C. Y. (2010). Willingness of residents to pay and motives for conservation of urban green spaces in the compact city of Hong Kong. *Urban Forestry & Urban Greening*, **9**(2), 113–120.

Louv R. (2008). *Last Child in the Woods*. New York, NY: Workman Publishing Company.

Martinho, G., Balaia, N., & Pires, A. (2017). The Portuguese plastic carrier bag tax: The effects on consumers' behavior. *Waste Management*, **61**, 3–12.

McIntosh, C. R., Shogren, J. F., & Finnoff, D. C. (2010). Invasive species and delaying the inevitable: Valuation evidence from a national survey. *Ecological Economics*, **69**(3), 632–640.

Mrosovsky, N., Ryan, G. D., & James, M. C. (2009). Leatherback turtles: The menace of plastic. *Marine Pollution Bulletin*, **58**(2), 287–289.

MSW Consultants (2009). National visible litter survey and litter cost study. *Keep America Beautiful*. Accessed 2, August 2020 at https://kab.org/wp-content/uploads/2019/08/News-Info_Research_2009_NationalVisibleLitterSurveyandCostStudy_Final.pdf.

NCLS (2020). States with littering penalties. Accessed 2 August 2020 at https://www.ncsl.org/research/environment-and-natural-resources/states-with-littering-penalties.aspx.

Nordlund, A. M., & Garvill, J. (2003). Effects of values, problem awareness, and personal norm on willingness to reduce personal car use. *Journal of Environmental Psychology*, **23**(4), 339–347.

Nowacek, R. S. (2009). Why is being interdisciplinary so very hard to do? Thoughts on the perils and promise of interdisciplinary pedagogy. *College Composition and Communication*, **60**(3), 493–516.

Oroeco (2020), *Oroeco: Turning Green to Gold*. Accessed 8 August, 2020 at https://www.oroeco.com/.

Pimentel, D., Wilson, C., McCullum, C., Huang, R., Dwen, P., Flack, J., Tran, Q., Saltman, T., & Cliff, B. (1997). Economic and environmental benefits of biodiversity. *BioScience*, **47**(11), 747–757.

Pimentel, D., Zuniga, R., & Morrison, D. (2005). Update on the environmental and economic costs associated with alien-invasive species in the United States. *Ecological Economics*, **52**(3), 273–288.

Rosa, C. D., & Collado, S. (2019). Experiences in nature and environmental attitudes and behaviors: Setting the ground for future research. *Frontiers in Psychology*, **10**, 763.

Rosenthal, Elisabeth (2008). By 'bagging it,' Ireland rids itself of a plastic nuisance. *The New York Times*. http://www.nytimes.com/2008/01/31/world/europe/31iht-bags.4.9650382.html.

Schippers, P., van der Heide, C. M., Koelewijn, H. P., Schouten, M. A., Smulders, R. M., Cobben, M. M., Sterk, M., Vos, C. C., & Verboom, J. (2015). Landscape diversity enhances the resilience of populations, ecosystems and local economy in rural areas. *Landscape Ecology*, **30**(2), 193–202.

Schwartz, S. H. (1977). Normative influences on altruism. *Advances in Experimental Social Psychology*, **10**(1), 221–279.

Seebens, H., Gastner, M. T., Blasius, B., & Courchamp, F. (2013). The risk of marine bioinvasion caused by global shipping. *Ecology Letters*, **16**(6), 782–790.

Soga, M., Yamanoi, T., Tsuchiya, K., Koyanagi, T. F., & Kanai, T. (2018). What are the drivers of and barriers to children's direct experiences of nature? *Landscape and Urban Planning*, **180**, 114–120.

Strong, A., Tschirhart, J., & Finnoff, D. (2011). Is economic growth for the birds? *Ecological Economics*, **70**(7), 1375–1380.

Thrupp, L. A. (2000). Linking agricultural biodiversity and food security: The valuable role of agrobiodiversity for sustainable agriculture. *International Affairs*, **76**(2), 265–281.

Toledo, Á., & Burlingame, B. (2006). Biodiversity and nutrition: A common path toward global food security and sustainable development. *Journal of Food Composition and Analysis*, **19**(6–7), 477–483.

Twohig-Bennett, C., & Jones, A. (2018). The health benefits of the great outdoors: A systematic review and meta-analysis of greenspace exposure and health outcomes. *Environmental Research*, **166**, 628–637.

TX DOT (2013). Don't mess with Texas leads to reduction in roadside trash. Accessed 2 August 2020 at https://www.txdot.gov/inside-txdot/media-center/statewide-news/2013-archive/043-2013.html.

Van den Berg, M., Wendel-Vos, W., van Poppel, M., Kemper, H., van Mechelen, W., & Maas, J. (2015). Health benefits of green spaces in the living environment: A systematic review of epidemiological studies. *Urban Forestry & Urban Greening*, **14**(4), 806–816.

Wakefield, J. (2017). Tomorrow's cities: Stockholm turns green. BBC. Accessed 2 August 2020 at https://www.bbc.com/news/av/39200838/video-game-cities-skylines-helps-plan-stockholm-development.

Westphal, M. I., Browne, M., MacKinnon, K., & Noble, I. (2008). The link between international trade and the global distribution of invasive alien species. *Biological Invasions*, **10**(4), 391–398.

Whitburn, J., Linklater, W. L., & Milfont, T. L. (2019). Exposure to urban nature and tree planting are related to pro-environmental behavior via connection to nature, the use of nature for psychological restoration, and environmental attitudes. *Environment and Behavior*, **51**(7), 787–810.

WHO (2017), *What is 'One Health'?* Accessed 2 August 2020 at https://www.who.int/news-room/q-a-detail/one-health.

Williams, A. T., Pond, K., Ergin, A., & Cullis, M. J. (2013). The hazards of beach litter. In *Coastal Hazards* (pp. 753–780). Springer, Dordrecht.

Wittenberg, I., Blöbaum, A., & Matthies, E. (2018). Environmental motivations for energy use in PV households: Proposal of a modified norm activation model for the specific context of PV households. *Journal of Environmental Psychology*, **55**, 110–120.

Young, R. N. (1999). Importance of biodiversity to the modern pharmaceutical industry. *Pure and Applied Chemistry*, **71**(9), 1655–1661.

Zeitlin, M. (2019). Do plastic taxes or bans curb waste? 400 cities and states tried it out. *Vox*. Accessed 2 August 2020 at https://www.vox.com/the-highlight/2019/8/20/20806651/plastic-bag-ban-straw-ban-tax.

12. Teaching natural resource and environmental valuation techniques

Peter W. Schuhmann

INTRODUCTION

Teaching non-market valuation (hereafter, valuation) can be fun, thought-provoking and challenging. Valuation has an interesting and controversial history and a deep body of literature that spans a wide variety of species and ecosystems. Valuation also connects economic theory to practical "real world" applications that students crave and can identify with. Because valuation can be connected to numerous other disciplines, instructors have flexibility in terms of the content that appears on the course syllabus.

Teaching valuation can also be challenging. The idea of monetizing the value of nature may be morally offensive to students who possess an ethical view of the natural world as "priceless." Further, most valuation methods require the application of statistical methods such as regression analysis that students may not have experience with. Calculations of welfare measures often involve nontrivial mathematics. Instructors should anticipate these challenges. Teaching valuation can also be rewarding. In my experience, the valuation unit of the course is often the first time that environmentally-minded students see that economics can play an important role in environmental policy, and that economic arguments for conservation can be more persuasive than moral ones.

The purpose of this chapter is to provide an outline of my approach to teaching non-market valuation to undergraduates. I'll cover the placement of the topic in my resource economics course, my use of stories and events to motivate the need for valuation, my approach to handling the technical nature of the content and other challenges that instructors might encounter.

For context, I teach natural resource economics at a public regional university. We do not have a graduate program in economics. My class size is typically between 50 and 70 students, with a roughly equal mix of economics majors and environmental studies majors. My teaching style is low-frills. I rarely use technology, classroom games or ancillary materials. I do require a good bit of reading and writing. I ask a lot of open-ended questions during class and expect students to respond and defend their answers. I have included many of these questions here, with a summary in Table 12.1. My principle area of research is the non-market valuation of coastal and marine resources using stated and revealed preference methods. When teaching non-market valuation, I rely heavily on my own research for real world examples.

PLACEMENT OF THE NON-MARKET VALUATION IN THE ENVIRONMENTAL OR RESOURCE ECONOMICS COURSE

Judging from its placement in most environmental and natural resource economics textbooks, valuation is commonly covered in the first half of the course. I follow this approach, placing the valuation unit about one-third of the way through my natural resource economics course, immediately following the topics of market failure (i.e. the economic perspective on the cause of environmental problems, including externalities, public goods and common property) and alternative solutions to environmental problems (i.e. command-and-control approaches vs. incentive-based policies and combination policies). At this point in the course we have already covered cost–benefit analysis and discounting. I find that an appreciation for these topics helps provide context for situations when valuation can be useful. For example, value estimates can be used in designing incentive-based policies such as user fees or Pigouvian taxes and can be used as an input into cost–benefit analyses regarding expenditures on public goods.

After covering market failure, I begin the valuation unit by reminding students that markets will often fail to provide the Pareto optimal or efficient amount of certain goods due to their non-rivalrous and non-excludable properties. If left to market forces, public goods and common property resources like parks, protected areas and healthy fish stocks will be under-provided relative to efficient quantities. This leads to the conclusion that collective action or government intervention is often required for the provision of these valuable goods, which means that decisions must be made regarding how much land or marine space should be protected and how the associated expenditures will be financed.

The idea of this short summary of the preceding topics is meant to motivate a simple policy question: "How do we decide what to conserve?" and to help students come to the obvious conclusions that, because of opportunity costs, we cannot conserve everything and that we should focus on conserving natural resources that are the most important to human wellbeing.

PRICES, COSTS, VALUE AND TRADE-OFFS

Valuation is the process of estimating what something is worth. After providing this basic definition, instructors can ask students *how we could go about figuring out what a good or service is worth (to people)* and then ask *if price and value are the same thing.* Instructors can ask students about the price and value of market goods and then ask similar questions about non-market goods related to the environment. Numerous examples from their lives can be used. For example, instructors can ask: *How much did you pay for that backpack, phone, sweatshirt, or laptop?* and then ask, *What is it worth to you?* Instructors can then ask about their experiences with environmental goods and services: *Have you been to the Grand Canyon? Have you been on a trip to the beach, the mountains or the rainforest? Have you been hiking, or surfing lately? What price did you pay for that experience? What was the experience worth to you?* If students struggle with this last idea, instructors can ask them what they would be willing to give up to have that experience again or how much they would have to be compensated to give up such opportunities in the future.

The goal of this discussion is to help students realize that price and value are not necessarily the same thing, and that there are many things in life that have value but do not have market prices. Hopefully students will quickly come around to the idea that price or cost is what you pay for something, but value is what it is worth to you. Goods and services provided by the natural environment have economic value and damages to those goods and services impose real costs on society. We want students to realize that economic values are (1) not always revealed in markets, (2) they are not zero, and (3) apart from wholesale losses of ecosystems, they are not infinite.

Some students will push back on this last idea and may argue that the environment is indeed "priceless." In my experience, this opposition presents a critical moment in the classroom and an opportunity to clearly illustrate the concept of economic value. My approach is a bit blunt. I ask students to raise their hands *if they believe that environmental quality has infinite value (or is "priceless").*[1] I then instruct students to keep their hands in the air if they do not drive a car, fly in airplanes, or use air conditioners in the summer. When students sheepishly lower their hands, I ask *why they engage in polluting activities if they believe that environmental quality is priceless.* Students' answers usually involve the "need" for comfort, convenience, or the necessity of travel. I respond by suggesting that they could give up these comforts if it was important enough. The goal here is for students to realize that if something were indeed priceless, we would be willing to make sacrifices for it: that is, value is revealed by what people are willing to give up. Another useful prompt here is to ask students: *What do you give up for the environment? Do you go through the trouble to recycle or compost some of your trash? Do you volunteer your time for activities such as beach or highway cleanups? Do you make monetary contributions to conservation organizations? Why do you do those things and what does this show?* The willingness to give up time and money reveals the value we place on things including the environment.

ILLUSTRATING COMPONENTS OF VALUE AND THE IMPORTANCE OF VALUATION

The next goal is to help students realize that people value things that they never actually use or interact with in any tangible way. The concept of non-use values can be abstract and difficult to grasp at first, so I like to start with questions directed at non-use values held by my students. *Can you value something that you never see in person? For example, do you care that blue whales exist on earth and are protected from commercial whaling?* When students confirm that people do indeed care about things they never actually interact with, I present the components of non-use values (existence, option, bequest) and remind students of the "evidence" of non-use values that we just discussed: people donate time and money to environmental causes, even though they will not necessarily interact with the species or ecosystems that they are supporting.

Having introduced economic values as being comprised of market and non-market values as well as use and non-use values, it is important to next establish the foundation for *why* we should try to estimate the value of environmental goods and services. Toward this end, I want to get students thinking about specific scenarios where having an estimate of the value of environmental goods or services or the value of environmental damage could be useful for making decisions.

One of the easiest ways for students to see the importance of valuation is to present them with a real-world scenario involving a trade-off where a decision was necessary. My approach here is tell a story involving a trade-off between market and non-market goods. Having grown up on the coast of New Jersey, the story of marine pollution from New York City showing up on New Jersey's shores in the late 1980s is one that I can recount from personal experience. New York's dated stormwater and sewer systems were operating at full capacity. During periods of heavy rain, sewage mixed with stormwater, resulting in waste material being flushed out to sea and arriving on the Jersey shoreline. Illegal dumping of waste at sea was also an issue. Beaches were closed during peak summer tourist months causing economic hardships to coastal businesses. Solutions included overhauling New York's sewer system and improving monitoring and enforcement of rules regarding illegal dumping. The estimated cost to New Jersey businesses in 1988 was over $1 billion. Numerous other stories of environmental damage can be used here such as the Exxon Valdez oil tanker spill in Prince William Sound, Alaska, British Petroleum (BP) Deepwater Horizon offshore drilling unit oil spill in the U.S. Gulf of Mexico, the Love Canal toxic waste pollution disaster in New York, ghost fishing harming marine life, spills of hog farm waste during heavy rains, etc. Instructors can also rely on examples from their coverage of externalities.

Table 12.1   Leading questions and learning goals

Leading question	Learning goal
How should society decide what natural resources to conserve?	Conserving everything would be costly. Not conserving anything would also be inefficient. Society must therefore make decisions about different sources of value.
How do we know what something is worth to people?	To make comparisons between alternatives we need to understand relative values.
Have you been to the Grand Canyon, beach, mountains, rainforest, hiking or surfing? What price did you pay for that experience? What was the experience worth to you?	Price and value are not necessarily the same thing. Many things in life have value, but do not have market prices. When prices are not available, we need another way to understand what some goods and services are worth.
Is the environment priceless? If so, why do you engage in behaviors that damage the environment?	Apart from wholesale destruction of ecosystems, the value of environmental goods and services is somewhere between zero and infinity. Environmentally damaging behaviors illustrate that people are willing to trade-off environmental goods and services for comfort and convenience.
What do you give up for the environment? Do you go through the trouble to recycle or compost some of your trash? Do you volunteer your time? Do you make monetary contributions? Why do you do those things and what does this show?	Value is revealed through trade-offs that people are willing and able to make.
Can you value something that you never see?	People can place real economic value on environmental goods and services without direct interaction (non-use values).
How do we know if clean-up or conservation activities are worth it?	Value estimates can help us decide whether to engage in an activity
What else could society do with money that would be used for environmental cleanup?	Resources spent on conservation initiatives can be spent on other things that society values. Spending on the environment carries an opportunity cost.

Leading question	Learning goal
Because of its remote location, Prince William Sound Alaska was rarely visited by people. Does this mean that the damages to Prince William Sound ecosystem from the Exxon Valdez oil spill had no value?	Value does not have to be associated with direct use of the natural environment. Value and preferences will not necessarily be revealed through human behavior. In order to understand the non-use components
Once we estimate the benefits that people derive from the environment or the costs that people impose, what purpose do these value estimates serve?	Valuation should be used to inform trade-offs.

I follow the NY/NJ pollution story by asking students what we should do in situations like this. Students will be naturally inclined to say, "Clean up the pollution!" This response leads to an important question that illustrates the use of valuation as an input into cost–benefit analysis. Instructors can ask a follow-up question such as: *Are you sure that cleaning up the beaches is worth it?* And, *How would we know if it is worth it?* We then discuss the idea that in order to judge whether this project is worth the expense we would have to measure the benefits of clean beaches and compare those benefits to the costs of cleaning up the pollution. This means that we must estimate the value of visiting clean beaches, which includes both market and non-market values which leads to the question: *How can we measure what those things are worth?*

An important side note: in addition to providing a real-world scenario where non-market valuation is useful for policy purposes, using a pollution clean-up story gives instructors a chance to remind students that decisions involve opportunity costs. During the dialogue about whether it is worth it to spend money on pollution cleanup, instructors should remind students that funds for public goods are limited, and can ask: *What else could society do with money that would be used for environmental cleanup?* Be sure to give examples that help students visualize the opportunity cost of spending money on an environmental problem. Ask them to name pressing issues in their community that are not related to the environment. They will probably mention things like crime, poverty, inequality, education and healthcare. Is $10 billion spent on environmental clean-up more valuable to society than $10 billion spent on hospitals, schools, poverty alleviation or law enforcement? The point here is not to get off track and discuss the relative value of different government programs, but rather to illustrate that budgets are scarce, and that spending funds on one issue often means spending less on other issues.

Once the basic ideas of value and valuation have been established and the idea of using non-market value estimates in a trade-off decision has been provided, instructors can present other scenarios where having estimates of non-market values would be useful for public decisions. Table 12.2 shows some of the scenarios that I use. Depending on where in the course valuation is covered, some of these may be familiar to students.

Table 12.2   Valuation scenarios and examples

Scenario	Example
Complete a benefit–cost analysis of a conservation project	Determine the net economic benefit of establishing a marine protected area or installing a system of mooring buoys to protect coral reefs from damage.
Analyze the potential economic impacts of a proposed policy or regulation change	Determining the economic and environmental implications of a proposed regulation that will decrease the allowable catch of a marine fish species.
Help to efficiently manage natural resources	Given that there are many ways to regulate fishing in order to protect stocks from depletion, what type of regulation will result in the highest net benefits from a given stock while ensuring it is economically and ecologically sustainable?
Assess the potential for user fees	Will tourists pay more for "environmentally friendly" recreation experiences? If so, how much more? Can revenues from user fees be used to finance protected areas?
Measure monetary damages from natural resource degradation or damage	What is the economic loss realized as beach width diminishes? How much should be spent on beach renourishment? What was the value of the damage imposed by the Deepwater Horizon oil spill? Should BP be responsible for payment? If so, how much?
Determine total economic value (TEV) of a resource	What is the contribution of coral reefs to the economy of Grenada? How much should be spent on reef protection?

To recap, important ideas to cover when introducing the topic of non-market valuation include:

a.   Price and value are not necessarily the same thing. There are many things in life that have value but do not have market prices. Goods and services provided by the natural environment have economic value and damages to the environment or losses of those goods and services impose real costs on society. Many of these costs and benefits are not revealed in markets.

b.   It's important to get students thinking about scenarios where having an estimate of the benefits from environmental goods or services or the costs of environmental damage can be useful for making decisions. Before covering the details of *how* we can estimate the economic value of environmental goods and services, it is important to first establish a foundation for *why* we should try to estimate the economic value of environmental goods and services.

c.   Presenting students with a real-world scenario involving a trade-off and decision involving the environment (e.g. should we spend money to solve this environmental problem?) is an effective way to illustrate that economic values should be understood before making decisions about resource use.

VALUATION METHODS

Having established that economic values are important to understand, the next step is to introduce students to the available methods for valuation in order to answer the question: *How can we estimate the economic value of environmental goods and services?* The basic idea behind non-market valuation is to observe and analyze trade-offs that people make when interacting with the environment. It is important to point out that because people interact with the environment in many ways, there are many approaches to valuation. A fun exercise here (Exercise 1, shown in Table 12.3) is to have students list specific benefits that people derive from the natural environment and list costs that people impose on the environment. Hopefully students will mention direct interactions such as recreation and aesthetics, indirect interactions such as pollution assimilation and oxygen generation, and passive interactions such as enjoying the knowledge that certain species and ecosystems exist.

With this context, I present an overview of valuation methods, providing basic definitions of market-based methods (relying on market data to estimate values), revealed preference techniques (observations of people's behaviors can help understand value) and stated preference techniques (asking people about value) before getting into details. I begin my detailed coverage of valuation methods with the travel cost method because it is intuitive and has an interesting history. I tell the story of the letter that Harold Hotelling wrote to the National Park Service (Hotelling, 1949), where he suggested that the cost of travelling to a recreation site (distance, time) can serve as a reasonable approximation for the price of accessing that site. I then describe the travel cost method in terms of data needs (often obtained through surveys of recreationists), the methodological approach to estimating the demand for a particular type of recreation, and how an estimate of demand can be used to calculate the monetary value of changes in the quality or availability of a recreation site. Some students will need a refresher on the ideas of demand and consumer surplus. I also provide a 15-minute primer on regression analysis, because most students in my course have not yet completed econometrics or advanced statistics.

After the travel cost method I cover the hedonic pricing approach, using simplified examples from the literature involving the value of views and open space (e.g. Morancho, 2003; Sander and Polasky, 2009), beach width (e.g. Landry et al., 2003), air quality (e.g. Bayless, 1982; Kim et al., 2003) and noise pollution (Cohen and Coughlin, 2008). Again, it is important that students have a basic understanding of regression modeling.

Next, I remind students that direct interaction with the environment is not a prerequisite for economic value. For instance, we need something other than observations of behaviors to estimate non-use values. The purpose here is to start the discussion of stated preference methods and to get students to realize that we must directly ask people about their preferences and value for environmental goods and services that they do not interact with. I set the stage by telling the story of the Exxon Valdez oil spill, showing headlines and pictures of Prince William Sound before, during and after the spill. After describing the damage to the pristine ecosystems of Prince William Sound, I remind students that its remote location means that people rarely visited the area. I then ask if this means that the damages to Prince William Sound ecosystem had no economic value. Students will hopefully identify this situation as involving market values (e.g. losses in commercial fishing revenues), non-market values and non-use values. We discuss which economic values can be estimated with techniques we've covered so far, and note that we need a new method to estimate the non-use components of economic value.

I then provide a basic overview of the contingent valuation method (CVM), covering the basic components of a CVM survey: respondent demographic information, a description of a program or scenario involving environmental change, a payment vehicle and a willingness to pay question. I spend a bit of time discussing each of these components, providing alternative ways that people can be asked to pay for public goods and alternative ways of eliciting willingness to pay (i.e. open-ended, bounded and payment card approaches). Important points to convey here are the ideas that asking people about value is not an exact science and variations in the method will produce variation in the resulting economic value estimates.

Before getting into various biases and difficulties with CVM, I recount the history of CVM as it relates to the Exxon Valdez spill. I have fun sharing this story with students and tell them about the two teams of "rock star economists" battling it out in the peer-reviewed literature with data and theory. The fall 1994 issue of the *Journal of Economic Perspectives* contains essential reading for those not familiar with the debate, but it's probably not necessary that students read these articles. I note that this debate among economists served a critical function: potential sources of bias were identified, and best practices were developed. We then discuss the many sources of bias and other difficulties associated with stated preference methods (information bias, strategic bias, starting point bias, hypothetical bias, objection to the payment mechanism, defining the appropriate market) and potential solutions.

Because I have been involved in valuation research using choice experiments (CEs), I also spend a good bit of time covering this relatively new approach, which also has an interesting history in transportation planning, marketing and health. I do not get too deep into the details of CE design or utility estimation, but I show them several examples of choice experiment surveys and I provide an overview of how regression analysis is applied to CE data. I conclude the valuation unit discussing other valuation methods such as the damage avoidance method and the replacement cost method, noting the benefits and shortcomings of these approaches.

If you spend enough time discussing data and estimation of welfare measures, students can get bogged down in the details. When covering valuation methods, it is important to provide reminders of the big picture. I try to present concrete examples for each valuation method and ask students to think about *what purpose the value estimates could serve*. The big point here is that valuation research should be designed to help society solve a problem, which typically involves a trade-off. Instructors can refer to the types of decisions outlined in Table 12.3.

DEALING WITH MORAL OPPOSITION TO VALUATION

One of the biggest obstacles to teaching valuation is moral opposition. Some students will simply reject the basic premise of putting a price tag on nature, as it goes against their ethical worldview that nature is "priceless." I address this opposition two ways. First, as noted above, I like to provide a little pushback on the notion of things being priceless by asking students how their daily life activities impact the natural environment. I also like to remind students that the process of valuation amounts to monetizing trade-offs that people are already making – that is, through our actions we are implicitly engaging in valuation anyway. This concept can be difficult for students to grasp, so I lean on examples that I've already introduced. For example, when you choose to drive your car to school or to work instead of walking or riding a bike, you are implicitly valuing your own comfort and convenience more than the damage to human and environmental health that are caused by your emissions. To sum up, valuation often amounts to simply measuring and monetizing the trade-offs that people are making.

ADDRESSING COMMON QUESTIONS AND MISCONCEPTIONS

Once students realize the value in valuation, it is important to remind them of a few realities. First, valuation research is often expensive, requiring costly surveys and other forms of data collection, plus time and technical skills for analysis and reporting. It is also important for students to understand that economists do not engage in valuation simply for the sake of knowing what something is worth. As noted above, we engage in valuation research when there is a reason why society needs to understand the monetary value of non-market goods and services, and that reason usually involves trade-offs. Students should be reminded that the purpose of valuation is to help society make better decisions about resource allocation, not to "prove" that the environment is worth conserving. While value estimates can be used for advocacy, advocacy is not the intended purpose. Sometimes valuation research will provide an economic argument in favor of conservation or reducing pollution, but not always. This is a good time to ask students whether estimates of "total economic value" are useful for policy purposes. To frame this question, I present an overview of "The value of the world's ecosystem services and natural capital" (Costanza et al., 1997) and the ensuing debate among economists regarding the usefulness and accuracy of the associated value estimates (e.g. Pearce, 1998; Toman, 1998; Bockstael et al., 2000). Hopefully students will grasp the idea that most environmental change is incremental rather than absolute. While it may be interesting to ponder the monetary worth of an entire ecosystem, and it may serve to raise awareness, such estimates are unlikely to be useful for specific policy decisions.

Finally, it is important to discuss the impact that valuation research has on environmental policy. There is a good bit of literature on this topic (e.g. see Kushner et al., 2012; Laurans et al., 2013; Waite et al., 2014) which suggests that while many valuation studies have had direct policy influence, the impact of valuation research on policy is often difficult to trace. Students should not be left thinking that estimates of economic value are the sole basis upon which policy decisions regarding the environment are made. Other important considerations include equity, budget constraints, and political will to make change.

ASSIGNMENTS

In addition to the assignment regarding lists of how people interact with the natural environment, I include two other assignments in the valuation unit of my course. These are outlined in Table 12.3 and detailed in the appendix to this chapter. One assignment involves presenting students with several scenarios where non-market valuation would be useful for a decision, and asking students to identify components of value and appropriate valuation methods. An important point of this assignment is that we often need multiple methods or approaches to understand economic value. A good tip for students is to focus on buzzwords. If the scenario involves recreation and travel, they should think about the travel cost method. If non-use values are involved, they should think about CVM. If multi-attribute goods are involved, they should think about CEs. Environmental goods and services that affect property values or wages can be estimated using hedonic pricing. The other assignment is for students to summarize a published non-market valuation study of their choice. Exposing students to the details of a valuation study provides important context for the lessons covered in class. Allowing students the flexibility to choose the environmental good or service that is the subject of valuation research can spark additional interest.

Table 12.3   *Valuation exercises and learning goals*

Exercise	Learning goal
How do people interact with the natural environment? a. List benefits that people derive from the natural environment. b. List damages that people impose on the natural environment that impact other people.	Help students realize the breadth of ways that people interact with the environment in order to motivate different valuation methods.
Valuation Scenarios (see appendix for full exercise) a. Present real or hypothetical cases where decisions must be made using estimates of costs and benefits. b. Ask students to suggest which valuation procedures could be applied to each scenario and explain why that method is appropriate. c. Ask students to explain how the resulting value estimates would be used to inform the decision or trade-off.	Help students understand the application of alternative methods and recognize that environmental change is often complex, requiring more than one valuation method.
Valuation research article summary Describe: a. The research question. What is being valued? Why are these value estimates important? b. The data used in the study. c. The methodology used to address the research question. What method is used to estimate value? d. The main results of the study. What did the researchers discover? e. How can the economic values estimated in this research be used to influence policy?	Expose students to peer-reviewed literature using the methods discussed in class. Highlight the importance of data and empirical analysis and objectively approaching valuation questions.

NOTE

1. Recall that my classroom typically has a couple of dozen students majoring in environmental studies. This question may not evoke as strong a reaction in economics students, but you are sure to get some takers.

REFERENCES

Bayless, M. (1982), 'Measuring the benefits of air quality improvements: A hedonic salary approach', *Journal of Environmental Economics and Management*, **9** (1), 81–99.

Bockstael, N.E., A.M. Freeman, R.J. Kopp, P.R. Portney, and V.K. Smith (2000), 'On measuring economic values for nature', *Environmental Science and Technology*, **34**, 1384–1389.

Cohen, J.P. and C.C. Coughlin (2008), 'Spatial hedonic models of airport noise, proximity, and housing prices', *Journal of Regional Science*, **48** (5), 859–878.

Costanza, R., R. d'Arge, R. De Groot, S. Farber, M. Grasso, B. Hannon, K. Limburg, S. Naeem, R.V. O'Neill, J. Paruelo, and R.G. Raskin (1997), 'The value of the world's ecosystem services and natural capital', *Nature*, **387** (6630), 253.

Hotelling, H. (1949), *An Economic Study of the Monetary Valuation of Recreation in the National Parks*, Washington, D.C.: U.S. Department of the Interior, National Park Service and Recreational Planning Division.

Kim, C.W., T.T. Phipps, and L. Anselin (2003), 'Measuring the benefits of air quality improvement: A spatial hedonic approach', *Journal of Environmental Economics and Management*, **45** (1), 24–39.

Kushner, B., M. Jungwiwattanaporn, R. Waite, and L. Burke (2012), *Influence of Coastal Economic Valuations in the Caribbean: Enabling Conditions and Lessons Learned*, Washington, D.C.: World Resources Institute.

Landry, C.E., A.G. Keeler, and W. Kriesel, (2003), 'An economic evaluation of beach erosion management alternatives', *Marine Resource Economics*, **18** (2), 105–127.

Laurans, Y., A. Rankovic, R. Billé, R. Pirard, and L. Mermet (2013), 'Use of ecosystem services economic valuation for decision making: Questioning a literature blind-spot', *Journal of Environmental Management*, **119**, 208–219.

Morancho, A.B. (2003), 'A hedonic valuation of urban green areas', *Landscape and Urban Planning*, **66** (1), 35–41.

Pearce, D. (1998), 'Auditing the earth: The value of the world's ecosystem services and natural capital', *Environment: Science and Policy for Sustainable Development*, **40** (2), 23–28.

Sander, H.A. and S. Polasky (2009), 'The value of views and open space: Estimates from a hedonic pricing model for Ramsey County, Minnesota, USA', *Land Use Policy*, **26** (3), 837–845.

Toman, M. (1998), 'Why not to calculate the value of the world's ecosystem services and natural capital', *Ecological Economics*, **25** (1), 57–60.

Waite, R., L. Burke, E. Gray, P. van Beukering, L. Brander, E. Mackenzie, L. Pendleton, P. Schuhmann, and E.L. Tompkins (2014), *Coastal Capital: Ecosystem Valuation for Decision Making in the Caribbean*, Washington, D.C.: World Resources Institute.

APPENDIX

Valuation Scenarios Assignment

For each of the following scenarios:
- (i) Determine whether the good(s) or service(s) to be valued are market goods or a non-market goods, or a combination of both. Explain your answer.
- (ii) Suggest which valuation procedure(s) would be best suited to determine the value of the good: the contingent valuation method (CVM), choice modeling (CM), hedonic pricing (H), the travel cost method (TCM), the replacement cost method (RC) or the damage avoidance method (DA). Justify your responses.

1. A marine management agency is considering a plan to decrease operating costs at marine protected areas (MPAs). You have been hired as a consultant to determine the economic desirability of the following actions:
   - (a) Part of the plan is to decrease the number of park managers and other personnel at each park. The labor cuts will be less maintenance of the shoreline and terrestrial areas within the parks, and less enforcement of no-take no-wake regulations within the marine area. Your task is to determine the value of the lost benefits to the park's users so that they can be weighed against the cost savings.
   - (b) Another part of the marine agency cutbacks is a proposal to close some MPAs. The land adjacent to the MPAs would be sold to private investors who would open the areas up for development.
2. In Southport, North Carolina, shrimp harvesters are currently using their boats and gear to clean up an environmental improvement gone bad. In the late 1970s the state of North Carolina submerged over a half million spare tires near Oak Island as an artificial reef to attract fish. The steel cables which once held the tires together have rusted through, and storms have released the tires into the sea. The state is currently paying the shrimp harvesters $4 per tire, but because of damage done to their nets by the tires, the shrimpers are demanding more. How can we determine if the fee should be increased?
3. Natural Citrus Products Corporation grows organic fruits in the Bahamas. Some consumers are willing to pay more for these products because they do not contribute to the environmental degradation caused by most pesticides and fertilizers. However, the organic fruits are less attractive visually (e.g. more blemishes) than those grown with conventional

means. The corporation would like you to explore the marketability of their products in the southern Caribbean area.

4.   To improve the viability of fish stocks in the Chesapeake Bay, the states of Maryland and Virginia are considering a ban on certain lawn fertilizers used primarily by golf courses. During heavy rains the fertilizer chemicals flow into rivers and streams which drain into the bay and harm marine life. Without the chemicals, the grass on the golf courses will not be as green and the owners feel this will adversely affect their business. How can we determine if the fertilizer ban will result in a net improvement in economic welfare?

5.   A proposal has been put forth to construct a large all-inclusive hotel on the Caribbean island of Tobago. The hotel would be built in the coastal zone, on an area of coastal wetlands and adjacent to a healthy coral reef. In order to facilitate water sports by hotel patrons, a small protected harbor would be constructed, requiring the destruction of approximately five acres of coral reef. The loss of nearshore coastal wetlands is expected to result in increased runoff and sedimentation and less absorption of land-based pollutants. These changes are also expected to have adverse impacts on reef health, fish biomass and fish diversity in the area. Over 200 jobs would be created during the two-year hotel construction period, and approximately 100 people would be employed by the hotel full time once it is open. The economic impact on the island is projected to be in excess of $2 million USD per year. You have been hired as part of a consulting team to provide the government with an objective appraisal of the economic costs and benefits associated with the hotel project.

Journal Article Summary Assignment

Use Google Scholar to find a published non-market valuation study that uses the travel cost method, hedonic pricing, the contingent valuation method, or choice modeling (choice experiments).
Provide:

a.   The full article reference.
b.   A description of the research question being addressed in the study. What is being valued? Why are these economic value estimates important?
c.   A description of the data used in the study. How were data collected? From whom? At what time?
d.   A description of the methodology used to address the research question. Describe the empirical approach to estimating economic value (e.g. the

authors estimate a travel cost model of demand or a hedonic house price function).

e. A description of the main results of the study (what did they find out?) and some thoughts about how and why these results might be used to influence policy.

13. Triangulated teaching: approaching environmental economics from multiple angles

David A. Anderson

INTRODUCTION

The importance of environmental economics compels us to convey its tenets in clear and captivating ways. To that end, triangulated teaching is the practice of explaining each difficult concept from three or more angles. As a lifelong learner, perhaps you use the same approach. To learn how to bake a soufflé, you might get instructions from a friend, consult a book, and watch a YouTube video. Each angle on the task adds valuable information that, in concert with information from other angles, leads to success. Yet as teachers, we may place too much emphasis on the instruction given in lectures, expecting students to master difficult material without the cookbook or the YouTube video.

Economic concepts are as challenging to learn as they are important. Differing perspectives from readings, videos, active learning exercises, guest speakers, field trips, documentaries, and other digital media add dimensions to environmental economics that, when properly exhibited, are clarifying and memorable. This chapter explains applications of triangulated teaching to environmental economics and cites evidence of the gains from providing multiple angles.

REASONS FOR TRIANGULATION

While some courses lack even the second angle a textbook provides, the value of multiple perspectives is both intuitive and established. When a student asks for help finding a tutor, that student is asking for another angle on the material. The same is true when a student asks for help understanding explanations given in a textbook or lecture. Every statement of "In other words, ..." is about the value of conveying ideas in more than one way.

Science backs up the intuition and anecdotes in support of triangulation. *Dual-coding theory* portends benefits from combinations of verbal and visual stimuli. The theory is that specialized subsystems in the brain handle information from each type of stimulus separately, and that interactive recall from these distinct subsystems enhances knowledge retrieval. (Paivio 1986; Clark and Paivio 1991). Mayer's (2009) *cognitive theory of multimedia learning* attaches the tenets of dual-coding theory to the notion that our minds synthesize the sights and sounds of multimedia presentations in an integrated way that supports the absorption of information.

Research by Choi and Johnson (2007), Brecht (2012), Vazquez and Chiang (2014), Yung and Paas (2015), and others indicates that videos and related visual aids significantly increase comprehension and retention. McDaniel and Einstein (1986) find that distinctive and bizarre imagery helps students remember things better. Motion and realism matter as well. Hoffler and Leutner (2007) performed a meta-analysis of 26 studies comparing the instructional value of static photos and animations. They concluded that animations make substantial contributions to learning outcomes and that the contributions are relatively large for realistic animations.

Anderson (2003) asked survey respondents to estimate the annual health and environmental damage caused by an oil refinery and a coal-fired power plant. Some participants were shown visual images of the operations and some were not. The median damage estimate of respondents who saw a photo of the oil refinery was 75 percent higher than that of respondents who saw no photo. The median damage estimate of respondents who saw a visual image of the power plant was 30.4 percent higher than that of respondents who saw no photo. As much as images matter, many lessons in fields that include environmental economics are devoid of the angle that visual aids provide.

An earlier phase of education theory promulgated the idea that people with particular learning styles, such as aural learners and visual learners, should receive information tailored to that style. Fleming and Mills (1992) summarize the earlier literature and discuss a questionnaire meant to reveal learning styles. More recent findings by Rogowsky et al. (2015), Willingham et al. (2015), Cuevas and Dawson (2018), Husmann and O'Loughlin (2018), and others suggest that narrowly focused teaching modalities do not pay off. Instead, students identified as auditory learners or visual learners, for example, learn well from a variety of modalities.

Public perceptions of the value of combining verbal or written information with visual aids are clear from the popularity of visually oriented magazines, websites, artwork, signage, and instructional videos. Despite the availability of written instructions on how to change a tire, several "How to Change a Tire" videos on YouTube have received more than one million views. People clearly prefer a visual addition to written and aural instructions. Despite the value of visual presentations, the teaching of environmental economics is far from replete with angles on the challenging material. This motivates further examination of the available options.

A FOUNDATION OF LECTURE AND DISCUSSION

The effectiveness of educational videos does not mean we can dismiss lecture and discussion. Almost since Telcan and Sony released the first home videocassette recorders in the 1960s there has been talk of recorded media replacing teachers. Some of that type of replacement is occurring now, with major universities helping their instructors transfer lectures, discussions, group work, and assignments onto digital platforms.[1] Research by Bridge et al. (2009), Dey et al. (2009), Traphagan et al. (2009) and others suggests that videos of class material show promise. Yet studies by McNulty et al. (2011), Fernandes et al. (2012), Varao-Sousa and Kingstone (2015), and others indicate that videos are no match for in-person instruction.

Beyond the documented evidence, the fact that most schools continue to provide relatively expensive in-person lectures reveals a preference for live instruction over recorded lectures. When present in a classroom with students, an instructor can customize the pace and content of lessons to the needs of the audience. The instructor can engage the students, assess their comprehension with verbal inquiries, answer questions from the students, and adjust the lesson plan on the fly. And by gathering for lecture rather than watching a screen in solitude, students bond and enjoy camaraderie. Although videos have failed to replace in-person lectures, short videos can enhance those malleable instructor-led lessons as discussed below.

The salient point is that advocacy for multiple sources of information does not imply large doses. As in most things, moderation is a virtue. Given the diminishing returns from any particular teaching style, and the capacity for chalk-and-talk lectures to be interactive and audience specific, the best practice involves a mix of approaches that retains the lecture component.

Figure 13.1 illustrates the idea that live lecture and discussion should be the focus of class time, and that other approaches are supplementary. In this spin on the classic food pyramid, movies of significant length take the place of sugar—they are delightful but we must use them with restraint. Their length is seldom justified and they need not take up class time. Field trips, guest speakers, and classroom activities (e.g., simulations or student presentations), along with short videos, are great for variety, but none of these should form the foundation for our time with students.

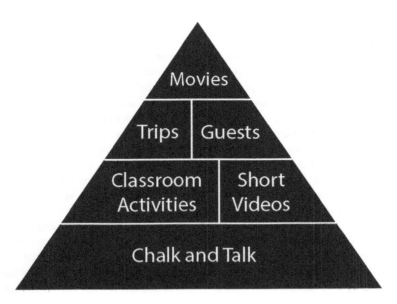

Figure 13.1   Pyramid of class activities

TEXTBOOKS AS A CRITICAL SECOND ANGLE

Like a kitchen without a cookbook, an environmental economics course without a textbook lacks the go-to source of ever-accessible information. Textbooks are credible sources of depth and details. They reinforce the lecture coverage and provide another angle on difficult material. There are options to purchase textbooks in digital or print formats, save them forever, and read them whenever a refresher is desired.

Environmental economics textbooks now come with a variety of resources that provide additional angles on the content, such as educational videos, problem sets, and PowerPoint slides. Available textbooks provide substantial visual perspectives within their pages, including large numbers of color photographs, diagrams, cartoons, charts, and graphs.[2] Many textbooks include application boxes that re-introduce key material in a real-world context. Some textbooks suggest online exercises and additional readings as extra angles on the content. In other words, as a supplement to lecture and discussion, a good textbook may fulfill the goals of triangulated teaching.

OPTIONS FOR THE THIRD ANGLE

Instructors can shed light on environmental economics from myriad additional angles. The ideal complement to lectures and textbook readings might be first-hand exposure to environmental problems and solutions. Field trips achieve that goal, but they present logistical challenges given liability considerations and large classes. When those barriers are surmountable, consider taking students to a home that is off the grid, a water treatment plant, a national park, a hydropower plant, or a municipal waste facility.

Guest speakers can provide fresh angles and expertise on the intersection of economics and the environment. Perhaps invite a policymaker, a forester, an environmental science professor, a miner, or a plant manager to class. If local experts are unavailable, experts from elsewhere can be Skyped into the classroom from anywhere with internet service.

Readings from sources other than textbooks are often timely and fruitful. Instructors can guide students to read the most recent posts on environmental economics blogs such as env-econ.net, news headlines on epa.gov, vital signs for climate change at climate.nasa.gov/evidence, or policy proposals from environmental organizations such as those of the Natural Resources Defense Council at nrdc.org.

Videos allow instructors to provide angles on environmental economics that go beyond the possibilities for chalk-and-talk lectures. With video clips, we can summon into our classroom environmental scientists, wildlife, externalities, resource markets, extraction sites, and energy sources. Higher education is evolving in ways that incorporate more use of videos. Experiments with "flipped" classrooms showcase a relatively new combination of live instruction and videos. For example, Caviglia-Harris (2016) compared the test scores for students in traditional classrooms with students who watched instructional videos and spent class time on exercises and applications. Her students in the flipped classroom, and students in a partially flipped classroom who watched videos but also received short lectures, performed better on exams than students who did not watch videos.

Other possibilities for the third angle include active learning exercises, podcasts, documentaries, student presentations, case studies, debates, and group projects (as discussed in the last section of this chapter).

TRIANGULATING WITH DIGITAL MEDIA

Modern technology expands both the allure and the options for multimedia presentations as complements to lecture and discussion. This section discusses the growing assortment of digital resources, instructor's ability to create their own resources, and assignments that engage students in the production of digital media.

Online Sources of Digital Media

The internet serves as a virtual library for digital angles on environmental economics. Websites, image collections, and video series that bring our field to life include:

- *Brookings Creative Lab* (www.youtube.com/channel/UCzDLNFY7Kg5 koLB157_gsFQ), a multimedia channel that showcases the stories behind Brookings research on topics that include water scarcity and climate change
- *Conservation Strategy Fund YouTube Channel* (www.youtube.com/chann el/UCSUx8XzYbinaF0whJYXHU8Q), a collection of videos on environmental and resource economics
- *Marginal Revolution University* (www.mruniversity.com), a website with teaching resources that include news articles and videos on environmental topics
- *TED* (www.ted.org), a high quality series of lectures by global authorities on environmental and resource topics and many other subjects
- *The Citizens Climate Lobby YouTube Channel* (https://www.youtube.com/ c/CitizensClimateLobby), a set of videos that explain the policy solutions to carbon emissions advocated by this organization
- *The EPA YouTube Channel* (www.youtube.com/user/USEPAgov/), a series of videos from the U.S. Environmental Protection Agency
- *Pexel Environmental Photos* (www.pexels.com/search/environment/), a source of free images of environmental assets
- *Unsplash Environmental Photos* (www.unsplash.com/s/photos/environ mental), a source of free images of environmental assets

Table 13.1 provides specific examples of videos on environmental economics from which students can benefit, along with videos for instructors on triangulated teaching.

Principles of Use

As educators ponder the use of digital media in the environmental economics classroom, three guiding principles may help us avoid pitfalls.

Keep it legal. Schools and their students are vulnerable to lawsuits. The many associated legal issues are beyond the scope of this chapter, but be aware that people are searching online for the unlicensed use of digital content

Table 13.1   Video examples

Concept	Program/Series	URL
Brownfield Cleanup	EPA YouTube Channel	www.youtu.be/AfK-Wd44DHA
Carbon Fee and Dividend	Citizens Climate Lobby	https://youtu.be/9oyguP4nLv0
Carbon Neutrality	TED	www.ted.com/talks/tshering_tobgay_this _country_isn_t_just_carbon_neutral_it _s_carbon_negative
Climate Change	Samantha Bee/Greta Thunberg	www.youtu.be/75UUiYUx1Fo
Cost–Benefit Analysis	Conservation Strategy Fund	www.youtu.be/7tdKkeNClPE
Fisheries Economics	Conservation Strategy Fund	www.youtu.be/Z4AXnZOsrK8
Green New Deal	Last Week Tonight	www.youtu.be/JDcro7dPqpA
Public Sentiment on Environmental Issues	The Daily Show	www.youtu.be/Wi3ujfXLYAc
Resource Depletion	The Story of Stuff	www.storyofstuff.org/movies/story-of -stuff/
Solutions to Externalities	Adventures in Economics	https://youtu.be/hKjhOxEuG5g
Triangulated Teaching	Adventures in Economics	https://youtu.be/c38vE5rEuPg
Video in the Economics Classroom	Macmillan Learning	www.youtu.be/OByogaUSlkU

including photos, videos, and music. If you make your own videos, it is also important to obtain signed release forms that grant permission to feature particular people and places. Examples of these documents are available online.[3]

Fair use guidelines allow instructors to show portions of various copyrighted media including video clips for educational purposes.[4] Among the restrictions for motion media, the duration of the clip cannot exceed 10 percent of the total length of the original, or three minutes, whichever is less. Background music is ancillary to the educational purposes of videos and cannot be used without permission. The purchase of music for personal use (e.g., on iTunes) does not make it fair game for use in videos. To license music for videos, see AudioBlocks.com, SongTradr.com, or PremiumBeat.com, among other sources.

Keep it short. Even in feature length films, the economic gems are often brief. An old favorite is Warren Beatty's speech about environmental ethics in the boardroom scene of *Heaven Can Wait* (Paramount Pictures, 1978), which lasts about four minutes. We must also be mindful of the short attention span of students. Conventional wisdom suggests a typical attention span of 10–15 minutes,[5] and possibly less.[6] Rather than showing long videos, we need to cut to the chase.

Keep it educational. It is tempting to share videos that are long on music or comedy and short on economic content. Consider emailing links to must-see but not-so-educational videos, such as the "Fear the Boom and Bust" Keynes vs. Hayek Rap Battle,[7] for students to watch outside of class. The discussion of assignments below includes guidelines for focusing student-made videos on educational content.

Video Production by Instructors

Unfortunately, many online videos are of questionable quality and some contain mistakes.[8] The challenge is to find the most worthwhile videos. One solution to the quality problem is to use videos from reputable organizations or textbook publishers. Another is for instructors to make their own quality videos. Most modern cameras record video and myriad video-editing software programs are available. The details about each of the programs are readily available online. What follows is a thumbnail sketch of some particularly useful options.

> *Adobe Premiere Pro CC* is a professional-level video editing program. Its seemingly endless capabilities come with corresponding complexity, but much can be accomplished after watching a few hours of training videos. This is part of Adobe's Creative Cloud. As of this writing in 2019, the price was $19.99 per month for educators for the first year, and $29.99 thereafter.
>
> *Apple iMovie* is Apple's popular video editing software program that comes free on Macintosh computers. It can handle basic editing functions and many special effects as well.
>
> *Final Cut Pro X* looks similar to iMovie but has professional-level capabilities. For instance, it can handle an unlimited number of video tracks. Final Cut Pro X works with many third-party apps. It's cost is around $300.
>
> *Filmora* is a relatively inexpensive video editing program for the PC and Mac that has many of the capabilities of Adobe Premiere and Final Cut Pro X, currently for $39.99 per year.
>
> *Videoscribe* produces the popular type of videos in which a hand is seen drawing things as the narrator describes them. Videoscribe users can make either stand-alone videos or clips to imbed into videos made with other video-editing software. Videoscribe currently costs $168 for an annual subscription.

A plethora of other video-related software programs and apps are available in every price range. The programs listed here are enough to accomplish most educational goals. For a more extensive list, see https://en.wikipedia.org/wiki/Comparison_of_video_editing_software, or pcmag.com/article2/0,2817, 2397215,00.asp.

Assignments to Find or Create Digital Resources

In light of the varying quality of online videos, the hunt for excellence itself can become an assignment for students. Consider culminating this hunt in an *Environmental Economics Video Festival*. As homework prior to the festival, ask students to go online and watch at least a dozen 3–6 minute videos about economic models they have not yet mastered. Have each student send you a link to the video that taught her or him the most. Then spend the Video Festival day watching and discussing everyone's favorite videos. In large classes, it becomes necessary to be selective, perhaps by showing only the first video submitted on each topic. Afterwards, you can send the students links to the videos in case they want to re-watch the best submissions or watch any for which there was insufficient time in class. This activity provides a useful review of important concepts before an exam, and if needed, a colleague can orchestrate the festival on a day when you must be absent.

An assignment to produce a video can be a great active learning exercise for students and a wonderful outlet for creativity. Smartphones have extensive video capabilities and students rarely (never in my experience) need help learning how to make basic videos. Students can edit cellphone videos easily with apps that include iMovie for iOS, PowerDirector for Android, and FilmoraGo for both iOS and Android. Most cameras also have video capabilities. In fact, DSLR cameras provide the footage for many high quality videos.

Videos that bring environmental assets into view are a real plus in the environmental economics classroom. Further, the process of *making* videos can take students into the field to see the relevant resources and sites firsthand. Instructors can encourage students to visit a water utility, a power plant, a recycling center, or sites where resources such as oil, coal, or timber are extracted or harvested.

For any video-production assignment, guidelines should emphasize the educational goal of the project. Without strict criteria, you can expect many music videos with economic terms thrown around but minimal reinforcement of challenging concepts. To avoid this, consider grading based on the following questions:

1. How challenging was the material covered?
2. How clear were the explanations?
3. Is it likely that after watching this video a student would earn a higher grade in this course?

4. Did the video display environmental assets or issues not normally seen in a classroom?
5. Did every student in the group play a significant role?
6. Did the video exhibit creativity and innovation?
7. Was the length of the video between 3 and 6 minutes?

Notice that production *quality* is not among the criteria. Students should focus on clarity, creativity, and education, rather than on perfecting the lighting, sound, and camera angles. It is easier for groups to make videos than for individuals, and by making it a group project, the number of videos becomes more realistic to watch even in a large class. The assignment can be either to explain a particular theory or policy, or to cover the topic the students most need to review.

For a narrower assignment with more emphasis on creativity, consider assigning a graph or concept for the students to explain and placing parameters on the location or props they may use to explain it. Here are some possible video assignments:

- Explain the Gordon fisheries model using only spaghetti
- Explain the tragedy of the commons using examples from your residence hall
- Explain how economists place values on environmental assets using only props found in nature
- Explain the prisoner's dilemma using an example you face at school
- Explain a solution to externalities using 3D props of any kind
- Explain how firms respond to environmental regulations with the help of a local entrepreneur
- Explain externalities using examples found within 100 yards of the student union

CONCLUSION

In environmental economics, as in life, sometimes the third time is a charm. Being lifelong learners, instructors know implicitly that a triangulation of perspectives on new material—commonly verbal, written, and visual—drives home concepts that are otherwise difficult to master. With intentionality about providing that triangulation for our students, we can both help them learn environmental economics, and model successful tactics for continued learning.

Lecture is the go-to modality in most classes. Textbooks offer a valuable second perspective, especially if they offer multiple angles within their pages, such as visual aids and real-world applications. The third angle is less standard, but options include field trips, experts, active learning exercises, and news reports. Perhaps the most convenient and flexible third angle is video. Like other digital media, video is popular and often compelling. When used wisely, video only supplements and does not replace more customizable and interactive classroom instruction. In some cases, video allows class time to be "flipped" and devoted to Q&A, discussions, and active learning exercises rather than lecture.

To capitalize on the versatility of digital media, instructors can use images and short clips to give students new perspectives on difficult content. Videos add context and motivation to environmental economics concepts that students might otherwise dismiss as lacking relevance. A video of rainforest destruction will pique students' interests in environmental economics in ways that words cannot. A video of Greta Thunberg provides a memorable opener for discussions of climate change and elicits interest in the graphs that follow. While watching videos can engage students, making videos brings activity to the educational process. Students are unlikely to forget challenging material after weaving it into the planning, filming, editing, and presentation of a video. In that process, they are also likely to make friends and have fun!

NOTES

1. See https://tech.msu.edu/teaching/course-guidelines/blended-online/.
2. See, e.g., Anderson (2019).
3. See, for example, www.videouniversity.com/articles/releases-for-use-in-film-and -video/.
4. The original document is available here: https://files.eric.ed.gov/fulltext/ED4029 20.pdf.
5. For a discussion of this popular assertion see Bradbury (2016).
6. See, e.g., Johnstone and Percival (1976).
7. See www.youtube.com/watch?v=d0nERTFo-Sk.
8. For example, videos in at least two economics online series show a unit-elastic demand curve as a straight line with a slope of -1.

REFERENCES

Anderson, D.A. (2003), 'A picture is worth $10 million: Adult object permanence and the neglected power of sight', *Association of Environmental and Resource Economists Newsletter*, **23**, 1.
Anderson, D.A. (2019), *Environmental Economics and Natural Resource Management 5e*, Oxfordshire, UK: Routledge.
Bradbury, N.A. (2016), 'Attention span during lectures: 8 seconds, 10 minutes, or more?' *Advanced Physiological Education*, **40**, 509–513.
Brecht, H.D. (2012), 'Learning from online video lectures', *Journal of Information Technology Education: Innovations in Practice*, **11**, 227–250.

Bridge, P.D., M. Jackson, and L. Robinson (2009), 'The effectiveness of streaming video on medical student learning: A case study', *Medical Education Online*, **14** (1), 4506.

Caviglia-Harris, J. (2016), 'Flipping the undergraduate economics classroom: Using online videos to enhance teaching and learning', *Southern Economic Journal*, **83**, 321–331.

Choi, H.J. and S.D. Johnson (2007), 'The effect of problem-based video instruction on learner satisfaction, comprehension and retention in college courses', *British Journal of Educational Technology*, **38** (5), 885–895.

Clark, J.M. and A. Paivio (1991), 'Dual coding theory and education', *Education Psychology Review*, **3** (3), 149–210.

Cuevas, J. and B. Dawson (2018), 'A test of two alternative cognitive processing models: Learning styles and dual coding', *Theory and Research in Education*, **16** (1), 40–64.

Dey, E.L., H.E. Burn, and D. Gerdes (2009), 'Bringing the classroom to the web: Effects of using new technologies to capture and deliver lectures', *Research in Higher Education*, **50**, 377–393.

Fernandes, L., M. Moira, and C. Cruickshank (2012), 'The impact of online lecture recordings on learning outcomes in pharmacology', *Journal of the International Association of Medical Science Educators*, **18** (2), 62–70.

Fleming, N.D. and C.E. Mills (1992), 'Not another inventory, rather a catalyst for reflection', *To Improve the Academy*, **11**, 137–143.

Hoffler, T.N. and D. Leutner (2007), 'Instructional animation versus static pictures: A meta-analysis', *Learning and Instruction*, **17** (6), 722–738.

Husmann, P. and V. O'Loughlin (2018), 'Another nail in the coffin for learning styles? Disparities among undergraduate anatomy students' study strategies, class performance, and reported VARK learning styles', *Anatomical Sciences Education*, **12**, 6–19.

Johnstone A.H. and F. Percival (1976), 'Attention breaks in lectures', *Education in Chemistry*, **13**, 49–50.

Mayer, Richard E. (2009), *Multimedia Learning*, Cambridge, UK: Cambridge University Press.

McDaniel, M.A. and G.O. Einstein (1986), 'Bizarre imagery as an effective memory aid: The importance of distinctiveness', *Journal of Experimental Psychology: Learning, Memory, and Cognition*, **12** (1), 54–65.

McNulty, J.A., A. Hoyt, A.J. Chandrasekhar, B. Espiritu, G. Gruener, R.J. Price, and R. Naheedy (2011), 'A three-year study of lecture multimedia utilization in the medical curriculum: Associations with performances in the basic sciences', *Medical Science Educator*, **1**, 29–36.

Paivio, Allan M. (1986), *Mental Representations: A Dual-Coding Approach*, New York, NY: Oxford University Press.

Rogowsky, B.A., B.M. Calhoun, and P. Tallal, (2015), 'Matching learning style to instructional method: Effects on comprehension', *Journal of Educational Psychology*, **107** (1), 64–78.

Traphagan, T., J.V. Kucsera, and K. Kishi (2009), 'Impact of class lecture webcasting on attendance and learning', *Educational Technology Research & Development*, **58** (1), 19–37.

Varao-Sousa T.L. and A. Kingstone (2015), 'Memory for lectures: How lecture format impacts the learning experience', *PLoS ONE*, **10** (11), e0141587.

Vazquez, J.J. and E.P. Chiang (2014), 'A picture is worth a thousand words (at least): The effective use of visuals in the economics classroom', *International Review of Economic Education*, **17**, 109–119.

Willingham, D.T., E.M. Hughes, and D.G. Dobolyi (2015), 'The scientific status of learning styles theories', *Teaching of Psychology*, **42** (3), 266–227.

Yung, H.I. and F. Paas (2015), 'Effects of computer-based visual representation on mathematics learning and cognitive load', *Journal of Educational Technology & Society*, **18**(4), 70–77.

14. Teaching the economics of environmental policy with applications to energy, air pollution and climate change

Jim Casey

INTRODUCTION

I have been teaching Environmental and Natural Resource Economics (ECON255) at Washington and Lee University for 20 years. This course is an introduction and requires only a Principles of Economics level background. Students from many disciplines outside Economics take this course to fulfill requirements in Environmental Studies and general education in the Social Sciences. My approach to the course is constantly evolving, from the assignments and assessments, to topics, and pedagogical approaches to presenting material. One aspect of the course that has changed and grown significantly, over the 20 years, is the section of the course titled "Energy, Air Pollution, and Climate Change." I spend approximately four weeks, which is 33 percent of the semester, on this topic.

Typically, this is Section III and follows a section called "Background, Theory, and Methods," and a section on Natural Resource Economics. At this point, in a standard semester, the students have been introduced to (1) market failure, (2) the role of government, (3) optimal resource allocation, (4) several seminal articles in Environmental Economics, and (5) valuation techniques with applications to forests, fisheries, agriculture, and biodiversity. With the rest of this chapter, I will describe the why, what and how I teach Section III.

WHY?

When I began teaching ECON255, in 1999, only 34 percent of Americans expressed concern about "global warming." By 2019, that number has almost doubled with 65 percent expressing concern and 70 percent of Americans, age 18 to 34, worrying about it a great deal/fair amount.[1] Although economists have been talking about climate change since the 1960s (Heal, 2017), the past two decades have seen an explosion of interest culminating with William Nordhaus's Nobel Prize award in 2019.

I take the sage advice of Paul Samuelson to heart – material in an economics course should be relevant and of interest to students. In the preface to the first edition of *Economics*, Samuelson (1948) offered advice to economic educators and the authors of economics texts. He implored teachers of economics (page v) to organize their course, the presentation of the tools of economic analysis and the associated insights, around "the topics people (i.e. students) find most interesting," and of "primary economic significance" such as unemployment and the public debt. In keeping with that spirit, I have significantly increased the amount of material and depth of coverage on the important topics of air pollution, global climate change (GCC) and its link to our need and increasing demand for energy.

WHAT AND HOW?

Part 1

I begin with basic textbook coverage on the connections between energy production, energy consumption and changes to the environment (land, water, and air). I introduce the students to some of the history of energy policy in the United States and its concerns with scarcity, price stability, and national security. I also want to be sure the students have a solid understanding that air pollution and climate change are primarily, though not exclusively, a function of the divergence between the marginal social cost and the marginal private cost in the market for energy. Given students in an introductory environmental economics course may be coming from different disciplines with different levels of sophistication, this provides a common knowledge base while acknowledging some students may have had significantly more exposure to the concepts.

Depending on the textbook you choose, you may need to supplement readings as there is wide variation in coverage across textbooks. Although most undergraduate textbooks have individual chapters on *energy, pollution*, and *climate change* – they are typically spread out across the text and can be many chapters apart. For example, Harris (2006) covers energy in chapters 12 and 13, but does not get to GCC until chapter 18, while Tietenberg and Lewis (2012) cover energy in chapter 7 and climate change in chapter 16. Covering these three topics in one contiguous unit provides students with a better understanding of the inextricable link between (1) our need for energy, (2) how it changes the environment, and (3) how we might manage these changes with public policy. An excellent introduction to the energy–climate change connection is provided by Schrag (2007).

Schrag (2007) discusses the components of a broad strategy to address the energy–climate challenge. The paper introduces students to the Keeling Curve and presents the current increase in CO_2 in the context of natural variability. The graphs and prose provide a simple explanation for what we know about CO_2 emissions and temperature variability in the past and how that allows us to make predictions about the future. The second half of the paper is focused on what can be done, focusing on both mitigation and adaptation. The emphasis is not on any particular strategy, rather, recognizing it will take a portfolio approach to dealing with the energy–climate challenge with everything from reducing demand, carbon sequestration, and the continued development of non-fossil-fuel systems.

After covering the basics, I introduce a simple overarching model I call TADCOM – the Total Acquisition and Dissipation COst Model. Starting from the premise that we need energy to fuel our economic activities, it provides a simple framework for calculating the full costs of producing and consuming energy resources. It borrows language from Physics arguing there are costs to the acquisition of energy resources in stage 1, and applying the law of dissipation of energy, there are costs when the unused portions of the original source are dissipated back into the environment in stage 3.

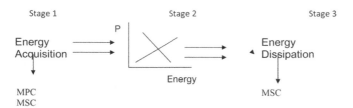

Figure 14.1   TADCOM – total acquisition and dissipation cost model

This model provides the students with a framework for thinking about the production and consumption of any form of energy and the accompanying externalities in addition to the private costs at each stage in the process. One way to motivate the model and start the conversation is to ask the students about the price of gasoline. Most college students have been driving long enough and have enough experience with filling their own tanks to know the price of a gallon of gasoline. They are usually able to describe how conditions of supply and demand lead to an equilibrium price and quantity in the gasoline market (stage 2). We have a quick conversation on the marginal private costs and marginal private benefits and then I ask the students if they think there are any market failures present? More often than not, they are able to identify changes in ecosystems from oil wells, water pollution from spills and air pollution from emissions, to name a few. Returning to the model, I illustrate graphically (in stage 2) the divergence between the MSC and the MPC curves. Lastly, I ask the students if anything happens when they "step on the gas" in order to get at stage 3 – the dissipation phase of the model. We then proceed to identify the primary pollutants – NOx, VOC, CO_2, CO, PM and O_3. Returning to the graph in stage 2, we shift the MSC again and determine the final equilibrium price and quantity accounting for the full cost of acquiring, using, and dissipating energy (in the form of gasoline). I think it is important to remind the students that this is simply a model and that the same pollutants, e.g. PM, CO_2, and other pollutants can occur in both the acquisition phase and the dissipation phase. I also want the students to recognize that any and every energy source can be plugged into this framework and each will have different acquisition and dissipation costs.

I finish the first part of Section III with a paper on full cost accounting from the Harvard School of Public Health (Epstein et al., 2011). This paper provides a thorough accounting of the marginal social costs of acquisition, use and dissipation of energy from coal. The TADCOM gives the students a framework to discuss and analyze the numerous externalities of the life cycle of coal as a primary energy input. The realization that the cost per KWh is more than five times the market price is an eye-opener for most students.

Part 2

In the second part of Section III, in keeping with an interdisciplinary approach to teaching ECON255, I emphasize the importance of understanding the basic science. Instructors may be more or less comfortable/confident in their ability to teach in an interdisciplinary way and if you are not inclined to do so, I point you to a quick read on interdisciplinary teaching (Goldsmith and Casey, 2011) that I hope will convince you to try.

Starting with air pollution, I ask the students to recall the primary criteria pollutants from our previous discussions. Usually, we will read a paper from the primary literature on the link between some or all of these pollutants and human health. If I do not have time to assign and discuss a specific paper, I still talk to the students about the literature on air pollution and human health with an emphasis on (1) ozone and children's health, (2) particulate matter and cardiovascular disease, (3) Pb and cognitive development, and (4) how many of the health consequences of exposure to air pollution start in utero. I suggest the following readings to start: Zhang et al. (2018), Jalaludin et al. (2000), and Nel (2005).

Zhang et al. (2018) estimates the impact of air pollution on cognitive performance with a rich data set from China. They estimate a simple econometric model with test scores as a function of daily exposure to differing levels of air quality. The analysis examines verbal and math test scores across age cohorts and finds particularly strong evidence for cognitive decline in those 55 and older, controlling for other covariates. The graphs in this paper provide easily interpretable results for beginning level economics students.

Jalaludin et al. (2000) look at the effects of low levels of ambient ozone on a cohort of Australian children. They find a statistically significant negative association between peak expiratory flow rates and same-day mean daytime ozone concentrations. This paper is an excellent read for stimulating conversation concerning safe levels of ozone exposure, EPA guidelines for non-compliance, and the health consequences found in the results with levels of ozone exposure below EPA standards.

Lastly, Nel (2005) is a very short read looking specifically at the effects of particulate matter on cardiovascular disease. An important point made by the author is that ultrafine particles have the most serious health impacts relative to PM10 and PM2.5, yet remain the least regulated. The paper concludes that we need more research into the adverse health effects and suggests an increased role for monitoring and regulating emissions.

I do think it is important to provide some good news and looking at the EPA's six criteria pollutant data and the progress that has been made since the 1970s is an excellent way to do this (https://gispub.epa.gov/air/trendsreport/ 2018/#highlights).[2] We can also begin to hint at the policy section by asking, "So, how do you think this might have happened and why have so many of these emissions increased since 2017?"

Shifting from the local and regional to the global scale, we turn our attention to global climate change (GCC). Most textbooks have a solid introduction to the causes and consequences of GCC, but I suggest supplementing this material with the Fourth National Climate Assessment (NCA), developed by the U.S. Global Change Research Program (USGCRP).[3] This document highlights the impacts of climate change in the different regions of the United States. Occasionally, I will have someone from our Geology Department, who teaches the science of global climate change, provide a guest lecture. Additionally, I try to assign outside articles from leading atmospheric scientists. In my experience anything written by Dan Schrag at Harvard (https://scholar.harvard .edu/dschrag) or Mark Jacobson at Stanford (https://web.stanford.edu/group/ efmh/jacobson/) provides the most accessible science on air pollution, energy and climate change.

During this part of the course I am constantly referring back to the TADCOM. Although I want the students to learn some of the basic science, more importantly, I want them to see how the science underlies our ability to model and quantify the social costs of air pollution and greenhouse gas (GHG) emissions and associated climate change. Ultimately, it is our (environmental economists) goal to estimate the full costs of our activities, but we are completely reliant on the scientific community for our understanding of what is actually occurring with respect to the physical and chemical changes in the environment.

Part 3

Now that the students have (1) an analytical framework for thinking about the full cost of energy, (2) a basic understanding of GCC, and (3) an introduction to the link between air pollution and health, it is time to read and discuss what leading economists think about GCC. Nicholas Stern has called the emission of greenhouse gases the biggest market failure the world has seen (Stern, 2008). William Nordhaus has described GCC as the ultimate challenge for Economics (Nordhaus, 2019). Paul Krugman and Greg Mankiw don't agree on much, yet they both want to regulate and reduce greenhouse gas emissions – and they are not alone (Casey, 2010).

In a 1991 address to the Woods Hole Oceanographic Institute, Robert Solow expressed that we should have no reason to believe that markets will solve environmental problems nor will they efficiently allocate natural resources (Solow, 1993). So what is it about economists that leads us to think we should curtail GHG emissions and limit the associated GCC as a result of these emissions? Clearly it is our understanding of markets and the limitations of markets. This is the time to return to the most basic of all economic models (supply and demand) and remind the students about the definition of a negative externality. Baumol and Oates (1988) define a negative externality as follows: the behavior must (1) effect production and utility, (2) change real variables (not prices), and (3) be unintended.

With a limited amount of time, I think it is very important to introduce students to the particular issues related to global climate change where economists can be most useful and where professional economists are spending their time in relation to global climate change. Issues related to risk and uncertainty, measuring social costs, the use of cost–benefit analysis, marginal analysis, discounting, and the role and limitations of economics in choosing policies are some of the areas where I focus my attention. Depending on how much time you have, you may choose to narrow your focus to a more in-depth look at fewer issues or broaden what I have suggested in terms of coverage.

Stern (2008), reminds us that "as economists, our task is to take the science, particularly its analysis of risks, and think about the implications for policy." Although there is a consensus on the relationship between GHG emissions and rising temperatures, there is still much uncertainty in predicting the actual changes to the environment. For example, the scientific models provide us with probabilities the ocean will rise by a certain amount over a certain time frame, they can predict increasing probabilities of drought, floods, storms, etc., but they can never give us precise pin-point estimates. On top of that we have economic models predicting those impacts on markets, and non-market activities with probabilistic statements pertaining to the costs associated with these changes. This is a great time to remind your students of the difficult task at hand – trying to predict the timing and magnitude of environmental and economic change. Additionally, due to the long time horizons associated with GHG emissions and GCC it is crucial to remind/introduce students to how economists think about costs and benefits over time and why the choice of a discount rate is central to the ultimate question of "What should we do?" i.e. what are the appropriate policy responses. Lastly, discussing the role of cost–benefit and marginal analysis is important in the context of trying to determine the "optimal" level of GHG emissions and/or the amount of temperature change. I think it is important to point out to our students that some economists see a substantial role for these tools while others are significantly more concerned about the limitations of using these tools to "determine" the optimal amount of climate change. Nordhaus (2019) originally suggested that a temperature increase of 3.5 degrees centigrade was optimal, but this has created a significant amount of controversy and discussion pertaining to the limits of cost–benefit analysis. As for assigned readings, Stiglitz (2007), Stern (2008), Heal (2009, 2017), and Nordhaus (2019) provide excellent and challenging articles to spark class discussions.

If you have not already done so, this is also an excellent time to introduce Coase's (1960) *The Problem of Social Cost.* I like to simplify the take-away from Coase as (1) how big is the externality, or how much of a difference is there between MSC and MPC, (2) determine if those affected can avoid it, and (3) determine the costs of government intervention. The last step provides an excellent transition to Part 4 of Section III.

Part 4

Although economists agree that something needs to be done to limit GHG emissions, hence reducing the damages from climate change that will occur, we are certainly not in agreement about how much to intervene and about which policy instruments to use. I think it is important to point out to the students that determining the optimal level of GHG emissions, or the optimal amount of temperature increase requires more than a simple economic calculation. Here, I return to the roots of our discipline – Moral Philosophy; reminding students that (1) there are limits to economics analyses, (2) climate change requires more than cost–benefit analysis, and (3) what we should and must do is ultimately a moral question. Stiglitz (2007) and many others point this out and have excellent discussions.

One of the first articles I assign is the seminal "Stabilization Wedges" piece from *Science* in 2004 by Pacala and Socolow. This allows the students to see that we already have the fundamental scientific, technical and industrial knowledge to solve the climate crisis. However, the paper makes very little reference to the economics associated with any of the potential solutions and therefore provides a nice transition to the discussion of how best to use economics to contribute to specific policy proposals.

Reminding students that firms and individuals respond to incentives and that economists prefer incentive-based policies allows us to step into one of our best known debates: *a carbon tax* or a *cap/limit on emissions*. Stern (2008) provides a nice summary of the debate over price controls (taxes) vs. quantity controls (permits). Additionally, Aldy et al. (2008) provide an excellent framework for discussing (1) how to choose a policy instrument, (2) the design of a carbon tax, and (3) several broad debates within the field. To provide some real world context I suggest looking at the tax in British Columbia (Murray and Rivers, 2015) and the RGGI[4] as a great way to help students see the application of different policy tools, the initial results of both examples and a discussion of the pros and cons of each.

I conclude this section of the course with readings from the World Bank.[5] This series of articles "provides a snapshot of recent scientific literature and new analyses of likely impacts and risks that would be associated with a 4-degree Celsius warming within this century." The focus is on developing countries and raises important ethical questions as well as providing a summary of many issues previously discussed.

CONCLUSION

My sense is that many of you already do many of the things I have suggested in this chapter. If so, I hope there are a few ideas that will help you as you continue to teach ENRE. If not, I encourage you to expand your coverage of this important topic. I know my students benefit from this exploration of energy, air pollution, and climate change and I think yours will as well.

NOTES

1. See https://news.gallup.com/poll/234314/global-warming-age-gap-younger -americans-worried.aspx?g_source=link_NEWSV9&g_medium=TOPIC& g_campaign=item_&g_content=Global%2520Warming%2520Age%2520Gap %3a%2520Younger%2520Americans%2520Most%2520Worried.
2. See https://www.epa.gov/criteria-air-pollutants.

3. See https://www.globalchange.gov/nca4 and the Chapter 14 supporting material at https://osf.io/dujas/.
4. See https://www.rggi.org/.
5. See https://www.worldbank.org/en/topic/climatechange/publication/turn-down-the -heat.

REFERENCES

Aldy, J.E., E. Ley and I.W.H. Parry (2008), 'A tax-based approach to slowing global climate change', *National Tax Journal*, **61** (3), 493–517.
Baumol, W.J. and W.E. Oates (1988), *The Theory of Environmental Policy*, 2nd edition, Cambridge, UK: Cambridge University Press.
Casey, J.F. (2012), 'New rules take important step toward clean energy', *Roanoke Times*, Point Counter Point, Invited Essay, April 16, 2012.
Coase R.H. (1960), 'The problem of social cost', *Journal of Law and Economics*, **3** (1), 1–44.
Epstein, P.R., J.J. Buonocore, K. Eckerle, M. Hendryx, B.M. Stout III, R. Heinberg, R.W. Clapp, B. May, N.L. Reinhart, M.M. Ahern, S.K. Doshi, and L. Glustrom (2011), 'Full cost accounting for the life cycle of coal', in R. Costanza, K. Limburg, and I. Kubiszewski (eds), *Ecological Economics Reviews*, *Annals of the New York Academy of Sciences*, **1219** (1), 73–98.
Goldsmith, A.H. and J.F. Casey (2011), 'Economic educators and the interdisciplinary approach to teaching economics', in K.-M. McGoldrick and G.M. Hoyt (eds), *International Handbook on Teaching and Learning Economics*, Cheltenham, UK and Northampton, MA, USA: Edward Elgar Publishing.
Harris, J.M. (2006), *Environmental and Natural Resource Economics: A Contemporary Approach*, Boston, MA: Houghton Mifflin.
Heal, G. (2009), 'Climate economics: A meta-review and some suggestions for future research', *Review of Environmental Economics and Policy*, **3** (1), 4–21.
Heal, G. (2017), 'The economics of the climate', *Journal of Economic Literature*, **55** (3), 1–18.
Jalaludin, B.B., T. Chey, B.I. O'Toole, W.T. Smith, A.G. Capon, and S.R. Leeder (2000), 'Acute effects of low levels of ambient ozone on peak expiratory flow rate in a cohort of Australian children', *International Journal of Epidemiology*, **29** (3), 549–557.
Murray, B. and N. Rivers (2015), 'British Columbia's revenue-neutral carbon tax: A review of the latest "grand experiment" in environmental policy', *Energy Policy*, **86**, 674–683.
Nel, A. (2005), 'Air pollution-related illness: Effects of particles', *Science*, **308** (5723), 804–806.
Nordhaus, W. (2019), 'Climate change: The ultimate challenge for economics', *American Economic Review*, **109** (6), 1991–2014.
Pacala, S. and R. Socolow (2004), 'Stabilization wedges: Solving the climate problem for the next 50 years with current technologies', *Science*, **305** (5686), 968–972.
Samuelson, P.A. (1948), *Economics*, New York, NY: McGraw-Hill.
Schrag, D.P. (2007), 'Confronting the climate–energy challenge', *Elements*, **3** (3), 171–178.

Solow, R.M. (1993), 'Sustainability: An economist's perspective', in R. Dorfman and N. Dorfman (eds), *Economics of the Environment: Selected Readings*, New York, NY: W.W. Norton and Company, pp. 179–187.

Stern, N. (2008), 'The economics of climate', *American Economic Review: Papers & Proceedings*, **98** (2), 1–37.

Stiglitz, J.E. (2007), 'The changing climate on climate change', *Project Syndicate*, Feb. 6, 2007, https://www.project-syndicate.org/commentary/the-changing-climate -on-climate-change?barrier=accesspaylog.

Tietenberg, T. and L. Lewis (2012), *Environmental and Natural Resource Economics*, 9th edition, Upper Saddle River, NJ: Pearson.

Zhang, X., X. Chen, and X. Zhang (2018), 'The impact of exposure to air pollution on cognitive performance', *Proceedings of the National Academy of Sciences*, **115** (37) 9193–9197.

Index

Printed and bound by CPI Group (UK) Ltd, Croydon, CR0 4YY

16/04/2025

14658484-0004